TIME'S WITNESS

Time's Witness

HISTORICAL REPRESENTATION
IN ENGLISH POETRY, 1603-1660

Gerald M. MacLean

The University of Wisconsin Press

The University of Wisconsin Press
114 North Murray Street
Madison, Wisconsin 53715

3 Henrietta Street
London WC2E 8LU, England

5   4   3   2   1

Printed in the United States of America

All illustrations are from copies in The Huntington Library, San Marino,
California, and are reproduced by kind permission.

Library of Congress Cataloging-in-Publication Data
MacLean, Gerald M., 1952–
    Time's witness: historical representation in English poetry,
1603–1660 / Gerald M. MacLean.
    374 pp.   cm.
    Includes bibliographical references.
    1.English poetry—Early modern, 1500–1700—History and criticism.
2. Historical poetry, English—History and criticism.
3. Historicism—History—17th century.   4. Literature and history.
I. Title.
PR545.H5M34   1990
821'.309358—dc20   89-40532
ISBN 0-299-12390-1   CIP
ISBN 0-299-12394-4 (pbk.)

In memory of
Margery Irene MacLean (1920–1982)
Irvin Ehrenpreis (1920–1985)
Christopher MacGregor (1947–1988)

Contents

Illustrations

Preface

All humane things are subject to decay.

—*Mac Flecknoe*

THE BEARING of the English civil wars upon contemporary British culture can be traced in a variety of forms and inflections across various social registers. During the 1984–85 miners' strike, graffiti on the wall of one of the men's toilets in the Bodleian Library accused Arthur Scargill, the leader of the Miners' Union, of being a traitor to the men and women whom he represented by comparing him to Cromwell. The heroic energies which had massed to resist the autocratic politics of Thatcherism were thus preserved at the expense of a leader who, I presume, was here being accused of selling out from a personal will to power. Although this analogy may well misrepresent the political careers of both Scargill and Cromwell, it nevertheless indicates something of the way the Thatcherite era has mobilized the living memory of the English revolution. And it indicates just how unstable such associations are. While it is hardly surprising that academics—especially at the university which had denied this prime minister her honorary degree—should be sensitive to the political analogies with the seventeenth century, it is of more interest to notice the extent to which popular musicians in Britain have turned to the seventeenth-century revolution for lyrics, symbols, icons, and directions for political intervention. Billy Bragg recorded a version of "The Digger's Song" on his 1984 album *Between the Wars*—which is dedicated to the work of the Miners' Wives Support Group. The same year Red London recorded an original song called "Kill a King" on their album *This is England*. Three years previously The Gang of Four's *Solid Gold* album reproduced a woodcut illustration of Strafford's execution on the back of the sleeve.[1] But perhaps the most interesting revival of anti-Stuart rebellion during the mid-1980s is a rock group called the New Model Army whose lead singer, called Slade the Leveller, claims, "I'm a

big fan of the seventeenth century. It was a great period of hope."[2] The
back cover of their 1985 album, *No Rest for the Wicked,* is probably the
first occasion on which the Magna Charta has been used by a rock group
to supply an epigraph—"To no man will we sell, or deny, or delay right
or justice." In popular culture, the memory of the seventeenth-century
revolution lives on clearly and distinctly.

The essays which make up this book are written from the conviction
that the living memory which connects revolutionary politics in the seventeenth century with oppositional cultural practices in the twentieth
century indicates the importance of (past) literary texts in the social production of consciousness. In a sense, then, the implicit subject of this
book is "the modern reader," a notion to be identified not with any real
historical persons or hypothesized social groups, but rather with the conditions of possible consciousness (still in the process of becoming)
brought into being by the texts which are here examined.[3] Again, this
reader is neither some exclusively seventeenth-century reader nor an
ideally "implied" reader, but is rather the possible product of those conflicting cultural discourses which emerged during the crises of the seventeenth century. If movable type began the age of modern communications, then among its major contributions to modern society must
surely be the individual reader, the consumer of printed texts, a species
whose Western hegemony would seem to be coming to an end. Advances
in print technology entailed alterations in the social status of poetic texts
with the shift from aristocratic patronage to consumer publishing, but
they also meant that texts reached a broader and larger readership. It
was partly because of this leveling tendency that the invention of print
was often deplored alongside the invention of gunpowder throughout
the seventeenth century.[4] Walter Benjamin oversimplifies these problems
when he writes that "the enormous changes which printing, the mechanical reproduction of writing, has brought about in literature are a familiar story."[5] As Elizabeth Eisenstein has shown in her synthesis of modern
scholarship, we are only just beginning to understand the printing press
as an agent of change.[6] Perhaps civilizations do, as they say of drowning
people, first come to understand themselves in the moment of ceasing to
be. Richard Helgerson argues that recent developments in telecommu-
nications are hastening the end of an age that began when the "King
James" Bible legitimated printed literature as an official mode of discourse.[7] In a sense, present conditions, especially the global dispersion of

information and capital, and the increasingly cultural cast of political opposition in Britain and elsewhere, can be apprehended only once they have been understood as the necessary and inevitable consequences of the crises which gave them birth. In significant ways, what we often mean when we say "now" began three hundred years ago.

The political importance of what went on in seventeenth-century England to people voting in Thatcher's Britain has been recently documented by Simon Barker as the continuing cultural reappropriation of Shakespeare for imperialistic purposes.[8] As the center of "English," not just a language but also an imperial discourse and so a way of looking at the world, Shakespeare played a role in the official explanations of the 1981 Anglo-Argentinian War, legitimating Thatcher's "resolute approach" to foreign policy by seeming to have predicted it. Barker notices how, commenting on the war in the South Atlantic, the distinguished Shakespearean G. Wilson Knight explained his belief in the prophetic power of the Bard's text with particular reference to what he called "Shakespeare's final words to his countrymen," those spoken by Cranmer at the end of *Henry VIII*:

> I have for long accepted the validity of our country's historic contribution, seeing the British Empire as a precursor, or prototype, of world order.... This [Cranmer's speech] I still hold to be our one authoritative statement, every word deeply significant, as forecast of the world order at which we should aim. Though democratic, it involves not just democracy alone, but democracy in strict subservience to the crown as a symbol linking love to power and the social order to the divine. For world-order, this symbol, or some adequate equivalent, must be supposed.[9]

The will to turn history into symbols, human lives into patterns of cosmic harmony, this use of aesthetics to resolve political struggle, displays that habit of thought which Benjamin calls "the logical result of Fascism" (p. 241) and the evils of which are so carefully documented in *Coriolanus*. "Shakespeare"—not only the man and the texts, but the productions and interpretations, the whole cultural institution, in short— has been at the center of the imperial reclamation of British culture, but his texts have also proved a productive focus for oppositional criticism. Less canonical figures have been largely ignored by recent critical interventions, and the contested domain of English civil war verse especially deserves better treatment. If the interpretation of the civil wars has continued to be a site of controversy for historians, civil war poets themselves struggled over historical matters of interpretation.

The struggle for control over the past is a different though related struggle when it is the civil war instead of Shakespeare that returns, like the repressed, to remind us how social being determines consciousness. The conditions of such a struggle first arose—as Timothy Reiss has argued—during the seventeenth century;[10] new ways of looking at the world developed when reading became an increasingly possible activity. These essays are concerned with the reading subject who may be supposed to have been brought into being by the activity of reading certain poetic texts. This is not a historical enquiry into readership. Nor is it concerned with how drama, the theater or the stage, made people feel about themselves, their lovers, lives, or monarchs, though drama was arguably the dominant literary mode in early modern "English" culture. Rather it concerns the invitation of a neat file of printed words the authority of which is the materiality of their being both printed and poetic. It is concerned with the moment in English history when people at large were first being asked to become readers, to give themselves over to the pleasures of a certain kind of textuality, to believe a necessary kind of truth was to be found by investigating and interpreting black marks on a page. Men and women living in seventeenth-century England faced political and textual interpretation on an unprecedented scale without the kinds of "institutional authority" over interpretation that Jon Klancher has recently traced in the period following the creation of a public sphere in the 1690s.[11] What made reading historical poetry especially seductive during the continual crises of the seventeenth century was no doubt the common sense that one was reading covert commentaries upon one's own times. But part of the engagement which most of these texts claim and the pleasures they offer (however remote they may seem when we don't know the characters and situations) also had to do with the construction of the desire to feel like an expert, a person of letters, someone in the know with access to the "Truth," whose understanding of poetry, history, and contemporary politics somehow counted. As Catherine Belsey puts it: "Sovereignty was transferred in this period from the monarch to those of 'the people' who were held to be authoritative because they possessed the truth (and a certain amount of property)."[12]

I would like to thank the following organizations for their generous assistance with research costs at various times: the Alumni Association and the Department of English of the University of Virginia; the Department of English of Queen's University at Kingston; the Ahmanson Foundation, UCLA; the Social Sciences and Humanities Research Council of Canada; the Humanities Computing Center at the University of Southern California; and the Department of English at Wayne State University. My thanks to Leo Braudy for arranging a visiting appointment at the University of Southern California that made regular visits to the Huntington and Clark libraries possible. At USC, Jerry Frakes made learning word processing with Notabene possible. A fellowship at the Society for the Humanities at Cornell University for 1988–89 to write an introductory study of feminist materialism allowed me time to reflect on questions yet to be asked of the English revolutions of the seventeenth century; my thanks to Dominick LaCapra, Jonathan Culler, fellows and visitors at the A. D. White House, and the students in ENGL 626 "Fantasies of Power: Gender, Class, and Print Culture in Seventeenth–Century England"—Heather Findlay, Sheila Lloyd, Michel Melia, Lisa Moore, Jennifer Summit, Charlotte Sussman, and Kim Tanzer—for providing so challenging an intellectual climate in Ithaca while I worked on final revisions.

While writing this study I have enjoyed the hospitality of librarians at the following institutions: Alderman Library, University of Virginia; Douglas Library, Queen's University at Kingston; the Freiberger Library, Case Western Reserve University; Harvard College Library; Humanities Research Center, University of Texas at Austin; Jackson Library, University of North Carolina at Greensboro; John Rylands Library, Indiana University, Bloomington; Newberry Library, Chicago; Olin Library, Cornell University; Wren Library, Trinity College, Cambridge; Library of Advocates, St. Johns College, Cambridge; the libraries of the University of Glasgow, the University of Edinburgh, the University of Tennessee at Knoxville, and Washington and Lee University, Virginia. University Microfilms, Ann Arbor, kindly sent an impoverished graduate student reel guides and a copy of Fortescue's catalogue of the Thomason Tracts without which I could not have begun this book. My thanks to P. W. Thomas of the Exeter Cathedral Library for a copy of the catalogue describing an exhibition held there in 1960. The Huntington Library, San Marino, and the William Andrews Clark Memorial Library, UCLA, make life and research in Los Angeles positively pleasurable; special thanks to Vir-

ginia Renner, Tom Wright, John Bidwell, George Guffey, and Max Novak. Overworked staff at the Bodleian Library, Oxford, the National
Library, Edinburgh, and the British Library, London, have always been
more than gracious. My thanks to them, and to Carol Briggs, David Scott
Cowan, Tim Dant, Molly Foxall, Christine MacGregor, Ian Shalders,
and Angela Tawn for making summer research trips in England so
rewarding.

   Thanks are also due to a variety of friends and colleagues. In 1981,
Ian Jack, Lester Beaurline, and Martin Havran asked questions of a dissertation which I hope I have answered. Over the years, Paul Alkon,
Lorrie Clark, Dan Cottom, Alastair Fowler, R. James Goldstein, Richard
Helgerson, Richard Ide, Arthur Marotti, Michael McKeon, Douglas Pa-
tey, Ross Pudaloff, Alan Roper, Len Tennenhouse, James Turner, Simon Varey, and Susan Wells read various sections in draft and made
encouraging suggestions. For various forms of encouragement during
the process of revising and rewriting, I would like to thank Jack Armi-
stead, Jay Clayton, Jack Cope, Jerry Herron, Christopher Hill, Elaine
Hobby, Jerry McGann, Marjorie Perloff, Nigel Smith, Gayatri Spivak,
Ernie Sullivan, Rachel Weil, Marilyn Williamson, and Steve Zwicker.
Fred Ahl took time out to help make sure the section on Lucan was free
of howlers, but is in no way responsible for the drift of its argument or
my ignorance of Neronian literature and politics. Special thanks are also
due to Annabel Patterson, Tilottama Rajan, and Harold Weber for rigorous commentaries on late versions of the manuscript; some of their
most exacting questions remain to be answered. Barbara Hanrahan at
the University of Wisconsin Press has been everything an editor should
be.

   The late Irvin Ehrenpreis directed my dissertation on vernacular
backgrounds to Dryden's political poetry; many of the topics pursued
here have their origins in our conversations. But his memory must share
this book with Donna Landry, who has helped make this book what it
is. All stubborn misjudgments are, of course, my own.

Whenever possible, I have used sound, modern scholarly editions, or first
editions of seventeenth-century texts when no reliable modern edition
exists. When quoting early texts I have silently modernized as follows:
long *s* is shortened; *u* and *v*, *i* and *j* are distinguished according to modern usage; *vv* is given *w*; extended passages of italics have been silently
reversed; and the irregular use of capitals in titles has been simplified.

Black letter has been romanized. Long titles have sometimes been short-ened in the text and notes, but not in the bibliography. The place of publication for seventeenth-century texts is London unless otherwise stated. Dates are given old style, though I have taken the year to begin on January 1.

Gerald M. MacLean

Ithaca, January 1989

TIME'S WITNESS

Introduction

It does not seem to me possible to understand the history of seventeenth-century England without understanding its literature, any more than it is possible fully to appreciate the literature without understanding the history.
—CHRISTOPHER HILL

THROUGH HIS Restoration appointments as poet laureate and historiographer royal, John Dryden combined in his career what were, and still are, most often thought of as different forms of writing. Writers of what we would now call literary theory distinguished poetry from history throughout the period, perpetuating a constant strain in neoclassical thought in terms largely derived from Renaissance interpreters of Aristotle's *Poetics*. Among the scholarly and critical accounts of Lucan's *Pharsalia* in seventeenth-century England, for instance, writers as diverse as Jonson, Hobbes, Dryden, and Temple asked: was it a poem or history? While not always agreeing on the answer, they all addressed the same problem in much the same way—by analyzing the manner in which the text purported to represent historical truth. Yet this distinction between poetry and history was evidently relevant to much more than learned debates over the status of certain complex texts carried on by literati, for we find it repeatedly asserted throughout the popular writings of the time (especially among the numerous guides to reading and writing history), continually reaffirmed in prefatory writings to collections of all sorts of poems, and ingeniously elaborated in iconographic title pages and the explanatory verses which frequently accompany them.

The engagement with this distinction between poetry and history both mystifies and helps characterize the complex ways in which the reading and writing of "poetry" and "history" constantly but variously functioned as socially constitutive processes in seventeenth-century English culture. To say this is to make both a general argument about how the writing and reading of printed texts produced social consciousness by encouraging people to think, believe, and act in certain ways, and a more specific related argument about how we should approach the problems of reading certain complex literary texts of the past in relation to their "historical contexts."[1]

Since this study primarily addresses problems related to reading seventeenth-century historical poems, I shall begin by considering how the terms poetry and history would most commonly have been encountered by readers of seventeenth-century English texts. But this is not to suggest that contemporary critical discourse alone can somehow provide a hermeneutic key that will tell us how to understand the precise relationship of these poems as literary texts to the otherwise-establishable historical record which they represent. We need also to understand the politics of how that record has come to be both constituted and interpreted. In tracing the terms "poetry" and "history," the first chapter offers not a general history but rather a particularized account of a series of contemporary critical utterances which typically set about reformulating the Aristotelian distinctions between history and poetry as a binary opposition. No attempt is made to offer a comprehensive view of seventeenth-century poetics or historiography. Rather, by focusing on moments in the debates when the two terms were brought together, I shall argue that discussion of the paradoxical status of historical poetry often stood in for discussion of its political agency at the same time that this conjunction of procedures from distinct generic domains made historical poetry self-critical.

Historical poetry is an uncomfortable category. During the revolutionary decades between James's accession in 1603 and the Restoration in 1660, critical theorists developed only rudimentary generic schemes that would account for how poets wrote about history, but in doing so they recognized the de facto existence of this kind of writing and assigned it various procedures and conventions within the hierarchy of genres. Even more important, they suggested a functional similarity between the writings of the poet and the historian by elaborating a theory of representation based on metaphors of space and sight. The tasks of historians and poets were typically described in spatial and visual terms that emphasized how the act of writing was always also a problem in reading, both the historian's reading of the past records and the subsequent reading of the "history" produced. Yet these visual metaphors also mark the site of an epistemological rupture between a residual providentialism which identifies the controlling gaze of an all-seeing divinity with that of an absolute monarch, and the emergent claims of scientific historiography.

Historians, and poets writing on historical topics, empowered themselves by appropriating the stance of the all-seeing and all-knowing witness, a position also claimed by and for the monarch in the cultural formations of early Stuart claims to absolutism. Court poets invite readers to see things from the point of view of monarchy, to take royal otherness for granted and to regard the past as a patrilinear catalogue comprising the reigns of mighty monarchs. And in doing so they were claiming for themselves only the traditional rights and privileges of court poets.

The development of oppositional poetry during the early Stuart decades cannot be simply associated with the development of scientific historiography. Although oppositional poets insist upon different ways of looking at history, they most commonly speak in the voice of vatic conviction, reading the signs of the present times within the larger text of (typically) a providentialism to which even kings are subject. The political reach of historical poetry, regardless of which position it articulates, remained circumscribed not only by its dependence upon the past but also by its reduction of time to space.

Formalist critics have long taken for granted the "spatial" character of Renaissance poetry generally when examining the important bearing of prosodic shape, iconicity, and numerical design upon poetic signification, meaning, form, and structure. Such writing oversignifies itself, draws attention to the conditions governing its own referentiality, and demands to be read in terms of its own shape. Spatial metaphors also characterized discussions of historical writing during this period when time was commonly imagined as though it were a matter of space and sight. The historical writer was imagined looking at the past and then reading and recording what she saw, having carefully focused her "perspective glass" on some important object, event, or person. The resultant text was typically a "serial narrative" of chronologically organized monuments and ruins that illustrated some "found" or discovered narrative presented from an "objective" point of view. Amidst the many advances in historiography—such as demographic and antiquarian research, local history writing, and precise chronology—which also helped direct the course of historical poetry, this visual/spatial mode of historical representation not only supplied historical writers with a means of imagining and representing the past, but also set specific limitations upon their ability to do so. In these respects, historical poems commonly resembled other historical writings of the time. But, as poetry, such texts also positioned themselves at a critical distance from the kind of truth claimed by historians: *Cooper's Hill* provides a well-known elaboration of this self-conscious preoccupation with how the poet's double vision produces the necessary supplement to the single objective view of the mere historian.

While the relation of any particular text to its genre is, perhaps, always problematic, the tensions are especially acute and highly nuanced when the genre is "historical poetry." "Historical poetry" in seventeenth-century English culture shares something of the oxymoronic status of "popular culture" in academic circles today since, in each case, there remain those who would speak as if no such thing could exist by definition, those who would acknowledge its existence by way of devaluing it to the ranks of the unspeakable and illegitimate, and those who would accord it due critical attention. When historical writers employed poetic form, they were performing a culturally constitutive yet at the same time potentially subversive activity. For such texts solicit generic and conventional expectations of a critical approach to historical facts and events. Poetic form persistently challenges the specialized claims to truth of the historical account as such. It demonstrates the need for a supplement to any narrative record of facts and events by displaying how "history" is a scene of writing—a collection of tropes, figures, metaphors, and conventions that have been selected for precise and determinable purposes— that demands interpretation, commitment, and imagination on the part of readers. The specific claims which historical poetry makes upon its readers are consequently complex, for the status of any historical record poetically rendered is at once called into question by the literary conventions that articulate it. This is both a repressive and a productive situation in which the poet is allowed to create freely from the otherwise knowable record of events (itself an empowering relation) by means of a necessarily circumscribed field of oversignificant literary tropes and conventions. In this sense we may speak of historical poetry as being "critical" history that demands the active participation of the reader.

Chapter 1 begins by examining various ways critical writers throughout the seventeenth century wrote about history and poetry as distinct, usually exclusive, categories of writing. That they did so at a time when a considerable body of historical poetry was actually being written is, perhaps, hardly surprising since if there were no such poetry there would have been little need for such an animated theoretical discussion. This debate directed attention away from the obviously political character of much contemporary poetry, especially that which purported to represent historical events. Although predominantly conservative in their political stances, poets became increasingly prescriptive as the Stuart regime sought increasingly centralized authority in defiance of what, to many, were more authentic traditional rights and privileges. Royalist versions of pastoral continued to defend a specific social and politicosymbolic order by idealization, but that very need—to write in defense—increased as that politicosymbolic order came under attack not merely from popular balladeer and "Digger" poets, but also from oppositional poets no longer prepared to tolerate the Stuart policy of nonintervention in the Thirty Years War. Examination of poems written on behalf of the Stuart court and others that were critical of it in various ways, however, shows how poetic strategies for representing historical events politically usually involved more than any simple distinctions between legitimation and opposition. Such was the urgency and complexity of contemporary politics.

Chapters 2 and 3 pursue the general politicization of English poetry by focusing on the struggle for control over the nation's identity and past in historical poems written during the decades between the first and the restored Stuart monarch, while also looking back to some Elizabethan poets and forward to some writing after 1660. Tracing the persistence of a Virgilian topos—*toto divisos orbe Britannos*—from a poem by William Camden (1596) to a play by Charles Hopkins (1697) demonstrates how the dominant image of the nation changes from that of an arcadian garden paradise to that of an imperial center of global power and culture rivaling Augustan Rome.[2] Changes in the way poets employed the topos signal not merely differing political attitudes on the part of the poets concerned but specific changes in the nation's social and political structure as well. In the case of poetic descriptions of the nation, literary change does not so much reflect as help constitute the terms in which political change becomes imaginable and negotiable. While the Elizabethan writers of heroic poetry had generally tended to address the present obliquely by way of allegory and analogy with the past, their Jacobean and Caroline successors began confronting the contemporary scene more directly and historically. The woodlands and pastures of arcadian pastoral give way to images of the island nation's global control over lands and economies not yet discovered. Although generic discussion of historical poetry confronted the overwhelming need to justify writing about contemporary events, the poems themselves focused on the event for which important precedents could easily be found, the search for past analogues to the present circumstance, and the belief that the solution to an immediate problem can be found in what the past leaves behind. Conceiving of the past as a storehouse of object lessons, a museum of monumental objects, persons, and events, poets explained the present in terms of the past by three major strategies: historical allusions, exemplary history, and the appeal to the past. By variously deploying these figures, poets were able to give shape to an image of how the nation might be, contributing in no small part to its social and political reconstitution during the central decades of the seventeenth century.

Arguing that poetry does not simply reflect an otherwise knowable historical reality but rather represents specific points of cultural, social, or political tension in order to resolve or displace implicit problems by aesthetic closure, the remaining chapters offer detailed critical examinations of selected historical poems written between the civil wars and Cromwell's death in 1658. Yeats was not, as T. R. Henn once claimed, the first poet to write great poetry out of the direct experience and emotional chaos of civil war: Cowley was. His largely neglected epic fragment *The Civil War* is arguably more significant for our understanding of the development of English political poetry in this period than Denham's *Cooper's Hill.* Interpreting the events of 1642–43 as they were taking place, Cowley's poem seeks to unite arts and arms by assembling a large arsenal of traditional figures, tropes, modal and generic configurations that will somehow legitimate the Stuart cause. Less than twenty years after Allan Pritchard's discovery and publication of the third book of *The Civil War,* we have arrived at a moment of critical debate through which we can now assess in a theoretically nuanced way the "unfinished" status of the text rather than dismiss it as an abandoned failure. The epic fragment, the brief epic, the mock heroic, *Annus Mirabilis,* Pope's *Brutus* fragment and his "Opus Magnum," even Cowley's *Davideis:* an intertextual reading of literary history would suggest that the piece of an unwritable epic might be considered a *typical* form of subsequent English poetry. This study addresses the politicosymbolic dynamics that made possible a cultural situation in which the fragmentary epic becomes a denigrated but nevertheless increasingly necessary form, in which the pressures of representing contemporary events make evident the inadequacies of a visual and spatial poetics tied to the past. Cowley may not have been able to complete his epic of England's delivery from the forces of darkness by Charles's army, but by closing the third book with a revelation of his direct involvement with the political events being described by his poem, Cowley achieves the only possible form of closure available. And if that very fact casts serious doubts upon the adequacy of Cowley's artistry, his reliance on traditional modes of historical representation, and on his political allegiances, then the key importance of his text in the history of English poetry is clear.

The limitation of historical poetry bound to images of past glory becomes more striking in the elegaic poems written on the king's execution, which frankly announce their inability to write about an event that has no precedent. They could express horror and dismay, but admitted that the entire historical and tropological orders upon which Stuart claims to absolutism rested had obviously been shattered. From 1649 until the Protectorate, poets writing on behalf of the new political orders characteristically develop analogies with Augustan Rome in order to legitimate the de facto government not for what it is, or has been, but for what it portends for Britain's future. Composed in anticipation of Cromwell's death, *The First Anniversary* by Marvell pushes the imaginative possibilities of triumphal form—a refined variety of spatial form— forward in a masterful artistic achievement that, nevertheless, can confront the certainty of Cromwell's eventual death only with a wish for millennial intervention. When Cromwell did die, an anonymous poet was able to use identical formal procedures in *Anglia Rediviva* (1658), to argue for the necessity of constitutional monarchy. Again, the commitment to the past reasserts itself within the very formal procedures poets used to represent the historical process, especially when tackling the future.

But the political history of historical poetry during the revolutionary decades of the seventeenth century is by no means restricted to limitation and failure. One could argue that if opposition poets had done a better job of imagining unprecedented futures that did *not* require monarchy, then there would have been less need for the Restoration. Yet to do so would surely be to misconstrue the tasks and responsibilities of poets however directly engaged they might be in changing the world. It's worth recalling that Charles arrived rather suddenly; many of the panegyrists comment about how they were taken by surprise. Even Milton, who was among the very first to realize that by the late summer of 1659 a return to monarchy was imminent, used the more immediate literary form of the prose pamphlet in his desperate struggles to steer the nation away from the Restoration.[3] What is nevertheless remarkable is the extent to which the official doctrine of Restoration panegyric recuperates oppositional ideology of the 1630s and 1640s. By documenting the vigor and variety of poems written in opposition to Stuart pacifism during the Thirty Years War, I show how the imperialistic militarism of tropes which had been developed to criticize court policy during the pre–civil war years became the very stuff of Stuart panegyric and policy after 1660.

While early chapters look beyond the Restoration in support of this and other arguments, *Time's Witness* ends its detailed survey of the relations between poetry and history with poems on Cromwell. Something remains to be said about general and connected questions of historical *period* and literary *canon*. The former is an especially fruitful problem for the English seventeenth century since specialist historians over the last half century—demographers and readers of legal records, economic historians, and parliamentary annalists—have documented and debated how to redivide the local and larger pictures for us. These inquiries and debates have frequently taken a partisan cast, often corresponding to lines of political division derived in no small part from alignments that were in the process of coming into being during the early modern period.[4] That this should be so stands testimony to the integrity of the historians on all sides as much as to the continuing political importance of what the English were up to—what they did, what they thought they were doing, and what records they left behind—during the revolutionary decades between the death of Elizabeth in 1603 and the death of Cromwell in 1658.

Far from being arbitrary or merely convenient dates within which to confine a literary historical study, the deaths of these heads of state were overdetermining occasions in seventeenth-century Britain that roughly set limits to the revolutionary period during which an entire assembly of sociopolitical relations was being shaken apart and reconstituted. Each died amidst constitutional uncertainty over not only who would succeed but how that decision would be made. In examining the historical poetry printed during this period, we can grasp something of the enormous shift in the functional and ideological status of complex poetic texts, a shift which might broadly be characterized as the difference in political method, manner, and achievement between Spenser and Dryden. In one of the best commentaries upon the question of the literary canon, Dominick LaCapra expresses his desire to problematize "the so-called 'great' texts of the Western tradition" as an exercise in intellectual history that will demonstrate "the importance of reading and interpreting complex texts."[5] While admiring LaCapra's purpose, to rescue from literary formalism the political edge of critical reading, I am here specifically concerned less with "great" than with "complex" texts produced during a moment of social and political crisis centered on the production of the terms which make up "English" culture. My purpose is to show how period and canon can be discussed only in terms of one another and only by closely addressing complex texts that lay claim, if not to greatness, then at least to the seriousness of poetic form which, when applied to historical themes, brings "into the world something that did not exist before in that significant variation, alteration, or transformation."[6] For the universalizing claims made for poetry serve not so much to remove or distance the immediate as to ask that readers look again and reread when the immediacy has passed. Historical poetry constructs its readers by insisting on the general "historical" importance, for *any* present moment of reading, of the events being represented as if to say "this may not be history, but it really is the way things are." Consequently, focusing too closely on the works of great poets can lead to misunderstanding the full political implications and conditions of the production of historical poetry.

Much of the best work on seventeenth-century English poetry in recent years has suffered, in various ways, from just this problem—an overconcern with "great" readers and writers. Jonathan Goldberg's (1983) focus on the reading and writing of poems at court, for instance, suggests that the politics of reading and writing concerns primarily the habits of the dominant classes.[7] Maureen Quilligan's (1983) important intertextual approach to Milton reading Spenser offers a major theoretical advance upon Harold Bloom's fantasy of literary history as oedipal conflict and Northrop Frye's myth of poetry as totalizing superstructure, yet needs to be developed to account for the positions of readers other than great writers reading other great writers.[8] In respect of the "English" seventeenth century, the "conservative" tradition which we are likely to discover from tracking "major," "great," or "strong" poets—a tradition that can domesticate the radicalism of Marvell and even recuperate Milton as the exceptional genius who proves the rule—corresponds as well to a compelling version of the historical "facts" which can then be adduced from the works of poets who prove, de facto, canonical. That the death of a head of state should prove as important for poets and other commentators on the possible political future(s) in 1658 as it had done in 1603 indicates the limited achievement of a largely bourgeois revolution when it confronts the tenacity within humanist ideology of the heroic belief that historical forces are directed by exceptional leaders. Surely Engels got it wrong when he observed of the period of transition from feudalism to capitalism generally: "The political order remained feudal, while society became more and more bourgeois."⁹ Dryden's achievement—signalized in his *Heroick Stanzas on the Death of Oliver Cromwell* (1658)—is that he persuades us to accept his terms and notice just how little the political order has changed. Humanist ideology helped make kings, but inevitably responded to succession as a crisis since another hero must somehow arise to take charge of the forces of history.

One of the key problems in writing literary history for the English seventeenth century has always been to account for the sheer abundance of great nondramatic verse; why should there have been so many exceptionally accomplished poets? and what generalizations about their work can we make that neither deny nor disregard that exceptionality? Even while we apply ourselves to the preliminary tasks of understanding the historical contexts which produced Donne and Jonson, Milton, Marvell, and Dryden, we are in constant danger of a reverse anachronism, a desire to believe in the values and attitudes which we have so carefully reconstructed.¹⁰ While no scholar of seventeenth-century literature has ever really doubted the interdependence of poetry and history and the political life of seventeenth-century Britain, there has nevertheless been a conscientious rehistoricizing of the period's literature over the last thirty years. Since Ruth Nevo's (1963) examination of "minor" poems of praise and blame established a serious tradition of political English poetry beyond canonical boundaries, many of the most important recent studies have, understandably, considered major writers. C. V. Wedgewood (1968) and Isabel Rivers (1973) broadly examined the work of several major poets to show how they favored conservative values of stability and tradition rather than change. Earl Miner's (1969, 1971, 1974) studies of the "metaphysical" and "cavalier" modes operating throughout the century centered aesthetic concerns on characteristic qualities of major writers. Steven Zwicker (1972) employed the hermeneutics of Protestant typology to explicate the politics of Dryden's poetry, while Michael McKeon (1975) brought sophisticated sociological analysis to bear upon the political circumstances of a single text, *Annus Mirabilis*. Michael Wilding (1987) has recently offered some close critical readings of poems by Milton, Marvell, and Butler against the backgrounds of "the English Revolution."¹¹ Other notable studies of single poets, by John Wallace (1968), Christopher Hill (1977), George MacFadden (1977), Annabel Patterson (1978), Warren

Chernaik (1983), and Steven Zwicker (1984), have summoned considerable research to help us understand the backgrounds of the singular achievements of Donne, Milton, Marvell, and Dryden as being crucially artistic *and* political.[12] Maureen Quilligan (1983) and Arthur Marotti (1986) have developed reception theories to explore the politics of reading Spenser, Donne, and Milton.[13] Recent criticism of Shakespeare and the dramatists of his age has produced some of the most theoretically and politically sophisticated studies of literary/historical relations in our times. Studies by Stephen Orgel (1965), Margot Heinemann (1980), Lisa Jardine (1983), Jonathan Dollimore (1984), Walter Cohen (1985), Catherine Belsey (1986), Leonard Tennenhouse (1987), and others have recuperated for us something of the complexity of the theater's political agency in engaging, shaping, and directing public opinion.[14]

What the new emphases in historical criticism have most convincingly shown is the problematic status of the authorial self.[15] Author-centered studies are necessary but limited since they can distort our sense of the broad range of printed poetry circulating at the time by relegating other poets and the conditions governing their work to the "background." Steps toward a more discursively focused understanding of the history and politics of poetry at this time have already been taken—by James Turner's (1979) important study of the production of the countryside in landscape poetry of the middle decades, by David Norbrook's (1984) survey of the political determinants of English poetry from Spenser to the early Milton, and by Annabel Patterson's important work on censorship (1984) and pastoral (1987).[16] While varying in method, purpose, and scope, these studies have all begun challenging the way literary historians have traditionally approached the textual history of seventeenth-century English culture.

Time's Witness examines complex verses produced largely by noncanonical writers with a view to asserting their importance, both literary and historical, and to redrawing the borders that contain the canon of seventeenth-century "English" poetry. It insists that the discourse of historical poetry between 1603 and 1660 must be understood in terms of both high or "elite" and popular culture, as a source of cultural continuity in the face of political discontinuity. Drama, as such, has been almost entirely bypassed since any performance of any dramatic text constitutes a public scene of political activity, of social reconstitution, unlike the private reading of a printed page. In offering a general history of how nondramatic poetry represents national history, this study seeks to isolate the literary conventions, to suggest how those conventions relate to sociopolitical formations, to provide critical readings of selected—and too frequently neglected—poetic texts that engage historical and political topics, and to offer some generalizations about the discursive relations between "English" poetry and history during the early modern period.

1
Poetry, History, and Seventeenth-Century English Culture

IN ORDER to come to terms with the cultural formations in which historical poetry was to function so crucially as a locus of ideological conflict, we might begin with descriptions of the writing of history by Renaissance critical theorists, in particular those who distinguished it categorically from the writing of poetry. I shall suggest that the distinction itself constituted an arena of struggle for control over the past in which aesthetic considerations commonly "disguised" or displaced covert political concerns.[1] When, for instance, English critics contested the generic status of Lucan's *Pharsalia* during the early seventeenth century, they politicized a previously formal debate by shifting the focus of attention from how this text came to be written to how it might be read. In doing so they were, it is true, developing a tendency already apparent in commentaries by Castelvetro and Tasso. But what gave their work its peculiar urgency can best be understood in the context of resistance to early Stuart claims to political absolutism, those attempts by James and Charles to rule without parliamentary representation that were to lead to the civil wars of mid-century. Political absolutism—and here I have in mind Perry Anderson's analysis in is *Lineages of the Absolutist State*—was never fully achieved in Britain, largely because of varying but persistent opposition to the doctrine that kings rule directly from god and so may not be held accountable by their subjects, an opposition fueled by market forces that were in contradiction with centralized, arbitrary authority.[2] This did not prevent Stuart poets from sometimes writing as if kings were Absolute Subjects, interpellating those over whom they rule from their divinely ordained position of transhistorical Otherness.[3] In historical poetry of the time opposition to Stuart ambitions subverted such claims and tactics, while theoretical disputes over an antimonarchist text like the *Pharsalia* provided a rallying point for writers hostile to James's policies. The general shift in English criticism toward the reception of Lucan's text, its possible uses by and effect upon its readers, represents not simply movement within an arcane debate over literary style, but the emergence of an oppositional poetics centered, for the most part, on the figure of Prince Henry whose courtiers sought to keep alive the heroic memory of protestant chivalry rather than follow Jacobean court style with its cultural forms and values imported from the imperial Roman past.

The second half of this chapter examines some of the ways this debate over historical representation entered the writing and reading of historical texts—especially poems—during the 1630s and 1640s. I argue that the objectivity claimed for historical writing was always in question in poetry written on historical themes, and demonstrate this argument with some instances of how poetry—and this is true of several genres— engages with historical matters in order to legitimate or oppose a presumed sociopolitical status quo. The illustration of oppositional poetics centers on some prefatory poems that invite us to read a heroic poem on the Thirty Years War. Since it was opposition to James's foreign policy that most excited poets to write critically of his government, this example is doubly appropriate, for these prefatory poems directly address questions of historical representation by way of instructing us how to read historical poetry critically.

What are the various typical strategies of naturalization and legitimation which enabled poets to identify a specific model of social and political values and attitudes with the interests of the nation as a whole? While Jacobean poets typically sought to legitimate the status quo, making it seem historically natural and inevitable by emphasizing continuity with the past in terms largely borrowed from imperial Rome, they were frequently caught up in the contradictions of the very forms and beliefs they sought to support. In poems written during the twenties and thirties, court poets increasingly defend (present) monarchy by appealing to (past) ideals of national unity in terms that barely disguise the contradictory claims of class and region. Even for court poets, the traditional identity of monarch and realm proved unstable. But it was early Stuart foreign policy which mobilized oppositional poets who saw the unwillingness of both James and Charles to defend the protestant cause in the Thirty Years War as the betrayal of Britain's historical destiny. For poets dissatisfied with Stuart policy, the distinction between historical and poetic truth offered strategies of dissent and resistance. Despite neoclassical strictures, they wrote ever more closely and critically of contemporary events. They revised and subverted Stuart conventions by variously claiming the greater authenticity of British national or Old Testament history compared with that of imperial Rome, or by asserting their own alternative version(s) of the Roman republic which could be used to legitimate models of government and society not structured in the interests of a dynastic monarchy.

HISTORICAL REPRESENTATION

Historical writing, and thought about history generally, developed rapidly in Britain amidst the political crises of the seventeenth century. It would be hard to overestimate the pervading interest in history and in the past throughout English society at the time, not only at court or public theater, in the universities and schoolrooms, but also among an increasingly influential reading public.[4] Then, as now, "history" covered a range of meanings that were subject to a continual scrutiny, both popular and learned, and that perpetuated traditional notions of the human past and its significance, while also modifying them to provide newer perspectives. The revolution in historiography of the late sixteenth and early seventeenth centuries established history as a self-regulating discipline of knowledge whose terms were increasingly subject to debate.[5] In the public theater and at court, plays and masques not only celebrated the glorious reigns and triumphs of past British and English monarchs, but also represented them with an eye to the present. The intrigues, alliances, and scandals that made up the stuff of previous reigns could, and did, provide dramatists with models of how current events might be interpreted. Elizabeth and James were accustomed to seeing themselves and their policies figured on the public stage in plays based ostensibly upon the stories of monarchs who had ruled, and misruled, before them. We have long been familiar with Elizabeth's recognition of herself in the figure of Shakespeare's Richard II.[6] Yet in recent years the so-called New Historicism has encouraged critics to examine just how complex the institutional significance of theatrical performance—especially of history plays—was at the time. Stephen Greenblatt has argued, "Within [the] theatrical setting, there is a remarkable insistence upon the paradoxes, ambiguities, and tensions of authority, but this apparent production of subversion is . . . the very condition of power."[7] One effect of this emphasis upon "power," which characterizes the New Historicism generally, is the reading of subversion as being finally authorized and contained by the dominant, or hegemonic, classes (i.e., the court). Against such readings of institutional containment, we might usefully pose the Marxist class analysis of Franco Moretti who has demonstrated how a good many of the subversive energies which led to the "deconsecration of sovereignty" during the civil wars of mid-century were generated in part, and given precise ideological form, in the historical drama of the previous decades.[8] In this context, let me rehearse again a central contention of the present study. The historical poetry of the prewar decades written in opposition to Stuart absolutism and pacifism helped to determine the imperialistic ideology used to legitimate *both* Cromwell and the Restoration of Charles. Far from containing oppositional ideology, Britain's monarchy was changed by it. By 1660 the very conditions of royal power had been transformed, partly by subversive and oppositional historical poetry produced during the previous three decades.

At a time when "ideas and values were being transmitted through books and print instead of verbally,"[9] historical topics provided a staple for many varieties of printed work. We should not underestimate the commercial interests of those printers and publishers who by supplying historical texts were also feeding the demand for them. From the elegant, aristocratic encomium to the popular broadside ballad that could be bought for a halfpenny, all kinds of verse compared current events to familiar episodes from the nation's past. The demand for such works was fueled, in part, by educational theories of the time which required that princes, courtiers, diplomats, gentlemen and gentlewomen be familiar with classical history, a requirement that gave rise to a rapid growth in the number of translations, editions, and popularizations of Greek and Roman historians. But increasingly even poets using elevated forms followed the balladeers and concerned themselves and their readers with current events.

The reading and writing of history also had immediately practical edges. The appeal to historical precedent in common law, and the authentication of claims to property rights and titles, generated an increasingly systematic approach to antiquarian research through historical documents, sparking constant theoretical disputes over the relative authority of other sorts of historical witnesses. In Parliament, heated political debates frequently were waged on the basis of appeals to tradition or to time-honored rights and privileges—the older the claim, the stronger the argument. Such was the growing importance of historical knowledge that chairs of history were first established at both Oxford and Cambridge during the reign of James Stuart. And if the first Camden Reader in History at Oxford lectured and wrote in Latin, those able to read only English could turn to several vernacular writers on the same topic.[10] While the establishment of chairs of history might lead us to reflect upon the splendid cultural achievements of Jacobean Britain, we might also wonder if there isn't evidence here of an urgent need to regulate "history," to pin it down and make it speak in the institutionalized forms of an academic discipline, because history writing had become, or was at least perceived to have become, especially dangerous. There can be little doubt that the increasing publication of political tracts issued in the name of crown and Parliament, this making public of political affairs, must have made traditional forms of government appear inadequate, especially after the collapse of censorship in 1641. But the political significance of history writing clearly cannot entirely be explained by the ways that printing changed the cultural map of who could take an engaged interest in history and politics.

History writing was recognized at the time to be what we would now call ideological, a question of how people were encouraged to view and judge the world around them unthinkingly, without reflecting upon how they might have come by those views or judgments. Reading history could help make the world seem natural and God-given. According to Thomas Bearde in 1597, history

> setteth before us such effects (as warnings & admonitions touching good and evill) and laieth vertue and vice so naked before our eyes, with the punishments or rewards inflicted or bestowed upon the followers of each of them, that it may ryghtly be called, an easie and profitable apprenticeship or schoole for every man to learne to get wisedom at another mans cost. Hence it is, that Historie is tearmed of the ancient Philosophers, *The record and register of Time, the light of Truth, and the mistresse and looking glasse of mans life.*[11]

Virtue and vice, punishments and rewards; this is a simplistic account, but a typical one in popular writings on the uses of reading and writing history. A "schoole for every man," history was recognized to be an important and generally available way of learning to look at, interpret, and understand both the world and one's place within it. History provided not only moral exempla but also a method of understanding and thinking about them. "History"—both the past and knowledge of the past—was considered a mode of thought, an instrument by which to understand and account for the human experience of time. Yet like other instruments it partly controls the shape of the tasks which it makes easier. And the task of the historian, in the language of seventeenth-century writers, is like that of the painter: to create "a picture which . . . setteth before our eyes things worthy of remembrance."[12]

This use of optical metaphors to describe historical representation expresses a habit of thought common throughout the century. Jonson, for example, translates the Ciceronian formula for defining history, also alluded to by Bearde in the passage above, as follows:

> Time's Witnesse, Herald of Antiquitie,
> The Light of Truth, and life of Memorie.

The lines appear in a sonnet written to explain the emblematic title page of Sir Walter Ralegh's *History of the World* (1614), one of the most important and controversial history books of the century (see Fig. 1).[13] Together, the poem and engraving exemplify the typically visual and spatial manner in which history was considered. The providential eye, Truth's "beamie hand . . . which searcheth the most hidden springs," the sunburst behind History's head, all express the dominant understanding that the task of historians is to *see* events and to record them; hence Time's Witness, the transformation of temporal process into visual images that are susceptible to human reception and recording. No other set of terms appears so persistently to describe the nature, range, and purchase of the historian's undertaking; so these tropes may be said to mark the limits of the possible historical consciousness of the time.

When, toward the end of the century, Dryden uses visual terms to describe how history achieves its heuristic function, his use of metaphors from optics and cognitive psychology marks the epistemic boundaries of his version of the world after Galileo and Bacon. "History," he writes, is "a prospective-glass carrying your soul to a vast distance, and taking in the farthest objects of antiquity. It informs the understanding by the memory."[14] The kind of vision that shapes—"in-forms"—the mind and brings us historical knowledge contracts time into space and, in doing so, converts human life into a visual panorama composed of monuments, static objects of sight that can be represented graphically. Historical rep-

Figure 1. Title page to Sir Walter Ralegh's *The History of the World* (1614).

resentation—truth to the particulars of sight—required the separation of continuing historical processes into observable, particularized objects that can be stored by the memory. This spatialization of temporal process was typically considered to be an essential characteristic of history writing. John Speed, for example, was praised in 1623 for portraying national monuments and institutions "as in a glasse we might rightly discerne the true shape, quality and condition of them in particular."[15] Lenses and mirrors, however, provide distorted images and can represent only objects, like monuments, but not processes, like Parliament, monarchy, the nation, or any human life. James Howell, the first English Historiographer Royal after the Restoration, writes that Lord Herbert of Cherbury's *Life and Reign of King Henrie the Eighth* (1649)

> holds forth a Glass
> Through which we may behold in every part
> This boisterous Prince.
>
> (Sig. A4ᵛ)

The dynamic processes of Henry VIII's reign—marking the beginning of the Reformation in England—become stationary objects that occupy space rather than time in order that we might apprehend them, allowing them to inform our understanding. And earlier in the century, Sir John Davies describes Speed's *History of Great Britain* as a direct confrontation between time and space over the "particulars" which otherwise constitute historical process:

> Here *Time* and Place, like friendly foes doe warre,
> Which should show most desir'd *Particulars;*
> *But Place* gives place, sith *Time* is greater farre:
> Yet *Place,* well rang'd, gets glory by these warres.
>
> (Sig. A5ᵛ)

Historical truth is here the product of a heroic confrontation that fragments temporal process into static, visual objects which can then be arranged serially—"well rang'd"—in chronological order as if temporal sequence were sufficient causal analysis: hence Time's victory over Place.

But history was not thought of merely as a way of looking at and understanding the world; it was also considered to be the product of its own gaze. In 1633 the engraver William Marshall, who created the famous portrait of the royal martyr *Eikon Basilike* (1649), portrayed Chronology as an emblematic female figure who views the figure of History through a "perspicill." This configuration appears in his title page illustration to Henry Isaacson's *Saturni Ephemerides* (see Fig. 2). Richard Crashaw interprets the emblematic relations in verses appended to the engraving:

> If on TIMES right hand, sit faire HISTORIE;
> If, from the seed of empty Ruine, she
> Can raise so faire an HARVEST: Let Her be
> Ne're so farre distant, yet CHRONOLOGIE
> (Sharpe sighted as the EAGLES eye, that can
> Out-stare the broad-beam'd Dayes Meridian)
> Will have a PERSPICILL to finde her out. . . .

Marshall depicts the female figures above twin pillars composed of books and gives to each a book of her own. Another poet, possibly Edward Rainbow, describes both history and chronology as books, subject to the viewer's gaze in their accountings of the effects of time:

> HISTORY is CREATIONS Booke; which showes
> To what effects the SERIES of it goes,
> CHRONOLOGY's the Booke of HISTORY, and beares
> The just account of DAYES, and MONTHES, and YEARES.
>   . . .
> Set then your eyes in method, and behold
> Time's embleme. . . . [16]

As the book of creation, History shows the "Series" of natural events that constitutes the "faire . . . Harvest" of Creation. Chronology, meanwhile, both looks at the past and organizes what she sees. In Marshall's emblem, she is a sort of mercantile Atropos, complete with a ruled ledger book in which to keep a "just account" of times past set down in order, and whose eagle eyes see everything. According to such a scheme, the continuous series of historical events becomes available to human understanding when transformed into observable, finite particulars that can be fitted into the general and prearranged order requisite to the historian's instruments of seeing and recording, of understanding and representing. Despite repeated assertions that history records a kind of truth unavailable and inappropriate to poetry, it was also recognized to be a way of looking

Figure 2. Title page to Henry Isaacson's *Saturni Ephemerides* (1633).

24

at the world that required a general principle of order little distinct from the perfect pattern of universal truth required of poetry.

Yet critical writers of the time maintained that the universalizing nature of poetry distinguished it categorically from history, from anything so potentially dangerous as political debate. Although admitting real, historical figures into epic and tragedy, critics insisted that poetry and history correspond with two distinct approaches to the truth; one universal, the other particular. As William Davenant wrote to Thomas Hobbes in the "Preface" to *Gondibert* (1650), there were two kinds of truth, "Truth narrative and past [which] is the Idol of Historians, who worship a dead thing, and truth operative ... the Mistress of Poets."[17] This sense that history is a transparent narrative of events was not reserved for philosophical minds only. Richard Braithwait, a popular writer of commonplace and courtesy books for aspiring gentlefolk, thought it necessary to inform his readers that history is no more "than a true narrative of what is done."[18] And Owen Feltham, in his highly popular *Resolves* (1623?) rescues poetry from the status of untruth by distinguishing figuration from "historical" literalism:

> Two things are commonly blamed in *Poetrie* ... and these are *Lyes,* and *Flatterye* ... Tis only to the *shallow insight* that they appear thus. Truth may dwell more clearly in an *Allegory,* or a moral'd *Fable,* than in a bare *Narration*. And for *Flattery,* no man will take *Poetrei Literal:* since in *commendations,* it rather shewes what men should be, then what they are.[19]

"Truth" comes in different forms according to whether it is poetic or historical, and informed readers are necessary for poetic truth to be discernible at all. Readers of poetry need to know how to construct meaning from allegory or fable; that's what makes poetic truth "operative." Conceived of in the forms of "true" or "bare narration" of "what is done," however, history gives up its meanings directly. Davenant writes of "Truth narrative and past" since history writing is concerned, in his (the poet's) view, with past truth, things already known and therefore not requiring interpretation. Turning his back on the past and on historians who make idols of its "dead" significations, he evidently prefers poetry since it makes available a truth capable of changing the way we consider the world—compelling logic, no doubt, for a poet writing in 1650, the year following the king's death.

These distinctions between poetry and history and their respective truths develop a long tradition of commentaries upon Aristotle's *Poetics,* a tradition rehearsed for seventeenth-century readers of English by Sir Philip Sidney. According to the Renaissance version of the Aristotelian argument, both poetry and history teach the truth of moral philosophy. But the one, associated with memory, teaches ideal truth by reporting examples of what men and women have done in the past. The other, associated with the fancy, teaches ideal truth in accounts of what might happen, or what should have happened. This categorical distinction is familiar and clear enough. What does require comment, though, is the curiously elaborated and often animated response which Lucan's *Pharsalia*—a text that J. P. Sullivan has recently called "a revolutionary work of art because [its] historical vision confronted issues of contemporary importance"[20]—solicited from critics working within these premises.

The Debate over Lucan's *Pharsalia*

The *Pharsalia* has occasioned a long critical controversy for several reasons. Lucan's career provides a resonant paradigm, that of a politically active poet who, though a senator who was highly successful at the imperial "court," changed allegiances and conspired to kill his emperor and sponsor. The text of the *Pharsalia,* moreover, creates the illusion of bringing poetry to the very threshold of history. From Servius in the fourth century through the Renaissance, critical commentators debated whether this historical epic on the Roman civil wars more resembled history or poetry. The product of this debate was the elaboration of a dualistic theory of truth by which one kind of truth, that of the historian, claims the authority of a "factual" account of events, while the truth peculiar to the poet demands the translation of history into myth or fable. Lucan's achievement in the *Pharsalia* is to show just how untenable such a distinction really is. In the words of three modern scholars:

> The "Pharsalia" is neither an annalistic chronicle in verse, whose poetic form is simply sugar to sweeten the pill, nor poetic fantasy on a historical theme. Lucan understood that epic must have a personal focus, and, above all, a dramatic and thematic integrity. Yet he also understood that there were boundaries he could not transgress if his narrative were to be historically credible. His extraordinary ability to reconcile the demands of both genres is everywhere evident. . . . He maintains apparent fidelity to history, yet he supplies, in somewhat different form, the personal struggles the reader of epic expects. While he is doing so, he assails and transforms traditional epic and history.[21]

Nevertheless, seventeenth-century English critics inherited the formalistic debate over generic epistemologies that had centered on Lucan's historical epic, mostly from the Italian commentaries on Aristotle's *Poetics* written during the previous century, and eagerly pursued it in terms that are worth recalling in some detail.[22]

The controversy over the status and meaning of Lucan's *Pharsalia* began with its appearance sometime between A.D. 61 and 65 and has persisted well into our own times. Although the documentary record is sketchy, this text evidently figured in the tensions between the young poet and the Emperor Nero, which led to an official ban on Lucan's works and his eventual suicide following his involvement with the Pisonian conspiracy against Nero. Modern scholars are still uncertain about what exactly happened and just how important the *Pharsalia* might have been in Lucan's fall from favor. Nero may have become insanely jealous of Lucan's successes as a poet. Or Lucan's prorepublican attack on tyranny in the poem may have been understood as an unacceptable attack on Nero's government.[23] Whatever the case, the *Pharsalia* became a touchstone in the debate over poetry and history among Renaissance literary theorists who were concerned more, it would appear, with its ambiguous generic status than its republican critique of arbitrary power.

Thirteen hundred years after Lucan's death, Boccaccio (1366) mentions Lucan in a way that suggests an audience of readers familiar with the debate over his epic. Boccaccio's emphasis falls squarely upon textual production:

> poets are not like historians, who begin their account at some convenient beginning and describe events in the unbroken order of their occurrence to the end. Such, we observe, was Lucan's method, wherefore many think of him rather as a metrical historian than a poet.[24]

By the time of Boccaccio's writing, the *Pharsalia*'s political significance has been suppressed by a concern for the formal distinctions between different methods of composition. Aesthetic—specifically, generic—considerations have displaced political ones.

In sixteenth-century Italy critical opinion remained generally concerned with questions of textual production, though without Boccaccio's emphasis upon narrative order. Scaliger (1561) declared emphatically that Lucan was a true poet for he not only wrote in verse but, like Homer, made history the "basis of poetry" by universalizing his historical narrative.[25] Castelvetro (1570), on the other hand, was equally adamant that Lucan had no legitimate claim to the title of poet because he "treated material already dealt with by historians." In his view, the crucial difference between the poet and the historian was twofold. While the historian's subject matter was "prepared for him by the course of worldly events or by the manifest or hidden will of God," that of the poet was "discovered and imagined by the talent of the poet." But the poet may not invent absurdities since "the subject matter of poetry ought to be similar to that of history, and resemble it, but it should not be identical."[26]

The further crucial difference in Castelvetro's account concerns language and reception. While the historian provides his own words, "they are the sort used in reasoning"; the poet's words "are not the sort used in reasoning . . . but . . . are composed in measured verse by the working of the poet's genius." In order to judge whether or not a poet has actually written poetry, the reader needs to attend to both content and style. Since a poet who takes his subject from history follows "events which have happened" instead of exercising the necessary invention, we cannot tell whether "he is either a good or bad poet, that is, that he does or does not know how to discover things like the truth and he cannot be praised for making resemblances." Or, and here Castelvetro recalls Plato's objection to poetry, the poet is engaged in description and trickery "if with the covering and colors of poetic language he has tried to dupe his readers or listeners into believing that there is poetic material beneath his words." Just such a case, he argues, is that of Lucan, who did not invent his subject matter but took it directly from the annals of Roman history. To both Scaliger and Castelvetro, despite the latter's more sophisticated distinction between form and content, the final critical decision is between the representation of historical truth and the discovery of "things like the truth." Their difference of opinion over Lucan hardly concerns the demonstrable artistic achievement of his text, but rather the kind of truth which he might be representing by means of that artistry. To both Italian critics, Lucan would deserve the praise reserved for poets provided he does not merely report actual events.

In France, Ronsard (1587) evidently thought that he did just that, for he dismisses Lucan from the ranks of poets altogether in terms that echo Castelvetro's description of the writer who pretends to poetry by using poetic diction that merely covers historical facts:

Les autres vieils Poetes Romains comme Lucain & Silius Italicus, ont couvert l'histoire du manteau de Poesie: ils eussent mieux fait à mon advis, en quelques endroits d'escrire en prose.[27]

[The other ancient Roman poets, such as Lucan and Silius Italicus, covered history beneath a cloak of poetry: in several places they would have done better, in my opinion, to have written prose.]

But an earlier Italian commentator, Carlo Signio (1562), argued on the contrary that both Lucan and Silius Italicus achieved the rank of poet by "feigning episodes at will and by interweaving the deliberations of the gods and goddesses with the meetings and discourses of men, and by seeking elsewhere gay narratives of events and pleasant descriptions of places."[28] Yet even so apparently straightforward a matter as that of whether Lucan did or did not interject invented and elaborated passages was disputable. In a blunt reminder that at issue in the debate over Lucan were the rival claims of two models of truth, Pellegrino (1585) insisted that the *Pharsalia* "is not poetry because Lucan wrote, precisely, the whole history of the civil war between Caesar and Pompey; he should have taken a part of it, filled it out with fictional means, and removed it from its particularity into the universality of poetry."[29]

In all these accounts, the emphasis falls upon the production of the written text, on questions of how Lucan set about composing and the origins of and status of the materials he employed. Does he adhere to the chronological order of events? Does he adopt a style appropriately different from that of reason? Is he covering over his subject matter in an attempt to deceive his readers? Does he offer fictional interruptions, "gay narratives" and "pleasant descriptions"? Does he follow the whole story or only parts of it? Throughout this debate, the historical facts, as such, are consistently presumed as being somehow given; Lucan may or may not adhere to them more or less closely and more or less completely. But the important epistemological question of how we come to know the historical facts, the "subject matter," in the first place is never once examined. Castelvetro and Ronsard argue that Lucan may be deceiving us by dressing historical material in poetic garb, but even so they take for granted the existence of otherwise knowable events that make up the body of history.

With Tasso, whose *Jerusalem Delivered* (1581) was itself often subjected to critical scrutiny for its use of historical material, we find the beginnings of a more fully nuanced critical approach to the debate over the *Pharsalia*. Tasso, while not questioning the assumption that history is knowable, nevertheless shifts the terms from an almost exclusive concern over whether Lucan followed history to theorizing the affective design of the text which he produced. In the *Discourses on the Heroic Poem* (1594), Tasso agrees with Pellegrino that the scope of even an epic poem should be limited; otherwise it will prove impossible for the poet to provide sufficient "digressions and other ornaments necessary to the poem."[30] He faults Lucan and Silius Italicus here, since both "embraced too ample and copious a matter." Their subjects, "vast in themselves, could fill the entire space allowed to epic magnitude, leaving no room at all for the poet's invention and ingenuity" (p. 55.) Part of the problem, then, is that of space, an argument that makes sense only if we infer a further unspoken assumption regarding the limited capacity, not of the poet to elaborate and ornament a truly vast work, but of a reader who is subjected to the affective design of the work being produced. Like Scaliger, Tasso notes that "the argument of epic should be based on some historical event or truth" (p. 60) but accompanied by a necessary process of selection. Here Tasso announces his own assumption regarding the ready availability of undeniable historical facts that were already known to the reader. "Let our epic poet," he writes, "leave as they were in fact the origin and end of the enterprise and the more famous and well-known matters, altering them slightly or not at all. Let him, if he pleases, change the means and circumstances, shift the times and sequences of other things" (pp. 60–61). There is something of a circle here in the claim that some facts are already "famous and well-known," but we also notice an important return to Boccaccio's position, that the formal ordering of events is of paramount importance.

Castelvetro's division of form and content does not trouble Tasso, who confidently assumes that poets and historians automatically set about writing in different ways: "They will regard them [the same events] differently, since the historian narrates them as true and the poet imitates them as verisimilar" (p. 61). With this introduction of the Aristotelian notion of verisimilitude, Tasso turns directly to Lucan, but begins to hedge behind a series of conditional clauses:

> And if I do not think Lucan is a poet it is not for the reason that persuades others, that he has lost his name because he narrated things that actually happened. . . . if the poet comes upon things that have really taken place,

he does not cease to be a poet. But if Lucan is not a poet, it is because he binds himself to the truth of particulars with little regard to the universal. (P. 61)

At this point Tasso drops the conditional in order to move on and elaborate his crucial point:

> Furthermore, the sequence Lucan used is not proper to poets, but merely the straight forward natural sequence in which what happened first is recounted first, the historian's customary practice. But in the artificial sequence, which Castelvetro calls distorted, some events that occurred first should be told first, some postponed, and some disregarded for the time being or put aside for a better occasion, as Horace teaches. Those must be told first without which we could not know the state of affairs, *but many that would diminish expectation and admiration may be omitted, since the poet should always keep the hearer in suspense, eager to read on.* (P. 61, emphasis added)

Like other European commentators, Tasso assumes that history moves in a "natural sequence" of worldly events displaying an overt or covert divine plan. He assumes such a sequence to be not only knowable but textually reproducible, the act of writing itself in no way contributing to or interfering with the "naturalness" of his sequential ordering of history.

Tasso looks beyond purely formal concerns and also considers the reception of the text. In addition to natural sequence, he postulates a latent form which the poet's artistry brings to the surface in an affective design, an "artificial sequence," that will stir the reader's "expectation and admiration." The key distinction which decides the status of Lucan's *Pharsalia* is one which sees poetry as a more efficient means of forming social attitudes, opinions, and expectations than history. For the affective design which the elaboration, ornamentation, and disturbed sequence of the poetic narrative brings about is not only one that was always already *there,* somehow mysteriously lurking within the events themselves, but also one that, once rediscovered, will be immediately apprehended as inherently true. It is this element of the debate over the *Pharsalia,* the concern for how it is to be read as much as for how it came to be written, that concerned English commentators in their continuation of the debate.

In general, seventeenth-century English critics agreed that the *Pharsalia* was poetry while they argued over its achievement. Critics typically compare Lucan with Virgil. In 1677, Dryden places Lucan and Statius alongside "the divine Virgil" as "men of an unbounded imagination, but who often wanted the poise of judgement" of Virgil.[31] But William Soames in translating Boileau's *Art of Poetry* (1680) dismisses Lucan's text with a contemptuous contrast which focuses attention upon its likely reception by readers: "Nay some there are, for writing Verse extol'd, / Who know not *Lucan's* Dross from *Virgil's* Gold."[32] Earlier in the century, William Drummond reports that Jonson accepted only selected passages of the *Pharsalia* to be true poetry while dismissing the work as a whole.[33] But in commendatory verses prefixed to Thomas May's 1627 translation of the *Pharsalia,* Jonson himself celebrates the Roman's text precisely because of its likely effect upon readers. In lines that rewrite Statius' comments on Lucan (*Sylvae* 2.7), he praises Lucan for achieving an artistic synthesis of contending elements that is bound to raise a rapturous response. "When," he writes,

> I veiw the parts so peiz'd,
> And those in number so, and measure rais'd,
> As neither *Pompey's* popularitie,
> *Caesar's* ambition, *Cato's* libertie,
> Calm *Brutus* tenor start; but all along
> Keep due proportion in the ample song,
> It makes me ravish'd with just wonder, cry
> What Muse, or rather God of harmony
> Taught *Lucan* these true moodes! replyes my sence
> What godds but those of arts, and eloquence?[34]

Here Lucan's synthetic ability, the skill with which his verses move the reader by means of harmonious truth which "arts and eloquence" make possible, impresses Jonson, who feels no need to comment upon the use of historical material. Unlike the early Italian critics who were primarily troubled over the production of the *Pharsalia,* Jonson and the English critics of the seventeenth century developed Tasso's lead and showed a particular concern for the effects of the work. This view agrees with the emphasis in Aristotle's *Poetics,* which does not prohibit the poet from basing his work on history, rather than that of Scaliger and Castelvetro. But after Jonson, English critics up to and including Cowley seem to have relied rather more upon Scaliger's commentary than on Aristotle, even though Theodore Goulston had produced an accurate Latin translation of the *Poetics* in England in 1623.

Assessments of the Roman poet by English critics associated with the Stuart court became increasingly severe as the century wore on. In 1650, for example, William Davenant judged Lucan unwise to have undertaken "an enterprize [that] rather beseem'd an Historian than a poet: For wise Poets think it more worthy to seek out truth in the Passions then to record the truth of Actions, and practice to describe Mankinde just as we are perswaded or guided by instinct."[35] Davenant's adherence to the Stagirite is less important than the emphasis—which he shares with Jonson and Tasso—on the poetic text as a key to understanding general human passion and as a means of relaying that understanding in the form of an instructive guide. In the same year Hobbes agreed, suggesting that Lucan was only an honorary poet, the title not being a just reflection of his deserts because "the subject of a Poem is the manners of men, not natural causes; manners presented, not dictated; and manners feigned, as the name of Poesy imports, not found in men."[36]

The debate over the status of Lucan's text endured through the end of the century. In the preface to *Annus Mirabilis* (1667) Dryden declared himself "apt to agree with those who rank *Lucan* rather among Historians in Verse, then Epique Poets."[37] While much of Dryden's argument in that piece concerns the lack of formal unity in his own historical poem, he did repeat this opinion in 1672 in a different context.[38] By 1674, Lucan's exclusion from Parnassus by English critics had become common enough to cause Thomas Rymer surprise at Cowley's choice of a historical subject for his epic, the *Davideis:*

> After all the heavy Censures that jointly from all Criticks have fall'n on Lucan, I do a little wonder that this Author should choose *History* for the Subject of his Poem, and a History where he is so strictly ty'd up to the Truth.[39]

Rymer's wondering strictures notwithstanding, Cowley had seen fit to follow Lucan's controversial example and attempt that paradoxical form, the historical poem. And in 1690, sixteen years after Rymer's views appeared in print, Sir William Temple still considered the question of Lucan's status as a poet sufficiently important to warrant publishing his opinion.[40]

We can account for much of the continuing engagement with the status of Lucan's work—and the various discontinuities that accompany and give that debate vigor and shape—by recalling that the text in question was notorious for its republican critique of arbitrary authority.[41] What these conflicting and contradictory tendencies, not only between critical theory and poetic practice but also within critical discourse itself, surely suggest is the suppression or strategic displacement of a key consideration: politics. As most of the Renaissance critics who commented on the *Pharsalia* would have known, Quintilian recommended Lucan to students of political discourse, as a model of political oratory rather than poetry.[42] Yet so long as doctrines of universal truth and particular truth could be evoked to distinguish poetry from history, historical poetry might seem detached from the social, cultural, and political conditions of its production and reception, and could then purport to represent, in an impartial way, a higher and more philosophically detached truth than the historian's, a truth which readers would intuitively grasp as timeless. Defenses of the *Pharsalia* stop just short of openly admitting that when poetry and history unite, the conjunction invariably has a specifically political function. Instead, as we have seen, they resort to epistemological arguments concerning aesthetic effect; "these true moodes" as Jonson put it, or "truth in the Passions" to recall Davenant. Even the English poets who write sympathetically of Lucan at this time commonly deny that he had any but the most high-minded purpose. Some go so far as to consider ways other poets use fable, exaggeration, and flattery for political ends only in order to "rescue" Lucan's text from such imputations by emphasizing its basis in history. Throughout this discussion of poetry and history, aesthetics typically replaces and disguises politics by elevating poetry beyond the political conditions of its production and reception.

Yet this hedging seldom hides the knowledge that poets, like Lucan, who write on historical themes are engaged in a fundamentally political activity. While much Lucan criticism remains conspicuously silent on political questions, those historical moments when critics have debated Lucan's text typically correspond, as Frederick Ahl has shown, with moments of specific political upheaval.[43] The general aim of such discussion in seventeenth-century Britain was to reverse a notion of historical truth that remains untouched by politics. In 1627, for example, Thomas May directly addresses the political significance of Lucan's text, which he calls a "true *History*," by describing it in terms of its poetic effects upon the reader: it is "adorned and heightened with *Poeticall raptures,* which doe not adulterate, nor corrupt the truth but give it a more sweet and pleasant relish."[44] May subsequently elaborates this defense of the poetic effect in verses prefixed to his own *Continuation of Lucan's Historicall Poem* (1630) by arguing that Lucan's "deathlesse" and "eternal song" rises above the historical conditions of its composition because of the "sound moralitie" of its satire:

> Thy verses teach no foule adulteries,
> Nor rapes committed by the Deities,
> Which may from guilt absolve the worst of men;
> But actions great and true: thy happie pen
> Adorning History with raptures high,
> With quicke conceits and sound moralitie
> Condemn'd the strong injustice of that age,
> And reines too much let lose to civill rage.
>
> (Sig. A7ᵛ)

Using terms that recall Jonson's commendation, May indicates how poetic truth, properly managed, constitutes a form of social power by means of which poetic writing about the past—"actions great and true"—controls and directs the reader's appetite for a certain version of justice. May points out that the very process by which the poet selects from among the available historical materials is itself political, since it helps to shape the kind of report being offered. Lucan's work does not provide mythical examples of vicious behavior that may be taken to sanction similar activities in the present; rather it documents the historical dangers of tyranny and political mismanagement. Only a tyrant could take offense.

In an age of censorship, May can so confidently describe the political force of poetry since he has dedicated his *Continuation* of 1630 to the king, who had admired his translation of 1627.[45] Verses prefixed to the title page of his 1627 translation, however, directly evoke the political history of Lucan's text by drawing one historical parallel that invites us to read another:

> THis dying Figure that rare *Lucan* showes,
> Whose lofty *genius* great *Apollo* chose
> When Roman liberty opprest should dy,
> To sing her sadd, and solemne obsequy
> In stately numbers, high, as *Rome* was great;
> And not so much to yeares indebted yet,

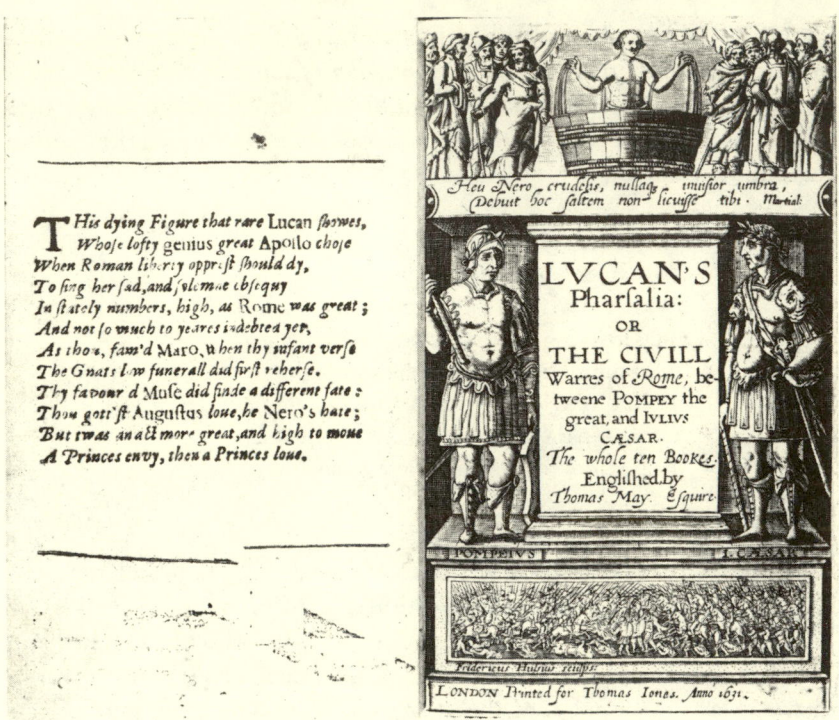

Figure 3. Title page and accompanying verses to Thomas May's translation of *Lucan's Pharsalia* (1631 ed.). The engraving and verses also appeared in the 1627 edition.

> As thou, fam'd *Maro,* when thy infant verse
> The Gnats low funerall did first reherse.
> Thy favour'd *Muse* did finde a different fate:
> Thou gott'st *Augustus* love, he *Nero's* hate;
> But twas an act more great, and high to moove
> A Princes envy, then a Princes love.

The strategic parallelism here destabilizes any possible reading of these lines as hostile to monarchy and hence assures the publication of May's translation (Fig. 3); Charles could not avoid choosing between the position of Augustus or Nero. If Lucan's text attacks Roman tyranny by way of singing its obsequy, then Charles must read May's translation the way Augustus did Virgil's youthful satire and accord it love not hate. Publicly, at least, the king appeared so delighted with May's translation that he commissioned two further narrative poems on historical themes, one on

Henry II (1633) and another on Edward III (1635). And when Jonson died in 1637, leaving vacant the post of poet laureate, the king personally recommended May as his preferred candidate. Despite the king's support, May lost out to Davenant. May's political career from this point curiously starts to resemble that of Lucan; after initial success at court, the poet changes allegiances in the cause of a republicanism at odds with the current government which has been supporting the poet's career. Throughout the 1640s May actively supported the parliamentary cause, becoming secretary to the Parliament in 1646. Yet the earlier favor of the king remained sufficiently well known to warrant epigrammatic treatment in *Wits Recreations* (1640) which recalls and rewrites that earlier parallel in order to compare May with Lucan: "Thou hast got Charles his love, he Nero's hate" (p. 12).[46] Far from being forgotten, the political circumstances of Lucan's text remained very much a part not only of this poet's career and reputation but also of poetic strategies for writing against the grain of any simple court hegemony.

Despite the aestheticizing tendency of much Lucan criticism, in seventeenth-century Britain discussion of the *Pharsalia* was explicitly bound up with political discourse, in particular with critiques of arbitrary or tyrannical power. Early in his own career as a poet, James appropriated a few lines of book 5 in an extended meditation upon the relationship between the king and his nobility to show how Lucan wrote in favor of royal authority. As elsewhere in his poetry, James displays his preoccupation with the absolute nature of royal power. "A Paraphrasticall Translation out of The Poete Lucane," which James published in 1584 when only eighteen, begins:

> If all the floods amongst them wold conclude
> To stay their course from running in the see;
> And by that means would thinke for to delude
> The *Ocean,* who sould impaired be,
> As they supposde, beleving if that he
> Did lack their floods, he should decresse him sell:
> Yet if we like the verite to wye,
> It pains him nothing: as I shall you tell.[47]

The verses continue by insisting that a king's power is by no means weakened by the absence from court of his nobles. That James should have undertaken this poetic exercise to assert the unconditionality of monarchical authority and power at so young an age may indicate something of his highly suspicious character: the lines being paraphrased (5.335–40) are spoken by Caesar to a group of mutinous officers. Since several manuscript copies of James's translation have survived, including one in Scottish, the verses no doubt circulated fairly widely among readers close to the court, perhaps as a warning. As Annabel Patterson comments, allusions to Lucan—like those to Virgil and Tacitus—"gradually came . . . to stand as signifiers in the code, the indirect language in which a later civilization could readdress the oldest question in the book: what was writing for, and whose ends could or should it serve."[48]

This very question, of how writing serves personal interest, was clearly of great concern to those who opposed Stuart claims to absolute power. It was raised early in the seventeenth century by one "W. R." in a sonnet prefixed to Sir Arthur Gorges' translation of Lucan (1614). The verses turn flattery against itself by praising both Lucan and Gorges for telling the truth rather than giving in to the pressures of court patronage. "W. R." praises those poets who challenge absolutist claims to control over the truth rather than give in to the temptations of self-advancement through flattering members of the ruling classes:

> HAd *Lucan* hid the truth to please the time,
> He had beene too unworthy of thy Penne:
> Who never sought, noe ever car'd to clime
> By flattery, or seeking worthlesse men.
>
> (Sig. A4ᵛ)

It is hard not to identify "W. R." with Sir Walter Ralegh, a cousin and close friend of Gorges who had been imprisoned in the Tower soon after the accession of the Scottish king to the English throne in 1603. Gorges had commanded Ralegh's ship on the 1597 expedition to the Azores and had been closely associated with the militant protestant group centered on Ralegh, a group deeply critical not only of James's claims to absolutism but also of his refusal to take a more aggressive stance against the power of catholic Spain. He became a member of the court of Prince Henry in 1611, a center of anti-catholicism and of optimism that the young Prince of Wales, once king, would reverse some of his father's foreign policy. The young prince's death in 1612, two years before the appearance of Gorges' translation, must have been an especially bitter disappointment to those who saw Henry as the champion of heroic English protestantism.[49] According to Roy Strong, Gorges' ties with Ralegh secured him a place at Prince Henry's court: "Undoubtedly his attraction lay less in his role as a man of letters ... than as an emanation of and a contact with the great man in the Tower. The steady stream of prose works is an expression of fervour for a revival of an Elizabethan policy against the old naval adversary, Spain, and the hand of Ralegh direct or otherwise is observable in all of them.[50]

But whether "W. R." was Ralegh or not, the verses invite reflection upon that "oldest question in the book," and there can be little doubt that the translation of Lucan by Gorges would have been regarded with suspicion at Whitehall: hence, no doubt, the anonymity of this and the other prefatory poems which appeared with Gorges' translation. It is with a clearly apotropaic intent, a hopeful warding-off, that "T. W.", another poet writing to recommend Gorges' translation, argues that Lucan's important contribution to poetry lies in having warned succeeding generations of poets to avoid the possible dangers of composing poetic fictions which might seem to have dangerous political implications. After such a prefatory gesture, how could any reader (not) imagine Gorges' translation to be politically motivated? Poets who wrote before Lucan, "T. W." explains, too often abused their freedom from literal truth in order to perpetuate evils, predominantly through indiscriminate and self-seeking flattery of those with power. Unlike Homer and Virgil, both of whom he accuses of writing in a self-serving way, Lucan offers only empirically verifiable facts—"what was seene, felt, donne"—not sycophantic fables. Gorges' function is that of *"Truch-man"* or interpreter of this wisdom:

> LUCAN, that first in the Imperiall tongue
> (In naked truth of acted history)
> The civill wounds made for an Empire song;
> Hath checkt precedent, taught succeeding *Poesy,*
> That flatteries and fictions may delight,
> May please a Tyrant, wrong a rightfull King,
> May please an Orphan Judgment, wrong the right,
> Envelop Truth, proclaime an untrue thing.
> *Lucan,* that first hath showne the force of verse,
> Relating onely what was seene, felt, donne,
> Of Conqu'rors triumphs, of the Conqu'reds herse,
> All as it left, all as it first begunne.
> Not like the *Trojan* Theamers, fit for schooles,

> Fabling of this and that in Heaven, Earth, Hell,
> Sober to mad-men, turning wise to fooles,
> Gods to be Neat-heards, men in starres to dwell,
> Hath match'd the faith, that History requires:
> Hath match'd best History in choyce of phrase:
> Hath taught, that History in nought aspires
> Above the truth of deeds, it self to raise.
>   This *Lucan* for his truth a *Truch-man* gaines
>   As true to him, as he to truth remaines.

(Sig. A6)

The claim for Lucan's originality here may seem excessively daring, and the terms in which it is made may seem rather too abstract to carry much conviction. But there is no mistaking the urgency of those remarkable lines which begin the second sentence in a bold assertion that "the force of verse" is its grasp of history in the form of the material processes of human life—"what was seene, felt donne." And the contemptuous attach on "the *Trojan* Theamers" must surely have been directed against James's attempt to legitimate his reign by recourse to a classicizing style that permits exaggeration and fable. Lucan, by contrast, has created a form of historical poetry that combines "the force of verse" with the "choyce of phrase" and the adherence to otherwise establishable facts which make "history" seem objective and politically disinterested.

Another sonneteer writing on Gorges' translation, "S. S.," also argues for radical revisions to neoclassical notions about poetry and literary history, coming very close to a full critique of the categorical separation of poetry from history. Writing from a clearly contentious stance that anticipates the dominant and opposing opinion, "S. S." praises Lucan in terms that challenge the neo-Aristotelian distinction between historical and poetic truth:

> HOMER and MARO, that did Poetize,
>   As much in matter, as in kinde of stile,
> Did thereby dimme the glorious deeds the while
> Of them, whose acts they meant to memorize.
>   So did not LUCAN, who (in other guize)
> The gests of two great Worthies did compile;
> S'deigning their high achievements to defile,
> Or inter-lace with idle vanities.
>   Therefore how farre from Fable Truth is set,

> So farre above all feigners LUCAN shines;
>   While in his Muse both faculties are met,
> That with sweet Number beauteous Truth combines.
>   And we to thee in endlesse debt must dwell
>   For making *Lucan* speake our tongue so well.

> (Sig. A5)

The attack on the "poetizing" of Jacobean neoclassicism could hardly be more direct. Yet "S. S." hedges his bet by framing his critique in aesthetic rather than political terms. Although clearly not intending a general theory of poetry, "S. S." nevertheless offers a bold departure from received opinion by treating versification as the definitive characteristic of poetry. He does not systematically challenge the critical distinction between historical truth and poetic fiction but, like "W. R." and May, suggests instead that poetry and history can indeed combine in the union of "sweet Number" with "beauteous Truth." Unlike May, "S. S." does not directly address the problems of how flattery and patronage lead poets to distort the manifest truth, but he achieves his subversive aim by dethroning Homer and Virgil. Just when his challenge to current critical thought comes closest to collapsing the dichotomy between the kinds, he sidesteps the political function of their fusion to offer an aesthetic one instead.

Such disingenuous disavowals of political concern should, however, not surprise us in an age when affairs of state were so jealously guarded by the king. They should, rather, warn us to be careful when assessing arguments about aesthetic detachment, especially at a time when poets and critical thinkers took the political function of poetry for granted. James himself, as we saw, translated a section of Lucan in order to affirm the independence of the king's authority, and was among those who openly addressed the political function of the poet's art. It was just as important for his political ambitions that he rule supreme over the realm of poetry as that he rule absolutely over his state. In his *Ane Schort Treatise, Conteining Some Reulis and cautelis to be observit and eschewit in Scottis Poesie* (1584) he warns poets to avoid translation since, he argues, it diminishes one's freedom to exercise invention. But the warning is more than simply about poetic creativity. He writes:

ZE man also be war of wryting any thing of materis of commoun weill, or uther sic grave sene subiectis (except Metaphorically, of manifest treuth opinly knawin, zit nochtwithstanding using it very seindel) because nocht onely ze essay nocht zour awin *Invention*, as I spak before, bot lykewyis they are to grave materis for a Poet to mell in.[51]

James's advice is carefully wrapped up in literary principles regarding the need for poets to stretch their inventiveness. But the caution indicates James's anxiety that poets would do just that—meddle in grave matters of state. And that was something he was not prepared to countenance; clearly James felt the need to restrict the freedom of poets as much as he did the need to restrict the freedom of his subjects.

Evidently, the debates over Lucan's text during the early part of the century indicate the emergence of a historically specific concern with the possibility of oppositional and subversive writing and the contingent need to theorize writing about contemporary events from the "objective" position of the historian. What makes the debate over the rival claims to truth of the poet and the historian a special case, one from which politics was so often suppressed or specifically displaced, is the need to create and maintain the possibility of a disinterested, objective position from which the present might be known and represented "historically." Given the traditional restriction that history-writing should exclusively concern the past, the need to write on contemporary events signaled an epistemological crisis over the position of enunciation and the "objective" representation of historical "reality." This crisis comes into focus most clearly in the attempt to install the belief—the "faith" which "T. W." wrote of as being "required" by "History"—that historical objectivity is possible and available to those writing on contemporary events. Historical poetry provided, by virtue of its paradoxical if not oxymoronic status, a position of enunciation that could claim to be politically unassailable since it was based upon historical truth and so beyond politically motivated exaggeration, fable, or flattery.

By the early 1640s, this need to write about the present with the objectivity usually reserved for the writing of history corresponds with the emergence of the propagandistic pamphlet. For if cheap printing made new literary forms possible, and if any particular genre may be held most responsible for making the development of political discourse centered on contemporary affairs explicit, it was the prose pamphlet aimed at encouraging people to take sides.[52] A brief glimpse at the struggle over terms like "party," "malignant," and "opposition" in the pamphlets published during the early months of the first civil war, long after court censorship had collapsed, might help explain why historically conscious poets anticipated the need to reserve a position of historical objectivity. "Party" invariably designates the enemy, the position of the diabolical Other who has designs on people and who operates against national self-interest. For instance, one parliamentary pamphleteer in 1642 attacks "that opposite and malignant party . . . the party which hath now insens'd and arm'd His Majesty against us and His other faithful Subjects in His kingdome."[53] Later in the same pamphlet, supporters of the king are called "the opposition" (p. 3). Both "party" and "malignant" seem to have been generalized terms of abuse during these months. A Parliamentary remonstrance of May 1642 characterizes "the Malignant partie about His Majestie" as "wicked spirits of division,"[54] but *His Majesties Answer* of later the same year reverses the terms of accusation against "a Faction of Malignant, Schismaticall, and Ambitious Persons, whose Designe is, and always hath been, to alter the whole frame of Government both of Church and State."[55] Picking up the term "faction," the Parliamentary response skillfully turns it against "party":

> A Faction prevailing against the Major part of both Houses, & pretending them to be a Malignant party, is like indeed to destroy the rights both of King and people. And we will adde too, the common right also of all the people, and the conservatory of all their rights, which is the Parliament. And because this is so, therefore doe we beleeve this is endeavoured to be done by the Malignant party about his Majesty, which by cunning and force, labours to prevaile against the true Major part of both Houses, pretending them to be a Faction of Malignant, Schismaticall, and ambitious persons, that would subject both King and people, to their owne lawlesse Arbitrary power and government.[56]

We might multiply examples of contending uses of "party" during the 1640s,[57] but what is of interest here is that this struggle over terms corresponds with a struggle to assume a position that seems not to be political. "Party" designates the divisive Other in order that the writer might claim the objectivity which legitimates the position of enunciation in the name of national unity. To mark history as an objective and disinterested sphere of knowledge, and to mark historical poetry as an objective and disinterested position of enunciation, enabled the historical poet to claim access to truth beyond that of historian or pamphleteer, a truth beyond that of "party." This is the position that the English Lucan, Samuel Daniel, claims for himself when he insists, "I versifie the troth, not Poetize."[58]

The suppression and aestheticization of the term "politics" in critical discussions of poetry and history suggests a particular need to conceive of events as being objectively knowable in one of two ways—that of poetry and that of history—which are never considered discursively as being the product of the mode of their representation. Historical truth as such seemed not to be a political issue of position at all in this formulation, since it simply *was* the way things *were* according to the natural order which constituted what was known of the past. But in the shift from the European formalistic concern for the production of the poetic text from the already-given subject matter that somehow is history, to the concern in Britain for the social and aesthetic reception of the finished text, we might follow traces of an awareness that different literary forms can, and do, have different effects.[59] This elaborate and highly nuanced debate over the formal and aesthetic components of representation constitutes a struggle for control over the means of producing "history," a struggle over the objective position of the historian. Of paramount concern during the twenties and thirties, as both an expression of and a vehicle for the growing immediacy of political opposition to Stuart claims to absolutism, was this recognition that literary form is always both a political and an aesthetic question, and the corollary need to maintain belief in an objectively "true" history not subject to the political constraints of tyrants. Here we can trace the emergence of a strategy of resistance to James's will to power which included his will to control the production of poetry. And the critical debate over Lucan's antimonarchist *Pharsalia* was precisely that, a struggle for control over the status and meanings of historical poetry.

THE POLITICS OF HISTORICAL POETRY

How did theoretical debates like those over the status and meaning of Lucan's text enter the writing and reading, the production in short, of historical poetry during the early seventeenth century? The history of Lucan's reputation illustrates how the objectivity claimed for historical writing was always in question in poetry written on historical themes. In the rest of this chapter, I shall explore this principle by observing how poetry—and this is true of several genres—engages history by legitimating and opposing a presumed sociopolitical status quo. The detailed illustration of oppositional poetics centers on the example of some prefatory poems that invite us to read John Russell's *The Two Famous Pitcht Battels of Lypsich, and Lutzen* (Cambridge, 1634), a heroic poem on the Thirty Years War. Since it was opposition to James's foreign policy that most excited poets to write critically of his government, this example is doubly appropriate, for these prefatory poems directly address specific questions of historical representation by way of instructing us how to read historical poetry critically. But first it is convenient to consider more generally the poetics of legitimation and opposition across a broad range of historical poems.

Whatever the discontinuities within seventeenth-century critical thinking on the topic, all sorts of poets wrote about history during the crises of 1603–60, with different but demonstrable political aims and consequences. When James was crowned king of England in 1603, Samuel Daniel was still publishing revised versions of *The Civil Wars*, his historical epic in the manner of Lucan, that describes war only in order to celebrate peace and warn against the evils befalling a nation with a disputed succession.[60] But not all poets who wrote on historical topics were trying to legitimate ruling class ideology, and not all of them wrote in the heroic mode. Satirists like George Wither turned critical eyes directly upon the present, especially the neoclassical culture of the Jacobean court.[61] Pastoral and georgic worked either way, sometimes praising, sometimes complaining.[62] Countless poems written throughout the century celebrate the natural social order found only in the countryside while glancing more or less directly at political affairs by constructing models of ideal social relations. Some country poems praise noblemen, their wives and estates as models of social and political virtue, while others advocate rural retirement away from the corruptions of political life at court and in the city. For readers living in London, balladeers supplied a "kind of commentary upon the political events" of the time.[63] At the universities in Oxford, Cambridge, Aberdeen and Edinburgh, students and fellows regularly wrote verses on traditional state occasions in Latin, Greek, Hebrew, Welsh, and Saxon, as well as in French and English. Some important political figures, including William Laud and John Locke, appear as contributors to these collections.[64] During the thirties and forties, propagandists of different persuasions adopted verse as a medium suited to rallying others to their causes.[65] And the writers of the newssheets that began appearing during the years leading up to the civil wars intersperse their reports with verses commenting on current events. In mid-century, Waller, Dryden, Marvell, and others composed formal panegyrics to Cromwell and the interregnum governments, later returning their encomiastic lyres to sing the Restoration of Charles Stuart.

A generic history of the politics of seventeenth-century historical poetry might start with Daniel's *The Civil Wars* for several reasons in addition to its convenient historical location at the start of a century and across the reigns of Elizabeth and James. The publication history of *The Civil Wars* stretches through five printings between 1595 and 1609, during which time Daniel constantly revised his historical poem to stay in tune with political events that changed the contexts in which it was likely to be read. Daniel's most recent editor comments that "every version has stanzas not in the others" (pp. 58–59), and that while many revisions are stylistic, or of no political consequence, Daniel tried "to keep up with the times: During the published career of *The Civil Wars* his patrons died or changed, political events had their repercussions on his interpretation of history, and, most far-reaching of all, the 'glory of Eliza's days' came to an end, and the celebrant of the Tudor dynasty had to make his way in a Stuart court" (p. 38). Although writing on behalf of the status quo, to legitimate rather than oppose, Daniel was clearly sensitive to how the political implications of his historical poem were liable to vary from year to year; as the present changed so did the implications of his representations of the past. It was no accident that both John Speed and William Camden called Daniel "our *Lucan*," and that other contemporary critics of Daniel's text compare it with Lucan's in aesthetic terms of style and poetic achievement.[66] Daniel does begin his poem with explicit echoes of the *Pharsalia*, but we might consider just what it meant for him to be critically associated with Lucan. Is the inference that Daniel's historical poem criticizes, directly or obliquely, the court which supports him? Or is the comparison simply a literary observation, that Daniel's text claims historical authenticity even though it is written in verse? Whatever the case, the association with Lucan suggests how English readers read Daniel's historical poem. Evidently they anticipated political commentary on their own time; poetry had, after all, always admitted allegorical readings. Daniel's experience as England's Lucan evidently led him to recognize that to write historical poetry was inevitably to engage in a potentially risky political discourse. The history of his revisions, at least, demonstrates his sense that the meaning of his text was up for grabs, as much a matter of when and by whom it is read as of his purposes and skills in writing. Hence his turn to prose, "the common tongue of the world" as he calls it, for writing his *Historie of England*.[67]

But the political range and character of historical poetry during this century are at once both more general and more detailed than accounts based on generic difference might suggest, partly because historical representation subsumes and infiltrates genres. Pastoral, for instance, perhaps the most politicized genre of the century, commonly disguised ideology in historical commentary. And when generic boundaries are most unstable, political commentary is most to be expected. In her recent study of Herrick, for instance, Ann Coiro shows how it is only once we have grasped *Hesperides* as "generic innovation" that we can attend to its complex political designs, its double action of commending and criticizing Stuart ideology even as it laments the passing era of royalist values and Charles's power.[68] In "The Argument of His Book," Herrick opens the *Hesperides* (1648) by announcing:

> I SING of *Brooks*, of *Blossomes*, *Birds* and *Bowers*:
> Of *April*, *May*, of *June*, and *July*-Flowers.
> I sing of *May-poles*, *Hock-carts*, *Wassails*, *Wakes*,
> Of *Bride-grooms*, *Brides*, and of their *Bridall-cakes*.
>
> . . .
>
> I sing of *Times trans-shifting*; and I write
> How *Roses* first came *Red*, and *Lillies White*.
> I write of *Groves*, of *Twilights*, and I sing
> The Court of *Mab*, and of the *Fairie-King*. . . . [69]

His "open challenges to the spirit of civil war," as Douglas Bush calls these lines, deliberately and concisely evoke an idealized version of those sociopolitical conditions that are disappearing even as he writes.[70] To Herrick's muse, social history often presupposes a once-available natural order that magically links seasonal change with human life and activity under merry monarchs. Maypoles, hock carts, bridal cakes, and other signs of rural plenitude symbolically evoke the time-honored social practices by which English countryfolk accommodate themselves to seasonal change and which, he would argue, should be as natural and as historically fixed and inevitable as the yearly round itself. Thus represented, a highly complex structure of social activities and values is announced and celebrated as though things should not be otherwise. Even monarchy can be made to seem as natural and inevitable as the seasonal cycle. Herrick's purpose, of course, is to lament the passing of such an age and, as Coiro says, to analyze the causes of Stuart failure. A central strategy of that purpose is this historicization of an idealized social order that seems natural, implicitly prior to any particular instance of monarchic success or failure, yet inextricably bound up with the magic of a benevolent monarchy.

Most poets seeking to legitimate a specific sociopolitical order, whether idealized or actually existing, employed such strategies of naturalization through historicization. Elsewhere in *Hesperides*, most notably in his epistle "To Sir Lewis Pemberton," and his georgic "The Hock Cart," Herrick laments the passing of Stuart power through this same procedure of naturalizing idealized historical conditions.[71] As Coiro points out, Herrick deliberated over the publication of *Hesperides* in 1648, just as the Stuart cause was hopelessly lost.[72] Dedicated "To the Most Illustrious and Most hopeful Prince Charles, Prince of Wales," *Hesperides* establishes and celebrates what a committed servant of the crown considers to be best in English social life—how things should be, naturally and historically. Challenges to benevolent monarchy are treated with epigrammatic irony that declares Herrick's complex but consistent political stance. For example:

> LEt Kings Command, and doe the best they may,
> The saucie Subjects still will beare the sway

> (p. 138)

This kind of wit presents us with a highly politicized view of the world in language that makes it seem as though it were natural, normal, and inevitable that kings should command. Herrick limits future possibilities by carefully studied language: how could "subjects" ever "bear sway" without the very burden itself becoming a cause of subjection? Indeed, can "subjects" control power and yet remain "subjects"? (This is the very paradox upon which Dryden plays in the remarkable opening lines of *Mac Flecknoe*.) If Herrick announces that he sings of Queen Mab and the Fairy King, he does so because he can, or will, imagine only worlds organized according to what have always been, in his view, the natural and historical conditions of the English nation: a benevolent hierarchy.

A characteristic and distinguishing feature of the historical poetry written on behalf of the early Stuarts, which reaches beyond immediate concerns for current events, and which cannot be fully described or accounted for in standard generic terms, is this legitimation of a social model as natural because it can be made to appear historical. Things should be the way the poet reports them always to have been. Since all kinds of poetry were recognized to serve didactic purposes, authorial intention was easily subsumed in generic function.[73] Any kind of poetry could offer general political advice, opinions, and attitudes in this way. And all genres commonly did, most frequently by urging readers to accept general models of ideal social relations based on a model of the idealized past. Nevertheless, within this broadly defined range of historical poetry, we can distinguish certain formal and ideological developments peculiar to the poetry written in English during the revolutionary decades of the seventeenth century. Distinct from poems which encourage us to accept idealized versions of the existing social order, new strains emerge that address specific social and political problems in order to advocate the doctrines of a faction or group seeking to influence national policy. Whatever their political alliances might be, poets profess the interests of a seemingly unified nation. But national unity itself was ever, at best, only a discursive ideal toward which people might strive rather than an actually achieved social condition. From the accession of James on, poets represented the nation as though it had a unified past, with political institutions already firmly in place, in order—directly or implicitly—to expose the features of social instability crucial to the central decades of the century and attempt a resolution that would constitute a return to social unity. But with growing regularity throughout the century, poets isolate specific problems which they then proceed to analyze from various oppositional perspectives, usually in order to advocate a solution as though it were best for the nation as a whole.

Even when advancing social doctrines that not all readers of English would be equally eager to accept, poets typically pose as incorruptible spokesmen of patriotic and civil virtues. In "On the Birth of Prince Charles" in 1630, for instance, Richard Corbett provides a schematic model of social relations in order to advance the interests of the royal family. But in doing so, he reminds other people to keep their place in no uncertain terms:

> This Child shall have attending his sweete raygne
> Reverence and Love; his Common vulgar Trayne
> Laborious and not wise; his Citizen
> A better Judg of wares than newes or men;
> A Gentry more Obedient than Learn'd;
> And his Nobility shal be discern'd
> By b'ing as Kings (for Love, not Powre) desiring
> The Crowne may flourish, to it not aspiring;
>   . . .
> That Peace, rich warlick Peace, I meane Consent

Betweene the Closet and the Parliament;
No Trumpet sounding Wars, and when it must
It shall be forrayne, fortunate, and just.[74]

Corbett's genethliaca, a "publike rejoycing . . . at the nativities of Princes chilren,"[75] addresses the entire nation, praising everyone able to read for presumed loyalty to the Stuart dynasty. Yet in forecasting the continuance of an apparently stable regime, this vision of national unity admits precise lines of social division that, increasingly, were seen as threatening Stuart claims to political absolutism. The poem displays considerable apprehension about evidence that laborers were starting to think, citizens to show an active interest in current events, landowners to become highly skilled in litigation, the nobility ("By b'ing as Kings") to seem increasingly jealous of power, and Parliament to appear reluctant to obey the Privy Council. With the recognition of class divisions such as these, a note of anxiety disturbs the confidence of Corbett's prophecy, which was written, after all, at a time of severe famine, plague, drought, and civil unrest.[76] Read in the context of its times, Corbett's poem serves as a warning as much as a celebration. Many politically influential Englishmen—like Sir John Eliot and the other eight Commons members held in the Tower for refusing to accept the king's supremacy, as well as the rioters throughout the West Country and parts of the Midlands—were obviously not accepting the limitations of their social position for the sake of national unity under the "personal" rule of Charles Stuart. And we can, I think, safely presume that many of those addressed by Corbett's poem—master craftsmen involved in city councils; merchants with overseas investments, many of whom granted substantial loans to the crown via royal agents; sons of landed families who had been trained for administrative duties at the universities and Inns of Court; power-hungry lords and bishops—would be far from content with the positions in the national model to which they are here assigned.[77]

Yet fewer still would have been content with the model of national order advocated in "The Digger's Song," an extreme example of the oppositional stances increasingly articulated in the years leading up to the civil wars. Where Corbett offers the illusion of national unity, the "Song" emphasizes social injustice and discord in order to advocate revolution. What is distinctively partisan about this poem is that the solution offered would satisfy only a precise and identifiable class—the disenfranchised.[78]

You noble Diggers all, stand up now, stand up now,
  You noble Diggers all, stand up now,
The waste land to maintain, seeing Cavaliers by name
Your digging does disdain, and persons all defame.
  Stand up now, stand up now.

Your houses they pull down, stand up now, stand up now,
  Your houses they pull down, stand up now, stand up now.
Your houses they pull down to fright poor men in town,
But the gentry must come down, and the poor shall wear the crown,
  Stand up now, Diggers all.[79]

A description of the obvious stylistic and generic differences between this song, Herrick's "Argument" and epigram, and Corbett's genethliaca would not fully distinguish their varying degrees of political commitment or, of equal importance, the central differences in historical and political attitudes which they represent. Professing to speak on behalf of the entire nation when advocating the continuity of the established political order, Herrick and Corbett evoke a tradition, powerful in Elizabethan poetry, of anxiety at the prospect of future change. The "Song," on the other hand, speaks directly on behalf of one portion of the nation when it advocates revolution to solve the problem of political inequity which it professes to have discovered in the current order. In 1648 Herrick's "Argument" confronts the inevitability of political change by praising the historicity of "natural" sociopolitical institutions under kings and queens. Corbett warns various classes not to disrupt the status quo. And whereas Herrick's epigram wittily confronts the threat of political change by describing the future in abstract terms ("subjects will bear the sway"), the "Song" makes change both imaginable and (to some) desirable, by characterizing the future in precise concrete terms of popular sovereignty: "the poor shall wear the crown."

This poem's program for political innovation, though unusually radical, nevertheless illustrates a characteristic development in seventeenth-century poetry. During the early years of the century, poets either avoided direct comment upon political matters or wrote about them in the most general terms, regarding the possibility of future change with apprehension, while, for the most part, conflating national interests with those of the royal house. But during the growing social and political unrest of the twenties and thirties, Stuart poets become increasingly partial in their portraits of the nation, frequently admitting—as in Corbett's poem of

1630—that the existing social and political fabric is being threatened and needs to be defended. By 1647, after the Commons had assumed control, one royalist balladeer was able to achieve a degree of ironic detachment from the transformation of kingdom into state:

> The hierarchy is out of date;
> Our monarchy was sick of late;
> But now 'tis grown an excellent state:
> Oh, God a-mercy, Parliament.[80]

But for poets who wished to write critically of early Stuart policy, the difficulties were obviously at once both more immediate and more intense than could be solved by ironic detachment.

Here, where irony fails, the discursive gap between the truths claimed by the poet and the historian provides a language for registering potentially subversive political designs: "historical poetry." In verses commending John Russell's *Battels of Lypsich, and Lutzen,* Thomas Riley, a fellow of Trinity College, Cambridge, engages familiar tropes that spatialize the historical subject into a textual object representative of the truth. He sets the terms of political contestation within the frame of encouraging a friend to publish his poems. *"Friend,"* he writes to Russell,

> thy first-fruits are sacred. GUSTAVES Name
> Is then (O *Muses*) more authenticall.
> Nor shall't be *Heresie* in verse to claim
> Aid from live *Names,* and still *Imperiall.*
> He shall preserve thy *Papers,* and vent more
> Then an enlarg'd *Edition.* His *Name*
> Shall be thy *Title* too, and fill the doore
> Of the rich Shop it lies in; like the Frame
> Of some rare *Frontispice,* with neat device
> Tying unto it the Spectatours eyes.
> So both in equall tye are excellent;
> Thy Book's His *Elegie,* He its *Monument.*
>
> (Sig. ¶¶2)

What is intriguing about these lines is their use of intimate address to engage a hot political topic. The apostrophe invites the reader to overhear one side of a dialogue between friends, one of whom is apprehensive about how this book will be interpreted. By reassuring Russell that the fame of his topic will legitimate publication of his poem, Riley both admits and avoids concerns over the very real risks involved; publishing news of the Swedish king's exploits had, after all, been prohibited back in 1632. Riley's familiar tone, with its bookish tropes and invocation of the writer-intellectual whose work bears directly upon international politics, encourages readers to think of Russell's poem as legitimate heroic discourse in which something potentially dangerous is going on. That danger is writing about Gustavus Adolphus who, before his death, had come to be regarded by many in England as the great champion of protestantism. The "official" attitude of loyal supporters of crown policy was best expressed in Thomas Carew's celebrated expression of Stuart *otium*, his *Answer of an Elegiacal Letter, upon the Death of the King of Sweden, from Aurelian Townshend, Inviting Me to Write on That Subject:*

> What though the German Drum
> Bellow for freedome and revenge, the noyse
> Concernes not us, nor should divert our joyes.[81]

Not everyone was happy with this solution. Those in England who disagreed with the Stuart policy of nonintervention were eager for reports of Gustavus Adolphus' military adventures during the Thirty Years War. David Norbrook has pointed out how the "Spenserians"—William Browne, Fulke Greville, Samuel Daniel, Michael Drayton, George Wither, and others who had long been critical of James's policy—viewed the accession of Charles in 1625 with renewed hope that England would finally take its rightful place as head of the protestant cause in Europe. Ralph Knevett, who began a continuation of *The Faerie Queene,* "took it for granted that Spenser's 'Faerie Land' included the fortunes of protestantism throughout Europe" and so named Gustavus Adolphus as his hero. But, as Norbrook concludes, by the time "Knevett had finished the supplement Charles had reverted to a pro-Spanish policy and the poem was never published."[82] Disappointment at Charles's refusal to commit himself more actively to the protestant war effort in Europe became especially acute with Gustavus Adolphus' "phenomenal wave of successes," beginning with his victory at Breitenfeld in September 1631 and continuing until the battle of Lutzen on November 6, 1632, when the Swedish king was killed in action.[83]

Other writers and poets critical of, or disappointed by, Stuart policy made a great deal of the Swedish king's heroic exploits. Public interest in "the king that had turned the wheele of Christendom with so swift a motion, the brave Swede," as Sir Thomas Barrington describes him in a private letter of April 1632,[84] had become so keenly discomfiting to Charles that, on October 17, Star Chamber banned the newsbooks reporting European events. "It must have been quite sickening," writes the Swedish bibliographer Folke Dahl, "for King Charles to read in the English newsbooks about 'our brave King,' 'our gracious King,' 'our gallant defender of the Protestant Church,' etc., knowing all the time that these expressions referred to a foreign king and not to himself."[85] Yet in commanding the ban, Charles was acting under pressure from the Spanish agent in London with whom he had been engaged in semiprivate negotiations since January 1631 concerning the partition of the independent Netherlands. Lord Cottington, Charles's ambassador to Madrid, was among the signatories of the decree. This secretive and, at times, hypocritical aspect of Charles's foreign policy was to feed dissent in the years leading up to the outbreak of civil war.[86] The ban was effective; at least the periodical newsheets reporting European events seem to have stopped appearing from London presses. But censorship at this time was never entirely enforceable, and the death of the Swedish hero weeks later provoked the appearance of several eulogistic books in England.[87] A third part of *The Swedish Intelligencer,* an irregular newsbook that had begun appearing in 1632 before the Star Chamber decree, somehow managed to appear during the early months of 1633. A 227-page quarto containing ten elegaic poems on Gustavus Adolphus, this third part was, apparently, printed in Lisbon and does appear without an additional "fourth" part.[88] And despite the ban, in 1634 a final reissue, *Compleat: All 4 Parts,* claiming to be "now the fourth time, Revised, Corrected, and augmented," appeared. The only augmentation, however, is the new title page over the 1633 text.[89]

Evidently the ban on news of the Thirty Years War was no longer strictly enforced by 1634, the year in which Russell's poem appeared. But the apparently straightforward fact that the ban existed at all may mislead us into imagining too simple a political scenario consisting of an official crown policy and an opposition. On inspection, both terms prove radically unstable; crown foreign policy during the thirties was often not to have one, while even the militant protestants keen to revive the reformationist zeal of Elizabeth's reign by drawing attention to Gustavus Adolphus represent significant social and political diversity. Even among themselves, the group of Cambridge friends and colleagues who wrote poems prefacing Russell's poem figure the political variability which makes generalizing about the status of any group opinion at the time highly problematic. In 1634 these men were all willing to publish their support for a poem that could not help but be regarded as potentially critical of Stuart pacifism and so likely to meet official hostility. In the cause of militant protestant propaganda, these men could all agree. But if we consider their careers over the next dozen years, we are forced to recognize how their willingness to voice public opposition in 1634 does not mean that these men constituted anything remotely like a consistent political opposition to Stuart government. Although associated here with anti-Stuart sentiment, Riley, John Pullen, and Richard Bulkley would prove supporters of the crown; at least all were ejected from their college fellowships in 1644 by the Parliament that had removed the king. At one end of the sociopolitical spectrum is Caesar Williamson who, like Riley, went up to Trinity with a scholarship from Westminster. Elected to a fellowship at Trinity in 1633, Williamson was ordained at Lincoln in 1640 and made canon at York in 1641. In 1642 he abandoned his Cambridge fellowship for Magdalen, Oxford, where he joined the king's army and fought at Edgehill the same year. Of humbler origins, John Saltmarsh was still a pensioner at Magdalene, Cambridge, when he was invited to write verses commending Russell's poem. This is the young man from Yorkshire who in 1646 would become the Calvinist chaplain to Fairfax and, eventually, the New Model Army. Of John Russell, the poet who brought this group together (with Stephen Jones of whom I can find no record), there is little to say: in 1634, the same year he published his poem, he was ordained and made rector at Chingford in Essex where he kept out of trouble and died in 1687.[90]

It is, perhaps, an indication of how issue oriented politics at the time tended to be that, in 1634, these men all agreed to take the risk of celebrating the military exploits of Gustavus Adolphus. In doing so, however, they specifically oppose other encomiasts and elegists. John Pullen complains bitterly of the poets who were inspired to write on the death of the Swedish king. "O inconsiderate Muse!" he complains, "Of him is't fit / That every budget brain and common wit / Should write a farthing Pamphlet?" (sig. ¶¶). For his part, Riley sardonically observes that the Swedish martyr "Suffers all Prose, or Verse" since "Deitie / Accepts an offring from the meanest trade" (sig. ¶¶ᵛ). Riley's larger design in drawing attention to both the riskiness of Russell's poem and the precise his-

toricopolitical moment of its appearance locates Russell's text in precise
opposition to *The Swedish Intelligencer* and other publications praising
the Swedish martyr. The immediate object of hostility was, presumably,
the 1634 reissue. Riley distinguishes the form, and affect, of Russell's
poem from those of the reissued *Swedish Intelligencer* with its elegaic
verses. Shifting his own verse into heroic couplets in imitation of Russell's
verse, he points an accusatory finger directly at the author of *The Swedish
Intelligencer* before proceeding to describe the importance of formal ma-
neuvers in the context of legal restrictions and the politics of publishing:

> WHat loose *Prose* could not pay to *Swedens* Herse,
> Thou has discharg'd in thy Heroick Verse,
> Th' *Intelligencers* Feet, on which he'l runne
> Now round the world, like a surveying *Sunne*.
> 'Twas greater art to chuse thy Theme, then write
> Some *Poems*. But to pen it in despite
> Of others grief, or silence, argues *Love*
> Great as thy *Art*. And if the People prove
> Thy hand hath rudely op't a publick wound
> Newly clos'd up; the *Magistrate's* not bound
> (As *Athens* mulcted *Phrenicus*) to be
> Their *Censor,* and to fine thy *Historie*.

(Sig. ¶¶2)

Precisely because Russell has written a poem in the heroic style, Riley
argues, his eulogy is acceptable since poetry organizes history and thus
distances it from immediate political circumstances in ways that newsbooks like *The Swedish Intelligencer,* with their "loose *Prose*" reports,
could not.

How might we account for Riley's obvious hostility to *The Swedish
Intelligencer?* Despite the rough syntax here, his verses clearly accuse the
author—or authors—of that publication of looking down upon global
events from the position of an uncommitted spectator. It is tempting to
imagine that Riley must have written these lines with a copy of the 1634
edition of *The Swedish Intelligencer* in front of him, so direct is the reference to the "loose *Prose*" tracts that contained "Some *Poems*" expressing
"others grief." Moreover, his argument that Russell's "art" achieves a
transcending and transforming *"Love* / Great as thy *Art"* reads like a
direct marginal commentary upon the pretensions of the writer of the
Intelligencer who, in the preface to the third part, writes:

I have done all, with as much diligence, as a Scholler (*morally*) might doe. . . . And something more than a common diligence, have I used in it. The *Italian Painter* hath 3. *degrees* of *Comparison,* in the preferring of his *Peeces.* If he saies tis but done *con diligenza,* with diligence, tis no great commendation of his paines, for he meanes no more than an ordinary diligence. His second degree of praysing it, is *con studio,* with study: and by that would he tell you, that his braine and hand; have a little more laboured, both upon the *designing* and the *colouring.* But if he addes *con amore,* that hee did it with a *love* and an *affection,* to the *Piece* or *Party:* oh! tis *di Madonna,* then: and the *Italian* himselfe is at the highest of his expression. (Sigs. *–*ᵛ)

Given that history writing required the transformation of temporal process into spatial objects—like paintings—which could be seen, we should be perhaps less surprised by this comparison with painting than by Riley's wishing to object to the overblown terms in which it is made. And in the context of contemporary critical discourse, we should observe in Riley an equally familiar move, that he should have appropriated from this preface the link between "love" and "art" while suppressing the term "*Party.*"

At issue here is the general understanding that the use of visual and spatial metaphors to articulate the historicity of a particular piece of writing clearly marks a political discourse. Even read apart from the *Intelligencer,* Riley's verses plainly argue that the formal artistry of Russell's heroic poem transforms contemporary events into a historical subject, thereby achieving a truth higher than any newsbooks. Yet this aesthetic distancing functions both as a means for insisting that Russell's account is not simply partisan but demonstrably true, and as a preamble to Riley's more precise accusation which follows and which takes us, indirectly, back to the reasons for his opposition to *The Swedish Intelligencer:*

> No: Let us know, our Guilt that *Matchlesse Man,*
> Whose *Dirge* thou sing'st, hath murdred. Nay, I can,
> And dare tell how too: 'Twas the fond excesse
> Of our big thoughts decreas'd his Happinesse;
> Whose modest *Soul* we vext with restlesse crie
> Of love pretended, Proud *Idolatrie.*
> His purer *Breast* divin'd asmuch, while we
> Mad men still tempted him with *Prophecie.*

(Sig. ¶¶2)

The syntax has again become rough, perhaps deliberately so here in order to leave more room for equivocation. For surely Riley is suggesting something rather dangerous by inviting his readers to ponder how responsibility for Gustavus Adolphus' death needs to be shared, how he was betrayed and murdered by those who (like the English) idolized instead of aiding him, by those who encouraged him (like the *Intelligencer*) with dangerous prophecies of success rather than material support. What began as oblique praise of Russell's epic style has become a rather cryptic accusation of general guilt that nevertheless keeps *The Swedish Intelligencer* clearly in focus. Readers of these lines might have recalled how the preface to the first part of the *Intelligencer*, published in 1632 before Gustavus Adolphus' death, ended with just the sort of prophetic encouragement being here condemned:

> For that it seemes impossible for us *English* to avoyde that observation of *Philip de Commines*, That in all great actions, we are still harkning after Prophecies; (which the well taking of some things in this kind, hath even now verified;) wee will therefore feed the humor of the times a little, with a *prediction* of a famous Astronomer of our own Nation, upon that great *Conjunction* of *Saturne* and *Iupiter*, Iuly 18. 1623. And with a *Prophecy* out of *Paulus Grebnerus* his Booke, now in *Trinity College Library* in *Cambridge*. (Sigs. A2–A2ᵛ)

Perhaps Riley had some vested interest in keeping this prophecy from his college library out of the public eye. In any event, the astrological forecast and prophecy which then follow tell how "famines, plagues, warres, etc." in Italy, France, Bohemia, Silesia, and Germany will "go hard with the *Romane* Empire" and of "a King of a true Religion that should do all this" (sig. A2ᵛ). With such assurances of the Swedish king's inevitable success, why should anyone in Britain feel the slightest inclination to lend him aid?

Read with an eye on the domestic struggle for control over news of the Thirty Years War, Riley's verses illustrate just how issue oriented and tentative oppositional poetics was during the early thirties. There really was no "opposition poetry" as such, but rather poetry written from a variety of positions that opposed aspects of or trends in crown policy. And crown policy was far from being consistent or coherent. Riley's tactic, generalizing the accusation by means of that ever-ambiguous first-person plural that links king and people ("we vext," "we . . . tempted him with *Prophecie*"), barely disguises the charge being directed at Charles's

European policy which had been consistent in little but its inconsistency. In May of 1629 he had permitted Gustavus Adolphus to levy volunteer troops in Scotland and England. Then, twelve months later, he instructed Lord Cottington, his ambassador in Madrid, to propose an alliance with Spain aimed at weakening the Dutch.[91] This temporary rapprochement with Spain effectively reversed the more aggressive stance toward England's traditional maritime rivals which, following Buckingham's lead, Charles had urged upon his father six years before when the Swedish king had first proposed a protestant alliance against the catholic powers of Spain and Austria.[92] Negotiations with Spain continued through the summer of 1630, but Gustavus Adolphus forced matters to a crisis by landing an army on the Baltic coast in June. Throughout August Charles hesitated in his response, finally granting the Marquis of Hamilton permission to raise six thousand volunteers to serve with Gustavus, "a course," Gardiner comments, "which would not implicate himself, whilst it gave him, as he fancied, a title to the gratitude of the King of Sweden" (7:174–75). To the extent that he had one, Charles's plan— "our big thoughts"—was to try to bring about a negotiated settlement that would return the Palatinate to Frederick, his brother-in-law, weaken the power of the Dutch mercantile fleet in favor of his own, and keep Anglo-Spanish relations sufficiently amiable not to endanger British shipping interests without offending the French and without involving himself in the sort of expenses that would require summoning Parliament. In November he proceeded to sign a treaty with Spain followed in January 1631 by a secret alliance through which England and Spain would partition the Netherlands.[93]

We can only guess just how much of Charles's politicking at this time would have been general knowledge, but—judging by the flow of letters to Lady Barrington, for example—public interest was considerable, rumors and suspicion traveled surprisingly quickly, and certain events were impossible to hide. Throughout the spring and early summer of 1631, Hamilton had been gathering troops to fight alongside the Swedish king. On the twentieth of June Sir Thomas Barrington wrote to his mother, "Now the drumm beates in London dayly and forces increase." And again, four days later: "The Marquis of Hambleton gathers his forces dayly, the king haveing written new letters to the lords lieftenants in all countyes to assist in their utmost" (pp. 195, 197). Hamilton sailed in July, just in time to assist at the Battle of Breitenfeld in September. Enthusiasm for Gustavus Adolphus' victories among English protestants—such as the Barringtons, and men like Simonds D'Ewes and Sir John Eliot—was great, even though Hamilton had lost over five thousand English and Scottish lives by November.[94] As winter approached, Gustavus Adolphus' "happinesse decreased." He applied to Charles for more men and money, but met with official silence from the English court since to finance his requests would have necessitated summoning Parliament. And that was something Charles was not prepared to do. However, by November Sir Thomas Barrington could report that Lord Craven—the soldier to whom Russell's poem is dedicated—"is goeing over with 300 of his owne charge and 1000 for the king of Sweden" (p. 217). Through the winter of 1631/32 negotiations between Charles and his Privy Council began to break down, and it was only under pressure that, in late April, Charles was prepared to make an offer of "love pretended"; ten thousand pounds a month to finance the restitution of the Palatinate. Gustavus Adolphus had already started out on a whirlwind campaign against the Hapsburgs.[95] "The papists," Sir Thomas Barrington wrote to his seventy-year-old mother in Essex,

> now interpret the prophecies of the Revelation concerning Antechrist upon the king of Swede, and say he shall continew the 3 yeears etc., but I hope God hath rayesed him to sett those in that stead, but not as the man-beast, I know, but the destroyer of that monster by God's blessing, or the preface to that greate worke. (P. 238)

Although this was a private correspondence, Sir Thomas invariably restricted himself to expressions of personal feeling, seldom even hinting at anything like a criticism of Charles's policy. But his letter home of May 25 makes it clear not only that information about the king's recalcitrance was available, but also that the forces at work behind the scenes were publicly recognized:

> Our king hath given way to the reayseing of 12 men for the assistance of the emperor of Russia, who rayses a greate armye for to side with the king of Sweden, which my lord Goearing tould me this day he had much adoe to procure by reson of the strong opposition of the Spanish partye. (P. 247)

The Barringtons, who were "typical of the Parliamentary gentry of England on the eve of the civil war,"[96] evidently followed the effects of official Stuart policy keenly and critically. Their correspondence is no longer available after October, but we can presume that they felt the death of Gustavus Adolphus, who had "turned the wheele of Christendome" in favor of European protestantism, as acutely as did Sir Simonds D'Ewes who wrote: "Never did one person's death in Christendom bring so much sorrow to all true protestant hearts . . . as did the King of Sweden's at this present."[97] Surely no reader interested in Russell's poem of 1634 could have missed the ironic weight of Riley's "our big thoughts" and that stinging "love pretended" which so accurately characterize the connection between Charles's personal rule and his minimal support of the great Swedish hero.

THE DISCOVERY OF THE PRESENT

The eagerness of poets to address contemporary issues in a relatively direct fashion indicates an increasing recognition—most often though not always reluctant—of social instability and, consequently, of the need for change in the political order. We can find early intimations of this development even among poems written to celebrate the accession of James to the English throne. Although James was refused the title of King of Britain, apprehensions over Elizabeth's successor easily gave way to momentary celebrations of the monarch who promised to unite the kingdoms of England and Scotland into a single nation-state. But within months of James's arrival, his scheme for a union between the two kingdoms encountered serious objections from the House of Commons.[98] Amidst disputes over the union, many poets wrote on behalf of the new king.[99] John Clapham, a member of Burghley's circle at Elizabeth's court, sounds anxiously hopeful about James's coronation:

> Those darksome clouds, which hanging o'er our heads
> Did threaten war, and miseries at hand,
> Are now dispersed. . .
>
> . . .
>
> "Success of time hath made two kindgoms one"
> Now link'd in league, never to be divorced.
> Such bliss, great Prince, doth thy fair entrance bring
> One God, one law, one people, and one King.[100]

Other poets writing to support the new regime mythologized not a stable and unified past but the *present* as the origin of a newly united British nation. Drawing his inspiration from Clio, the muse of history, Joshuah Sylvester (1605) recalls past division in order to show how it has been ended by the political and religious unity introduced under the new regime:

> JAMES, Thou just Heire of *England*'s joyfull UNION,
> UNITING nowe too This long sever'd ILE
>   (*Sever'd for Strangers, from it Selfe the while*)
> *Under One Scepter in One Faith's Communion.*[101]

In 1608 Morgan Coleman had also noted that "All rights conjoined in STEWARTS foure-fold crowne."[102] But the gap between poetical statement and political reality was all too evident. In 1628, Richard Verstegan suggested that the Stuart union was merely a political fiction based on James's claims to power rather than a social reality. He writes that "Jacobus Magnus" holds sway not only over England and Scotland, but over Ireland and France too, an arrangement in which the political symbolism of monarchy bears little relation to the socially and culturally diverse composition of the body politic: "Foure Nations now are subject to his might, / Though each to other strange accounted be."[103]

    With James's accession, Stuart poets were predominantly concerned with pretending that the currently existing realm, symbolically headed by the monarch, was a unified nation. In attempting to generate belief in the nation as something that already existed, court poets clarified the extent, limits, and ambitions of monarchic rule. Once patriotic optimism began to encounter widespread disenchantment with James's political ambitions, poets became preoccupied with the inseparable issues of whether there was a nation, what its historical status might be, and how it was to be governed best. They set themselves the task of defining, as precisely as their own political stance and their artistic endeavor would allow them, the nature, range, and legitimacy of existing institutional mechanisms of political representation. Clearly influenced by rapid developments in antiquarian research, local history, and the history of social, civic, religious, and legal institutions, poets mapped out versions of the national landscape, in both its internal configurations and its global relations, in accordance with discernible political ideals and motives. The Virgilian dual perspective of the island-nation at once apart from and yet within the world at large—"*toto divisos orbe Brittanos*—provided them with the necessary contradictions, ambiguities, and paradoxes needed to represent a complex social formation undergoing rapid political and cultural transformation.

To account for the development of historical poetry in seventeenth-century Britain is to account for the ways poets historicized the present by representing the emergent nation in terms of its past in support of their own class interests. Commonly represented as a "world without the world," as the second Eden, as Albion, as New Troy, or as the Fortunate Isles, the island nation appears as a garden haven separate from European wars during the halcyon days of the early Stuarts, as a war-torn landscape during the forties, as a refuge for victims of political injustice under Cromwell, to emerge, in the final decades, as the center of civilization and power for the world from which it is geographically separated. But each of these constitutes a strategic positioning rather than a simple reflection of an otherwise knowable condition. For the garden haven of pro-Stuart poetry served to distract attention from what many felt to be Britain's obligations toward the protestant cause in a Europe being devastated by the Thirty Years War. Even when defending Stuart policy, Jacobean and Caroline pastoralists instructed and informed their readers that there was an adversary lurking within the island. They did not always provide an accurate definition of this adversary, but nevertheless they warned of national instability and, in doing so, began to shatter the myth of a unified nation even as it was being formulated.

With the collapse of censorship in 1641, militant protestants seized the opportunity to write poetry that redefined images of the nation, recasting neoclassical versions of an arcadian world apart by introducing an apocalyptic strain which made the island kingdom the center of divinely instigated reformation that would eventually involve the world. Poets could hardly ignore the events taking place around them, but characteristically blamed the nation's chaos on the moral degeneracy of the present, either by harking back to some glorious past era of peace and prosperity which existed only negatively in the conventions of pastoral poetry, or by defining the Stuart peace as an age of repression and darkness. "During the civil wars," Patterson observes, "the pastoral myth of the halcyon days was undoubtedly recognized for precisely what it was, a proposition designed to ratify the behavior and circumstances of the ruling class."[104] Faced with the unprecedented task of defending the interregnum governments, governments without hereditary monarchs to serve as symbolic heads, poets shifted their sights overseas to adopt an international perspective that would displace discontent at home, a strategy later adopted and refined by poets writing to defend the Restoration. Let us consider in more detail how these changes came about.

2

English Poetry and the Struggle for a National History

AT THE beginning of the Stuart era, poetry and history were considered separate discursive strategies, but the distinction was commonly described in visual and spatial metaphors common to both. Among the arbitrary powers to which James laid claim was that of giving laws to poets whose writings he evidently considered peculiarly dangerous, sites of possible ambiguity and political resistance. Dutifully representing the island kingdom from above, court poets supported such claims by associating the perspective of the monarch with an all-seeing providential gaze that controlled everything it surveyed. What Jonathan Goldberg has called the "Jacobean 'style of gods,'"[1] a style that sought to impose classical Roman tropes and figures upon English culture generally and poetry in particular, was a crucial ideological instrument of James's will to power. But it was also one that contained within itself the conditions and terms of its own critique. For in writing on contemporary political themes in defiance of classical theory, poets were, in part, engaging the already present counterclaims of the new historiography which also purported to see and describe the world and the past objectively. And allusions to Roman history could be used against the court.

This chapter pursues echoes of a line from Virgil's First Eclogue which appear throughout English poetry of the century, the sort of trope which George deForest Lord has recently called a "classical presence," but which Fredric Jameson would call an "ideologeme." In *Pastoral and Ideology,* Annabel Patterson has mapped the political history of Virgilianism for Western Europe in general.[2] By the end of the fourteenth century, Patterson argues, the *Eclogues* "were found to enable a wide range of ideological activity, whose center was the concept of the writer-intellectual at work *sub umbra,* defending himself and his responsibilities in relation to the power structure of his own place and time" (pp. 60–61). Patterson continues by showing how, as early as 1502 with the publication of Brant's illustrated *Virgil,* pastoral had come to be associated with "the language of the common people" (p. 105), and so was particularly suited to addressing relations of labor to landownership and tenancy in seventeenth-century Britain. Following insights from Raymond Williams' *The Country and the City* and James Turner's *The Politics of Landscape,* Patterson's version of seventeenth-century pastoral maps out the coordinates of a crisis of cultural legitimation that resulted from the failure of James or Charles to sponsor the Baconian educational project[3] which she characterizes as "a pastoralized georgic, or vice-versa."

> Had it taken hold, and particularly had it been given royal or institutional support, it might well have protected England from the polarization that followed, with all its political consequences. What happened instead, as the policies of James I and Charles I became increasingly unpopular and hence on the defensive in terms of their cultural expression, was a split in class lines between intellectuals (a group increasingly conceived in aesthetic terms) and those involved in "work," whether commercial or agricultural."
> (P. 138)

Patterson's class analysis of pastoral covers several centuries. For the seventeenth in Britain, which she treats in some detail, we still need to know more about those invisible laborers before we can fully understand how pastoral and georgic mediated the capitalization of land, on the one hand, and mercantile expansionism on the other.[4] In the first part of this chapter, I am interested in the more limited question of how the use of a line from the First Eclogue in seventeenth-century historical poetry documents the various ways "poetry" figures the common discourse of political subjects, the ordinary language of those whose lives depend on others with power over them, as a means of defining both the nation to which they are subject and the conditions of that subjection.

In Dryden's version of Virgilian pastoral, for instance, specific shape is given to John Pocock's observation that "any formalized language is a political phenomenon in the sense that it serves to constitute an authority structure."[5] Dryden's dedication to Hugh, Lord Clifford, with which his translation of Virgil opens, reminds us how the culture's classical inheritance focused several interrelated modes of power, especially the prin-

ciples of patrilinear inheritance which informed both literary history and
political succession, and the drive among politically ambitious men to
fashion themselves by means of learning to read and imitate classical
poetry, especially Virgil's. Dryden's witty turns upon "master" and "shepherd" in his dedication bring the potentially reversible relations between
poet and patron into steady critical relief: through the very act of writing
dedications, the poet takes care of the cultural legitimacy of the hand
which feeds and rules him. While recommending his translation and
himself to the care of a former patron's son, Dryden speaks of the Eclogue as Virgil's "first Essay in poetry," thereby recalling how memoriz-
ing and translating passages from Virgil were commonly among the
more prestigious tasks assigned students at schools like Westminster.[6] So
pervasive was the general influence of the *Eclogues* via the educational
programs of the time that Patterson has argued that "Virgilian semiotics
became a kind of public shorthand. Because the conceptual structure of
this language was so well understood, its units could be used elliptically,
without, as it were, the syntax showing. Brief quotations could stand for
larger arguments or even an entire ideology" (pp. 140–41). In one reading, Dryden's version of Virgil's poem offers a modified model of political
absolutism in which only kings rule. Ordinary men, we can infer from
his translation, should concern themselves not with politics but with
writing poetry that will attract them a wife. This freedom to compose
erotic poetry is the privilege of those, like Tityrus, who occupy positions
of relative security in an unstable world. To the recently exiled Meliboeus, such license seems like a gift from some "Heav'nly power" (line
27). But it is also the reward for dutiful service to the state, this being
permitted the leisure to woo a wife who—ideally at least—once courted
and wed can be controlled. The use of gender hierarchy within the family to model the relations of rulers and subjects within the state is traditional enough, though it was a notably favorite trope in James's own
writings. In Stuart pastoral, the freedom to compose verses itself represents a form of power that becomes more desirable because of the presence of those, like Meliboeus, who lack it and are forced into exile.

   This structure of inclusion/exclusion, centralization/marginalization
aptly characterizes the politics of seventeenth-century English pastoral
since it not only "assures the stability of cultural explanations [such as
pastoral] in general,"[7] but also helps explain the oppositions, divisions,
and contradictions within pastoral descriptions of the nation aimed at
legitimating royal authority. Stuart poets typically adopt a long view that
looks in upon the nation from outside in order to support a centralizing

ideology that disables social and political threats by exclusion and displacement. The neoclassical emphasis in Jacobean and Caroline pastoral typically inscribes national unity by dividing the nation into court, city, and country, and then variously assigning perceived social dangers to a marginalized or displaced Other; landowners should leave the court and return to their estates, city lawyers and merchants should stop interfering in the running of the country, and women should quit the public stage and reenter the private sphere of domestic management.

But as we saw in the first chapter, while poets writing in support of the status quo became increasingly prescriptive and critical of particular policies or events, various forms of anti-Stuart poetry were emerging, especially among militant protestants such as those associated with Ralegh and the court and cult of Prince Henry. During the thirties and early forties oppositional poets described the nation by looking in different directions from those pursued by court poets, not in and down as if from some great height, but across and out to the greater world from which Britain was supposed to be apart. They saw the nation in terms less of insularity and neo-Virgilian pastoral than of Old Testament prophecy and the (commonly pastoral) discourse of Elizabethan protestantism. This shift in stance enabled the development of various oppositional poetics that sought to destabilize the isolationist vision of Stuart absolutism while commenting directly upon present concerns within broader historical and literary contexts.

FROM ARCADIA TO IMPERIUM: REPRESENTING THE NATION

Much of the enduring significance of Virgil's First Eclogue can be attributed to the way it gives precise dialogical form to political differences of subjectivity, class, and nationality. Like many Roman farmers during the period of civil war following the assassination of Julius Caesar in 44 B.C., Meliboeus has just been evicted from his farm.

> Round the wide World in Banishment we rome,
> Forc'd from our pleasing Fields and Native Home:
> While stretch'd at Ease you sing your happy loves:
> And *Amarillis* fills the shady Groves.

> (2:873)

After listening to Tityrus sing the praises of his patron, under whose protection he can continue his rural life, Meliboeus sets out to wander with the other exiles:

> But we must beg our Bread in Climes unknown,
> Beneath the scorching or the freezing Zone.
> And some to far *Oaxis* shall be sold;
> Or try the *Lybian* Heat, or *Scythian* Cold.
> The rest among the *Britans* be confin'd;
> A Race of Men from all the World dis-join'd.
>
> (2:876)

> [At nos hinc alii sitientes ibimus Afros,
> pars Scythiam et rapidum Cretae veniemus Oaxen
> *et penitus toto divisos orbe Britannos.*
>
> (Lines 64–66, emphasis added)

The characters of Tityrus and Meliboeus articulate both the contrast between and the interdependence of pastoral retreat and political struggle in a dialogue that figures a major shift in the politics of seventeenth-century historical poetry. For while Britain appears as an arcadian garden in Shakespeare, Daniel, Sylvester, and other poets writing early in the century, the "Race of Men from all the World dis-joined" emerges as a more fully developed nation with imperial ambitions in the poetic representations of mid-century. Changing images of the British Isles can be traced across generic lines in the various ways poets of the late sixteenth and early seventeenth centuries treated the island's separation from the rest of the world—often echoing Virgil's line. By tracing some of the differing uses poets made of the Virgilian topos, we can see how the imperial ambitions of the second half of the century were latent in earlier representations of the nation as an insular garden paradise. Imperial ambition appears as an oppositional poetic trope that anticipates and subsequently determines social policy.

Tropes based on Britain's insularity—and on Virgil's formulation of it—articulate the contradictions between social values based on national identity, independence, power, and destiny, and material conditions of social and political struggle. The notion of Great Britain as a world beyond the end of the world, we are told, "caught the fancy of the Elizabethans." It "has its roots in ancient geography and mythology, and . . . support for it was found in Elizabethan etymology and even in Biblical exegesis."[8] The idea endures long after the Elizabethans, though it receives its best-known expression in *Richard II* where Gaunt's famous vision brings together most of the commonplaces of the time: the island's remoteness as a sign of special grace, the island's fertility, its natural abundance, its isolation from and protection against a ruder world beyond its marine boundaries. Once geographical isolation has thus been accommodated within a providentialist history, the island's inhabitants can be treated as though they naturally constituted a unified political entity, a people united by their mutual separation from all others.

But the nation's isolation, like any topos, is self-deconstructing and liable to undergo changes at least as significant as its perpetuation. Virgil separates Britain and the Britons from the rest of the world in order to stress their remoteness from the known, habitable world familiar to his civilized readers. Such was the purpose too, no doubt, of the third-century grammarian Solinus who, in his *Polyhistor,* writes:

> the Sea coast Gallia had beene the ende of the worlde, but that the Ile of Brytaine for the largenesse thereof every way, deserveth the name almoste of an other Worlde.[9]

English writers of the late sixteenth and early seventeenth centuries, however, commonly transformed this sense of remoteness into a sign of peculiar grace and distinction. Insularity became a source of national pride rather than a cause for disparagement. Commonly attributed to the benevolence of some divine agency—Neptune, Fortune, and Nature are common, but so are political and military leaders—the remoteness of the island signifies a covenant of highest favor that gives Britons a special place in the world, marking them out for freedoms and privileges unknown elsewhere.

A typical Elizabethan formulation appears in a song, "The Marriage of Thame and Isis" (1586), by William Camden. Better known for writing chronicle history than poetry, Camden plays with the Virgilian line in a conventional manner that is interesting precisely for its conventionality. Natural and national differences are mystified by personification so that any possible political difference may be displaced into sexual difference and then resolved by marriage. The figure of Britona sings of

> how Brittany from all
> The world devided was,
> When *Nereus* with victorious Sea
> Through cloven rocks did passe.[10]

Imagined as a triumph of sea over land, the island's separation from the mainland enables Camden to displace national into sexual politics through a celebration of internal coherence—the marriage of the two rivers. Despite the political contradictions entailed in imagining the Britain of 1586 to be a unified nation, geophysical isolation from "the world" provides seemingly undeniable evidence of a higher unity based upon precise and "natural" gender hierarchies. In Camden's verses this unity is achieved, literally, in language—the "English" that takes over, embodies, and transforms the Virgilian echo. It is also a language that unsatisfactorily seeks to resolve the problem of an original violence—figured as the "victorious" passage of the sea "through cloven rocks"—in terms of sexual violation and dominance. When one form of violence figures another, any form of unity or resolution is but precariously achieved.

The Virgilian trope fascinated poets, no doubt partly because of its expressive range. Shakespeare employs it twice in *Cymbeline* (1609) to indicate differences of national character and political outlook. Responding to Lucius Cassius' demand for tribute to the Roman emperor, Cloten exclaims: "Britain's a world by himself, and we will nothing pay for wearing our own noses".[11] But the abrasiveness of his pompous self-reliance and unmediated patriotic fury contrasts sharply with Imogen's more reflective speculation later in the same act:

> I'th'world's volume
> Our Britain seems as of it, but not in't:
> In a great pool, a swan's nest: prithee think
> There's livers out of Britain.
>
> (3.4.139–42)

Faced with banishment, she feigns an indifference to the political force which she must obey. Some scholars have rejected the metaphor of the "swan's nest" for being un-Shakespearean, but the contrast between this formulation of Britain's insularity and Cloten's neatly distinguishes differing forms of national identity by means of the same literary figure.[12]

Further edge is given to the expressive range of the Virgilian topos in Samuel Daniel's *Civil Wars* (1599–1609) where it enables the poet to conflate popular discontent with geophysical isolation:

> "Why Neptune, Hast thou made us stand alone
> "Divided from the world, for this, say they?
> "Hemd'in, to be a spoyle to tyrannie,
> "Leaving affliction hence no way to flie?

"Are we lockt up, poore soules, heere to abide
"Within the waterie prison of thy waves,
"As in a fold, where subject to the pride
"And lust of Rulers we remaine as slaves?
"Here in the reach of might, where none can hide
"From th'eye of wrath, but onely in their Graves?
"Happie confiners you of other landes,
"That shift your soyle, and oft scape tyrants hands." [13]

Daniel explicitly distances his own sympathies from this position by insisting that it represents the views of "the malecontented sort [that] never can the present State comport" (1.70). But in giving voice to rebellious discontent, the lines rework familiar pastoral motifs—the need to fly from tyranny, and envy of other peoples who are freer to move beyond a tyrant's reach. And tyrannic power is here associated with the ability of "Rulers" to see—"th'eye of wrath"—what people are doing.

Such a range of expressive possibilities must have contributed to the popularity of the topos, but we need also to remark the contexts in which it was used. The single, undeniable fact of the island's separation from the mainland by the sea offers a double perspective. For, by being cut off from the world, the island could, as in Camden, seem capable of achieving a greater internal cohesion of parts than the larger world outside. But again, as Daniel's lines and Imogen's lament forcefully remind us, that very isolation might make it impossible to flee from tyranny and oppression. Tropes are always reversible. So while English writers generally agreed to disagree with Virgil and Solinus and insisted instead that remoteness was a sign of special privilege, they nevertheless used the trope in significantly different ways. Many represent the Britons as an island nation separate from the rest of the world in order to celebrate—directly or indirectly—the person or groups with greatest political power. Emphasizing geographical isolation serves to legitimate the current regime by making it seem structurally integral to the nation's political identity.

Examples of the use of Virgil's line to legitimate a current monarch by identifying ruler with the area ruled are common throughout the century. In 1608, Morgan Coleman employed the topos in the opening of a verse genealogy written to support the succession of James to the English throne: "Britaine: The various fortunes of this noble land, / (Once thought a world) lo heere abridged stand." [14] Two years later, in his masque *Love Freed From Ignorance and Folly,* Jonson praises the divinity of royal power by attributing to James the ability to see in its entirety the land over which he rules in much the same way that the king's position during the performance of masques was the only one which permitted a view of the entire spectacle. The topos provides the initial motif in the riddle with which the Sphinx confounds Love:

> First, Cupid, you must cast about
> To find a world, the world without.[15]

Through the centralizing language of divinely ordained absolutism, the riddle develops from here in an ornate fashion suitable for a courtly entertainment. But few of those watching the performance could possibly have taken as long as the character of Love seems to need to discover the solution, which is a transparent compliment endowing James with the godlike ability to rise, like the sun, and look down upon the "world without":

> 'Tis done, 'tis done, I have found it out:
> Britain's the world, the world without;
> The King's the eye, as we do call
> The sun the eye, of this great all;
> . . .
> Now Sphinx, I've hit the right upon
> And do resolve these all by one:
> That is, that you mean Albion.
>
> (Pp. 85–86)

Island nation and king are here "resolved" into that single but composite figure of Albion through a typical paradox that merges the monarch with—while elevating him above—the realm he rules.

But as echoes of the Virgilian line became increasingly commonplace in the language of Jacobean absolutism, the trope's application became increasingly complex and potentially self-critical. By 1613 Virgil's phrase had become so hackneyed that George Chapman could blithely misquote it while commenting on its use by other poets. In his masque for the marriage of Princess Elizabeth to the Elector Palatine he writes:

> For (according to our rare men of wit) heaven standing and earth moving, her motion (being circular) hath brought one of the most remote parts of

> the world to touch at this all exceeding isle: which a man of wit would image must needs move circularly with the rest of the world, and so ever maintain an equal distance. But poets (our chief men of wit) answer that point directly, most inginiously affirming that this isle is (for the excellency of it) divided from the world (*divisus ab orbe Britannus*).[16]

Here, as David Norbrook has pointed out, Chapman's achievement is to make "a speaker declare that the Britons are no longer . . . divided from the world; the Palatinate match had brought Britain into the mainstream of European Protestant politics."[17] The world apart from the rest of the world had indeed become a part of it.

The enduring usefulness of the Virgilian topos to differing political arguments and positions indicates how its precise formulation at any given time can be fully understood only as a constitutive element of a prevailing political discourse, an element that changes in direct relation to the stance of the text toward ideal or existing political conditions. These discontinuities can be illustrated across the century by considering two differing textual deployments of Virgil's line, one by Samuel Daniel in a sonnet from his *Delia* sequence of 1592 and one by Charles Hopkins in his play *Boadicea* written in 1697. After closely examining these particular instances, I shall trace some of the more general strategies poets used to forge an image of the nation—most often but not always using Virgilian allusions—in poems written during the intervening years in order to demonstrate how that changing image gave precise shape, meaning, and value to many of the vexing political disputes of the period. Rather than simply reflecting contemporary conditions, poetic images of the nation's internal organization and foreign relations commonly provided the terms in which social and political struggles were waged. For poets eager to celebrate the Stuart peace, the Virgilian line provided a convenient means of turning their backs upon the rest of the world and looking in upon the island nation from the divine heights of providential detachment. But for those seeking to criticize what they considered to be irresponsible insularity, it could provide a means of deploring Stuart isolationism.

Daniel's *Delia* (1592) and Hopkins' *Boadicea* (1697)

In sonnet 53 of the *Delia* sequence, written "at the Author's beeing in Italie," the lover praises his beloved as the fairest jewel of the fairest land. This guise of geographical exile from the loved one enables Daniel to achieve a seemingly objective stance for articulating erotic desire and patriotic longing. In this most typical of Elizabethan poetic forms, the object of desire slides quickly from mistress to nation illustrating how the language of sexual desire gives shape to political ambition—a phallic will to identify with the godlike power of kings to possess, control, and protect. Like the magnetized needle of a compass, the lover's "heart" responds to the natural and inevitable force of the beloved's eye:

> Drawne with th'attractive vertue of her eyes,
>   My toucht heart turnes it to that happy coast:
>   My joyfull North, where all my fortune lies,
>   The jewell of my hopes desired most,
> There where my *Delia* fairer than the Sunne,
>   Deckt with her youth whereon the world doth smile.
>   Joyes in that honor which her eyes have wonne,
>   Th'eternall wonder of our happy Ile.
> Flourish faire *Albion,* glory of the North.
>   *Neptunes* best darling, held betweene his armes;
>   Divided from the world, as better worth,
>   Kept for himselfe, defended from all harmes.
>   Still let disarmed peace decke her and thee;
>   And Muse-foe *Mars,* abroad farre fostred bee.[18]

After the octet's ardent contemplation of the distant residence of his beloved, the sestet shifts to a direct apostrophe to Britain. For it is here the poet's true desire resides, in the ability not only to command Albion to flourish, but also to order "Muse-foe *Mars*" to stay away from his woman/nation. The insistence upon peace in the final lines recalls how the closing years of Elizabeth's reign, when Daniel wrote the *Delia* poems, were a period of constant anxiety lest civil war should erupt at the queen's death. Daniel himself wrote *The Civil Wars,* in part, to warn against the evils of internal strife.

We might also consider the more general political implications of Daniel's manipulation of generic convention. During the 1590s it was the fashion to address sonnet sequences, like *Delia,* to queens and ladies at court, powerful women who could offer poets patronage, money, status, and influence. But, as Arthur Marotti has shown, the vogue for writing amorous sonnet sequences served "as a form of mediation between socio-economic or sociopolitical desires and the constraints of the established order."[19] Here, the sonneteer pays tribute both to his loved one and to his nation by comparing Delia with Albion, both of them worthy of the highest love and praise. Political loyalty is constructed within the heterosexual norms of phallic desire which here begins in apparent subordination, aroused by the "attractive virtue" of the beloved's eyes, but ends with the achievement of a language that can both command and warn.

Certain notable poetic features of this erotics of domination survived Elizabeth's reign. Stuart poets often portrayed the nation as the desirable body of a virgin-nymph worthy of the highest adoration. In 1635, for example, Crashaw identifies the queen with the nation in his panegyric "Upon the Duke of Yorke his Birth" first published in *Voces Votivae Ab Academicis Cantabrigiensibus.* It is Henrietta Maria's sexuality, her ability to generate a race of heroic warriors who will defend the royal house, that provides the logic of praise and allows the poet to figure her body as the site within which all Britain's hopes for the future find imagined "roome" for realization:

> Illustrious sweetnesse! In thy faithful wombe,
> That Nest of *Heroes,* all our hopes finde roome.
> Thou art the Mother *Phaenix,* and thy Breast
> Chast as that Virgin honour of the East [i.e., Cynthia],
> But much more fruitful is. . . . [20]

While such conflations of the nation with the queen's body were especially common during the reign of Elizabeth, whose problematic virginity resembled that of the untouched and untouchable island, Edmund Bolton writing in 1632 observed that poets had traditionally conflated the nation with its queen regnant. Again the emphasis falls on virginity as the condition of royal power:

> But ever under Virgins was our Ile.
> The blessed Virgin had it in her style,
> After *Diana* had the title lost;
>
> . . .
>
> *England* was after call'd, Our Ladies Dow'r.
> And we have seen it under maidens pow'r;
> *Eliza,* Maiden Queen, her title reft:
> *Dian'* to *Mary, Mary* t'her it left,
> *Eliza* so was by another name,
> Enstyled *Cynthia;* nor amisse the same.[21]

As Peter Stallybrass comments regarding the Ditchley portrait of Elizabeth, "The state, like the virgin, was a *hortus conclusus,* an enclosed garden walled off from enemies. . . . As she ushers in the rule of a golden age, [Elizabeth] is the imperial virgin, symbolizing, at the same time as she is symbolized by, the *hortus conclusus* of the state."[22]

When Daniel personifies the nation as Albion, he manipulates the conventions of his genre and the associations of the untouched because untouchable figure to comment upon his own times, representing at once the will to power typical of the dependent courtier class to which he belonged as well as a wish for peace common to all loyal subjects of the crown. While his sonnet may be described in these general terms as political, it is by no means partisan in the sense I discussed earlier, but nationalistic in support of an existing status quo. The institution of monarchy as such was not seriously in question at the time. What mattered was patrilinear succession. Rather than questioning that principle, Daniel in his desire for peace displaces potential civil conflict into the realms of sexuality and aesthetics; for poets who would be lovers, Mars is "Muse-foe." Daniel comments on his own times in terms that make the current political order seem unquestionable, as "natural" and "ahistorical" as heterosexual desire.

Later poets, by contrast, criticize the current form of the political order by discovering problems to which they purport to offer a solution, usually one that is constructed in light of the past. They tell us that something must be done in order to advance the interests of a group engaged in political dispute. The point is best clarified by a contrast that illustrates how what began as a critical position had become dominant by the end of the century.

In 1697, when the structure of English society had altered as the result of at least two political revolutions, Charles Hopkins in his play *Boadicea* employed the Virgilian topos to portray the nation in ways that register specific changes in political relations. Following the Williamite Revolution of 1688, when Parliament had shown its effective ability to control the appointment and election of the monarch, royal claims to arbitrary power had greatly diminished from the days of the early Stuarts. Given a broader base of political representation than would have been thinkable under Elizabeth, Hopkins addresses a public oration to those in command, encouraging them to accept the opinions of one group in the name of national unity. During the century dividing Daniel from Hopkins, the erotics of political ambition have been replaced by the rhetoric of imperialistic zeal. The Virgilian trope of Britain's Otherness persisted. In Hopkins' tragedy, the character Cassibelan protests the growth of foreign power over the independent Britons:

> Let her [Rome] make all the World besides her own,
> Nature has made us for our selves alone.
> She fix'd our Isle, cast the wide Seas around,
> Made the strong Fence, and shall not hands be found
> In *Britain,* to maintaine the *British* bound?
>
>   (P. 4)

The invocation of ancient rights against the imposed control of a foreign power might invite speculation that Cassibelan is a late-seventeenth-century Jacobite, calling for armed resistance against the recently imported king, William of Orange. At the time of writing *Boadicea,* moreover, Hopkins was a protégé of Dryden, the great old man of English letters lately dispossessed of all public offices at the Revolution.[23] In performance too, the play's celebration of the legendary heroism of an ancient British queen would surely have generated similar speculations about the play's potential Jacobitism.

Whether Jacobite or not, Cassibelan's lines articulate partisan interests that contrast with Daniel's more generalized wish for peace. They analyze political divisions within the nation in order to offer a solution. Whatever the implications of the lines might have been at the time—and they are, after all, spoken in context by a character in a play—this partisan element signals marked changes in style and deployment of traditional ideas and motifs. In place of Daniel's legendary Albion, this later poet refers to a political location with rights that require defense. Gone is the divine lover Neptune, replaced by the more abstract "wide Seas" commanded by "Nature." And this supreme natural force, in the balanced couplets, marks off the nation for special favors, giving her the seas to protect her from foes. While Daniel personifies and then addresses Albion directly, ensnaring the reader's agreement with his celebration of royal absolutism by writing of war as an enemy to the muses, Hopkins assumes a more public tone that speaks to a wider audience in the hortatory style of political oratory. Daniel assumes unquestionably the reader's acquiescence in his myth and commitment to the principle of monarchy; Hopkins aims to move a divisible audience to act in a certain way for love of country. Although both poets employ a similar trope to characterize the nation, the personification and erotic sensuality of the sonnet give way to the rhetoric of political persuasion and dramatic enactment.

Between Daniel and Hopkins, these stylistic and generic changes in the uses of the Virgilian line increasingly encouraged readers to think and feel about the dominant political institutions in relation to a particular conception of national identity and independence. The rest of this chapter concerns representations of the nation built from alternative tropes and conventions. During the reign of James, when Parliament began challenging royal authority, poets wrote ever more directly about current circumstances, variously identifying monarch and nation but also indicating the lines of social and political tension that were dividing the body politic into distinct interest groups. With the increase of political unrest during Charles's reign, contemporary events came to be treated ever more directly and forcefully, often by elevating pastoral tropes into the high style of epic and tragedy. The national image comes to be transformed from a garden paradise free from foreign conflicts into both the theater of a seemingly universal tragedy and the heroic center of a newly emergent global empire rivaling Augustan Rome in both arms and arts. At any given moment we can find poets deploying familiar images, tropes, and themes in complex vehicles that portray the nation in ways which legitimate the authority of those in power. But we also find this same arsenal of poetic weaponry being used for more subversive ends that call into question the very terms in which it was possible to imagine national unity. During the early 1640s a more virulent poetry appears that redefines the nation through appropriating and subverting the neoclassical island tropes, sometimes replacing them altogether. Counter to the classicizing tendencies of court poetry, the oppositional poets of the thirties and forties do not pretend to be kings pretending to be gods looking down at the island nation in order to direct the course of its history. Instead, they typically represent contemporary events by turning to the Old Testament in order to understand how the signs of their own times were to be taken for wonders.[24]

THE NATION TAKES SIDES: STUART POETICS, 1603–1648

During the early decades of the century, many poets sought to legitimate the new dynasty by resuscitating Elizabethan tropes of the nation as an idealized garden paradise, an "earth of majesty," and mingling them with Virgilian allusions. Such figures were in general accord with

James's isolationism and Charles's personal rule since they commonly disguised social and political unrest beneath an arcadian rhetoric of natural, rural simplicity. Shortly after James's accession, Joshuah Sylvester hailed the nation in typical terms:

> All-haile (deere ALBION) Europes Pearle of price,
> The Worlds rich Garden, Earths rare Paradice.[25]

By this time the parallel between the political state and the garden had long been established as a stock figure.[26]

While tending to idealize the nation in seemingly apolitical ways, this isolationist and arcadian image was by no means unresponsive to shifts in the social and political order and could be put to oppositional uses. Meliboeus' banishment from his farm is, after all, an essential part of Virgil's version of the pastoral which was "devised . . . not of purpose to counterfait or represent the rusticall manner of loves and communication: but under the vaile of homely persons, and in rude speeches to insinuate and glaunce at greater matters, and such as perchaunce had not bene safe to have beene disclosed in any other sort. . . ."[27] As a metaphor for the nation, the garden already contained, as it were, the serpent of its own destrucution. Even in Gaunt's vision, this other Eden is also a "sceptered Isle" and a "seat of Mars." The symbols and icons of imperial power seem to have been integral to arcadian conceptions of Britain's garden state. Although imperialistic elements provide only a minor part of Gaunt's vision—where they are carefully submerged within the naturalizing imagery—they accumulate increased force in Sylvester's apostrophe to the world's rich garden. He personifies Albion as a composite figure, thus naturalizing military expansionism by means of an agricultural metaphor:

> Thrice-happy Mother, which ay bringest forth
> Such Chivalry as daunteth all the Earth,
> (Planting the Trophies of thy glorious Armes
> By Sea and Land, where ever *Titan* warmes).

> (1:463)

Like Daniel, Sylvester wrote at a time when, for rhetorical purposes at least, political power resided exclusively in the person of the monarch. Political divisions between crown, commons, and commerce have not yet been recognized publicly, it seems, so the poet may direct the reader's attention by focusing on providential peace and prosperity at home as the necessary prior condition of colonial expansion.

When Sylvester was writing, James had, by acceding to the throne, but recently ended a period of considerable uncertainty regarding the succession, so we might expect poets to emphasize the continuity of royal power at home. In keeping with James's views on the structural homology of the patriarchal family and the absolutist state, Sylvester characterizes Albion as a fertile and generous mother who guarantees her influence abroad by "raysing *STUARDS* to [her] Regal Throne":

> Yet are thy *Woolls, Corne,* thy *Cloath,* thy *Tinne,*
> Mines rich enough to make thee *Europes* Queene,
> Yea Empresse of the *World.* . . .
>
> . . .
>
> And last, not least (so farre beyond the scope
> Of *Christians* Feare, *Anti-Christians* Hope)
> When all, thy *Fall* seem'd to Prognosticate,
> Hath higher rais'd the glory of thy State;
> In raysing *STUARDS* to thy Regal Throne,
> To Rule (as *David,* and as *Salomon*)
> With Prudence, Prowesse, Justice, and Sobrietie,
> Thy happy People in *Religious Pietie.*
>
> (1:464–65)

Sylvester's Albion both legitimates and qualifies James's authority by recalling the anxiety over Elizabeth's death and making his rule contingent upon a supreme female. Unlike Daniel's, Sylvester's personification openly supports the current regime by claiming to be the authority that instituted it. These strategies enable the poet to set limits to James's claims to absolute power since the king must live up to the terms— "Prudence, Prowesse, Justice, and Sobrietie"—by which his reign has been legitimated. In contrast to the sonnet by Daniel, we have a poem verging upon being partisan, and it is clear that in each poem the traditional figure of Albion shapes and is shaped by differing political conditions.

Further reason to see poetic descriptions of the unified nation as attempts to disguise undeniable political tensions appears in a text that conflates legendary and historical material in order to construct obviously fictitious solutions to very real political problems. Although written in support of James's highly unpopular policy of nonintervention in the Thirty Years War, this poem signals the always already critical stance of historical poetry, though like Sylvester's poem it offers no precise alignment with an organized opposition as such. Once again, sexual difference provides a code for inscribing political opposition. Since the text is not readily available I shall give it in full here:

> A Stately Nymph of *Nereus* traine,
> Wave-bred in the *Virginian* Maine,
> Ycleped *Albion,* kept ere whiles,
> So famous erst the *Fortunate* Iles!
> Whose treasures, as of equall price,
> With *Hesperid's* fruit and *Colchos* Fliece,
> Brave Knights to seeke Adventures came,
> To winne this wealth, and court this Dame;
> From *Syria* one, a next from *Greece,*
> The third a home-bred churlish peece,
> A *Brute* from *Troy,* the fift neere kinne,
> The one quels Devils, t'other Men;
> A sixt from *Rome,* and next from *Rhene,*
> The eighth from *Cymbria,* ninth from *Seyne:*
> All these were Warriors, all these came,
> By dint of Sword to purchase Fame!
> But comes a tenth in shewe more milde,
> A crowned King even from a Child,
> And though new-Lords, new-Lawes! yet strange,
> Nor Lord, nor Law nor State did change;
> Because, perhaps this peace-full Impe,
> Or so lov'd *Albion,* or faire *Nymph*
> Most lov'd by her: To see their Glories,
> Wherof they vaunt; behold their Stories.
> To win this *Nymph,* her wealth or favour,
> The *Syrian* first, who came to crave her,
> Bore Armes through eld, obscure and darke,
> Seemes his great Grandsire *Noah's* Arke;
> Next *Neptunes* sonne of *Paynim* Race,
> Talkes of his Fathers *Trident* Mace,
> The third a *Gyant-Satyr* wilde,
> *Pan*-like in shew, and *Cham*-bred stilde!
> The fourth from *Troy, Venus* his Guide,
> *Brute* doth one crowne in three devide.
> The fift agen of five makes one,

Happie *Cornish* Prince, blest union.
Sixt *Caesar* vaunts his gods at *Rome,*
His *Eagle* and *Troyes* Trophees some:
The seventh next with his sevenfold Crowne
And *Saxon* Horse, would beare all downe.
The eighth the *Dane,* in armes by stealth,
Sought win, or wed, or weare her wealth.
And ninth, advanc'd 'mongst these Misrules
His *Norman* Leopards, bath'de in Gules!
But now the tenth sans strife or Warres,
Brings Peace and Union, stints all Iarres.
Give sentence then, if any crave;
Who best deserves this Nymph to have.

These lines are printed opposite the emblematic title page of William Slatyer's *The History of Great Britanie from the first peopling of this Iland to this present Raigne of our happy and peacefull Monarke K. James,* published in 1621 (see Fig. 4), in which heroic portraits of the eight semilegendary and historical warriors—Samothes, Albion, Gygas, Brutus, Malmuth, Caesar, Hengist, and Swanus—preceding William the Conqueror are arranged to form twin columns on either side of a central arch surmounted by James's coat of arms. Below them larger portraits of William and James form bases on either side of a splendid emblem of Albion. These portraits of Albion's military lovers, who came to woo with swords, are presumably stock engravings since their arrangement here upsets the numerical inscriptions on the engravings and their usual chronological relations. (The top two pairs from either side need to be moved down and to the left, thus forming four rows two high, rather than two rows of four.) Each of these warriors is portrayed with armorial shield and sword or club, including the figure of William. James's relationship to him and to Albion's earlier lovers is graphically clear since he figures as both the culmination of this historical sequence and its final transformation. James completes the modern period started by the Conqueror since he replaces the arts of war with those of peace; he wears stately robes, not armor, and carries a scepter but not a sword. Separating the heroic past from the even more glorious present, Britain appears as a female figure of peace and prosperity. In one hand she holds an olive branch, in the other a cornucopia.[28] Behind her and to the left, we glimpse Britain's mercantile fleet returning fully laden to native shores with Nature's providential bounty. (Is the land to the right too hilly to

Figure 4. Title page to William Slatyer's *The History of Great Britanie* (1621).

be the Thames estuary?) Enclosed within the fold of Albion's mantle, even the castles evoke the exoticism of chivalric romance rather than the political crisis of their aristocratic tenants under the economic impact of mercantile expansion.

In keeping with this sense of history's fulfillment in the romance of the present, Slatyer's prefatory poem describes the attempts of these various knights to court the "Stately Nymph" Albion. The first nine seek to dominate her by "dint of Sword" for none were native sons but foreign invaders. With James Stuart, however, comes a new kind of lover, "in shewe more milde / A crowned King even from a child." In contrast to the previous nine warriors, this tenth worthy is suited to win Albion by reason of his peacefulness.

Slatyer here combines poetic fiction with contemporary politics more directly and explicitly than either Daniel or Sylvester. Like them he personifies the realm as Albion, but in his version she is neither a mother nor a docile object of desire. Rather she is a "Stately Nymph" with a mind of her own whom the king must woo. While Slatyer contends that James deserves to win the fair more than any previous ruler, in order to do so the poet must first represent monarch and realm as separate figure linked by sexual difference, the one worthily pursuing the other. In contrast to traditional conflations of king with kingdom, Slatyer's separation of king from nation conforms to James's own practice in 1603.[29] But in 1621, this representation of their connection can be read only as an attempt to mystify significant alterations in the relations between James and his kingdom. When Slatyer's work appeared, such a separation was taking place and for reasons and in ways directly signaled by the poem. From within the complexities of Jacobean political history, two aspects may be isolated that are relevant to the argumentative strategies of Slatyer's poem: the king's intransigent claim that he should rule without consultation and the emergence of hostility to royal policies, both foreign and domestic, within the existing institutions of government.

The Jacobean House of Commons consistently challenged James's attempts to establish and maintain arbitrary control of national policy. When the Commons assembled in the year of Slatyer's poem, James had pretty much lost direct control over the proceedings of the Parliamentary assembly.[30] Although Daniel can represent a unified nation in his figure of Albion, and Sylvester can portray Albion as a bountiful mother figure who appoints and nurtures her own dynasty of kings, by 1621 Slatyer figures the nation as a nymph who must be wooed by the king. James was, however, by no means as conciliatory toward the increasingly aggressive Commons as Slatyer suggests. Indeed, Slatyer's design vindicates those aspects of James's policy which had offended and angered many of his most powerful subjects. Slatyer refers directly to certain controversial issues from early in James's reign. He asserts, rather than argues, that the king "though new-Lords, new-Lawes! yet strange / Nor Lord, nor Law nor State did change." Yet throughout his reign, James had sought to establish and maintain absolute personal power by elevating favorites, such as Robert Carr and George Villiers, from relative obscurity into a dependent court élite. By the end of his reign James had almost doubled the number of secular peers by such new creations, a practice that consistently angered the Commons.[31] James also provoked the anger of the legal profession. "New-Lawes" may refer to the legal disputes between the crown and the courts of law over traditional privileges, disputes that were a fundamental element of the redistribution of power during the early decades of the century.[32] Or the references may be more specifically aimed at the highly unpopular economic legislation which had been inaugurated under James.[33] But however we understand "new-Lawes," Slatyer's general strategy of legitimating James's claim to the stately nymph by emphasizing his peacefulness seeks to defend the king's foreign policy as the best course for the nation to follow. Although James prided himself on his ability to avoid war and to bring peace,[34] this very aspect of his rule was consistently unpopular, especially at the time when Slatyer's poem appeared.[35] By then James had stubbornly been following a policy of nonintervention in the Thirty Years War for three years, despite enormous popular support for the protestant cause of his own son-in-law, Frederick.[36] James's intransigence exacerbated his relations with the Parliamentary gentry who largely made up the House of Commons. Following the defeat of Frederick in 1620, James found himself confronted with "a hostile council urging war."[37] "Profoundly affected by considerations of foreign policy," writes J. R. Tanner, "the Parliament which met in 1621 openly challenged royal authority with the Protestation of Liberties which the king tore from the records with his own hands."[38]

That love of peace, which Slatyer urges in support of the royal claim to Albion, was highly controversial when his *History* appeared. This personification of the nation as Albion, and this portrait of James as a suitor who deserves to win her love, represent the existing political crisis in terms carefully designed to urge acceptance of royal authority in the face of specific hostility while also encouraging the king to find some way to ameliorate a dangerous situation. Although supporting the king, this poet no longer writes that generalized variety of political poetry which assumes—rightly or wrongly—an identity of political interests among the various groups composing the nation as a whole. Instead, he varies known poetic conventions in such a way that the resulting version of political relations seems to be the historical one.

Other partisan poems written between the accession of James and the outbreak of civil war represent the nation as a whole, while pointing to broader political divisions less easily and accurately describable. With care, one may still usefully speak of the country, the crown, and the city as distinct interest groups, although the terms are so hackneyed that they tend to obscure actually existing relations. The city is best understood, as Valerie Pearl has shown, to be a collection of heterogeneous men of variable and varying political opinion rather than a unified power group.[39] But as such, the city still represents a collection of political interests that can be distinguished from those of the crown and, often, the country. The country, in this sense, presents even greater difficulties than the city, and has been the subject of heated debate among historians for at least the last thirty years.[40] Nevertheless, these terms remain indispensable if only because political poets—and thinkers—frequently employed them at the time and, in doing so, established the terms in which contemporaries often framed their political differences.[41]

It may well be that poets used these sociogeographical categories as political classifications simply because they thought such groups actually existed as distinctive gatherings of mutually exclusive political interests or kinds of power. But during the early decades of the century, so many poems were written in imitation of classical celebrations of the country as a retreat from the corruptions and vicissitudes of court and city that the nation itself often came to be defined in terms of these traditional antitheses. Here pastoral remains most relevant because, as Frank Kermode notes, "the simplest kind of pastoral assumes that the quiet wildness of the country is better than the cultivated and complex life of the hurrying city and court."[42] English pastoral of the seventeenth century demonstrates how the genre is variously and subtly adapted to serve political ends. I have already suggested ways in which the arcadian version of the pastoral dominant during the reign of Elizabeth developed into specifically contemporary political commentary during the early decades of the seventeenth century. The emphasis shifts from the idyllic pleasures of Tityrus' traditional life to the politically governed future of Meliboeus. In well-known versions of the pastoral like Jonson's "To Penshurst" and Herrick's "The Hock Cart," the country is by no means wild and uncultivated, but represents, rather, a complex social order that stands for the nation as a whole. And, in poems like Jonson's "To Sir Robert Wroth," Sir Richard Fanshawe's *Ode on the King's Proclamation*, and Thomas Randolph's "Ode to Mister Anthony Stafford," the divisions of country, court, and city appear in specifically politicizing terms that generate both urgency and alarm at developments in contemporary sociopolitical life.

This political use of the pastoral effected other changes in the genre, especially its use of historical materials. "Where there is any expression of the pastoral vision," write two recent scholars of seventeenth-century English pastoral:

> it is either from poets looking back ... to an aristocratic culture that had all but passed, or ... as an implicit assumption in urban and court satire. At the same time, however, the seventeenth century sees the emergence of a different kind of pastoral voice, one that expresses no longer a merely idealized view of the countryside surrounding the town which housed the poet, and one which makes for the first time hesitant moves in the direction of "realism."[43]

In part, at least, this mixture of kinds and this new realism emerged to give meaningful shape to the increasing breakdown of traditional social alliances, especially with the increasing capitalization of land tenure shaking apart the domestic sphere.

Sir Richard Fanshawe's famous pastoral *Ode upon Occasion of His Majesties Proclamation in the year 1630. Commanding the Gentry to reside upon their Estates in the Country* is an especially illuminating case, a poem that, while written in support of the Stuart peace, nevertheless helped to establish the categories in which social and political disputes were to be conducted.[44] Fanshawe adopts a Horatian stance and tone that would appeal to the aspiring urbanity of his declared audience; he employs a public style suited to his political purpose rather than the more highly wrought style suited to coterie poetry. He represents Britain as a haven of peace, separate from the wars then raging across Europe:

> NOW warre is all the world about,
> And every where *Erynnis* raignes,
> Or else the Torch so late put out
>   The stench remains.
>   . . .
>
> Onely the Island which wee sowe,
> (A world without the world) so farre
> From present wounds, it cannot showe
>   An ancient skarre.
> White Peace (the beautiful'st of things)
> Seemes here her everlasting rest
> To fix, and spreads her downy wings
>   Over the nest.
>
>   (Pp. 5, 6)

Employing the Virgilian topos, Fanshawe not only treats insularity as a sign of peculiar grace, but also adopts a point of view that enables him to mark off the island for close scrutiny while maintaining a sense of global context.

Focusing attention within the island's borders, Fanshawe represents social and political divisions from the sublime stance of a spokesman for tradition and absolutism. Under this gaze the nation appears as a farm rather than as an arcadian garden paradise. Fanshawe defines the nation as that island "which wee sowe." a marked alteration from the "Garden of the World" which, according to Giles Fletcher in 1612, "God hath planted,"[45] or which, in Sylvester's lines, grows by some sort of spontaneous generation. An active participation in the rural economy is essential to the logic of Fanshawe's poem, for he could hardly urge landowners to return to the country if God and Nature were there to do their work for them.

But Fanshawe has other readers in mind too. He takes pains to represent country pleasures suited to the tastes of those whose power lodges within the families of citified gentry:

> Beleeve me Ladies you will finde
> In that sweet life, more solid joyes,
> More true contentment to the minde,
>   Than all Town-toyes.
>
>   (P. 8)

Like that of queens and great ladies at court, the power of wives within landowning families had greater social importance than was once recognized by male historians who evidently do not take Fanshawe's poem very seriously.[46] Yet Fanshawe was not the only male poet of the time to address the "Ladies" since his poem was written in direct imitation of verses by James. The royal verses were composed, presumably, at the time of his "Proclamation commanding all persons Noblemen, Knights and Gentlemen of Quality, to repayre to their Mansion houses in the Country, to attend their servises, and keepe hospitality, according to the ancient and laudable custome of England" of November 1622. James's verses are exclusively directed at married women, though the confusion of personal pronouns in line 4 suggests that he was reluctant to address them directly for very long:

> You women that doe London love so well
> whome scarce a proclamacion can expell
> and to be kept in fashion fine & gaye
> Care not what fines there honest husbands pay
> you dreame on nought but vizitts maskes & toyes
> And thinke the cuntrye contributes noe joyes
> Be not deceiv'd the cuntrey is not so bare
> But if your trading lacke there's ware for ware
> or if you musicke love know every springe
> Both Nightingale & Cockoe there do singe.[47]

To Fanshawe's credit, he avoids the harshness of James's unrelenting misogyny, though by imitating the former king's verses, the courtier was engaged in flattering his son. Nevertheless, this flattery achieves a political seriousness absent from the original. In Fanshawe's poem, the natural pleasures of the countryside appear as analogues for life at court. Love and sexual adventure, tales of violent passion, intrigue, and horror, finely tuned airs, the ceremonial pomp of court and splendid panoply of state—all these, he assures the ladies, can be found in the country:

> Nor *Cupid* there lesse bloud doth spill,
> But heads his shafts with chaster love,
> Not feathered with a Sparrowes quill
>   But of a dove.
> There shall you heare the Nightingale
> (The harmelesse Syren of the wood)

How prettily she tells a tale
            Of rape and blood.
The lyrricke Larke, with all beside
Of natures feathered quire: and all
The Common-wealth of Flowres in'ts pride
            Behold you shall.
The Lillie (Queene), the (Royall) Rose,
The Gillyflowre (Prince of the bloud),
The (Courtyer) Tulip (gay in clothes),
            The (Regall) Budd,
The Vilet (purple Senatour),
How they doe mock the pompe of State,
And all that at the surly doore,
            Of great ones waite.

                                        (P. 8)

But underlying Fanshawe's analogy lurks an anxiety that all is no longer well. While seeing the "blest Isle" as a "safe retreat to all that come," Fanshawe also ponders the belief that an enemy within the nation's boundaries threatens the social and political order. Writing in a characteristically partisan fashion, he outlines a problem for socially responsible male readers in a manner befitting their rank:

Yet wee, as if some foe were here,
Leave the despised Fields to clownes,
And come to save our selves as 'twere
            In walled Townes.
Hither we bring Wives, Babes, rich clothes
And Gemms; Till now my Soveraigne
The growing evill doth oppose:
            Counting in vaine
His care preserves us from annoy
Of enemyes his Realmes to'invade,
Unlesse hee force us to enjoy
            The peace hee made.

                                        (P. 6)

Landowners might have been more easily persuaded if Fanshawe had spoken of "your lands" rather than "his Realmes," but the class alliances are clear throughout the poem as Fanshawe defines the categories in which political and ideological dispute take shape. In this version of the pastoral, Fanshawe documents the fragmentation of the realm into various contending factions—court versus city, city lawyers and merchants versus the landowning nobility, with women, the mob, and country "clowns" confined to the margins of social being.

The immediate occasion of Fanshawe's *Ode* was an ordinance issued by Charles on September 9, 1630, requiring those with country estates to return to them. Similar orders had been issued by James in 1622, 1623, and 1624. But there were peculiar conditions of widespread social discontent and political unrest at the time of Fanshawe's poem. Since a 1632 government census found that less than one percent of the gentry were resident in London "without good reason," the ordinance of 1630 seems likely to have been a measure designed to distract attention from more pressing social problems.[48] The year 1630 was one of especially bad harvests and plague that "coincided with a trade slump in 1629–31,"[49] and began the so-called Eleven Years Tyranny (1629–40) of Charles's personal rule during which the king, aided by Laud and Strafford, implemented "Thorough" a political program which "gave all classes a common grievance" against Charles.[50] In 1630, aiming to support the crown's recent policy meant setting oneself a difficult task. Fanshawe tackles it by displacing the source of all possible discontent away from the court and the king's policies, focusing instead on moral corruption within the city: a traditional strategy carried over from Roman satire. Political comment, as so often during the century, appears in moral terms directed at a class antagonist:

> Who would persue
> The smoaky glory of the Towne,
> That may goe till his native earth,
> And by the shining fire sit downe
> > Of his owne hearth,
> Free from the griping Scriveners bands,
> And the more byting Mercers books;
> Free from the bayt of oyled hands
> > And painted looks?

> (P. 7)

Having already attributed the recent bad harvests to the absence of the country landlords, Fanshawe must carefully avoid antagonizing them by too strident an accusation here. Instead, he seeks to reconcile the landed families with their rural lives: first, by blaming corrupt city lawyers and covetous merchants for any and every possible civil disturbance; second, by celebrating the delights of the country life to which he wishes them to return.

This tearing of the social fabric into rural and urban components dominates an important group of poems which G. R. Hibbard first identified as "country-house poems."[51] Aimed at flattering a more specifically aristocratic audience than Fanshawe's, these poems portray one kind of rural economy as a model for the nation as a whole. By harking back to traditional if not feudal values of personal loyalty to land and lord, such poems offered a means of opposing social innovation while seeming to remain loyal to the court. As Raymond Williams suggests, these poems "use a particular version of country life as a way of expressing, in the form of a compliment to a house or its owner, certain social and moral values."[52] In Cowley's ode *Solitude* (1656), "the woods, the birds, the poets and the gods are seen literally ... as the social structure—the natural order—of seventeenth-century England" (pp. 26–27). Jonson's familiar poem "To Sir Robert Wroth" celebrates "the life of a country gentleman ... as an explicit contrast to the life of the court and the city. The figures of city lawyer, city capitalist, and courtier, are brought in to point the moral" (p. 28). Country-house and rural retreat poems of the time register equally precise alterations in the political life of seventeenth-century England by representing this increasing separation of political interests between country, court, and city.

The formal difference which Williams recognizes between Jonson's "Penshurst" and "Wroth," which compliment an estate and a lord respectively, controls not only what Jonson says but the manner in which he says it. "Wroth" looks outward from aristocratic life toward the city and the larger world beyond the seas. "Penshurst" looks inward upon the estate, as Fanshawe looks in upon the island nation, concentrating on what falls within its geographical domain, thereby inviting us to think of similar houses and comparable lords. By looking inward upon the Penshurst property, Jonson can portray the aristocratic institution of the Sidney estate as a benevolent and hospitable social order that, while it seems sealed off from the nation as a whole, nevertheless admits guests from the country, city, and court since hospitality constitutes an essential and integral part of that order.[53] Indeed, the visits of the countryfolk, poets, and even King James and Prince Henry, give the estate and house their legitimate social role within the larger political order of the nation.

A social institution, Penshurst represents an aristocratic ideal of political order which makes a benevolent and fruitful inclusiveness possible; everything wanting is provided there. In "Wroth," on the other hand, the poet's outward-looking perspective favors explicit exclusion and condemnation of what can be seen outside. Praising country gentlemen for repudiating those struggles for wealth and position characteristic of life in the city and at court, Jonson assures us that Wroth is "though so neere the city and the court, / . . . ta'en with neither's vice." In "Wroth" Jonson presents a wider version of the political order than in "Penshurst," and in so doing must condemn much of what he sees. The dismissive moral attitudes of much of "Wroth" becomes possible once the poet locates himself and his reader within the country estates and then looks out toward the city and court—not dispassionately, by any means, but with a sense of security that here, at least, all is still well.

The ideological significance of Jonson's formal strategy in "Wroth" becomes clearer if we compare this poem with Thomas Randolph's "Ode to Mister Anthony Stafford" written two decades later, where the strategy is exactly reversed. Writing on the eve of civil war, Randolph looks longingly from the city to the country, replacing Jonson's poised and secure rural perspective with the impatience and hauteur suited to the urbane style of a man highly conscious of his rank and contemptuous of those beneath it. The highly elaborate moral analysis of cityfolk in Jonson becomes mere snobbish jibing at city wits and lawyer's clerks, a style that demands a looser diction suited to sneering and the apparently confident ease of strong, personal expression. No one really needs to be convinced of anything, especially the other courtly gentleman being addressed:

> Come, spur away
> I have no patience for a longer stay
> But must go down,
> And leave the chargeable noise of this great town.
> I will the country see,
> Where old simplicity
> Though hid in grey,
> Doth look more gay
> Then foppery in plush and scarlet clad.
> Farewell, you city wits, that are
> Almost at civil war;
> 'Tis time that I grow wise, when all the world grows mad.
> More of my days

> I will not spend to gaine an idiot's praise;
>   Or make sport
> For some slight puisne of the Inns-of-Court.[54]

The dominant tone of the poem suggests a nervous anxiety found in neither Jonson nor Fanshawe. Amidst the convivial bombast and impatience there emerges a note of stress that replaces the former sense of security with urgency. Randolph responds to social and political changes in the urban scene by seeking to defend a former way of life against what he perceives as encroaching madness. In a typically pastoral gesture, a former way of living is associated with the country and with "old simplicity"—a key phrase in the poem with its sense of things being better in the past, a truly arcadian attitude.

Like Jonson in "Wroth," Randolph attacks that class of cityfolk who secured political power by accumulating independent wealth not tied to the land. Merchants, capitalists, and lawyers were certainly becoming conscious of their political power in the years before war broke out. Uncertain as a class, and by no means a political front, these men sparked a growing fear and resentment amongst those poets whose livelihoods still depended upon traditional forms of royal and aristocratic patronage. Addressing themselves to specific class and political allies, Jonson and Randolph condemn the ostentation and vulgarity of those slowly emerging as a social, political, and economic force with interests contrary to those of dependent poets. But in so doing, they implicitly acknowledge the very real social and political tensions fracturing the island "nation."[55]

Many poets writing in support of royal policies during the thirties defend the status quo as an idealized present more glorious than had ever been known before. National insularity could still, as in Fanshawe, provide a rhetorical guarantee of security and divine benevolence to the world beyond the rest of the world. In 1635 Richard Crashaw employs traditional figures in his panegyric "Upon the Duke of Yorke his Birth." But even Crashaw opens his poem in praise of the continuing Stuart dynasty with an address to the personified island in which he plays with the reader's recognition that all is not well:

> BRittaine, the mighty Oceans lovely Bride,
> Now stretch thy self (faire Ile) and grow, spread wide
> Thy bosome and make roome; Thou art opprest
> With thin own Gloryes. . . .

(P. 176)

The wit here is to raise expectations and then deflect them, a typical "Cavalier" maneuver for dealing with political tension and stress.[56] What starts out looking like a call to empire—"and grow, spread wide"—becomes a rather smutty joke involving the pregnant land; what first looks like a warning—"thou are opprest"—becomes witty hyperbole. For poets writing to defend the Stuart regime, like Crashaw, there are no tropes like the old ones, and before very long he alludes to Virgil:

> Thou by thy selfe maist sit, (blest Isle) and see
> How thy Great Mother Nature doats on thee:
> Thee therefore from the rest apart she hurl'd
> And seem'd to make an Isle, but made a world.

> (P. 177)

Again, the wit of Crashaw's portrait of the nation depends upon the slide between the indisputable geographical fact and its attributes. Here the island nation is secularized—no longer, as in Sylvester, identified with the "Great Mother Nature," but something apart. Hence the force of "maist," which admits that isolation is, in part at least, a matter of choice. And it is this very element of choice in the ruling powers' decision not to become too closely involved with European wars which Thomas Carew celebrates in the infamous closing lines of his reply to Townsend, who had invited him to write on the death of Gustavus Adolphus:

> these are subjects proper to our clyme.
> Tourneyes, Masques, Theaters, better become
> Our *Halcyon* dayes; what though the German drum
> Bellow for freedome and revenge, the noyse
> Concernes not us, nor should divert our joyes
> Nor ought the thunder of their Carabins
> Drowne the sweet Ayres of our tun'd Violins;
> Beleeve me friend, if their prevailing powers
> Gaine them a calme securitie like ours,
> They'le hang their Armes up on the Olive bough,
> And dance, and revell then, as we doe now.[57]

Like Harold Macmillan in the 1960s, Carew obviously thought that Englishmen had never had it so good. Yet, through the smug and complacent insularity, the note of defensiveness also heard in Randolph accompanies a sense that a former way of life needs a vigorous defense against an enemy who, working inside the nation's borders, can no longer be warded off with tropes, no longer be banished from the blest island paradise that Neptune defends with his watery arms. As in Daniel's *Delia* sonnet, war is enemy to the Muses; but Carew surely knew that halcyon days are short-lived.

THE NATION TAKES SIDES: ANTI-STUART POETICS, 1634–1641

In part, we can identify this enemy with the militant Protestants angered that Charles had betrayed the cause of true religion by failing to support Gustavus Adolphus in his crusade against the Hapsburgs. The following passage from John Russell's "The Battle of Lutzen" (1634) provides a singularly appropriate contrast to Carew's complacency since, even out of context, the hard-edged irony with which it turns the traditional tropes against Stuart claims to divine appointment sounds out unmistakably:

> Oh happie *England,* who wilt scarce confesse,
> Drunk with securitie, thy happinesse;
> That dost enjoy such Quietnesse, such Ease,
> Such calme Tranquillitie, and blessed Peace;
> And that not purchas'd by laborious Toil,
> By fire, and sword, by ruine, and by spoil;
> Nor by the losse of thy choice *Youth,* whose *Fate*
> Thou wouldst not fear 'gainst *Heav'n* t'expostulate:
> But it hath cost thee nothing: for behold,
> On thee th'Almightie hath his blessings roll'd,
> Without all labour or desert of thine,
> Meerly by instinct of his love divine;
> And hath enricht thee with a gracious *King,*
> At whose blest Birth *Angels* of peace did sing.[58]

Striking in their emphatic insistence that the English are free not only from "laborious Toil" but also from "all labour or desert," Russell's lines, written as though in direct reply to Fanshawe and Carew, neatly subvert the defensive features of Caroline pastoral. If that "drunk," following so close behind "scarce confess" with its implications of catholicism and guilt, isn't a sufficient signal of ironic intent, then surely the strain with which the long apostrophe to England builds through the expository couplets, constantly deferring something not quite sayable, betrays the poet's lack of conviction in the values of the all-too-conventional tropes.

The style could hardly be more different from the "vicious ease" of Carew's condescending indifference.[59] But it is also unlike the rest of Russell's poem which, from the start, has employed the pentameter couplet in the voiced manner of John Cragge, William Browne, and George Wither, "to give the effect of personal spontaneity" that "becomes a symbol of imaginative freedom as opposed to courtly restraint." This style was, according to David Norbrook from whom I have been quoting, one "which drew attention to its own artifice and thus highlighted the inability of language fully to embody transcendent truths" but rather "revealed transcendent truths" as an "expression of an apocalyptic world view" (pp. 212, 209, 200, 201). This, it seems to me, is just what Russell is up to.

Oppositional poets relied on imitating the excitement of the voice. Pressing against the constraints of the loose pentameter, the energy of conviction builds and sometimes makes a lot of din and clatter, a noise quite distinct from court pastoral. Following the rather offhand compliment to the king, Russell's apostrophe to "happie *England*" becomes increasingly excited and scornful as it turns to its major concern, the European wars from which England has been shamelessly absent:

> Oh look upon thy neighbour *Germanie,*
> Drown'd with a floud of tears and miserie;
> Whose towns are ruin'd, and whose Cities burn,
> Whose fields do flow with bloud, whose people mourn;
> Think but on this all you that cannot weep,
> Who in the arms of happie *Peace* do sleep.
> Is't irksome to your eares? Your tender Heart
> At these molesting sounds (methinks) doth start:
> From *Warres* and *Woes* y'have been so long secure,
> That now you cannot their rough Name endure.
>
> . . .
>
> Shall these my verses, that with clatt'ring ding
> The strokes of Warre and furious Rage do sing,
> Displease our *British* eares, who are of late
> (It seems) grown tender and effeminate?
> Your *Amorettoes* think them farre to rough,
> Not smooth, nor pleasing, nor half low enough:
> They cannot screw them any wayes to suit
> Or consort with their sweet-tun'd warbling *Lute.*
> They are too lofty for a *Womans* voice,

> And drown all sweetnesse with a ratling noise.
> Some hollow-sound *Drumme,* or *Trumpet* shrill,
> Or thundering *Cannons,* that the eare do fill
> With frightfull sounds, fit Instruments would be
> To Echo forth my lines melodiously.
> The smaller shot shall serve for repetition,
> While clatt'ring swords shall represent division:
> And the more *Discords* that my verses show,
> The better *Harmonie* from thence will flow.
>
> (Pp. 32–33)

The attack on court style is about as hostile as it could be without becoming treasonable. Drowning out sweetness with a "ratling noise," Russell's version of the heroic seeks to force readers to look again at the contemporary scene and see how being English involves responsibility for events taking place beyond the island's boundaries. The voice of directly expressed poetic commitment becomes a means of arousing moral sensibilities and is aimed at stirring readers to the immediate apprehension that something needs to be done, rather than offering, as an end in itself, the harmonious closure of an easy solution.

But the poetic voice of opposition to Stuart policy was also being raised in Scotland, where Charles had no doubt insulted many by waiting until June 1633 to be crowned. While English protestants spoke of responsibilities to anti-catholic forces in Europe, the Scottish writer William Lithgow complained of "the grosse enormities"[60] inflicted by the Stuarts on their native land. Readers of seventeenth-century travel literature will know Lithgow's story from his own accounts, how this traveler from Lanark who visited the Pope in Rome came to be saved from execution in Madrid and subsequently housed by James at Theobalds until he was evicted after publicly insulting Gondomar.[61] Here was a poet who could claim to be a personal friend of the late king. His *Scotlands Welcome To Her Native Sonne, and Soveraigne Lord, King Charles* (Edinburgh, 1633) dutifully opens with a formal welcome describing Charles's reception in Edinburgh, before digressing to praise the past valor of Scottish soldiers defending the Scottish crown. After commemorating this coronation, and praising the Scottish church and Parliament, Lithgow gets down to the more serious business of complaining about unemployment and the loss of capital investment in Scotland since the court left for London with the Stuarts. Lithgow complains in the voice of Scotland:

Have I not *Floods* and *Seas*, good *Ships* and *Ports*?
Brave *Sea-Men, Pilots, Skippers*, and *Consorts*;
But where's the *Merchant* that will freely enter
To put these *Men* to work; and byde the venter
Of doubtfull successe; nay; there's none I see,
That now dare hazard further than his eye.

         . . .

    As for my *Trades*, they're ruind with decay,
There few or none imploy'd: My *Nobles* play
The curious *Curtezan*: that will not bee
But in strange fashions; O! what Noveltie
Is this? that *London*, robbes Mee of my gaine:
Whilst both my *Trades* amd *Merchants* suffer paine.

                                     (Sig. B2ᵛ)

When the Stuarts left Scotland to unify Britain, they took all the land's mobile wealth: everything flowed to London and nobody was left with anything to invest in developing Scottish resources.

Besides my *Nobles* see my *Gentry* too
Post up, post downe; their states for to undoe:
Nay, they will morgadge all; and to bee breefe,
Ryde up with gold, and turne againe with greefe:
Who better far might stay at home, and live
And not their meanes to loveless labour give.

                                     (Sig. B2ᵛ)

In imitation of the court, even small landlords have started turning on their tenants, taking full rents but failing to improve the land and estate, "thus they take my money all away / To spend abroad; whilst it should rather stay, / For to enrich my *Bowels* . . . (sig. B3). Since the Stuarts left, everything has gone wrong. At Lithgow's bidding, the voice of Scotland rails against the growing corruption of lawyers, against deforestation without replanting, against the misuse of tithes and the decay of schools, against witches, moneylenders, and tobacco, against the courtly fashion for young men to wear long hair and kilts, as well as against "vagabounding *Greeks*" to be found in the city streets (sigs. B3ᵛ–D4). Since the Stuarts left, public buildings are falling down and not being repaired, the Spanish are having too much say in British foreign policy, and something must be done to aid the Germans (sigs. F–Fᵛ).

> So with this grievance, I bequeath the rest
> To be reformed by *Thee,* and soone redrest:
> Then weight them right, into thy judgement just,
> That these confusions may be brought to dust:
> So shall this *Land* be happy, live in rest,
> By thy good *Government.*
>
> (Sig. F3)

Like the protestant reformers, Lithgow relies on the direct address of a specific voice to convey strong personal conviction. Although it provides an acute analysis of how the centralized Stuart court enabled the capitalization of the Scottish economy, Lithgow's poem is thick with nostalgia for feudal hospitality and patriarchal privilege. Perhaps it is the memory of having known the king's father which authorizes this bold appeal, in the voice of Scotland, to the king who waited eight years to be crowned.

Between Charles's visits to Scotland in 1633 and 1641, the white bird of Stuart peace prepared to abandon Britain's shores. Crashaw revised his poem on James, Duke of York, by adding forty lines that anticipate impending civil disturbance.[62] And it is, perhaps, ironic that Carew's own death in 1639 was probably precipitated by illness suffered during Charles's march on Scotland during the first Bishops' War.[63] Ignoring Scotland, Waller opens the new decade by displacing the tumult growing within the island's borders by anticipation of the birth of the queen's fourth son. Resorting to an Elizabethan procedure, the court poet eroticizes Henrietta Maria as a goddess whose fertility will assure the nation's future peace. The verse, though, is far from Elizabethan in its delicacy and the conversational ease of the enjambment:

> Fair Venus! in thy soft arms
> The God of Rage confine;
> For thy whispers are the charms
> Which only can divert his fierce design.
>
> What though he frown, and to tumult do incline?
> Thou the flame
> Kindled in his breast canst tame
> With that snow which unmelted lies on thine.
>
> Great Goddess! give this thy sacred island rest;
> Make Heaven smile,

> That no storm disturb us while
> Thy chief care, our halcyon, builds her nest.
>
> Great Gloriana! fair Gloriana!
> Bright as high heave is, and fertile as earth
> Whose beauty relieves us,
> Whose royal bed gives us
> Both glory and peace,
> Our present joy, and all our hopes' increase.[64]

But Waller's prayer went unanswered; the halcyon fled and the "God of Rage" broke out of confinement to roar in strains more virulent than Russell's.

Assembled in November 1640, the Long Parliament abolished the Star Chamber the following July, and with it disappeared the court's control over the press.[65] The response—and reaction—were almost immediate: more than thirty times as many printed books appeared in 1641 as during the previous year.[66] Many writers took the opportunity to publicize their long-suppressed views of the crisis in church and state. In the very month that the Star Chamber was abolished, John Vicars published *Englands Remembrancer, or, A thankfull acknowledgement of Parliamentary Mercies to our English-Nation,* which opens with the injunction to his readers to "see" how history was being made around them:

> COme hither, each true Christin heart and see;
> But, bring a joyfull, thankfull heart with thee.
> Come see (I say) to Gods eternall praise,
> His miracle of mercies in thy dayes.
> How, though two former Parliaments were broke,
> A third is cal'd, hopefull to strike the stroke
> Of blessed reformation.
>
> (Sig. A2)

In the excitement of free speech, Vicars took upon himself the task of chronicling the events leading up to the summoning of the Long Parliament in the form of an anti-catholic and anti-Spanish diatribe that insists his readers participate by seeing the profound changes taking place throughout the nation. Peace with Scotland, the defeat of the Spanish fleet by the Dutch, the promise of Church reform in England, agreement between king and Parliament are all signs of great changes taking place in a world centered on England, where, after years of darkness, it is now possible to see that "good men sit in seates of high renown" (sig. A2ᵛ). Poetic figures which the Stuart poets had used to celebrate national isolation take on renewed energy as Vicars vehemently details the grievances that Parliament will set straight in forging a new protestant union. He asks us "to see, with exultation,"

> From Both the Houses a blest Protestation,
> Together, all true English-hearts to tye,
> In a blest league, *Romes* Strumpet to defie,
> All Popish Innovations to disdain,
> Christs Truth to th'death constantly to maintain.
> O, who cannot these Halcyon-dayes admire,
> And with enflamed Zeale to be set on fire.
>
> (Sig. A3)

Vicars structures the entire poem rhetorically through repeated exhortations to rejoice that we are now permitted "to see" the signs of the changing times. Among them is freedom of the press:

> To see Gods Sabbaths more sincerely kept,
> Of Carryers, Fruit'rers, Taverns soyle well swept;
> And Presses open wide to vindicate
> The Sabbaths precious honour. . . .
>
> (Sig. A3)

But not everyone was as enthusiastic as Vicars about the new freedoms of speech, and we can sense something of the immediate force of unrestricted publishing through the horror which it stimulated in others. Having lamented the upsurge across the nation of radical preachers—especially the sectarian women who "would needs be men of God, and preach"—George Barlow deplored the activity of the presses:

> Others write bookes, which the adulterous presse
> Unhappily brings forth; and is no lesse
> Guilty, then their first authors. Oh what quill
> Can possibly expresse, the gall they spill
> In these base Pamphlets, which no light can clayme
> But what proceeds from their own funerall flame,
> Else everlasting darknesse; where no eyes

> May ever see those monstrous Calumnies,
> And thrice accursed Lyes which vented be
> 'Gainst holy Church, and sacred Hierarchy![67]

Many of the other Oxford poets who contributed to *Eucharistica Oxoniensia* of November 1641 defended the "sacred Hierarchy" of Stuart rule by identifying Charles and his return from Scotland with the sun that dispels northern darkness.[68] Henry Vaughan, however, is the only one of the Oxford poets to allude to the Virgilian topos, perhaps in anticipation of his own pastoral retirement from England when war broke out:

> This is great *Brittaines* blisse;
> The *Island* in it selfe a just World is.
> Here no commotion shall we find or feare,
> But of the *Courts removeall,* no sad teare
> Or clowdy *Brow,* but when You leave Us, then
> *Discord* is loyalty professed, when
> *Nations* doe strive, which shall the happier bee
> T'enjoy your bounteous ray's of *Majestie.*
>
> (Sig. A2ᵛ)

But that very image of darkness as a metaphor for the moral, spiritual, and political corruption which the presence of the sun king could magically disperse was being constantly appropriated by the Parliamentarian and militant protestant writers whose "base Pamphlets" Barlow deplored. Many agreed with Vicars that the meeting of the Long Parliament signaled deliverance from the Egyptian darkness of Laudian Arminianism and Charles's personal rule. "THe times being now open," writes the anonymous author of *Machiavel. As He lately appeared to his deare Sons, the Moderne Projectors* of 1641,

> and the mists of errour being by our bright English Sunne (the parliament) expelled, and scattered, I thought it a point of my duty (worthy reader) to expand in its right colours some of the fatall clouds that occasioned our darknesse: Projectors being principall vapours that dimm'd both our quiets and our profits; behold them here defin'd generally and specially.... And render due praise to this high and honourable Court of Parliament. (Sigs. B–Bᵛ)

Attacking crown monopolies and the projectors who proposed new methods of manufacturing commodities was, even after the breakdown of censorship, a fairly safe and traditional method for criticizing crown policy since Charles himself had canceled several patents back in March 1639 hoping to improve his popularity, and Parliament had recently expelled monopolists from the Commons.[69] But it was also a means for redefining the nation in terms that ran counter to those appropriated from Virgilian pastoral.

Anti-Stuart poets constructed alternative images of Britain that either abandoned or subverted Virgilian conventions. In the antimonopolist poems and tracts of 1641, the island emerges as a breeding ground for vermin, disease, and corruption. The projector, we read in *Machiavel,* "is the *Egyptian Frog,* that creeps into every mans dwelling, nay into his dish, and sometimes into mens beds, for often he has beene given to Venerie, and invaded mens wives" (sig. B2ᵛ). In the more formal language of the pentameter couplet, John Cragge gave voice to *Great Britains Prayers in This Dangerous Time of Contagion* of November 1641:

> In mercy Lord behold great Brittains Land,
> To stay thy plagues Lord give thy sweet command,
> From fearfull plagues and all diseases ill,
> For evermore defend and keepe us still.
>
> (Sig. A2)

The memory of how monopolists had served as prime conveyors of the nation's disease continued throughout the years of civil war. In analyzing the causes of the wars from the hindsight of 1648, one poet employed a familiar political metaphor for describing their influence throughout the land:

> THe spring being thus corrupt, the streames can be
> Nothing but currents of impuritie:
> From this red Sea of sin a crew there came,
> Differing in naught from Locusts, but in name;
> Monopolists, that (Priest-like) had a share
> In every trade, but more than Tythes they were.
> These did so spawn, they got nine parts at least,
> Th'right owner scarce was to his own a Priest.[70]

Although playing off tithes, the analysis here is surprisingly accurate since, according to Hirst, "the crown received about 13 per cent of the proceeds on monopolies overall. The courtiers and contractors scooped the rest" (p. 172).

Writers not committed to defending the court often wrote about recent events by reversing the usual priorities of pastoral; instead of typifying the nation in idealized terms of rural life, they represented urban corruption spreading nationwide. Back in 1641, a pamphleteer writes in the idiom of that year: "Monopolers by their nefarious Projects, and impious exactions, have contaminated the Land with such a contagious exulceration of wicked impositions, that I may with a coequall sympathie, assimilate them to the *Frogs of Aegypt*."[71] Resounding with the fury and moral indignation of Old Testament prophecy rather than the decorousness of neoclassical modes, these attacks draw for us an image of a sick and degenerate nation that is not adequately governed by its appointed head of state and traditional political institutions, but is rather controlled by the self-interest of corrupt individuals who have used the king's name to insinuate themselves into positions of power. The author of *Machiavel* describes one of them for us:

> He is neither foole nor Physitian, yet undertakes to reforme all abuses in the body politick with those three words, *Caroli Dei Gratia*. . . . Hee is one whose Arse makes buttons by the Bushell at the noyse of a Parliament, more than the *Scots* do at the noyse of *English* Drummes, and hath wrought under hand with Seminaries and Jesuites like a Mole, to set dissention betweene the two Kingdomes, on purpose that he avoyd a Parliament, and hath gotten a Patent or Grant of all the Blew Bonnets that are taken in the first battell; but meanes not to be there himselfe, but stay behind, and engrosse all the Carrots and Parsnips that come to *London,* to make Dildoes for the Citizens wives, old maidens, and poore whores that staid behind the *Progresse*. (Sigs. C2, C3)

Fierce hatred of women and sexual activity, paranoid fears of catholic plots and conspiracies undermining political stability like "moles," these themes were central to oppositional accounts of the national decay. But not all attacks on monopolists resorted to character assassination, or seemed as afraid of independent female sexuality as this one.

Oppositional poets helped turn the world upside down in 1641. Abandoning the decorums of Stuart pastoral, they describe the contemporary scene in subversive and irreverent detail. Rather than celebrating the cultural achievements of the peace-blessed island, they attack the corruption which they see spreading nationwide from the court, which they can then attack for its increasing control over domestic markets. *A Pack of Patentees. Opened. Shuffled. Cut, Dealt. and Played* (1641) offers a fantastic and disturbing view of the problem of monopolies by presenting several of the commodities under controversial patent—coal, "sope," starch, leather, wine, salt, tobacco, gold wire, war horns, butter, and rags—in the form of personified playing cards that dominate the poor poet's vision before being shuffled up together, cut, dealt, and then played.[72] This bizarre fantasy dehumanizes the figures of oppression while displacing the problem of patents into an inverted world in the time-honored manner of carnivalesque reversal. It opens with what seems to be a double paradox in evoking the effects of the patent on coal supplies:

> FAine would I write, but that I quake with cold,
> The seasons of the yeare, are bought and sold
> By *Patentees:* yet underground like Moles
> They have their cells. The devill trades for *Coales,*
> For Brimston's very scarce (all fiendes by kinde)
> Ile blow my nailes, and then Ile write my minde.
>
> (P. 3)

The poet who cannot write because he is too cold manages to write nevertheless, while the purchase of the seasons by patentees offers a hyperbolic exaggeration suggestive of how capitalists have taken control, not of the yearly round itself, but of the means by which people might cope with seasonal variation. Once we have entered this imaginary world, one that becomes increasingly popular with poets writing during the civil wars and—as Margaret Doody has shown, the "Augustan" poets who followed them[73]—familiar shapes and traditional forms become slippery and unstable. Even material objects become unreliable and subject to unnatural transformation under the whim of the license holder:

> BEware the Horner comes, he can transport
> The Calves defence, the Oxe, or any sort
> Which are within his List, this Beast is free,
> He'l suffer none to trade in hornes but he.
> Speak, will you have them rough? then they are put
> In universall termes; If they are cut
> He'l change them into Combes, with privy theft

> He'l barrell shame, he'has a Coxcombe left,
> Which he will use himselfe....
>
> (P. 10)

When the logic of maximum profit turns the world upside down and inside out "in universall termes," questions of national identity become merely irrelevant. The unrestricted will of self-interest abolishes social cohesion. Here is "Butter," as pithy a critique of the spirit of free enterprise as we are likely to find anywhere:

> NOw here a slippery Merchant, hold him fast,
> His Patent seal'd with Butter, at a cast
> He'l venture all his worth, he would be rich,
> And make ten thousand pay for't....
>
> (P. 11)

But this poem uses the carnivalesque mainly to reverse order and control; even entrepreneurial will proves insufficient in the end. Once the various cards have all appeared and a dealer is assigned to them, they refuse to be organized by the laws of any game:

> WEll now he deales about, & yet their game
> With free allowance had not got a name.
> The Cards prove bad, they are mad at what they doe,
> They're every one a scurvie trick or two.
>
> (P. 14)

Nevertheless, play continues—or rather it degenerates—as identities and fixed numerical relations dissolve into oblique and unreliable allusions to the madness and nonsense of life at court:

> When three were flush of foure, eldest hand
> Had got a great paire Royall; he did stand
> Upon his priviledge, and cast a plot
> To win the Game; but he was out a spot.
> But having spi'd a Courtier, up he starts,
> To while his partner turn'd the knave of Harts
> For Noddy knave....
>
> (P. 15)

As Doody observes, "It is a theme of Civil War poetry, as of Augustan poetry in general, that words are inadequate and slippery" (p. 55). Here words seem to be abandoning the attempt altogether, leaving only the verse itself—which remains regular to the end—to remind us that there is a referent outside the free play of signifiers.[74]

In developing their satiric arsenal of tropes, oppositional poets typically characterized the nation in terms of political disputes rather than pastoral geography. Poets and pamphleteers of 1641 often grounded their criticism of crown policy in direct analysis of immediate social and political controversies. No less fantastic than *A Pack of Patentees,* perhaps, T. B.'s *News from Rome. Or a Relation of the Pope and his patentees Pilgrimage into Hell, with their entertainment, and the Popes returne back againe to Rome* of June 1641 subverts epic convention in making a common equation between the monopolists and a long history of catholic conspiracies against the British crown (see Fig. 5). More than any other topic, fear of catholic subversion provided the radical poets of 1641 and 1642 with a focus for their redefinitions of national history.[75] The island paradise becomes a prize for which Manichaean forces of light and darkness contend in apocalyptic struggle. The traditional association of the monarch with the sun is frequently reassigned to the Long Parliament in its divinely inspired efforts to rid the land of all forms of Roman intervention and darkness. An anti-episcopal satire of 1641, *Lambeth Faire: wherein you have all the Bishops Trinkets set to sale* (see Fig. 6), begins with an implicit identification of Parliament with the sun:

> NO sooner was the sable darknesse past,
> And *Sol* his eye on our Horizon cast
> By whose bright beams those clouds dispersed were,
> Which did benight the land with horrid feare;
> But presently the people heard strange Fables,
> The Bishops went to *Lambeth* with their Bables,
> Where a *new Faire* was lately consecrate
> For Popish Garments, that were out of date.
>
>   (Sig. A2)

Presumably written to support the "root and branch" petition against episcopacy which Alderman Pennington presented to Parliament in December,[76] *Lambeth Faire* offers a rather jocular and festive approach to

NEVVES
FROM *ROME*.
OR
A Relation of the Pope and his Patentees
Pilgrimage into Hell, with their entertainment, and the Popes returne backe
againe to R ò m e.

With an Elegiacall Confabulation betweene
D e a t h and H o n o u r.

A Lecture which may be read to the greatest Monarch
in the world.

Printed in the Yeare
1 6 4 1.

Figure 5. Title page to *Newes from Rome* (1641), signed "T.B." The collapse of Star Chamber in this year effectively ended government control over the press. One result was the sudden appearance of many poems opposing King and bishop. Fears of a catholic counter-revolution in Britain figured large in these works.

Lambeth Faire:

Wherein you have all the
Bishops Trinkets set to sale.

I sit thus groveling in S. *Peters* Chaire,
Ore-prest with griefe to thinke on *Lambeth Faire.*

Time brings all to light.

Death close mine eyes with thy eternall doome,
Before this Faire be thus proclaim'd at *Rome.*

O mihi præteriros referet si Jupiter annos
Qualis eram

These tricks and whimseys have been long conceal'd,
But now the pack's laid open, al's reveal'd.
The little *Patriarke* frets and fumes to heare
How cheap his knacks are sold in *Lambeth Faire.*
        You that delight in Popish *ware,*
        Come fit your selves in Lambeth Faire.

Printed in the Yeare, M. DC. XLI.

Figure 6.   Title page to *Lambeth Faire* (1641).

110

the highly vexed disputes over the Arminian prelates, an approach that is at once reassuring—with its homely and familiar description of a market—and firmly committed to a radical position.

Of writers for whom the collapse of censorship in 1641 offered an opportunity to wage holy war against Stuart absolutism by associating it with encroaching catholicism, the presbyterian John Vicars was among the most prolific and outspoken. Carlyle may have thought him "a poor human soul zealously prophesying as if through the organs of an ass,"[77] but Vicars was not alone in regarding the opening reforms of the Long Parliament as the beginnings of divine direct intervention in state affairs. "From 1640," writes Bernard Capp, "many moderate parliamentarians believed that the Long Parliament would take over the duty long ignored by the Stuarts and at last erect the New Jerusalem through a godly, ordered reformation of church, state, and society."[78] Vicars' long narrative poem *November the 5. 1605. The Quintessence of Cruelty, Or, Masterpeice of Treachery, The Popish Pouder-Plot, Invented by Hellish-Malice, Prevented by Heavenly-mercy* (1641) was designed to help establish and confirm this conviction (see Fig. 7). An earlier and shorter version of this piece, based on a Latin poem by Francis Herring, had appeared in 1617, entitled *Mischeefes Mysterie: Or Treason's Master-peece.* Vicars had attempted to publish the expanded version during the 1620s when James was at loggerheads with his Parliaments. But, as he explains in a marginal gloss to *November the 5,* his attempts had been thwarted:

> D. *Baker* a late most impudent Apostate, who would not license this my Historie, because, as he said, we were not so angrie with the Papists now a dayes (though wee never had greater cause than in these our daies) as they were 20. or 30. yeers agoe, and one Mr. *Crosfield* a Senior fellow of Queenes Colledge in *Oxford,* could not (as he endeavoured) get it licensed for the Presse there. Nor could Mr. *Daniell, Cambridge* Printer (who would have printed it there) get it licensed at *Cambridge,* Dr. *Brumrick* being then Vicechan. *O tempora! O mores!* (Sig. A3)

It is hardly surprising that Vicars should have viewed the abolition of the Star Chamber and its control over publishing with millennial hope and optimism. As in *England's Remembrancer,* he relies on visual metaphors, insisting that his readers see contemporary events as signs of England's central position in the approaching confrontation between forces of darkness and light. Sight puts true believers in touch with the work-

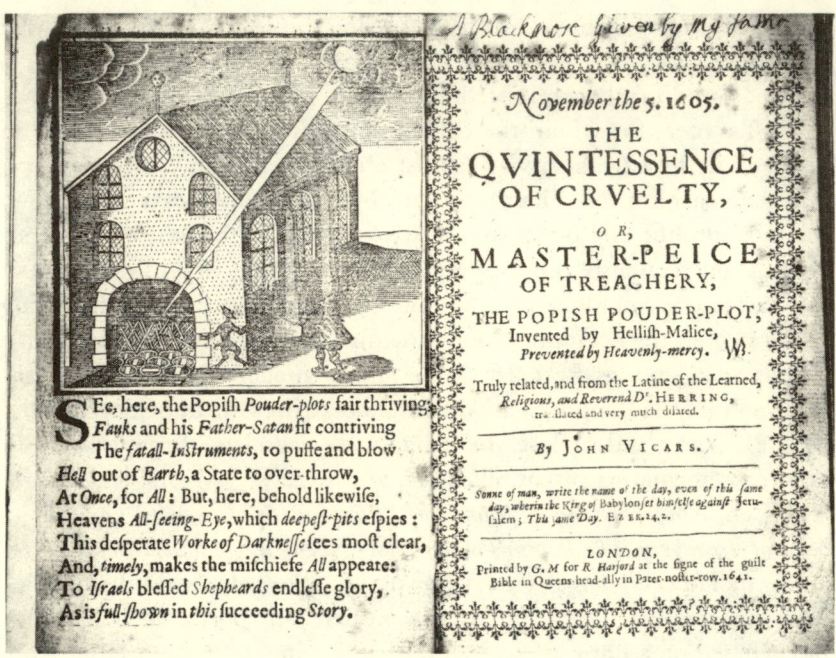

Figure 7. Title page and engraved frontispiece to John Vicars' *November the 5. 1605. The Quintessence of Cruelty* (1641).

ings of the divine plan for human history, as verses describing the engraving opposite the title page explain (see Fig. 7):

> SEe, here, the Popish *Pouder-plots* fair thriving;
> *Fauks* and his *Father-Satan* fit contriving
> The *fatall-Instruments,* to puffe and blow
> *Hell* out of *Earth,* a State to over-throw,
> At *Once,* for *All:* But, here, behold likewise,
> Heaven's *All-seeing-Eye,* which *deepest-pits* espies:
> This desperate *Worke of Darknesse* sees most clear,
> And, *timely,* makes the mischiefe *All* appeare:
> To *Israels* blessed *Shepheards* endlesse glory,
> As is *full-shown* in this succeeding *Story.*

The engraving illustrates the House of Commons at night; a shaft of light emitted from a providential cloud at top right shines on piled barrels just inside the doors; a devil leads inside a cloaked figure armed with a lantern and spurs.

The offhand manner of the comparison here between Israel and England should not mislead us as to its crucial importance in the rhetoric of Parliamentarian poetry on the eve of the civil wars. For the redefinition of the nation in which these poets were engaged frequently relies on the style of Old Testament prophecy while claiming England to be the chosen land. Yet Vicars is typical of poets of the early 1640s in not seeking to elaborate a systematic parallel, such as Dryden offers in *Absalom and Achitophel*. Rather, Vicars and others construct a more general comparison: England, like Israel, has been wickedly ungrateful regarding the special favors which God has granted it, but being the chosen land it can recover its privilege by acting decisively.[79] Vicars addresses the constant danger of forgetting this destiny, either because of ingratitude and sloth, or because of the pervasive powers of the diabolical forces of darkness—including the censors. Such is the purpose in the prefatory verses of his "succeeding *Story*" of the Gunpowder Plot, where again the emphasis falls upon analyzing the contemporary scene rather than elaborating carefully detailed literary parallels with paradigmatic narratives from the Old Testament:

> THe richest rarest mercies, daily sent
> (Right Christian brethren) to us of this land;
> From Gods ore-flowing grace, al-filling hand
> May be compar'd to th'Sun in firmament.
>
> Whose glorious rayes all creatures hearts revive,
> Whose light enlightens all the world throughout,
> Whose heat doth cherish plants that spring and sprout.
> Whose shine to want doth us of joy deprive.
>
> Yet since, so daily, man doth it enjoy,
> Who is't (almost) that valews it aright?
> Who yeelds due praise to heaven for heavens sweet light?
> O few or none. *Abundance does us cloy.*
>
> From whence, we (therefore) justly may conclude,
> That Gods rich mercies, which we oft possesse,
> Where with he daily, hourly doth us blesse,
> We all receive with great ingratitude.
>   . . .
> For this cause, therefore, I have ta'ne in hand,
> Again to sing (to Gods due praise and glory

In this revived and most faithfull Story)
How powerfully God to our Church did stand.

Which, now, at last (though, with much strugling) I,
(By Gods aid, in our pious Parliament)
Have brought to publike view, thus to prevent
Our times dough-*Bakers* base malignity:

Who, heated had their Ovens, extremely hot,
To burn-up in Oblivions smoaky-flame,
The memory (to our eternall shame)
Of this nefarious Popish Pouder-Plot.

(Sigs. A2–A2ᵛ, A3)

These lines demonstrate a remarkably complex and nuanced range of expression if they were, as we are supposed satirically to imagine, composed through the organs of an ass. After the easy flow of the call to prayer in the opening three stanzas, the verses turn at the emphatic admonition of "*Abundance does us cloy*" to become, themselves, increasingly clogged by parenthetical struggles with syntax in the effort to demonstrate how the history of the poem that follows is itself part of the history of struggle for control of the nation's memory. The genial light and vital warmth of the sun's rays have been diabolically transformed into the "extremely hot . . . smoaky-flame[s]" of the censor's ovens. Once, under control of divine benevolence, we had "plants that spring and sprout"— a little ludicrous, perhaps, but no more so than often admired passages by Herbert, Vaughan or Traherne, enraptured at the workings of providence. But times have changed, and now we must contend with the plosive disturbance of harsher consonants in "dough-*Bakers* base malignity"—alluding to Laud's chaplain, Samuel Baker, who had refused to license the earlier version of Vicars' work.[80]

In fashioning the 1641 edition of *November the 5* with an eye toward contemporary events, Vicars has shrewdly assessed the importance of control over the living memory. The course of poetry writing during the thirties and forties substantiates, and inflects with a degree of historical complexity and longevity, Michel Foucault's observation that "memory is actually a very important factor in struggle. . . . If one controls people's memory, one controls their dynamism. . . . It is vital to have possession of this memory, to control it, administer it, tell it what it must contain."[81] As part of this struggle for control of the nation's memory, the memory of what the nation has been, has become, and might be, Vicars seeks to revive "the memory . . . / Of this nefarious Popish Powder-Plot."

Like George Wither—with whom he is bracketed in a satirical aside by Butler in *Hudibras* for being inspired "with ale, or viler liquors"[82]—Vicars favors the jingling rhyme of the loose pentameter couplet for conveying the excitement of his message. The story, which bears contrast with *Paradise Lost* in its political manipulation of epic narrative and divine machinery, begins in Hell where Pluto becomes "enamoured of *Romes Strumpet*" and has her carried down to the underworld. She is by no means an unwilling victim, however, since

> *mutuall-love* their *liking* did expresse.
> Strait, they enjoy'd *infernall copulation*,
> Whose foule effects had present *procreation*.
>
> (P. 1)

It is to Treason, the offspring of this *"infernall copulation,"* that she turns soon after when, the thrills of marriage and motherhood having grown thin, she becomes jealous of England. Her complaint about "Britans nation" offers a precise example of what Margaret Doody has termed "ventriloquism," a popular device of civil war poetry by which "the voice of the 'real' speaker (speaking for the poet, and his audience) is momentarily cast into the personification of the Opposite or Other; a dummy puppet-speaker" (p. 44). Here, complaint functions as celebration of the most anti-catholic nation:

> Long have we in our sacred Cath'like chair,
> Even we thy holy-Mother, full of care,
> Sat mourning and bewailing (but in vain)
> The matchelesse losse wch Rome doth (still) sustain,
> And long, yea, too-too-long hath felt and found,
> And therwith ta'ne a desperate, deadly wound:
> I mean by Englands foule Apostacy,
> From *Peters* chair to *Luthers* heresie;
> For, since that time, no land in *Europe* fair,
> Hath labour'd, more, our welfare to impaire,
> Hath born more open and intestine hate
> To our Apostolike, imperiall-State,
> Than those damn'd hereticks of Britans nation,
> Endeavouring daily our dire extirpation.
>
> (Pp. 2–3)

Since this view of the nation is presented within a specific dramatic context, we need examine it neither as an accurate description nor as a reversal of Vicars' opinion. We know that he was by no means pleased with Britain's record in striking against Rome: in *Englands Remembrancer* of the same year he strongly advises Charles to participate more actively in the struggles of European protestantism:

> Remember also and Commiserate
> Thy royall Sisters poore *Palatinate,*
> Sad *Germanies* long lamentable woes;
> *Rochell,* like *Rachell* in her childlesse throwes.
>
> (Sig. A3ᵛ)

Rather, the complaint/praise of Britain's stand against catholicism serves both to fire national pride and to provide a rationale for assuming a catholic conspiracy in the first place. Before the Reformation, more wealth flowed to Rome from Britain than from any other country, according to Rome's complaint. Since then, all forms of social and political disturbance have been carefully engineered by Rome to recover her lost source of income:

> I tell thee (Son) this only *Albions*-Isle
> Through daily discord, variance, fraud and guile,
> Which, twixt them rais'd, for bribes, we quickly ceast,
> Hath Romes revenues mightily increast.
>
> (P. 4)

Having represented the island kingdom as the invaluable prize which she aims to conquer, Rome instructs Treason in how she has formerly—and unsuccessfully—employed Spain to do her business of recovery for her (pp. 5–9), and it is to Spain that she sends Treason to arrange the destruction of Parliament and King James.

From here, Vicars narrates the inception of the diabolical plot in detail, recounting the debates between the members of the conspiracy (pp. 16–20) and reminding us of their constant communications with Rome (pp. 21–22). He describes the undercover activities of digging beneath the House to plant the powder with all the verve of a writer of modern thrillers aiming to create suspense and arouse the reader's horrified anticipation (pp. 22–24). A digression on what would have happened had the plot worked sidesteps political considerations in order to arouse disgust—or, perhaps, vicarious delight—by piling up detailed descriptions of various dismembered nobles and their spouses (pp. 26–31). But God, who has been keeping an eye on the whole procedure, protects his chosen people:

> Our great Jehovah, God omnipotent,
> Who sits in Heaven, above the firmament,
> His *Israels* carefull *keeper, shepheard* great,
> Who mans affairs views from his mercy-seat . . .

calls a passing angel—

> You, saith Jehovah, now shall understand,
> How Satan that *sly-hunter* takes in hand
> With *Cholchos spels* and *spight* by agents proud,
> Great Britanes *soyle* to *spoyle:* yea and hath vow'd
> To root-out of the Earth the English-nation,
> Who to our *name* perform *pure* adoration.

> (P. 31)

God explains that allowing Rome to recapture England would contradict "*Prophecies* of old" (p. 32), and so announces that "I purpose with all expedition. . . / This hasty, hatefull enterprize to stop . . ."

> And, although Englands sins my wrath deserve,
> Yet, for my names-sake, I will them preserve,
> Although (I say) Englands ingratitude
> Justly deserves judgements amaritude.

> (P. 32)

With these qualifications, which are essential to Vicars' design, God dispatches the angel to contrive the letter which warns King James of the plot (pp. 33–39).

The plot discovered and disabled, Vicars devotes more than a thousand lines to a detailed account of the trial, torture, and execution of Fawkes, followed by a description of the tracking and capture of the other conspirators (pp. 41–74). He then turns to Hell, where the Devil decides to leave England alone until better occasion offers itself (pp. 75–80). A marginal gloss removes us from the fantasy by announcing that

"This hath bin most fully confirmed by Satan and his Agents, our Church & State projectors, in this lately discovered plot, by our blessed Parliament, 1641 which would have far transcended this of the powder-plot had it taken effect" (p. 80). Following a thanksgiving prayer for past and present deliverances (pp. 80–84), Vicars exhorts his readers to make themselves worthy of future divine assistance. The nation must be kept pure,

> That so, that ancient Prophets true prediction,
> Of *Babels* bane, of Roms proud *Whores* conviction,
> This age (in Gods due time) to passe may bring;
> This conquest great, Lord, grant unto our King.
>
> (P. 84)

The apocalyptic urgency helps to redefine the special privilege of the island, not as the nesting place of swans and halcyons, but as the battle-ground over which Manichaean forces contend. Vicars recasts Caroline tropes in order to insist that catholic infiltrators must be routed:

> O, if we will persist them (still) to spare,
> Let's blame *our-selves,* if we fall in their *snare.*
> Thee, thee (ô England) I may happy call
> Thou *little-isle,* whom father *Neptunes* wall,
> And mighty arms embrace; I past all doubt,
> May term thee happiest, all the world throughout;
> If thou didst *truly* know thy blest estate,
> Or heaven's rich *mercies* would'st commemorate.
>
> (P. 86)

Vicars' emphatic use of the conditional in his apostrophe here—"I may happy call . . . / May term thee happiest . . . / If . . ."—points to the crucial recognition that social well-being and political stability are not, as they often seem in Stuart poetry, the results of arbitrary divine indulgence magically assured by the mere fact that there is a king on the throne. At issue, rather, are the very terms in which national identity is conceived. As Keith Baker has observed in a different context:

> Politics in any society depends upon the existence of cultural repre-
> sentations that define the relationships among political actors, thereby al-
> lowing individuals and groups to press claims upon one another and upon

the whole. . . . Political contestation therefore takes the form of competing efforts to mobilize and control the possibilities of political and social discourse, efforts through which that discourse is extended, recast, and—on occasion—even radically transformed. (Pp. 134–35)

Vicars, and other militant protestant poets and writers of the early 1640s, were engaged in just such a contest over the terms in which to recast national identity and stability. They appropriated metaphors, tropes, and topoi used by Stuart poets to legitimate the claims of the ruling dynasty and transformed them by insisting that their truth was subject to the collective agreement of a people who had not forgotten their own past. "Yea," Vicars concludes his poem on the Powder Plot:

> canst thou (England) canst thou possibly
> Be so orewhelmed in *stupidity?*
> So sottish, senselesse, impiously ingrate,
> As to forget, or to *obliterate*
> Out of *thy thankefull-heart,* the odious smell
> Of this projected *pouder-smoake* of hell,
> So long as ever *thou* a Kingdome art?
>
> (P. 90)

We cannot, with any certainty, know just how successful Vicars was in his campaign to ensure that people not be lulled into a sense of false security by official representations of a volatile political situation. After the Restoration, Anthony à Woods claimed that Vicars "did affright many of the weaker sort and others from having any agreement with the Kings Party, by continually inculcating into their heads strange stories of Gods wrath against the Cavaliers" (2:85), and he was certainly not alone in turning to verse in order to argue that all was not so well within the island kingdom as the court poets would have had readers believe. Whoever those "others" who were not "of the weaker sort" may have been, they were repeatedly assured by Vicars, and other militant protestant poets such as Cragge and Taylor, that the British nation was a special place that God had set aside to bring about the workings of his mysterious plan.

THE HEROIC PRESENT: CIVIL WAR AND AFTER

With the collapse of social and political stability at the outbreak of civil war in 1642, we should not be surprised to find poets writing on behalf of the Stuart monarchy once again turning to those familiar neo-classical tropes which they had once used to celebrate the peaceful kingdom. But now heroic has subsumed pastoral utterance. In 1643, echoing Virgil, Cowley asks in utter amazement:

> What rage does *England* from it selfe divide
> More then Seas doe from all the world beside?[83]

By 1648 another poet seems almost resigned to social fragmentation and civil disturbance as deplorable but somehow undeniable conditions of the times:

> we that be
> Sever'd from other Nations by the Sea,
> And from our selves divided by our sin,
> Need now no forraign foes, wee've foes within.[84]

But in Cowley's *The Civil War,* insularity becomes part of a plea for an end to the darkness of civil war:

> If wee're resolv'd and fixt our Way to loose,
> Let's some false Road before false By-wayes choose.
> But rather let our Isle the Oceans Tyde,
> As from the World, from the Worlds Faults divide.
> Let other Lands love darkness; 'tis our Right,
> Our Countries Priv'eledge to have lest of Night.
>
> (3.77–82)

In the same poem, written from the exiled court at Oxford during the course of the first civil war, Cowley describes the outbreak of armed conflict as a transformation within the poetic character of the nation. England changes from a georgic farm to an epic battlefield when Alecto, the goddess of discord, displaces the plowmen from the island. Once again, his lines recall Virgil:

> dire *Alecto,* ri'sen from *Stygian* strand,
> Had scattered *Strife* and *Armes* through all the Land.
> . . .
> The fatall seede still dropt shee as shee went,
> And her owne clowds with a shrill *Trumpet* rent.

Great *Brittaines* aged *Genius* heard the sound,
Shooke his gray head, and sunck into the ground.
The'astonisht *Plowmen* the sad noyse did heare,
Look'ed up in vaine, and left their worke for feare.

(2.5–6, 11–16)

If in Stuart poetics the image of Britain as a pastoral garden was forced to give way to that of a georgic farm, then the farm gave way, in turn, to the epic battlefield. Since, as Margaret Doody argues, "there is no style or form which will not be capable of being used by the enemy ... the question of genres has to be worked out again, and all style is recognized as concealing lurking dangers" (p. 32). A lot depends on whom one considers the enemy to be, of course. Foe to the Muse no longer, Mars inspires Suckling and Lovelace to go off to the wars, far from their mistresses. But not before offering new tunes which poets might sing to their loved ones. Marvell understood the urgency driving young men to forsake poetry for war, and composed one of the finest English Horatian odes in response to contemporary events. Waller, no doubt still longing for the comfort of Venus' fair arms, has a less reputable account to give of himself and the political poetry he wrote between 1640 and 1660.

Not until the relative calm of the fifties, and the years of Cromwell's Protectorate, did the Virgilian image again suit the proud confidence of those who would celebrate the nation. Waller's notorious *Panegyric on My Lord Protector* of 1655 may, indeed, have been fiction as he later told Charles II, but it reinvests traditional tropes and themes with a clarity of tone and a sureness of rhythm that reaffirm their values. Waller once again looks in upon the island from a global perspective in order to offer a mystified account of the natural order found there:

Our little world, the image of the great,
Like that, amidst the boundless ocean set,
Of her own growth has all that Nature craves;
And all that's rare, as tribute from the waves.

(2:12)

This relationship to the world is not, however, purely parasitic since the island "was sure designed / To be the sacred refuge of mankind" (2:11). Under Cromwell the island has become a haven that serves the entire world instead of retreating from foreign strife as in Carew's earlier lines.

But despite the inward perspective, Waller's more expansive scope constitutes part of his poem's larger design, which is to endorse the Protector's rule by celebrating successful overseas conquests. The nation assumes its destined role as a center of world empire under the Protector. Traditional conceits take on a new life as both sea and Cromwell encircle the island:

> What may be thought impossible to do
> For us, embraced by the sea and you?

> (2:11)

In these revolutionary times, Cromwell, the center of power and might, has also assumed the encircling role formerly reserved for divine, monarchic figures.

In order to legitimate the Protectorate, Waller shows the landscape to be flourishing as it was supposed to have done before the civil wars. Moreover, under Cromwell the nation achieves the imperial dominion for which it has always, apparently, been destined. The past has finally found fulfillment in the heroic present:

> Things of the noblest kind our own soil breeds;
> Stout are our men, and warlike are our steeds;
> Rome, though her eagle through the world had flown,
> Could never make this island all her own.

> Here the Third Edward, and the Black Prince, too,
> France-conquering Henry flourished, and now you;
> For whom we stayed, as did the Grecian state,
> Till Alexander came to urge their fate.

> (2:12–13)

By showing how, under Cromwell, England has surpassed classical precedent in conquering the Scots, the Irish, and European nations, Waller ignores entirely the Jacobean union of Britain and represents England as an imperial state with a destined role in world history. He replaces the earlier emphasis upon insularity by a chauvinistic perspective that accords praise to the Protector for bringing about England's manifest destiny. This global sense of England's imperial future dominates the historical poetry written during the revolutionary decades and after, partly accommodating itself to the internationalism of prewar militants who had challenged Stuart isolationism, and partly displacing certain distressing sights, the devastation of the land wrought by wars at home.

When Charles II arrived in England in 1660, no longer an exiled prince but a king with claims to a dynastic inheritance, poetic tributes poured forth from all over the country, tributes that legitimated his power even as they defined its conditions and limitations. Dryden opens the best known of these poems by constructing a historical perspective that rehabilitates the Stuart dynasty within a broader European context:

> NOW with a general Peace the World was blest,
> While Ours, a World divided from the rest,
> A dreadful Quiet felt, and worser farre
> Then Armes, a sullen Interrvall of Warre.

> (1:16)

By 1660, when *Astraea Redux* appeared, the Virgilian topos had become a cliché listed in Joshua Poole's *The English Parnassus* of 1657—a rhyming dictionary and catalogue of stock epithets for poets in need of a little assistance.[85] Nevertheless, Dryden turns the trope to good effect here, calmly depicting the world apart in historical and political terms that, in true partisan fashion, pose a problem: what can be done to rectify the situation so described? Dryden's praise of the returned king, in part, describes how Charles effects a solution merely by his return. But the text contains advice too—be merciful at home while starting a war against the Dutch that will strengthen British control over the seas and boost trade.[86]

By the end of *Astraea Redux,* Dryden has demonstrated—by selectively reporting the events surrounding the king's return—how the Restoration betokens a reversal in the circumstances with which the poem opens. The world divided from the rest of the world will now assume its rightful place as the imperial center of the world:

> Our Nation with united Int'rest blest
> Not now content to poize, shall sway the rest.
> Abroad your Empire shall no Limits know,
> But like the Sea in boundless Circles flow.
>
> . . .
>
> Oh Happy Age! Oh Times like those alone
> By Fate reserv'd for Great *Augustus* Throne!

> When the joint growth of Armes and Arts foreshew
> The World a Monarch, and that Monarch *You*.
>
> (1:23–24)

Dryden's panegyric closes with a carefully detailed vision of the nation's future under the restored Stuart dynasty, one that emphatically turns inside out the insular perspective of Jacobean and Caroline pastoral to announce a global empire achievable through the "joint growth of Armes and Arts."

One striking feature of Dryden's Restoration panegyric is that he evokes the name of the Roman emperor which militant protestants summoned as an anagram for their Swedish hero thirty years before when protesting the first Charles's foreign policy. What was once oppositional has become part of the "official" view of the Restoration settlement.

> *Sweds* Great *AUGUSTUS!* Oh how could I dwell
> Upon that Name! How often could I spell
> Its every sacred syllable; and when
> I've done't a thousand times, begin agen!
> That Name who honours not, Oh may he be
> O'rewhelm'd with never-dying infamie![87]

Margaret Doody has argued that "Civil War verse and its interests, poetic as well as political, had a part in shaping what we know as Augustan poetry" (p. 42), but we may need to reach back further still to the poetic and political interests of those poets who, not content with the isolationism of the early Stuart kings, urged an aggressive foreign policy in the years before civil war broke out.

During the final decades of the century, political poets became preoccupied with shaping England's future global empire in a variety of heroic forms that had lost the religious urgency of the 1630s and early 1640s. Howard Erskine-Hill has shown the marriage of arms and arts to be a constitutive feature of Augustan poetry, and clearly this union marks a reversal of procedures from the time when Daniel spoke of "Muse-foe Mars."[88] Marvell's *On the Victory Obtained by Blake* (1657), Waller's *Instructions to a Painter* (1665), and Dryden's *Annus Mirabilis* (1667) come to mind as well-known examples. But this innovative tendency to represent England's future imperial power in the elevated terms of heroic poetry by no means entirely replaced the nostalgic insularity of pastoral verse preoccupied with an idealized countryside and an idyllic past. Representations of the land play a central part in the emergent heroic enterprise as poets historicize the national landscape by describing places precisely as sites of significant past events.[89]

This habit of associating places with their past may be linked to the development of local history writing during the century, a general movement arising from the desire to understand the nation's political character by knowing its various regions. Concern with local history had entered English poetry with Drayton's *Polyolbion* (1612) at the beginning of the century; other poets quickly adopted the habit of describing a place by reminding us of its significant history. By the forties, with local loyalties at issue, the question of region became crucial. In his *Iter Boreale,* written during the twenties, Richard Corbett describes Leicester by mentioning its links with former kings. In doing so he naturalizes monarchy for being as much a historical part of the national landscape as the city itself. Metaphors of sight fuse movements between time and space together in what sounds distinctly like the language of educated tourism:

> And now wee are at *Leister* where wee shall
> Leape ore six steeples, and one Hospitall
> Twice told; But those great Landmarkes I referr
> To *Camdens* Eye, England's *Chorographer.*
> Let mee observe that Almesmans heraldrye,
> Who being ask'd, what *Henry* that should be
> That was their founder, Duke of *Lancaster;*
> Answer'd: twas *John* of *Gaunt,* I assure you Sir;
> And so confuted all the walles which sayd,
> *Henry* of *Grisemond* this foundation layd.
>
> . . .
>
> Is not th'usurping *Richard* buryed there,
> That *King* of hate, and therefore *Slave* of feare;
> Dragg'd from the fatall feild *Bosworth,* where hee
> Lost life, and, what he liv'd for; Cruelty?[90]

Corbett endeavors to help us imagine we are there with him, eye witnesses to the place, knowing Leicester because of our shared knowledge of what has happened there. The landscape itself becomes legible as a book of national history.

But it was alongside this retrospective tendency characteristic of the pastoral commitment to the past that a more global view developed, one linked to belief in the nation's growing imperial power. Civil war and exile make educated tourists with a knowledgeable interest in foreign property; in Restoration panegyrics Charles was frequently praised as the best of kings since his education in foreign courts peculiarly fitted him to rule the world. After the Restoration, poets justified current policy for being most conducive to an imminent age of English global imperium. What distinguishes the imperial and heroic from the arcadian and pastoral representations of the nation is a concern for international politics that entails a shift in historical perspective from one concerned exclusively with the national past to one that engages with the future by looking beyond national borders to the world at large.

3

Representing the Past

This VOICE. doth to your sight, and hearing come.
— GEORGE WITHER, *Vox Pacifica* (1645)

GENERIC CONVENTIONS embody class positions and normative values, most commonly by specifying the sites of ideological tension and social dislocation. But though necessary, generic analysis can prove both limiting and misleading for seventeenth-century historical poetry.[1] In *Marxism and Literature,* Raymond Williams develops the notion of *stance*—"a mode of basic (social) organisation which determines a particular kind of presentation"[2]—to enable us to distinguish the political predispositions of literary texts in ways that generic analysis tends to blunt. For any literary text, "stance" serves as an intergeneric procedure for including or excluding textual possibilities: in the production of a poem directly involving topics of contemporary political interest, certain narrative forms and literary conventions are put aside while others become textual material. Court poets favored neoclassical forms and allusions to imperial Roman history, while oppositional poets, criticizing royal policy in the decades leading up to the civil wars, tended to favor references to the Old Testament, Saxon law, and the Elizabethan era. Although Renaissance genre theory restricted historical poetry to past topics, many poems were occasional in the sense that some specific current event—a birth, marriage, or death in the royal household, a battle, dispute, or policy affecting the public at large—called them into being, while other historical poems generated their own occasions from contemporary crises. We could construct an ideal contemporary reader who would have had some idea of what such works were about; and the difference between that more or less reconstructible experience of the text, that ideal reading in the past, and our own is important. But if we are to consider how literary texts such as historical poems actively engaged in the social construction of contemporary readers—as any historical account of such works surely must—then those readers will most usefully be understood as already knowing something of the events being described, but not necessarily in the versions that poets offered. Here differences in class attitudes and values between the two different kinds of occasional poem become important. A neoclassical panegyric or masque written to celebrate a formal state occasion will constitute an immediate coterie readership quite differently from the way a broadside by a Martin Parker or an outburst of poetic fury from a George Wither urge their readers to participate in constructing a critical understanding of contemporary history. While formal court verse confirms the values of its conventions, historical poetry that creates its own occasion addresses readers differently in the attempt to impress upon them the historical significance of some topic which might otherwise pass unnoticed. Wither and the other Spenserians commonly tell us that they felt moved to write because of some entirely personal conviction or experience, and so they might be considered among the earliest to attempt voicing the political from the personal.[3]

But in thinking about what writers say they are doing, we ought not to forget that readers in all ages can misread, deliberately and strategically, inadvertently through carelessness, or compulsively through ideological blindness. Even if we don't know what readers of historical poems in the seventeenth century actually thought, we can nevertheless historicize the problem of "reading" by bearing in mind how the texts in question are evidence of the way poets, who were also readers of and in their own times, sought to control meanings. Both in the ways they represent otherwise knowable events and in the ways they limit and direct their readers' activities within the general range of expectations that we call genre, these texts have designs upon their readers. Writers might fail to fulfill, understand, or articulate their literary purposes. But historical poetry, understood as a political discourse, is necessarily tendentious and instrumental. After surveying some typical critical statements regarding the nature, range, and status of "historical poetry" as a genre, this chapter analyzes the politics of some of the conventions which poets of the seventeenth century most commonly used when writing about the present by representing the past.

Historical Poetry and Generic Form

Since competing versions of the nation's identity rely throughout the century upon competing versions of the past regardless of genre or stance, representing the past was in every way a political endeavor, a "contestation" in Baker's term, for control over the reader's memory. The attempt by Renaissance theorists to preserve history as a value-free heuristic category was, consequently, both a strategic move that enabled poets to write as if from an objective position, and an ideological blindness to the necessarily political character of any form of historical representation. Whatever traditional theorists may have claimed, facts about the past exist only within precise discourses that determine which "facts" are produced—made available and subsequently shaped into significant formal designs. We have seen how literary theorists most commonly concentrated upon this latter concern for shape and style, but we have also seen how in practice partisan interests modified not only formal procedures but also the range of facts chosen for poetic treatment. Although there was, strictly speaking, no independent genre of historical poetry, many poets during the seventeenth century wrote poems which they called "historical" and something like a generic theory developed during the course of the century.

Renaissance critical theorists seldom treated "historical poetry" as such since the concept was something of an oxymoron. Those critics who did write about historical poetry tended to restrict its concerns exclusively to past persons and events. In *The Arte of English Poesie* of 1589, one of the first English critical texts of the period to give the genre extended treatement, Puttenham describes "historicall Poesie" as that class "by which the famous actes of Princes and the vertuous and worthy lives of our forefathers were reported."[4] Accordingly, the only criteria which Puttenham offers for selecting facts for historical poems are derived from an explicit class hierarchy requiring a corresponding decorum of styles and exclusivity of subject matter:

> because the actions of meane & base personages, tend in very few cases to any great good example: for who passeth to follow the steps, and maner of life of a craftes man, shepheard or sailer, though he were his father or dearest friend? yea how almost is it possible that such maner of men should be of any vertue other then their profession requireth? Therefore was nothing committed to historie, but matters of great and excellent persons & things that the same by irritation of good courages (such as emulation causeth) might worke more effectually, which occasioned the story writer to chuse an higher stile fit for his subject.... (P. 41)

While admitting that historical facts are chosen in accordance with particular interests, Puttenham sidesteps the question of how some men came to be considered "great & excellent" in the first place, and turns to a concern for an appropriate style that "might worke more effectually." Literary form determines social effect even as it is shaped by sociopolitical determinants.

To Puttenham, and Renaissance humanists generally, history writing offered heuristic strategies for preserving the memory and inculcating the values of those who gained, exercised, and maintained power: those, in other words, who made the production of poetry, history, and literary theory both possible and necessary by means of the circuits of patronage. Puttenham dedicated *The Arte of English Poesie* to William Cecil, Lord Burghley, who, alongside the queen and the earl of Leicester, "was one of the three most prominent dedicatees of printed books" in Elizabethan England.[5] Burghley, in turn, relied upon the poets and writers who dedicated works to him for cultural legitimation almost as much as he did upon the crown for his rise to a position of wealth and influence. Under such circumstances, we should not be surprised to find Puttenham outlining a theory that disguises these social functions of historical poetry by using epistemological terms that suggest social structure is a matter of à priori truths commonly available to all. "There is nothing in man," he begins,

> of all the potential parts of his mind (reason and will except) *more noble or more necessary to the active life* then memory: because it maketh most to a sound judgement and perfect worldly wisedome, examining and comparing the times past with the present . . . it came upon this reson, experience to be so highly commended in all consultations of importance, and preferred before any learning or science, and yet experience is no more than a masse of memories assembled, that is, such as man hath made in time before. (P. 39, emphasis added)

From amidst the indiscriminate "masse of memories assembled" constituting the past, historical poets select those which are "more noble & more necessary to the active life" and therefore best suited to serve as examples for those readers who would themselves be great. The historical poet, whose task it was to discover and describe the circumstances and conditions by which some realized their greatness, was not, however, tied to the truth like the historian.

Puttenham recognizes how poets will often forego their duty to the facts when shaping the past to form exempla suitable for providing the knowledge that makes self-advancement possible. This artistic freedom enables poets to avoid the problems of unmalleable material. Unlike Sidney, Puttenham does not take a controversial view of the problem, admitting instead that even historians frequently fake the facts in practicing their art, while insisting that they do so only from the highest moral principles (p. 40). Historical poetry, however, achieves the same purpose as history without compromising the integrity of its genre for the "fained matter" distinctive of historical poetry

> works no lesse good conclusions for example, then the most true and veritable: but often times more, because the Poet hath the handling of them to fashion at his pleasure, but not so of th'other which must go according to their veritie none otherwise without the writers great blame. (P. 40)

Yet in the cause of moral instruction, historical facts were invariably seen as being tractable to the higher truth attainable through the poet's art since, as John Hall observed in 1631,

> Truth is the historian's Crowne, and art
> Squares it to stricter comlinesse.[6]

Puttenham insists, however, that both poet and historian write only about the past since "the good and exemplarie things and actions of the former ages, were reserved only to the historicall reportes of wise and grave men" (p. 40). Historical poetry should not concern itself with contemporary events since doing so would—though Puttenham does not say as much—compromise its pretense to objectivity and truth and thus its moral purpose. Nevertheless, he admits that historical poetry invites its readers to compare past and present matters that they might conclude "with a stedfast resolution, what is the best course to be taken in all . . . actions and advices in this world (p. 39). And if "the Poesie historicall is of all other next the divine most honorable . . . for the common benefit as for the speciall comfort every man receiveth by it" (p. 39), then it most certainly served a social function even when deliberately ignoring current events.

By the second half of the seventeenth century, poetic theory had altered sufficiently to account for poets who wrote directly on contemporary events. Dryden offers a modified conception of what was permitted a historical poem by applying the term to *Annus Mirabilis* (1667), a poem written about events as they were happening. Yet in his prefatory comments Dryden distinguishes historical poetry from epic, calling his own work the former since, while the subject and persons are of epic stature, the poem lacks certain formal and artistic properties required of epic proper—such as unity of action, theme, and length. "I have chosen," he writes, "the most heroick Subject which any Poet could desire . . . the motives, the beginning, progress and successes of a most just and necessary War."[7] Despite the suitability of his subject, Dryden regards his poem as historical rather than epic:

> I have call'd my Poem *Historical,* not *Epick,* though both the Actions and Actors are as much Heroick, as any Poem can contain. But since the Action is not properly one, nor that accomplish'd in the last successes, I have judg'd it too bold a Title for a few *Stanza's,* which are little more in number then a single *Iliad,* or the longest of the *Aeneids.* (1:44)

Dryden's emphasis here differs from Puttenham's for while both agree that historical poetry must praise and inspire emulation, Dryden stresses the artistic problems of composing a poem in praise of contemporary men and their deeds rather than the difficulties of shaping past events to suit a morally instructive purpose. The intractability of a contemporary rather than a past subject caused Dryden to write the preface. He originally designed a unified poem on the Dutch Wars of 1666 that would glorify the English fleet, its commanders, and their heroism. But he was interrupted in this task by the Great Fire, a disaster of sufficient magnitude to demand attention from an aspiring state poet.[8] Dryden's preface offers a theoretical justification for his change in subject matter and his consequent violation of those artistic rules traditionally governing heroic poetry.

Both Dryden and Puttenham, though separated by almost a century, develop a primarily functional theory in which historical poetry seeks to praise some national figure, institution, or event. For Puttenham, the historical poem does so by freely shaping past events to fit a moral design; for Dryden it should follow chronological events, even to the detriment of artistic principles, in the pursuit of its argument. Yet Dryden's professed adherence to historical events does not stand in the way of his poem's political purpose. And as for the factuality of his account, few of his readers would have expected it to be entirely reliable. Dryden was by no means the first to admit that his poem on contemporary events mixed historical and panegyrical elements. In 1660 John Crouch had described his panegyric on the Restoration as "A Mixt Poem, Partly Historicall, Partly Panegyricall." And even before this, in 1648, a poem entitled *London, King Charles His Augusta* had appeared, declaring itself to be "An Historicall and Antiquarian Work." This latter text provides an interesting instance of the links between poetry, history, and politics, and deserves fuller comment as a self-proclaimed instance of that oxymoronic category "historical poem."

Although *London* was ascribed to Davenant on the 1648 title page, Thomas Blackburn has shown that it was originally composed as a Latin work—*Augusta Caroli*—by the catholic historian Edmund Bolton in 1632.[9] Bolton himself died in or around 1634 and so could have had no part in the publication of the English version in 1648, but he was, according to Blackburn, likely to have undertaken the translation. Blackburn argues that Bolton's purpose was to yoke king and capital together in a paean of praise that would encourage the aldermen of London to grant him three or four thousand pounds to write "the Institution, and History, &ct., of the citie, in Latin and English."[10] Bolton's scheme, like his earlier more ambitious project to found a Royal Academy under James, came to nothing.[11] And the Latin poem, *Augusta Caroli,* does not seem to have survived. But the English version, *London,* remains to show how this writer combined the arts of poetry and history into a self-proclaimed historical poem that was eventually published for immediate political purposes which would have been inconceivable to its author.

Yet Bolton evidently had a political design when writing this "historical poem" since *London* compares various legends concerning the foundation of London in order to demonstrate how, under the power and might of King Charles, the city deserves the glorious title "Augusta" (p. 12). Using titles to link city and king in mutual praise, Bolton adapts early seventeenth-century historical method to a political program.[12] He searches into the origins of London, using etymology to evaluate the historical reliability of the various accounts of its foundation, in order to praise its glorious past and its equally glorious present ruler. The poem is presented as an impartial enquiry into the past. To further this impression of historical impartiality, the reader is provided with a multitude of learned notes to seemingly irrefutable authorities, both ancient and modern, as various as Pliny, Diodorus Siculus, Suetonius, Julius Caesar, and Selden, Cotton, Camden, and Stow (pp. 2, 6, 9, 1, 11). But the poem's profession of historical impartiality hardly masks overt partisan sympathies.

Bolton's primary object no doubt was, as Blackburn suggests, to "persuade the aldermen to support his scheme" (p. 323), but he does so in a more generally political manner by praising the imperialism of "royall *Charles*" and his capital city in terms of their dynastic past. Prefatory verses addressing the king describe the task and purpose of the poet-historian who searches into past times in order to praise the present ruler:

> Fames old reserves my verses subject be,
> Who LONDON built, most prosp'rous King for thee.
>
> (Sig. A4)

This task involves reporting what can be found amidst the relevant historical records rather than inventing—"Things found, not fain'd are here." Like a careful historian, the poet recognizes that the records are not necessarily accurate; but his solution to the problem is that of the poet—"I tell not which is true, but what is heard" (sig. A4^v). *London* itself largely follows this program by writing Charles's reign into an internationalist history of the progress of empire. It begins by recounting the legend of a Trojan foundation that links the origins of London with the legendary kings of Rome. London was founded by Brutus,

> That valiant Worthy, who did not bely,
> With deeds dengenerous, his ancestry,
> Equall to Kings of *Troy*. . . .
>
> (P. 1)

By establishing a personal dynastic empire centered in London, Brutus heroically advanced the imperial bloodline to a position superior to that of the Trojan founder of Rome who cowardly fled his native city:

> "As for *Aeneas*. Crownes no cowerds gain,
> "No more then unstirr'd flames the roof attain."
>
> (P. 2)

Once London's originary claim to a glorious imperial destiny superior to Rome's has been linked with dynastic principles, the poet switches tactics and begins surveying various etymologies of *London*:

> being found for ships a port secure;
> (The *Welsh* a ship call *Lhong*) it did enure,

> In after-ages far another name,
> Even *London,* which it beareth still the same.
> And this, if some wise men rove right, is true;
> *Dinas,* in *Welsh* a City. Thus it grew.

(P. 2)

Having already warned us to "part doubtfull things from sound," the poet offers additional versions of the origins of the name *London.* "There others are" he reminds us

> who think it call'd *Llan-Tain,*
> And of *Dianas* temple there did gain,
> That famous title: *Llan,* a temple is,
> And *Tain, Dian. London* grew from this.

(P. 2)

Lest we should feel in need of guidance amidst these questions, the poet comes to our aid as every dutiful historian should. But his preference for the derivation through Diana, whom he then associates with Brutus, owes more to the poet's art of turning facts to praise. We might have anticipated the Virgilian closure:

> Of all conjectures this to me seems best.
> For under her, as Goddesse, to the West,
> Beyond the *Celts* land, where the Sun goes down,
> That brave heroick Prince, born to renown,
> Great *Brutus* bravely came, and fixt his seat,
> Within the *Oceans* bosome, fixt that great,
> Imperiall state, beyond the worlds known end,
> Shut out, where he his own known world did tend.

(P. 2)

The preferred etymology of *London* legitimates dynastic "British" imperialism for being divinely ordained. In much the same fashion the rest of the poem follows etymological paths posted with the city's various names through different legends and stories, all of them structured by the values of imperial dynasticism, and all of them pointing to Charles.

This poem's rhetorical skepticism barely disguises the poet's stance and political design—the nation's imperial destiny is a natural, geographical fact intimately linked to the origins of its capital city and to the Stuart dynasty. The poet historicizes political judgments by hiding them beneath a surface quest for accuracy. His preference for one account over another invariably stems from a desire to associate Charles Stuart with the capital of a nation whose past has been one of glorious imperial conquests under mighty monarchs—even though such was not quite the case during Charles's reign. In accordance with this intent, the poet suggests London should be renamed Augusta to express the city's present status as the seat of world empire under Charles:

> if she had not heretofore been taught,
> That stately style, now certainly she ought,
> When royall *Charles* the *British* empire swayes,
> *London,* which royal *Lud* did newly raise,
> And newly name, now ought *Augusta* be,
> Well able to make good that old decree.
>
> (P. 12)

Such may have been Bolton's view in or around 1632 when, presumably, he wrote *Augusta Caroli* (provided that the English version accurately follows the lost Latin original). But when his poem, duly "translated into English Couplets" (sig. A1), was published during the spring of 1648— Thomason dates his copy March 7[13]—the political situation in England had so far altered from 1632 that we can have little doubt that the publishers' concerns were quite different from Bolton's.[14] The anonymous preface which ascribes the work to Davenant—clearly not the work of Bolton who died before he could have known Davenant—indicates a new purpose beyond that of praising city and dynastic king:

> And now I shall cleare the *Title* from some aspersions which malice might be ready to cavill at, because, happily, it may be thought not *Calculated* for the *Present Times:* yet who knows not that *LONDON* hath always had the honour to be, (as well as to be call'd) *The City Royall;* and I hope, Learning is not so much forgot, but by that easie figure it may still be tearmed, the *City Loyall;* and then why not *King Charles* his *Augusta?* although, for more then the last Lustre of yeares it hath been *Divorc'd* from it's greatest lustre, namely, the presence of *Him,* who only made it *Famous.* (Sigs. A2–A2ᵛ)

Political tensions were specially fierce in London during the spring and early summer of 1648 when *London* was published, and a poem praising Charles and his royal city could hardly have avoided engaging in the disputes. During 1647, the Levellers had gained support among the lower-middle classes in London; by August the Army Council—following their seizing of the king in June—was using force against the House of Commons, thereby asserting itself as the group with preeminent political power. But the Army Council fractured along class and religious lines, as became clearer with the Putney debates of October. With the king's escape in November, the possibility of counterrevolution increased, especially among the Parliamentary gentry and Army grandees who looked to Scotland for support. Political unrest during these months was fomented by an abundance of verse propaganda advocating various policies for resolving the struggles for power among Cavalier, Parliament, Army, and Citizen.[15] In the midst of these events an English version of Bolton's poem—*"Calculated* for the *Present Times"*—appeared in March 1648. By celebrating London's historical links with dynastic rulers in general, and Stuarts named Charles in particular, *London, King Charles His Augusta* aimed to encourage pro-Stuart feelings among those living in the city and environs on the eve of the second civil war.

Yet if this "historical poem" was published with a view to contributing to pro-Stuart sentiment, the preface opens with what presumably sought to pass for impartial literary criticism:

> Thou art here presented with an *Historicall Poem* of the antiquity of this (yet) famous *City;* where thou shall finde the *Ancient Honours* with the severall *Names,* and *Founders* neatly cast into this elegant composure as well be fits so excellent a *Subject.* (Sig. A2)

Once again, as in Puttenham and Dryden, the emphasis upon historical poetry as a means of praising national institutions in an appropriately elevated form quietly seeks to announce a propagandistic purpose. Since adherence to historical method provides the very subject matter of Bolton's poem, this "historical" enquiry becomes, with publication in 1648, a clear instance of propaganda. Amidst the social and political turmoil of the thirties and forties, the surface quest for objective truth served as a point of departure for political rhetoric: my side is right since it bases its version of events upon undeniable historical precedent.

Important historical poems of the 1630s featured chronological narratives of national glory under strong, warlike kings. Thomas May offered an encomiastic rationale for his *The Reigne of King Henry the Second* (1633), dedicating this "Historicall Poem" to King Charles since it was "Borne by his Command."[16] Two years later he apologized lest his *The Victorious Reigne of King Edward the Third* (1635) intrude upon political matters more suited to a "Historian in Prose" than to "straines of height for an Heroike Poem" (sig. A3ᵛ). Yet, like Charles Aleyn's *The Battailes of Crescey, and Poictiers under the leading of King Edward the Third* (1631), to which May wrote a Latin dedicatory poem (sig. A2), and Aleyn's subsequent *The Historie of . . . Henrie . . . the Seventh* (1638), May's poems were written to celebrate the king regnant as much as the king titular. In verses appended to the second edition of Aleyn's *Crescey* in 1633, Henry Blount described how, foe to the muses no longer, Mars cooperates with the poet to praise England's monarchy. Just as Aleyn's "*Bayes* advance" the king's "*Sword*," so does "his *Sword* thy *Bayes* / So joynes with *Mars* his dread, thy *Muses* praise" (sig. A3ᵛ). Whatever the claims of theorists, the truth offered by royalist historians invariably legitimated the power of rulers by representing them as integral to the very nature of things and hence not subject to political dissent.

A further instance of a self-proclaimed historical poem is a work of quite different intent and character from any of those mentioned so far. Often incorrectly attributed to Marvell, *An Historicall Poem* (1680) satirizes the return of Charles II. The title is suggestively ironical, for the poem belittles the restored king by reporting true but unheroic facts about the conditions of his return.[17] The king, we are reminded, could not even afford to pay his own way:

> At length by wonderfull impulse of Fate
> The People call him home to helpe the State,
> And what is more they send him Mony too,
> And cloath him all from head to foot anew.[18]

Truth to history in the hands of a satirist has an effect opposite to that of the encomiast's truth, for it can expose the duplicity of claims to historical objectivity.

Evidently the term "historical poem" encompasses a range of ideologically disparate strategies and meanings in seventeenth-century critical thought and practice. In the case of historical poetry, at least, generic difference often proves more significant than similarity. Although Puttenham had insisted that poets should consider only past subjects, a historical poem like Bolton's *London* represents the past specifically in order to construct a partisan version of national history directly relevant to present needs. Crouch's panegyric and the satirical poem written on the Restoration, however, treat contemporary events as though they were already historical, a procedure that receives theoretical justification in Dryden's preface to *Annus Mirabilis*. Sometimes historical poets acknowledged that their real subject was the present, but in doing so suggested that what they had to say about the present was as true as history.

THE ANALOGY OF PAST AND PRESENT

During the course of the century, the need to write about the present became more urgent, so that the present intruded upon the former dominance of the past to become itself a valid subject for direct treatment in historical poetry, against traditional prescriptions. This shift in the subject matter of historical poetry suggests the emergence of a general— and by no means fully conscious—sense that current events themselves are as much a part of history as past events. As Robert Weimann argues in his study of the poetic elements in Thomas Nashe's historical narratives, the seventeenth century was "a historical moment of cultural change and experiment, which the combined use of poetic and historiographical modes of discourse ... significantly helped to constitute."[19] Support for such a view—which might lead us to speak of the historical consciousness of the period—could be found in the growing interest in varieties of historical writing. In addition to the development of news sheets, corantos, and broadsides detailing contemporary events,[20] we might cite the development of contemporary history during the century as men and women from various classes and political positions began keeping detailed records of the events of their own times: the important work of May, Vicars, Ludlow, Clarendon, and Burnet comes to mind.[21] And we could find a different kind of evidence in the spiritual autobiographies of the century which, together with the more secular autobiographical writings of the famous diarists—Pepys, Evelyn, Lady Anne Halkett, Lucy Hutchinson, Simonds D'Ewes and others—suggest an increasing need to find appropriate literary forms to express a sense of direct and immediate personal involvement with shaping the course of history.[22]

Some such shift in historical consciousness clearly seems to have been taking place.[23] More precisely, the different ways poets wrote about the past demonstrate how, despite their increasing commitment to contemporary issues and topics, formal and artistic concerns restricted their ability to understand and represent their own times without reference to some idealized or (mis)remembered past. As was recognized at the time, this is an epistemological matter because the available modes of historical understanding and representation—by means of which poets spoke of viewing the world, and by means of which they recreated it for their own purposes—turned historical process into a narrative series of objects that could be closely observed, recorded, and understood rather than into a complex network of sociopolitical relationships.

How poets represented the past sheds light not only on their strategies of political argumentation but also on some of the more general connections between poetry and contemporary political thought. The dominant analogical method of comparing past with present enabled poets to ignore or blend radically different historical theories—fate, providence, patrilinear inheritance, dynastic succession, cyclic repetition, linear progression—since the analogy between past and present provided a common ground for all of them.[24] Arguments from pagan notions of fate and Christian providence happily cohabit in historical poems of the time. Yet the analogy also restricted poets from being able to imagine the future as anything other than a replication of the past, and hence from representing complex historical relations as anything other than a chronological list or series of completed, discrete, and finite events. In consequence, the belief that there is nothing new under the sun becomes, as it were, a self-fulfilling prophecy.[25]

The past was of special importance in seventeenth-century political life for several reasons. Constitutional disputes concerning power and authority most often appeared in terms of appeals to ancient rights and privileges; the older the claim, the better. Many who rebelled against the claims to absolutism of the early Stuarts—even if they did not wish to wrest power from or execute the king—did so from a sense that their own traditional rights were being violated. Consequently, it was crucial to demonstrate that those rights were, indeed, historical. Common law, moreover, institutionalized a belief that past judgments were true for all time. This historical basis underlying political and legal disputes was facilitated, in part, by a growth of systematic and secular historiography, and by an increasingly skeptical tendency toward distinguishing fact from fable. But, in theory at least, the controls placed upon the historian did not fully apply to the historical poet who was free to invent as necessary. Nevertheless, many poets did, as we have seen, increasingly purport to provide factual accounts, often of contemporary events, thereby signaling the importance of adopting an objective stance. During the seventeenth century contemporary history became, in practice, a suitable subject for serious poetic treatment. When poets referred to the past— however recent or remote—they increasingly constructed an idealized version that exemplified the proper workings of whichever political system suited their purpose. The past lent credibility to partisan versions of the present, frequently evoking the pastoral sense that things were better once upon a time.

The arcadian myth of the golden age proved especially suitable for poets who wished to use familiar and traditional ideas to locate all peace, plenty, security, liberty, and justice in "that age of old," as Jonson called it, "which boasts to have had the head of gold."[26] In this view the past always appears better than the present and is most often linked with idealized attitudes toward rural life. Midway through the century Herrick writes "Upon the Troublesome Times":

> O! TIMES most bad.
> Without the Scope
> Of hope
> Of better to be had!
> Where shall I goe,
> Or wither run
> To shun
> This publique overthrow?[27]

Randolph, as we saw, would have directed his fellow poet to the "old simplicity" of the countryside. Indeed, pastoral writers adopted the view of Fulke Greville that "the *Golden-Age* was when the world was yong,"[28] and that its ideals and benefits could still be found in rural retirement. But the longing for the past was by no means restricted to poems on country matters or to poets writing in defense of the status quo.

There are three main ways in which poets represent the past for current political purposes: historical allusions, exemplary history, and what I shall call the appeal to the past. Each elaborates upon the basic model of the analogy between past and present and in doing so reaffirms the spatialization of time. Historical allusions are subordinate elements of a poem, designed to illuminate some particular aspect of a current situation by specific comparison and contrast with a comparable person or event from the past. Exemplary history provides a narrative account of the past so constructed as to encourage us to accept an attitude toward a comparable situation in the present as though it were impartially right and necessary. Exemplary history is thus diachronic, offering a comparison between a discrete pattern or sequence of events that occurred in the past and one occurring in the present. Historical allusions, on the other hand, are synchronic, designed to clarify and validate an analysis of a present situation. In a more general way, exemplary history tacitly assumes the reader's prior understanding of and interest in the current situation and then, by comparing it with past events, offers either a new perspective or one that confirms existing presuppositions. Allusions are more directly concerned with conveying information about the present that may or may not have been known to the reader but, either way, advances a particular interpretation as historically accurate. The appeal to the past is a more openly evaluative procedure than either of these: the poet makes a summary contrast between past and present governed by a set of judgments or preconceptions that it is assumed the reader already shares. The contrast itself invariably works through some form of emotional appeal, some nostalgia for, or pride in, former ways of life and national triumphs.

Belief in the analogous relation of past and present pervades the century and constitutes the model of historical analysis by means of which poets understood and represented historical events. "The importance of implied analogy of all kinds," as Patterson observes, "but especially between 'this time' and episodes from past history, cannot be overestimated" (p. 47).[29] Its political and literary importance at the opening of the century is well illustrated by the familiar case of Sir John Hayward, imprisoned from 1599 to 1601 for writing a history book. *The First Part of the Life and Raign of King Henry the IIII* was published in 1599. Before the year was out Hayward had been tried and convicted in Star Chamber by the renowned spokesman for common law, Sir Edward Coke. The attorney general's case against the historian rested upon his ability to prove that in Hayward's treatment the notorious Richard II bore a close and apparent resemblance to Queen Elizabeth. We might say, then, that Hayward spent three years in prison because of the prevailing belief in the analogy between past and present.[30]

Besides influencing legal practice and, surely as a direct consequence, the practice of poets eager to keep out of trouble, the analogy constituted a major crux in the historical thought of the Renaissance and early seventeenth century, especially in the development of a secular and specifically political view of history writing.[31] "Hystories," writes Sir Thomas Blundeville as early as 1574,

> bee made of deedes done by a publique weale, or agaynst a publique weale, and such deedes, be eyther deeds of warre, of peace, or else of sedition and conspiracie. Agayne, every deede, be it private, or publique must needs be done, by some person, for some occasion, in sometyme, and place, with meanes & order, and with instruments.[32]

With the emergence of secular explanations, all historical events become politicized. Once the past is thus understood, not entirely as the pageant of divine judgments and retributions, but as the deeds of men acting within a political state that they themselves have helped to create, it becomes a storehouse of practical wisdom for politicians. Blundeville, here echoing recent developments in European historical theory, continues with a common religious and social goal turned to a political end: peace. The new secular emphasis is clear:

> The way to come to that peace whereof I speake, is partly taught by Philosophers in generall precepts and rules, but the Historiographers doe teache it much more playnlye by perticular examples and experiences. (Sig. D3ᵛ)

In order to function, the analogy between past and present requires the belief that like causes produce like effects. From our knowledge of the past "we may learne," continues Blundeville, "how one selfe effect springeth of one selfe cause, and how the contrarie proceedeth of his contrary" (sig. E4). If the past consists of deeds performed by human agents of determinable motive, goes the argument, then surely those deeds can be repeated at any other time under comparable circumstances. The past can repeat itself because, in the biblical epigram with which King James prefaced the *Basilicon Doron, "Nihil novum sub sole."*

Historical Allusions

Seventeenth-century poets constantly *allude* to the past when representing current events. In its simplest form the historical allusion directly compares some well-known figure or event from the past with some comparable figure or event of recent interest, a comparison so constructed that certain attitudes are transferred from the former to the latter. Poets invariably select those aspects of the past which contribute to their design and seldom leave the point of their comparison vague or ambiguous. Specificity and clarity are essential requirements of historical allusions.

This procedure of drawing historical analogies was by no means new with the English poets of the seventeenth century. Looking back to a long European tradition of representing the past as a series of exemplary figures and actions worthy of emulation or careful avoidance, they often rely on past analogues that have traditionally established associations requiring little or no further explanation. Classical figures often alluded to in this way were Nero for tyranny and Alexander for successful imperial conquest. Allusions to mythological and biblical characters and events operate in much the same way: Absalom for rebellion, Abraham for faith, Eve for female treachery, Phaeton for ambition, the Scylla for envy, Diana for chastity, and the Medusa for cruelty.[33] But we would mistake the full range and political importance of the poet's artistry in deploying historical allusions were we to imagine that the past—human, mythical, or biblical—was in any way a set of fixed and unchanging points of reference, a typology of immutable symbolic meanings. Even when alluding to familiar past figures, poets were normally very careful to remind their readers precisely what the figure in their poem signifies. And we will notice that poets frequently vary traditional past analogues in order to suit particular current needs.

Of special interest is the way that preconquest national history conveyed preformulated political associations which poets brought to bear upon the politics of the present. During the middle decades of the century, political disputes were often argued by reference to the conflicts between ancient Britons and Saxons. The history of the Britons, linking Trojan with national history and emphasizing the legitimacy of dynastic succession, was often adopted by supporters of the Stuart dynasty, while Saxon history, stressing constitutional agreement between the head of state and a representative assembly, appealed to critics of Stuart absolutism. Supporters of the Stuart dynasty claimed that the royal line was descended from ancient Britons who had come to the island with Brutus from Troy. On the other hand, Parliament's claims to representative authority independent of the crown were commonly based upon Saxon precedents.[34] Writing to support James in 1608, for example, Morgan Coleman declares that

> The *Britains* ancient Lords of Britaine were,
> These (as the rest of Europ) long did beare
> The *Romane* yoke: yet often did repine;
> Untill the raigne of greatest Constantine:

He being British by the mothers side,
Made that the sea no longer did divide
This Iland from the maine, as joined by love.[35]

From legendary British origins, Coleman's genealogy traces the various fortunes of "this noble land" until the seventeenth century when

All rights conjoined in STEWARTS foure-fold crowne:
Whose mystical high name the heavens decree
Shall of their gifts sole dispenser bee.

Rejection of British legend, on the other hand, could signify an attack upon the house of Stuart. When Milton abandoned his proposed Arthuriad he also dismissed this legendary king from his *History of Britain* (1650).[36]

Richard Rowlands, or "Verstegan," an Anglo-Dutchman, was one of the major proponents of Saxon history as the key to understanding the nation's past. In his modestly titled *A Restitution of Decayed Intelligence* of 1628, he shows "how the antient noble Saxons the true Ancestors of Englishmen, were originally a people of *Germanie*."[37] One of the dedicatory poems to this work explains how Verstegan's researches bear directly upon national law and current political institutions:

Behold here *England:* learne thy name, thy race, thy offspring:
Perisht, or forgotten, by time and ignorance,
VERSTEGAN will tell thee, what by discontinuance,
Thou hast left or lost, in writing, speaking, doing.
    Here shalt thou find thy ancient Nobilite,
Thy eldest offspring, honour and worthinesses,
Thy lawes, thy manners, thy armes, thy manlinesse,
Searcht out of registers of most antiquitie.

(Sig.***ᵛ)

And indeed, ancient Saxon laws were evoked in justification of the revolt against the king. James Harrington's Oceana, for instance, was founded upon Saxon principles.[38] As Roberta Brinkley comments, "Upon the ancient laws of the nation depended the right of the people to revolt and depose a king" (p. 74).

Saxon laws, such as those contained in William Lambarde's collection *Archaionomia* (1568), which was reissued in 1644, were often cited

to justify opposing the king.[39] In *The First Defence* (1651), Milton cites
Saxon legal precedents for limiting royal power in a manner which assumes these laws to be both well known and generally accessible:

> Come we now to the Saxons; since their laws are extant I shall quote none
> of their deeds. Remember that the Saxons were sprung from Germans,
> who never gave their kings absolute or unlimited power, and who used to
> hold a council of the whole tribe upon the more weighty affairs of govern-
> ment ... the early Saxons, when they had subdued Britain and set up
> kings, required an oath of them to submit to the judgement of the law as
> much as any of their subjects. (7:437–39)

By alluding to preconquest British history, then, writers of either persuasion could rely upon certain ready-made political associations to carry
over from current political debate into the ways their texts could be read.
It was not by chance that the catholic monarchist Edmund Bolton should
so loudly regret the victory of the Saxons over the ancient Britons in
London:[40]

> This mov'd King *Arthur* to advance in sheild,
> The Virgins semblant, who from every field,
> Returning victor vanquished in fight,
> The *Saxons* powr's (in vain, through fates despight,
> The *Britans* bravery withering in his death)
> And crown'd her forhead with a twelvfold wreath.
>
> (P. 8)

Poets also used other kinds of historical allusions. In addition to
adopting the political associations currently being applied to conflicts
that had taken place in the nation's remote past, poets often alluded to
notable persons and events from more recent times to illustrate topics of
current interest. In countless references to certain English kings—and
some of their more eminent advisers and adversaries—poets helped to
construct and consolidate the variable reputations of such figures as a
means of directing their readers' understanding of their own times.
Richard I and Henry V invariably appear as figures of successful overseas
conquest,[41] while Edward II and Richard III commonly suggest various
forms of political tyranny and mismanagement.[42] Roger Mortimer, notorious among supporters of royal government for his part in the assassination of Edward II, often appears as a representative of outrageous

ambition in poems throughout the century,[43] as does Simon de Montfort.[44]

Although kings and nobles were the historical figures most often alluded to, some figures of lesser status rise from their graves to haunt the imaginations of poets writing on contemporary events. Stuart poets were specially tormented by the specters of those who had led popular uprisings. But even the antimonarchist Alexander Ross who espoused what were, for the time, democratic principles expressed fear at the anarchy of popular rebellion. In *Englands Threnodie* (1648) he imagines the nation recalling its past:

> All insurrections of rebellious men
> The wisdom of my Governors brought down:
> When Anarchy was likely now and then
> To get possessions, and abase the Crown:
>   *Jack Cade, John Wall, Wat Tyler,* and *Jack Straw*
>   With *Wyat* knew what 'tis to'pose my Law.
>
> (P. 2)

The uprisings led by Tyler and Straw produced frequent anxiety in political writers of the century,[45] but it should not be surprising to find poets dwelling upon past rebellions in an age of continual social, political, and religious unrest. And it is suggestive of the increasing emphasis which poets placed upon contemporary history that, while there had been few poems written to celebrate the English victory over the Spanish forces in 1588, the Gunpowder Plot of 1605 was constantly referred to in poems throughout the century. It was even used as an academic topic as we know from Milton's *In Quintum Novembris.*[46]

An implied simile underlies the construction and use of historical allusions such as these: these aspects of a present ruler's reign are like those of a past ruler's reign. A direct variation of the analogy between past and present, this formula owes much, in its precise attributions of particular reputations, to the stock judgments of the "mirror for magistrates" tradition, which operate on just such parallels. These traditional reputations were so tenacious that a particular king could be compared with widely different present rulers to carry the same signification. We are, for example, required to think of Edward III's victories over the French when thinking of both Charles I and Oliver Cromwell.[47] But we should not too rashly assume that reputations did not require constant reaffirmation. Poets invariably recognized the need for direct exposition when alluding to the past. In his *Historie of That wise and Fortunate Prince, Henrie of that Name the Seventh, King of England* (1638), Charles Aleyn suggests that a historical poem should have the same clarity of detail found in a painting by Van Dyck. Anything not fully known should be relegated to the shadows:

> A constant cleernesse is above the law
> Of *Mortall,* nor within that *Region* stands.
> As those *elaborate peeces,* which doe draw
> Breath from exact *Van-Dyks* unerring hands
>   Are deeply *shadow'd,* and a *duskie Sable*
>   Doth *Clow'd* the borders of the *Curious Table.*
>
> (Sig. L3ᵛ)

In practice poets normally highlight those colors of a past analogue most relevant to their present design.

The poetic portrait of King John provides an especially interesting case of this artistic control since it undergoes, for evidently political reasons, considerable shifts in lighting and coloration during the century. While poets generally agreed about the facts of John's reign, they did not fully agree about how to interpret or represent them, in what colors to paint them, or on which of them to cast light. The rabid anti-catholic king portrayed in John Bale's pseudo–morality play *Kynge Johan* (1548) receives mixed favor and criticism in Shakespeare's play (circa 1595) and in Richard Niccols' compendious *Mirour for Magistrates* of 1610. In *Albions England* (1602), William Warner, like Foxe, goes so far as to treat John as a royal martyr. Drayton returns to the more severe portrayal in *Polyolbion* (1613).[48] For the most part these disagreements can be ascribed to differing moral emphases: poets stress those human and personal qualities of a king most suitable for instructing us in kingly virtues and vices. Daniel, who omitted John from the early versions of *The Civil Wars,* introduces him with the revisions of 1609 in order to attack certain vices that make a bad and unnatural king:

> contrary to course,
> False *John* usurpes his *Nephew Arthurs* right;
> Gets to the Crowne by craft, by wrong, by force;
> Rules it with lust, oppression, rigour, might;
> Murders the lawfull heire without remorse:

> Wherefore procuring all the world's despight,
> A tyrant loath'd, a homicide convented,
> Poysoned he dies, distrac't and unlamented.[49]

But Daniel's further purpose here stresses the need for a stable line of dynastic succession. While attributing John's usurpation of power to his own moral decay rather than contemporary political necessity or any inherent problems with monarchy in general, he nevertheless warns readers of the specific dangers of disputed succession.

John's portrait in historical allusions alters significantly with the civil wars of mid-century. He assumes a new importance to many poets as the king who signed Magna Charta, thereby assuring the English people of their rights and privileges. Stuart poets of the 1640s stress the political office of kingship rather than the morals of the incumbent by showing how the current wars are misdirected rebellions against the throne, which already assured popular liberty during John's reign. Denham invokes Magna Charta in order to stress the inviolability of royal office—provided, of course, that the king does not assume the power of a tyrant. At Runnymede, Denham writes:

> was that Charter seal'd wherein the Crown
> All marks of Arbitrary power lays down:
> Tyrant and slave, those names of hate and fear,
> The happier stile of King and Subject bear:
> Happy, when both to the same Center move,
> When Kings give liberty, and Subjects love.[50]

In *The Civil War* Cowley paints a more lurid scene in expressing anger at the treachery of those who wrested power away from its proper and natural place, the king. He portrays a vision of hell:

> There thowsand stubborne Barons fettered ly,
> And curse their old vaine noyse of Liberty.
> They who their angry Soveraigne to oppose,
> The hatefull yoake of France and Lewis chose.
> A vaine pretence from Johns bad acts they bring;
> John was a fond wild man, but yet their King.

> (2.457–62)

Writing during the early months of the war, Cowley, like all good Stuart propagandists, is anxious to demonstrate that rebellion against the king is inherently evil and will be punished eternally.

John's changing reputation in historical allusions suggests that in referring to figures such as kings, poets felt free to vary stock reputations according to the specific requirements of their design. Shifting their focus from John's usurpation to the correct limits of power, poets were all the more careful to make their points clearly and unmistakably, seldom relying too much on the reader's prior knowledge. Reputations were, to some extent, traditional and circumscribed by historical facts, but they were by no means fixed or assumed to be common knowledge.

So far we have considered only the simplest kind of historical allusions, those which compare a single past term with a single current analogue. Often, however, poets gather together a collection of past kinds, usually by common reputation, to suggest a dynastic pattern underlying the nation's destiny. Such chronological series of kings lead, relentlessly and inevitably, to a certain present situation. Clearly this procedure was especially useful for legitimating the current regime as historically inevitable: Bolton, we saw, uses it in *London,* both Denham and Cowley use it to legitimate Charles I, while Waller and the writer of *Anglia Rediviva* (1658) use it to legitimate Cromwell. In *Cooper's Hill* (lines 65–68) Denham brings together past national leaders as disparate in their historicity as Brutus, his son Albanact, Julius Caesar, Canute, and Edward III and his son the Black Prince, all by virtue of a common military heroism that outdoes that of the pagan gods. Last in this line, and indeed the seemingly inevitable product of the sequence, is none other than Charles I, for whom Denham creates a suppositious genealogy. Cowley also uses the procedure in *The Civil War* to vindicate the Stuart war effort.[51]

A most intriguing use of the kingly series occurs in *Anglia Rediviva,* in which the poet constructs two quite different series in order to justify Cromwell's rule. One series defends monarchy, by showing how single heads of state bring the nation imperial success, and is directed against recent attempts at constitutional reform. The other illustrates those potential dangers in monarchic government that will certainly *not* trouble a nation with a virtuous king—like Oliver—on the throne. The first advocates "the lawfull use of Kings" against that kind of oligarchy currently in force under the purged Long Parliament:

> For *Parlaments* which some cry up again,
> Rare helps of Government, whilst Kings did reign
> As formerly with Members all compleat,
> But not as now, all maim'd and mutilat.
>
> (P. 6)

This poet suggests that we recall the nation's glorious conquests when kings alone ruled supreme in the land. He alludes to three former kings, all of whom extended England's foreign empire:

> *Edgar* as far extending our command
> By Sea, as our third *Edward* did by Land,
> Or our fifth *Henry,* glories of their name
> And ours, and *Englands* everlasting Fame.
>
> (P. 7)

The second series of kings in *Anglia Rediviva* illustrates some of Cromwell's many personal virtues by opposing them to vices found in former kings. The poet uses the outdoing topos. Although demonstrably open to abuse, the monarchic form of government is better than others, especially when the king displays as many virtues as Cromwell. Marginal notes make sure we recognise the unnamed former kings alluded to here—Henry VIII, Richard II, and Edward III—while prose notes remind us of the various abuses of royal power which these kings supposedly exemplify (pp. 22–23).

Serial allusions to past persons and events could carry a variety of possible political implications that could be suited to the poet's requirements. But in its structural dependence upon the analogy between past and present, the device remains committed to an inherently conservative political stance, as in *Anglia Rediviva,* where the potentially revolutionary character of Cromwell's heroic leadership cannot transcend the traditional benefits of a righteous monarchy. Precisely because of its dependence upon analogy, the historical allusion, even in its serial form, fails the interregnum poet seeking to legitimate radical social or political change. For analogy binds the present instance to the law of a preformulated past, a past already shaped and molded according to the prescriptive orthodoxy of monarchist historians, a past selectively constructed from that raw experience which Puttenham called "no more than a masse of memories assembled" to serve the interests of those for whom it was written. Radical change was, quite literally, unthinkable in the terms provided by allusions to the past since it would necessitate the displacement of the analogical frame which made historical knowledge possible. So long as the only imaginable forms of government and political leadership depended upon the stories of heroic individuals who had already been written into history as the prefigured manifestations of "man" in an anthropocentric universe, then the legitimacy of any political system was invariably tied to the personal qualities of its leader. For poets, historical knowledge consisted of re-presenting past figures who fit a story that would prove illuminating to the present by reason of its demonstration of exceptional moral strength; and to the extent that it performed this function, then this form of knowledge was protected from verification by appearing in suitably elevated verse. The isolated and synchronic allusion could lend a moment's credibility to an otherwise fictitious interpretation of contemporary events, but the most even the serial allusion could do was suggest that what the poet wanted the reader to believe about the present was the most likely truth since the past seemed to lead to the present.

One problem with heroes that humanist ideology and its attendant figures of representation—such as the allusion—could never solve was the inevitability of mortality: heroes die. When they happen to be leaders of the state, this problem presses directly upon material considerations with some force and urgency. The crisis over Elizabeth's death lent a certain short-term legitimacy to James's accession since it could be claimed that he achieved a peaceful union of the two kingdoms. Confronted with Cromwell, there were those, like the author of *Anglia Rediviva,* who could entertain the idea of Cromwell as a national leader only by considering him as a "king." Dressing him up in all the topoi of Stuart panegyric might seem an unsuitable way of making nondynastic leadership legitimate. But he did make a fine imperial hero—like Edgar, Edward III, and Henry V—whose ascendancy could be marked by his difference from those kings who abused their hereditary power. What the form of the allusion could not achieve was a representation of political power that was not androcentric. The analogical frame of the dominant ideology—which we now name "humanism"—not only privileged the center and the limit with the names of "man" and "God," but also supported a complex epistemology that Baconian thought was only beginning to challenge. If the poetic use of the allusion became lodged here, incapable of imagining Cromwell as anything but a monarch, incapable of imagining any political state other than one ruled by a heroic leader, the epistemological bases upon which the allusion rested were by no means incapable of being elaborated, restated, and reinvested with explanatory force in forms other than the synchronic allusion.[52]

EXEMPLARY HISTORY

The analogy between past and present also underlies exemplary history, a procedure by means of which the poet shapes a diachronic report of past events to fit a narrative model of how certain constant forces are at work in the present. The selection of appropriate events and forces—fate, providence, destiny, whatever—invariably depends upon present needs.[53] The poet so represents the past as to illustrate political precepts. As the case of Hayward's *Henry the IIII* suggests, this was commonly thought to be the true and inevitable purpose of writing history—the problem with Hayward's work being that it was considered treasonable.

The analogy provided the basis for drawing comparisons between not only events but also their causes. In the preface to his *The First Part of the Historie of England* (1612), Daniel provides "a perfectly clear statement of the dominant seventeenth-century attitude towards historical change":[54]

> We shall find still the same correspondencies to hold in the actions of men: Virtues and Vices the same, though rising and falling, according to the worth, or weaknesse of Governors: the causes of the ruines, and mutations of state to be alike: and the trayne of affaires carried by precedent, in a course of Succession under the like colours. (Sig. B2)

Principles such as these had earlier governed his historical epic *The Civil Wars,* an exemplary history which Daniel wrote during the final years of Elizabeth's reign. He abandoned it in 1609 to write his prose *Historie.* When he first began the poem, England faced a major political crisis: Who would succeed the Virgin Queen? So long as this question remained unanswered, there persisted the anxiety that the country might face civil disruption. Daniel's account of English history addresses the problem in a suitably indirect way. Except to praise Elizabeth for having brought peace to a once divided nation (5.9–10), he does not refer to contemporary events at all.[55] But his account of the Wars of the Roses specifically assigns the evils of civil war to disputed succession. His version of the past represents political issues of current interest, and in the manner of a typical Renaissance humanist he draws precepts of general use—false claims to the throne lead to bloodshed, while peace, even under an unjust ruler, is preferable to civil war in the name of justice.

After the fact Daniel acknowledges his political intentions in writing this poem:

> this Argument was long since undertaken (in a time which was not so well secur'd of the future, as God be blessed now it is) with a purpose, to shewe the deformities of Civile Dissension, and the miserable events of Rebellions, Conspiracies, and bloudy Revengements, which followed (as in a circle) upon that breach of the due course of Successsion, by the Usurpation of *Hen. 4;* and thereby to make the blessings of Peace, and the happinesse of an established Government (in a direct Line) the better to appeare.[56]

In the opening of the poem itself, he links his instrumental purpose with the epistemological rationale of the analogy: knowledge of the past helps us to think about our own times. He invokes the muse of History to come to his aid:

> And to the ende wee may with better ease
> Discerne the true discourse; vouchsafe to showe,
> What were the times foregoing, neere to these,
> That these we may with better profit knowe:
> Tell, how the world fell into this disease,
> And how so great distemperature did growe.
> So shall we see, by what degrees it came,
> "How things, at full do soone wax out of frame."
>
> (1.7)

In accordance with this opening statement of his intent, Daniel shapes the past so that he can, by means of the immutable causes of past events, legitimate a monarchist status quo with its clear lines of succession.

Within the general epic framework he represents civil rebellion from the time of Richard II to Elizabeth as a degeneration—a "disease" into which "the world fell"—from a former time of glory. He immediately indicates the epic frame of his poem and declares the historical perspective from which he writes. "I Sing," he begins, "the civill Warres, tumultuous Broyles, / And Bloody factions of a mightie Land" (1.1). But he also admits that he represents civil struggle in order to praise the current monarch. After reminding us of the horrors and waste of civil war, he asks:

> Yet now what reason have we to complaine?
> Since hereby came the calme we did injoy;
> The blisse of thee *Eliza*.
>
> (1.3)

The glories of the present time have been brought about by divine providence which "no other way . . . could finde, but to unite againe / The fatall sev'red Families" (1.3). The interests of national unity under a monarch precede those of personal dispute.

In Daniel's historical epic, the past provides a measure for the present. Before the period of civil war that will constitute the poet's theme, there was an even more distant time when the nation was fully united as it now is "againe" under Elizabeth. Daniel devotes a dozen stanzas (1.8–20) to a summary history of this period, which he represents as an age of growing English might and glory under a series of kings between the Conquest and Richard II. He invariably stresses the contribution which these early kings made to national unity and overseas empires while pointing out the persistent dangers of a disputed succession. Of Henry II, for example, he writes:

> When *Henrie,* sonne to *Maude* the Empresse, raignes,
> And *England* into forme and greatnes brought,
> Addes *Ireland* to this Scepter, and obtaines
> Large Provinces in *Fraunce;* much treasure gote,
> And from exactions here at home abstaynes:
> And had not his rebellious children fought
> T'imbroyle his age with tumults, he had beene
> The happiest Monarch that this State had seene.
>
> (1.13)

The true hero of Daniel's epic is evidently "this State" itself, united under the successful imperialism of powerful kings. This heroic subject is the political nation of conflicting social, economic, and political interests. In the interests of a national unity that makes overseas conquest not only possible but both necessary and probable, Daniel returns to his central argument—civil war must be avoided at all costs—repeatedly throughout *The Civil Wars* by drawing precepts from the events he describes. He varies his historical stance to suit both historical circumstances and his interpretation of past and present. While the rabble, for example, openly lament Richard II's expulsion of Bolingbroke, the wiser sort think differently because they have been educated to understand the lesson of history:

> When-as the graver sort that saw the course,
> And knew that Princes may not be controld,
> Lik't well to suffer this, for feare of worse:
>   . . .
> "They saw likewise, that Princes oft are faine
> "To buy their quiet, with the price of wrong:
> And better 'twere that now a few complaine,
> Then all should mourne, aswell the weake as strong:
> Seeing still how little Realmes by chaunge do gaine;
> And therefore learned by observing long.
> "T'admire times past, follow the present will,
> "Wish for good Princes, but t'indure the ill.
>
> (1.71, 72)

The wise patriot has, in all times, "preferred farre / Th'unjustest peace, before the justest warre" (1.73). Rebellion against a de facto monarch—even when it is carried on by a virtuous nobleman—can only lead to unjustifiable killing (see 2.116–17). Accordingly, the poem openly condemns men like Richard, Duke of York, for claiming the crown to which he has a right since such an action can only lead to civil bloodshed. "How much better for him," writes Daniel,

> had it beene,
> T'indure a wrong with peace, then with such toyle
> "T'obtaine a bloody Right? since Right is sinne,
> "That is ill sought, and purchased with spoyle.
> But, this so wretched state are Kingdomes in,
> Where one mans Cause, shall all the rest imbroyle.
>
> (5.47)

Moreover, the victory of a successful rebel leader must necessarily be limited since he can never rule supremely over those who helped him to gain power:

> So wretched is this execrable Warre,
> "This civile Sworde: wherein, though all wee see
> "Be foul, and all things miserable are;
> "Yet most distresse-full is the victorie:
> "Which is, not onely th'extream ruiner
> "Of others; but, her owne calamity:
> "Where, who obtains, what he would cannot do?
> "Their powre hath part, who holpe him thereunto.

(7.99)

Within the epic framework of the poem, Daniel celebrates the benefits of hereditary monarchy by shaping past events to illustrate seemingly universal precepts and hence historical truths that are of special significance for his own times. This exemplary account of the past does not require him to mention current events directly, but rather offers general observations that readers are urged to recognize as applicable to their own times.

In certain respects, an exemplary history like *The Civil Wars* can be distinguished from a parallel history like Dryden's *Absalom and Achitophel* in which the narrative pattern of past events invites systematic application to a contemporary situation in order to advocate a specific analysis and course of action. In a parallel history, the analogy between past and present makes the two courses of events seem interchangeable, and the future thus seem determinable. The known biblical story of Dryden's poem bears directly upon contemporary events in this way, since it embodies political doctrine throughout a narrative structure that advises Charles to recall David when considering his own son and chief minister—assuming he wishes to avoid civil discord. What happened once is happening again for the same reasons, and requires similar political wisdom to achieve the desired end, a determinable future.

THE APPEAL TO THE PAST

A final way in which poets represent the past for political purposes might be called the appeal to the past, though by this term I wish to suggest something different from golden age nostalgia. What I have in mind is a common structural procedure that governs the overall design of a poem and employs nostalgia, and other feelings, for political purposes. Poets carefully represent the past in order to make an emotive appeal to former conditions, an appeal that can then bear directly upon the present. Unlike the allusion, the appeal commonly controls the poem's overall design, while differing from an exemplary history by representing the past less for its narrative analogues than for its affective possibilities. As an artistic procedure, the appeal to the past operates by inviting us to feel a certain way about the past that will cause us to judge the present. An ensuing nostalgia for the past and consequent discontent with the present commonly provide poets with an emotive means of making a judgment about the present *felt* to be true, even when it clearly isn't, thereby encouraging readers to accept highly charged interpretations as historical facts.

The general sense that current conditions represent a degeneration from the past was common throughout the century and has, of course, endured to our own times. Marvell opens one of his earlier poems, dedicated to Lovelace, with a richly explicit version of this notion which locates it at the intersection of precise socioliterary coordinates:

> Our times are much degenerate from those
> Which your sweet Muse which your fair Fortune chose,
> And as complexions alter with the Climes,
> Our wits have drawne th'infection of our times.
> That candid Age no other way could tell
> To be ingenious, but by speaking well.
> Who best could prayse, had then the greatest prayse,
> Twas more esteemed to give, then weare the Bayes:
> Modest ambition studi'd only then,
> To honour not her selfe, but worthy men.
> These vertues now are banisht out of Towne,
> Our Civill Wars have lost the Civicke crowne.
> He highest builds, who with most Art destroys,
> And against others Fame his owne employs.
> I see the envious Caterpillar sit
> On the faire blossome of each growing wit.
>
> (1:2–3)

The poet's art directs cultural change, affectively working upon the structure of feeling of the age in which it is produced. In Lovelace's "candid Age," poets could only be true to the dictates of their calling, so they only praised the virtues of the worthy. More recently, poets have commonly misused their art by attacking the work of other poets rather than celebrating virtue, and thus they have brought about civil discord.

But nostalgia—however complexly described—was not the only emotion suited to appeals to the past. Indeed, the thirties—that "candid Age" against which Marvell measures and deplores the late forties—was highly praised by some of the poets writing then. In James Shirley's masque *The Triumph of Peace* (1633), for example, the Hours sing:

> They that were never happy Hours
> Till now, return to thank the powers
>> That made them so.
>> The Island doth rejoice,
> And all her waves are echo to our voice,
> Which, in no ages past, hath known
>> Such treasures of her own.[57]

Stuart poets of the time also frequently celebrated, by negative comparison with the past, the glorious reign of Charles and Henrietta Maria as the most blessed of all ages. Throughout the so-called halcyon days of peace and prosperity, Charles's reign figured as the harbinger of an age more glorious than any other in known times. So writes the youthful Cowley in 1637, praising Charles for keeping the nation out of war:

> In what Playne or what River hath not beene
> Warres story, writ in blood (sad story) seene?
>> This truth too well our *England* knowes,
>> 'Twas civill slaughter dy'd her *Rose:*
>>> Nay then her *Lillie* too,
>>> With bloods losse paler grew.
>
> Such griefes, nay worse than these, we now should feele,
> Did not just *Charles* silence the rage of steele;
>> He to our Land blest peace doth bring,
>> All Neighbour Countries envying.
>>> Happy who did remaine
>>> Unborne till *Charles* his reigne!

(2:64)

Yet at the same time, other poets did disagree with the Stuart version of the decade. Some blamed the age for the decay of their art. In his first published work (1634), John Saltmarsh, the antinomian preacher who would become chaplain to the New Model Army, expressed dislike for the softness of contemporary poetry, and he confidently proclaimed the affective power of martial poetry when recommending Russell's *Battels of Lypsich and Lutzen:*

> these *Rhymers* of our silken Age
> Unlade their Fancies on an emptie page.
> *Mars* is thy theme; thy *Muse* hath learn'd to talk
> The *Cannon-language* of the Warre, and walk
> A loftie March; while thy faint readers dread
> And tremble at each syllable they reade.
> Leade on, Stout Poet, in thy Martiall state.[58]

Once the thirties were over and civil war disturbed the silken age of peace, however, the decade itself became a former age suitable for nostalgic comparison with the present—as in Marvell's lines. Along with others, Cowley wonders in *The Civil War*, "How could a *warre* so sad and barbarous please / But first by sland'ring those blest Dayes of *Peace?*" (1.109–10). Structurally, the appeal to the past could work either way, depending on the poet's stance toward contemporary events. As we have already seen, Stuart poets took considerable pains during the thirties to ignore or to dispel the discomfiting possibility that the nation might not be so blessed as they had hoped. From the perspective of a hundred years later, Swift would write:

> I have found . . . a great Number of Pamphlets printed from the Year 1630 to 1640, full of as bold and impious railing Expressions against the lawful Power of the Crown, and the Order of Bishops, as ever were uttered during the Rebellion, or the whole subsequent Tyranny of that Fanatick Anarchy.[59]

Yet court poets of the time continued lavishly to praise the Caroline court, the splendor and opulence of which they insisted were surely a sign of special grace and favor to Charles, his queen, and reign.

With the advent of war in the early forties, Stuart poets acknowledged how the times had taken a turn for the worse; but the previous decade remained a touchstone. As C. V. Wedgewood writes, before supplying several examples of poems that support her comment,

> The 1630s, that blessed time of peace, seen through the smoke and smother of the ensuing years of Civil War, acquired a magical beauty even for those

who had not at the time been in close sympathy with the royal government.[60]

Perhaps: but to accept this view we must ignore the many poets who expressed opposing views in their retrospections upon the thirties. As Swift noticed, the poetic challenge to the Stuart myth of the glorious thirties was under way before the outbreak of war in 1642. We have seen how, in 1641, John Vicars revived the memory of November 5 in order to redefine recent events as an era of catholic insurgency directed against traditional political institutions. John Taylor and John Cragge were also among the poets who, during the final weeks of 1641, set about revising the Stuart version of the thirties by taking a longer view of recent events, typically by having recourse to prophetic urgency based upon appeals to Old Testament stories or protestant myths of a chivalric and reformist Elizabethan age. In *Englands Comfort, and Londons Joy: Expressed in the Royall, Triumphant, and Magnificent Entertainment of our Dread Soveraigne Lord, King Charles, at his blessed and safe returne from Scotland on Thursday the 25. of Novemb. 1641,* Taylor compares the relations of Scotland and England with those of Judah and Israel in order to suggest how the recent past was a similar period of betrayal. What makes the analysis of the present so compelling is our assumed belief in biblical analogy, not the evidence:

> WHen *Israel* with *Judah* did contest,
> Which of them ought to love King *David* best;
> *Judah* claim'd Kindred of the King, and said
> That he (by Right) should still with them have staid:
> But *Isr'el* boldly to them straite reply'd,
> That *David* (onely) was with them t'abide:
>   . . .
> I wish Great *Britaine* the like Song to sing
> In love, who best shall love and serve the King:
> Let *Sheba's* head be lost, and let us be,
> *England,* and *Scotland,* both in Unity.

(P. 7)

Where Taylor employs the parallel in order to advocate policy—ridding the land of those Shebas who would bring dissension—John Cragge speaks more boldly in the voice of prophetic inspiration, calling upon

the young earl of Essex to fulfill the aggressive foreign policy of his
martyred father.

> God hath ordain'd you for some other end:
> Then in great Britaine all your dayes to spend.
> Your fathers fame, and good report I heare,
> It made all Irish rebels stand in feare.
>   . . .
> He made a vow, which made proud *Rome* to storme,
> You are his Son, you must his vow performe.
>
>   (Sigs. A2, A2ᵛ)

The appeal here to the belief that the past can answer an immediately
pressing crisis deflects any desire for analysis of facts about that crisis.

    The voice of prophetic conviction characterizes oppositional poetry
of the time. In the second part of *A Prophecy Concerning the Earle of Essex
that now is* of December 1641, Cragge turns to the larger audience of the
nation as a whole in vatic impatience with the tropes of court ideology.
But he also provides a specific version of the present:

> Although our foes doe daily still increase,
> Our god's a god of war as well as peace,
>   . . .
> God loves dispatch, he can brooke no delay,
> Let us make haste, to *Ireland* take our way:
> Let all our votes in Parliament agree,
> With quicke dispatch, with heart, with courage free,
> To send our forces thither with supply,
> We shall in Christ the rebels force to flye
> Let us with hearts, with minds with votes consent,
> To send forth Ayd by Act of Parliament.
>
>   (Sigs. A3, A3ᵛ)

Cragge balances his prophecy with a pragmatic recognition that even the
divine will works through the agency of human institutions. But the
urgency of his call to arms stems, precisely, from a directly popular appeal to the memory of the Elizabethan period; as Norbrook observes of
the Spenserian poets writing in 1613–14, "the golden age lay in the time
of Protestant chivalry rather than the corrupt present."[61] The voice of
the plain-speaking shepherd has, by the early 1640s, become the voice of

the inspired prophet reviving the memory of earlier glory under the great queen.

Appealing to an assumed collective memory of national glory under Elizabeth, this visionary, prophetic strain in oppositional poetry which supplements the arcadian elements of pastoral was no less populist in its use of voiced, colloquial idioms and visceral appeal. Like Cragge, the poet who wrote *The Humble Petition of the Wretched, And most contemptible, the poore Commoners of England,* which appeared in July 1642, mere days before Charles raised his standard in Nottingham, fully exploits the first-person plural.[62] The poem begins in collectivity, with the plea of the people to "S^t. Elizabeth of Famous Memory." Nostalgia for the days of feudal relations here reminds us just how reactionary forms of populist opposition can be:

> Looke on our sufferings, thinke but on our wrongs,
> That hardly can be told with mortall tongues;
> Oh be not now lesse gratious then of old,
> When each distressed vassell might be bold
> Into thine open hand to put his griefe,
> And timely thence receive a faire reliefe,
> Be not lesse good, lesse gratious then before,
> In heaven the supplications of the poore
> Are heard as soone as suites of greatest Kings.
>
> (Sig. A2)

After admitting to unspecified sins that made "This sinfull land" unworthy of so great a queen (sig. A2^v), the voice of the people concedes how Elizabeth's death might have been a just punishment for the sins of the nation. Without historicizing those "sins" so that we might connect them with the conditions that brought grief to distressed vassals, the voice immediately turns, in the second part of the poem, to a direct petition to God:

> wast not enough we pray
> That at the first thou took'st that Queene away,
> Was not that done, that lambe of innocence,
> Sufficient sacrifice for our offence.
>
> (Sig. A3)

Elizabeth's death heralded the end of England's glory and "the sad beginning of our misery" (sig. A3^v) when the nation fell into an Egyptian

darkness further compounded by the death of Prince Henry "in whom
great Britaine set up her last rest" (sig. A4).

   In Cragge's version of the years of Charles's personal rule, conditions
degenerate from bad to worse as plagues more severe than those with
which God punished the Egyptians overtake the nation. This language
was common during 1641 and 1642. Here is *The Humble Petition* again:

> *Egypt* did Grasshoppers bring forth, and yeeld,
> That eate the fruite and corne of every field,
> And we have Skip-Jacke Courtiers I dare say,
> That devoure farre more in one poore day,
> Then they in *Pharoahs* age could e're have done,
> They bounded were, praid but from Sun to Sun:
> But these for three apprenticeships have eate
> The fruite of all our laboures, all our meate.
>
>   (Sigs. A4ᵛ–B)

A long and bitter attack on "Busie Intelligencers, base informers ... /
Promooting Rascalls" (sig. B) ensues, but finally turns into nationalistic
fury at the memory of conditions before the Stuarts:

> Was there a nation in this universe
> More daring, once, more stout, more bold more fierce,
> And is there now upon the worlds broad face
> Any that can be reckoned halfe so base?
> Is there a people so scorn'd, so much despis'd,
> So laught at, trod on, and so vassalis'd?
>
>   (Sig. B)

So much for the "magical beauty" of the thirties.

   But what makes *The Humble Petition* especially interesting is that in
the third and final part, the voice of "the blessed Saint *Elizabeth*" herself
admonishes the "people" who have been complaining. By shifting voice
from people to queen, the poem criticizes its own critique.

> I doe confesse poore soules, the truth of all,
> And wish a period to your miseries,
> But first your infinite inequities
> Must have an end ...
>
>   . . .

> How dares an unjust servant once require
> Of his just master, either grace, or hire.
>
> . . .
>
> . . . I left you rich 'tis true,
> But proud with all, you feare none, all feare you.
>
> (Sig. B2)

By offering its final section in the voice of the dead Queen, this poem
can at once confirm and qualify the complaint against Charles's recent
policies. The voice of the dead monarch analyzes political events from a
position of heavenly omniscience similar to the absolute regal otherness
of Stuart verse. Here regal otherness turns against its own familiar tropes
as Charles's personal rule is criticized by the "true" voice of English
monarchy:

> Princes like the Sunne should from the floods exhale
> The wealth they raise therein, and let it fall
> In every place, as they have cause a share,
> And not consume it, like the wanton heire,
> The'r full Exchequers must like Conduits be,
> Open to all, to rich and poore, like free.
>
> (Sig. B2ᵛ)

Having established that the commonwealth should follow this version of
natural exchange, Elizabeth condemns the attempted union with Scotland (sigs. B2ᵛ–B3) before reminding us of how stable and wealthy was
the realm she left behind.

In this dialogic presentation, the appeal to the past modulates
expressions of righteous fury, anger, bewilderment, and the systematic
rewriting of conventional Stuart tropes. At the time of her death, Elizabeth claims, she not only left the nation strong (with a powerful navy
and army whose men were properly paid), but also supported friendly
foreign countries in their struggles against catholicism, and passed on a
well-managed economy. Since then Stuart mismanagement has taken
over, much to her obvious horror:

> In briefe I seldome borrowed, oft did lend,
> Yet left enough to give, enough to spend;
> How comes it then, that neither Fleete nor Fort,
> Mony nor Garrison, nor House nor Court,

Wages nor debts, nothing repaid or paid,
Nought purchast, nought lent, nought built, wrought, playd,
And yet ther's nought remaines, nought to be found,
All is not perfect sure, all is not sound.
I no lesse muse to see the woods cut downe
The ancient woods, revenues of the Crowne
Dispos'd of so to favorite or friend....

(Sig. B3)

Yet even oppositional poetry was limited in its critique of existing political institutions. Voicing these criticisms through the ghost of Elizabeth implicitly supports the institution of monarchy. The past continues to provide meanings for the present. Far from casting doubt upon monarchy in principle, this poem concerns itself only with exposing recent abuses by appealing to the contrast with an earlier age of strength, success, and glory. The very terms which poets like Sylvester had used to legitimate the accession of James have returned to haunt the reign of his son.

Thus the analogy between past and present continued to exert a conservative influence even over poems—like *The Humble Petition*—ostensibly critical of the Stuart regime. Elizabeth is adamant in defense of monarchic authority since the divinely ordained condition of royal knowledge is that it remain secret. The double action of this passage authorizes what is to follow as the divine knowledge of its martyr-queen:

Princes are gods on earth, and subjects eyes
Upon their actions should not stand as spies,
It is a dangerous and ungodly thing
To pry into the Chamber of a King.
The arke of State is sanctified, and must
Be onely toucht by them, are put in trust.

(Sigs. B3–B3ᵛ)

While this defense of monarchy intensifies the attack upon recent abuses of royal power, it also makes the remedy more necessarily violent. Birth imagery provides the controlling metaphor for imagining the future:[63]

Your sorrowes yet alas, like womens throwes
Doe come and goe, but there will follow blowes,

Ere England will be delivered, it will make
Your very entralls bleed, your soules to quake,
The time shall come when bravest mindes shall mourne
And children wish they never had been borne.
The Sword shall eate, what plagues have over-slipt
And fier consume what famine hath not nipt.

(Sig. B3ᵛ)

There will be war, famine, and chaos in the manner of the punishments visited upon Israel for faithlessness in Old Testament prophecies:

Englands disease is desperate, and 'tis decreed
That e're shee can recover, she must bleed.

(Sig. B4)

Not all poets who appealed to the past to discredit the Caroline years, however, resorted to Old Testament rhetoric and nostalgia for the reign of Elizabeth. One anonymous ballad, published in 1642, ignores the smoke and smother of the present to focus upon how conditions have actually improved under the rule of the Long Parliament. The so-called halcyon days were, in this version, little more than a period of severe economic exploitation:

Like silly Sheepe they did us daily sheare,
Like Asses strong our backs were made to beare,
Intolerable burdens, yeare by yeare,
No hope, no helpe, no comfort did appeare,
    But from the great Counsell of the King,
    And the Kings great Counsell.[64]

They versus us; the political lines are clear. The scornful irony of the refrain modulates throughout the fifteen stanzas of the ballad in a thinly veiled attack upon abuses of class privilege typical of the genre. Directly opposed to the halcyon days version of the thirties as an age of prosperity, this ballad accuses the court of directing the exploitation of the honest citizens:

With taxes, and Monopolies opprest,
Ship-money, Souldiers, Knighthood, and the rest,
The Coate and Conduct-mony was no jest,

> Then thinke good neighbours how much we are blest
> *In the great Counsell of the King,*
> *And the Kings great Counsell.*

The refrain turns the analogy between past and present to create an ironic ambiguity that praises the present, under the Long Parliament, in the same terms it faults the court. It looks both ways, as it were, toward a recent past characterized by the royal abuse of political power, and toward the present in which these abuses are being rectified by Parliament. Some poets did indeed, as Wedgewood points out, represent the thirties as a blessed time of peace. But others argued and represented the past differently since retrospection can work either way depending on the poem's stance. And as Annabel Patterson has recently shown, "During the civil war the pastoral myth of the halcyon days was undoubtedly recognized for precisely what it was, a proposition designed to ratify the behavior and circumstances of the ruling classes."[65]

While the appeal to the past could legitimate, oppose, and criticize the current state of things, its structural dependence upon the analogy of past and present nevertheless restricted its field of operation. Even opposition poems commonly imagine nothing better than a return to feudal relations, as we've seen in William Lithgow and John Cragge. In a loyal Stuart poem like *The Foure Ages of England,* the appeal to the past archives structural importance leading to self-contradiction and absurdity. Published in 1648 and—incorrectly—ascribed to Cowley, this poem employs the traditional myth of four ages to lament current discord as a divinely ordained judgment upon the nation's decay into profanity and immorality. Conventional characteristics of the myth of a golden age appear in explicitly politicized terms. Since the poem is not readily available I shall quote at length:

> Gone are those golden Halcion daies, wherein
> Men uncompell'd, for love of good, fled sin:
> When men hug'd right & truth, whose souls being clear,
> Baffled the threats of punishments or fear.
> No Lawes, no penalties, but there did rest
> A Court of equity in each mans brest;
> No trembling pris'ner to the Bar did come,
> From his severer Judge t'xpect his doome;
> No need of Judge or Executioners,
> To keep by Law that which by right was theirs.

> The Pyne not then his mother-mountaines leaves,
> To dance Lavalto's on th'unconstant waves.
> Walls cloath'd not Towns, nor did mens safety stand
> In moving Forts by Sea, on fixt by Land.
> They understood not Guns, nor Speares, nor Swords,
> Nor Cause, nor Plunder, and such Martiall words;
> No armed Souldier stood for their defence,
> Their chiefest Armor was their innocence.
> Mans quiet nature did not feel that fire,
> Which since inflames the world, too great desire.
> Kings did not load their heads with Crowns, nor try
> By force or fraud, t'invade the liberty
> Of their obedient Subjects; nor did they
> Strive with Annoynted Soveraigns for sway;
> But Prince and people mutually agree
> In an indissoluble Sympathie.

> (P. 1)

These opening lines from *The Foure Ages* introduce the poem's argument from original human nature and typify its moralistic analysis of the civil wars as the result of increasing vice within all parts of the nation. Corruption in social and legal institutions brings about war and tyranny. The preface polemically advises readers of the poet's design in which they will find themselves continually implicated:

> Thou hast here the Causes, Effects, and conjecturall consequences of these unnaturall Divisions: the times Looking-Glasse, wherein (be what thou wilt) thou shalt see thy face, and find something that concerns thee. And (if thou wilt lay aside thy *philautia*) here thou shalt read thy own selfe a main cause of this War. (Sig. B3)

Churchmen—high and low—separatist preachers, lawyers, country gentlemen, and the many-headed multitude are all variously invited to put aside self-love and recognize their complicity in causing the civil wars. All classes of Englishmen are represented as giving in to the base desires which have destroyed the "indissoluble Sympathy" of the golden age. That primordial natural state, without laws or the need for them, when conscience acted as judge, and when military defenses were unknown because unnecessary, was an age when everyone was, by nature, a good member of a state and so without personal political ambitions:

> Then right
> Spurn'd the proud thoughts of domineering might;
> And lawrell'd Equity in triumph sate,
> Upheld by vertue, which stood candidate,
> And curb'd the power and craft of vice; maintain'd
> By the instinct which in mens nature raign'd:
> Th'unspotted soul could not attainted be
> With Treason 'gainst the highest Majestie;
> Vice was a stranger to't, nor could it'bide
> To club with Av'rice, or converse with Pride.
>
> (P. 2)

But like Gonzalo's utopian projections in *The Tempest,* this version of the golden age entertains some strange contradictions. Despite repeated assurance that laws and restrictions were needless when nobody desired power, this golden age is peopled by anointed kings and obedient subjects. Within the given logic of this first age, what—we might wonder—could kings have governed, or subjects obeyed? With no laws to uphold or wars to fight, the royal office itself could have had little reason for being. If such an age existed, then according to this poem its political form must unquestionably have resembled a royal state even though any and all political institutions were, by the same account, unnecessary. In this version of the appeal to the past, the use of legendary material prevents the poem from constructing an ideal state that does not require the apparatus of monarchy.

The *Foure Ages* slides easily between politics and morality in support of its argument that the current civil strife results from progressive moral decay common to all classes, rather than problematizing the "natural" state of monarchy which it posits. Virtue, it seems, has been replaced by vice, "unblemisht harmony" by "these degenerate times." The residual emphasis upon how moral decay brings about political degeneration continues throughout this version of how the golden age decayed into the silver, the "Brazen," and the iron. The account of the last describes the events of the 1640s thematically, in terms of moral and social issues, rather than giving a chronological record of events that would, perhaps, need to defend Stuart policy (pp. 27–35). The seemingly natural political harmony of the golden age gives way to political chaos as the nation fractures along class lines, each group driven by common self-interest:

> Our Councell's thwarting, and our Clergy heady,
> Gentry divided, Commonalty unsteady;

> That alwaies to the rising party run,
> Like shadowes, Ecchoes to the shining Sun.
> Religion rent with Shismes, a broken State,
> Our government confus'd, and those, that hate
> The Realm, still undermining, those that brought
> A civill war, which all our ill hath wrought.
> The King in danger; and the Kingdome roul'd
> Into inevitable ruine, sold
> Unto her foes.

> (P. 56)

In *The Foure Ages* a rigorous class determinism underlies the poem's moral comparison between past and present as well as its treatment of historical causation. Applied systematically, the myth of historical degeneration through four ages enables the poet to convey some idea of temporal movement and inevitability.

Other poems appeal to the past by purporting to be simple narrative reports of recent events in which the present appears the inevitable result of past conditions. Poets construct tendentious versions of contemporary history that have all the appearance of inevitability when they are commonly little more than highly partial accounts of selected incidents. This strategic use of historical narrative enables partisan poets to disguise judgment as fact. Two familiar Stuart poems, Fanshawe's *Ode* of 1632 and Cowley's *On His Majesties Return out of Scotland* (1641), exemplify how the appeal to the past makes partisan narratives of current conditions seem "objectively" historical. Both poems shape events while claiming the status of historical reportage. They locate selected emotive values in general past formations in order to persuade readers to accept their solutions to pressing political problems: solutions offered as though they were historically based impartial assessments.

As we have seen, Fanshawe's pastoral celebrates rural life as a means of encouraging the errant gentry to return home. But he opens with a discussion of war and foreign affairs:

> Now warre is all the world about,
> And every where *Erynnis* raignes,
> Or else the Torch so late put out
> > The stench remains.
> > . . .
> Onely the Island which wee sowe,
> (A world without the world) so farre

From present wounds, it cannot showe
An ancient skarre.

(Pp. 5, 6)

And so the *Ode* moves inward from the world at large to the little world
of the peaceful island haven. Given the unusual peace and prosperity
made possible by divine benevolence and royal power, Fanshawe suggests
that the movement of the gentry to the city is needless folly (lines 49–
60). He offers recent European events as an excuse for country landlords
to have abandoned their estates in fear, but it is an excuse which he
proceeds to demolish. This straw argument depends upon the poet's
careful manipulation of contemporary events, since in comparing Britain's present with Europe's past Fanshawe diverts attention away from
the real social problems at hand. But in order to maintain the contrast
which is essential for his argument, he paints a very distorted picture of
recent events. The portrait of the "Island which wee sowe" fits the
georgic emphasis of the poem as a whole, while reminding us that it was
only in the strict geographical sense that Britain enjoyed peace in 1630
since no battle had recently been fought in the British Isles. But, contrary
to Fanshawe's account, not only had the nation ruled by the Stuarts been
engaged in international wars since 1629—months before the occasion
of the poem—it had also been subject to serious domestic political discord. During the first three years of Charles's reign, widespread unrest
had been directed against the duke of Buckingham, whose foreign policy
resulted in costly and politically disastrous wars with France and Spain.[66]
Despite the English defeats at Cadiz (1625) and La Rochelle (1628),[67]
Buckingham's aggressive foreign policy, and the highly unpopular taxes
levied to pay for his blunders, ended only with the duke's assassination
in August 1628. For the English, peace abroad began after this event;
with England and Spain technically at war at the time of Buckingham's
death,[68] the prospect was one of continued international military adventures. Peace at home came later, too, when domestic discord was defused
by the king's prorogation of Parliament in 1629: even Clarendon dates
the halcyon days of Charles's reign from the dissolution of Parliament
and not, like Fanshawe, from ancient times.[69] The nation's recent past,
which Fanshawe represents as having been one of constant and enduring
peace, had until very recently been marked by unsuccessful foreign war
and domestic discord. The poet misrepresents the past in order to give
apparent historical authenticity to his partisan analysis of the present.

Poets could also advocate particular courses of action by appealing to the past. We have seen John Cragge calling upon the earl of Essex to fight catholicism in Ireland. In his poem *On His Majesties Return out of Scotland,* written in 1641 after Charles had successfully negotiated a peace agreement with the Scots, Cowley also calls for foreign war by appealing to England's successful and heroic imperial past. Cowley's poem appeared in *Irenodia Cantabrigiensis,* a collection of poems celebrating the king's return from Scotland written by members of the University of Cambridge and published in November 1641.[70] Political events during the six months before the king's return largely precipitated the outbreak of civil war in the summer of 1642. In May, Strafford had been executed for intervening in Scottish affairs.[71] His trial and execution mark a watershed in the struggle between crown and Commons which had begun nearly twenty years earlier during the reign of James. Mere weeks after Strafford's death, Charles left London for Scotland, where he remained until the late autumn. A Parliamentary commission was appointed—by both Houses—to accompany the king, against his will. "Apparently," writes Godfrey Davies, "to issue an ordinance of parliament without the concurrence of the king was unprecedented" (pp. 105–6). Charles's visit north was one of the final episodes in the conflicts for power that would result in the outbreak of civil war less than a year after his return. Undertaken despite Parliamentary opposition, Charles's visit was aimed at securing Scottish support for the crown in case of domestic discord in England.[72]

Cowley's poem generalizes these events in order to encourage the English to prepare for war, and to think of their enemies as foreigners:

> No *Blood* so loud as that of *Civil War;*
>   It calls for Dangers from afar.
> Let's rather go, and seek out *Them,* and *Fame;*
> Thus our *Fore-fathers got,* thus *left* a *Name;*
>   All their rich blood was spent with gains,
>   But that which swells their *Childrens Veins.*
> Why sit we still, our *Spir'its* wrapt up in *Lead?*
> Not like them whilst they *Liv'd,* but now they're *Dd?*[73]

The avowed purpose of Cowley's poem is to celebrate peace; the first five stanzas of eight praise Charles for having averted the possibility of war with Scotland. We might, then, be entitled to wonder why, in a poem that purports to celebrate peace, Cowley should wake the martial spirits of English ancestors to encourage the living to fight? Early in the poem Cowley speculates upon the evils of war to show the benefits of Charles's peace:

> This happy *Concord* in no *Blood* is writ,
>   None can grudge heav'n *full thanks* for it.
> No *Mothers* here lament their *Childrens* fate,
> And like the *Peace,* but think it comes *too late.*
>   No *Widows* hear the jocund *Bells,*
>   And take them for their *Husbands Knells.*
> No Drop of *Blood* is spilt which might be said
> To mark our joyful *Holiday* with *Red.*[74]

Cowley celebrates peace not by directing the attention of readers to the obvious benefits of that condition, but by dwelling on the evils that have been averted. Although occasioned by the supposed threat to England from Scotland, the poem constantly emphasizes the evils of civil war, a peculiarity that surely indicates a further purpose beyond that of the avowed occasion.

That purpose can best be understood through Cowley's distortion of recent events which has the effect of diverting attention from continuing threats to the political order in England; threats that were greater than those recently dispersed by the king. Although other English poets at the time commonly slandered the Scots in contemptuous terms, Cowley never questions the union of England and Scotland.[75] He recognizes nevertheless the persistence of a political problem and he offers a solution: since the English want war, they should direct their martial energies abroad rather than at each other.[76] This strategy removes any real emotional force from the lines on the anguish of war: we are not invited to consider too closely the sufferings that attend civil war—which won't come about now anyway—lest we should recognize that foreign wars cause just as many widows and sonless mothers. Charles appears as a king of undeniable and unquestionably divine authority. The poet doesn't mention Parliamentary opposition to the king's journey north, though that journey must surely have been in the minds of contemporary readers. Indeed, Cowley localizes any and all danger in the Scottish threat which the heavenly king has recently removed. Nowhere does he admit to the already apparent and equally persistent threat of war within

England itself, though he does insist that war should only be waged abroad.

The design of Cowley's poem depends upon the reader's anticipation of civil war since he draws attention to it by the constant use of martial imagery. Acknowledging that the threat of war with Scotland has raised warlike spirits, Cowley offers a policy whereby those spirits might be accommodated. In contrast to war at home, he shows foreign war to be integral to the national destiny and inheritance: a move in that direction will mark a return to past imperial glory.

Cowley's appeal to the past evokes national pride in ancestral glory while subordinating the sufferings of widows and others to national destiny. This appeal to a highly selective and generalized concept of the nation's past—we are not required to think of past defeats, periods of peace, or of previous civil wars—urges us to accept a partisan version of current political events as historically accurate, factually true. In Cowley's *On His Majesties Return,* as in *The Humble Petition* to Elizabeth, the appeal unfolds through the poem and thus exerts a controlling influence over the structure. Both poets try to persuade us to accept one version of the present as indisputable by means of an emotional appeal to the past that clearly aims at preventing us from noticing the historical distortions, and in Cowley's case, the poem's contradictory attitude toward human suffering. Nowhere does his analysis of political conditions in 1641 indicate the specific issues involved in the royal visit to Scotland. Rather the poet praises the king while suggesting that he follow a certain policy—a speedy foreign war to channel domestic unrest.

During the early and middle decades of the seventeenth century, poets relied on seemingly objective knowledge of the past to lend credibility to their partisan interpretations of the present. Basing their procedures on an assumed analogy between past and present, poets commonly represented current conditions by selective comparison with similar conditions in the past. In practice, at least, the art of analogy invariably indicates a specific stance toward current affairs—whether or not we may speak of the analogy as being entirely deliberate or within the poet's control. We have seen how the reputations of past kings alter with changes in political conditions; how poets frequently distort recent events in order to promote their own analyses of current policy; but we have also seen how they can become involved in needless contradictions and absurdities. In other words, poets invariably and even uncontrollably represent the past with an eye to the present, forcing what they see to fit an interested design that makes their version of the present seem historically accurate. Equally, when they come to represent the present, they do so by keeping an eye on the past.

Throughout the historical poetry of the period, past and present bear a reciprocal relationship controlled by the political values governing the poet's conscious or unconscious perception of the world. In a sense all historical writing is contemporary history, and poetry was by no means as detached from the historical circumstances of its own production and reception as seventeenth-century theory would have us believe. The poet who writes on historical themes, then, fits E. H. Carr's description of the historian in general—"a social phenomenon, both the product and the conscious or unconscious spokesman of the society to which he belongs." And the poet is also, like the historian, "part of history" since "the point in the procession at which he finds himself determines his angle of vision over the past."[77]

4
Contemporary History and Epic Form: Abraham Cowley's The Civil War

A Muse stood by mee, and just then I writ
My Kings great acts in Verses not unfit.
The trowbled Muse fell shapelesse into aire,
Instead of Inck dropt from my Pen a Teare.

—The Civil War, 3.545–58

BUT WHAT of the poet writing about contemporary matters, whose vision is directed at the present, and whose concerns are for events still in the process of becoming? While we are experiencing them, the phenomena which make up contemporary history may commonly seem little more than a series of random incidents connected primarily by temporal sequence. To these the historian of the early modern peiod brought significant order, usually claiming to discover that significance in the events themselves rather than imposing it. Poetry declares itself to be neither chaotic nor meaningless. Like historical writers generally, poets writing on historical events selected incidents to shape into a coherent and comprehensible design that imposes meanings while seeming to discover them. A poem's design is that tendentious *formal* link between the aesthetic or universalizing pattern poets give to chosen events, and their discernible design upon the reader in so representing those events.

The relation of any text's particular instrumentality to the conventions of its genre is always surprising unless we believe there are "unproblematic realms of discourse, illustrated by texts that fall within them."[1] This chapter offers a detailed critical reading of a single historical poem by one of the most influential poets from the generation before Dryden that illustrates many of the procedures and generalizations offered in previous chapters. It argues that Cowley's unfinished epic, *The Civil War*, demonstrates how Augustan poetics have their origins during the revolutionary civil wars when the "heroic" couplet emerges to dominate the poetic scene for more than a century. Written in support of the Stuart war effort, Cowley's *The Civil War* demonstrates how some of the poetic conventions of militant protestantism—which had founded an oppositional politics upon a commitment to a righteous war—were at once assimilated by Cowley's epic and yet blunted by his loyalty to the Stuart cause. In polishing the native pentameter into the predominantly closed "heroic" couplet, Cowley's text articulates tensions that question the premises of heroic form and value: with its characteristic use of balance and antithesis, Cowley's heroic couplet invariably contains the terms of its own possible negation. As the mode of the poem's militaristic designs upon contemporary readers, the antithetical couplet imposes a rational frame of binary oppositions unlike the direct expression of personal rage in the startling language and loose pentameters of a Russell, Vicars, Cragge, Wither, or Taylor. If John N. King is correct, then these poets writing critically of Stuart claims to absolutism inherited "a broad consensus concerning doctrine and devotional life, based upon the central tenets of justification by faith alone and the absolute primacy of the scriptures."[2] Since religious discourse was inseparable from political debate throughout the early modern period, it was the potential for critical discourse within doctrines of "justification by faith alone" that gave the languages of Reformation protestantism their radical edge. Even the Elizabethan historical epics of Drayton, Daniel, and Warner, a central genre of the official court poetry against which—if we remodel King's general argument—the plain style of the protestant tradition formed an oppositional margin, operated looser, more heterogenous, styles of stanzaic patterning than the closed pentameter couplet with which Cowley set out to legitimate the Stuart cause.

Yet Cowley's reputation is based upon his development of an English "pindaric," a varietal form associated with the strong expression of excessive and complex personal feeling; *The Civil War* is his most significant attempt at the heroic couplet, a measure he himself abandoned when he stopped writing this poem. Perhaps it was while contemplating the death of friends that Cowley came to realize how the real conditions of civil—or any—war dislocate military heroism from its available poetic packaging. Cowley's problem was inevitably but not entirely a formal one: how could the traditional values and neoclassical conventions of heroic poetry legitimate the Stuart war effort when not only the civil wars but also the poetic values and conventions of representation invariably contained the terms of their own critique? The normative balance and antithesis of the closed pentameter typically articulate heuristic binaries—us versus them, the here/now against the there/then—as the mode of the reading public's becoming. In a sense, the most admired qualities of the heroic couplet were responsible for generating readers too critical to believe what they read in a poem. As Dryden was to discover, the best way to use the heroic couplet if you had to write on behalf of the Stuarts was loyal satire: "we may be bad, but they are worse."

Cowley's Epic Design

The visual and spatial metaphors which, for the English seventeenth century, characterize the discourse of the poetic imagination, understanding, and method of historical representation are largely familiar from the prospect section of *Cooper's Hill* where Denham explores the dialectic between poetic sight and the topoi of historical knowledge. The observing poet actively participates in the historical construction of the national landscape by perceiving, understanding, and representing what he sees in the form of static tableaux. The reader is directly implicated in this perception and participation through imaginative involvement with reconstructing the particular scene. And the reading public is specifically defined—both engaged and restricted—by the literary pleasures and demands of Denham's diction, use of allusion, historical reference, syntax, and dazzling command of rhetorical figuration. The politics of seeing, reading, and writing which Denham's poem announces was not, however, entirely restricted to courtly, aristocratic registers.

Two years before *Cooper's Hill* appeared, Martin Parker had published a broadside on the opening of the Short Parliament (my italics):

> The order how they rode that day
> To you I will in briefe display,
> In the best manner that I may,
>   for now my minde is bent
> To publish what *my selfe did see,*
> *That absent (Loyall) hearts may be*
> *Participants* as well as wee
>   *Ith'joy oth' Parliament.*[3]

More directly and explicitly than the antitheses and ellipses of Denham's couplets, Parker's ballad informs a wider possible audience how the dialectic of poetic sight and knowledge of current circumstance necessitates political commitment and participation. But what, more precisely, does it mean for a poem to "participate" in this way? A traditional answer might describe how a poem participates by offering a version of events which an unwary reader (one incapable, perhaps, of understanding *Cooper's Hill*) could mistake for historical truth. So we might account for Parker's ballad in order to dismiss it as not really poetry at all but propaganda in verse.

But once we turn to a text such as Cowley's *The Civil War*, composed during those months of war in 1642 and 1643, the problem becomes both more intriguing and more sophisticated since this text cannot so easily be dismissed as "mere" propaganda. Yet Cowley's poem directly participates in the events it describes by offering a tendentious version of the present, one that would demand readers accept a normative position. The text manipulates heroic conventions to analyze the war as a problem of historical causation. In this account, the present degenerates from a glorious past because of an infernally generated reformist zeal threatening the fabric of traditional social behavior and political relations. The battles and sociopolitical crisis of 1642–43 are given generalized import as particular instances of more enduring moral conflicts. Here the poetics of English Augustanism emerge from the revolutionary struggle of mid-century in an attempt to employ the balance and poise of the closed couplet to achieve a civilized and seemingly impartial voice that is both socially conscious and responsible enough to offer an incisive and persuasive analysis of contemporary disputes. What is most distinctly "Augustan" is the contradiction between such a socially reflective voice and its deployment in attempts to justify punitive violence in the name of civilization and social order.

In Cowley's version of history, England's natural and historical order, the true conditions of its claims to civilization, are represented by the Elizabethan model of successful war abroad and peace at home under just monarchs. The poem opens in characteristically partisan fashion by posing a political problem about the present state of things in historical terms:

> What rage does *England* from it selfe divide
> More then Seas doe from all the world beside?[4]

Professing to solve this problem by treating the wars as an interlude— one of tragic and heroic proportions—in the continuing epic of England's glorious monarchy, the poem postulates an eventual future that will be made even more glorious by the victory of the Stuarts over the self-divisive rage currently fracturing what is supposed to be a united nation. *The Civil War* provides a chronological narrative of contemporary events in specifically literary terms governed by Cowley's stance as poet of the Caroline cause. He marshals a vast army of conventional rhetorical figures, epic and georgic topoi, literary and historical allusions, stock conceits and images to transform contemporary history into a poetry which will arouse readers' "hearts to participate" by accepting the poet's cause. The initial heroic optimism with which the poem sets out, however, gives way to a more fully tragic note of desperation by the time Cowley stops writing. Far from being mere propaganda, Cowley's *Civil War,* perhaps even more than Denham's *Cooper's Hill,* heralds the arrival of English Augustanism, its characteristic forms of the heroic couplet and the unfinished or unfinishable epic forged from the conflicts of the seventeenth century.

Cowley himself invites us to consider the politics of the poem in the repudiation published more than a dozen years after he abandoned the work. "I have," he writes in the preface to his *Poems* of 1656, "cast away all such pieces as I wrote during the time of the late troubles, with any relation to the differences that caused them; as among others, *three Books of the Civil War it self*" (1:9). But he had not destroyed every copy of the three books. Although a version of the first appeared in 1679, the full text had to wait three hundred years for Allan Pritchard's excellent edition of 1973.[5] In its newly restored state, *The Civil War* remains the earliest attempt to write an epic poem in English on contemporary events as they occurred.

Even so, *The Civil War* began as a party poem designed to further the cause of the Caroline war party amongst potentially royalist sympathizers otherwise reluctant to fight against fellow countrymen and, often, kinsmen. Effective propaganda was in considerable demand during the months of 1642 and 1643 when Cowley was beginning the poem and was soon recognized to have exacerbated the fighting. Looking back from 1648, one poet argues that "the effeminate warr of words, / Which did enlarge the jarrs" between factions was directly responsible for incensing men to fight:

> First they fall to't by pen, which did incense
> Both parties with a greater vehemence;
> From hence names of disgrace at first arose,

> And each to other made more odious:
> And the amazed people did invite
> To lay aside their tedious peace, and fight.
> They plainly saw the warr, before they could
> Discern the Cause on't; and they might behold
> Th'effects, though not the quarrell; they well knew
> That they must feel the warr, and end it too.[6]

It is nearly impossible to assess precisely how and to what extent poetic propaganda contributed to the war. Yet during the early months, there were doubtless many—like Colonel John Birch—who had difficulty deciding if, and for which side, they should take up arms:

> I never had an intention, nor yet have, of taking up arms of either side, my reasons this, my protestation already taken binds me both to king and parliament. I am not so senseless (though it were almost to be wished I were) that there are two armies, the one the king's, the other the parliament's, each seeking to destroy [the] other, and I by oath bound to preserve both, each challenging the Protestant religion for their standard, yet the one takes the papists, the other the schismatics for their adherents, and (for my part) my conscience tells me they both intend the Protestant religion. What reason have I therefore to fall out with either?[7]

Before they could be swayed one way or the other, people needed to be assured that they would be fighting on the right side, and even then they needed constant reassurance that they had made the correct decision. Birch, for instance, fought for and subsequently supported Parliament. But only until the execution of Charles. By 1654 he was actively engaged in opposing Cromwell's Protectorate.[8] Back in the early months of civil war, poetic representations of recent events, like Cowley's, aimed to persuade readers that if they couldn't fight for the king, they should at least support his cause.[9]

Cowley's version of what was happening in 1642–43 constantly refers current events to past analogues in order to analyze events as a movement in the larger framework of national history. He thereby displays, to borrow Herbert Butterfield's term, "historical mindedness," the sense that problems are open to historical treatment.[10] Although frequently assigning moral causes to historical events, Cowley locates his own times within the nation's political history as a whole. But his adherence to a heroic view of history also determines his version of a war

which, he attempts to persuade us, is one of those diabolically instigated
rebellions against the divinely—and historically—sanctioned authority
of the crown which have periodically occurred throughout the past, but
which have never yet overthrown the established and seemingly natural
institutions of monarchy. Within this general pattern, Cowley represents
specific incidents by historical allusions and, commonly, by reference to
some previous historical events that transpired at the scene of battle.

COWLEY'S VERSIONS OF THE PAST

Cowley twice offers potted summaries of the nation's past, each time
with distinct designs. First, in order to displace the political crisis which
marks the scene of his writing, Cowley opens with a summary military
history filled with appeals to glorious ages of England's imperial successes. This strategy resembles the one he used in his 1641 ode *On His
Majesties Return out of Scotland* to demonstrate how Englishmen should
do what they have always done—direct their martial energies against
foreign enemies. If they aren't prepared to attack otherness abroad, they
should stay home and enjoy the peace (1.72–76). But in either case, they
should leave politics to the king. The second time Cowley describes the
past at length, he ranges beyond national boundaries and concerns in
order to trace the diabolic origins of revolution in general. Book 2 opens
discussion of the current war with a general history of rebellions that
places the opposition leaders at the end of a long line of biblical as well
as English rebels. Cowley's devil claims certain leaders to be his own
infernal agents on earth:

> by my great selfe, I sweare,
> Had I another Heav'en I'de venture't here;
> The Cause is ours, ours the cheife gaine will bee;
> Is Say, or Pym concern'd soe much as Wee?
>
> (2.534–37)

Devils were not infrequently invoked as the instigators of rebellion in
English political songs and ballads; cavalier satire commonly associated
figures such as Peters, Pym, Cromwell, and the regicides with diabolic
and infernal forces.[11] We have already seen how the Presbyterian John
Vicars used the devil to satiric effect in *November the 5,* though Cowley's
use of this device indicates how little poets respected the aesthetic decorums which might have made personal invective inappropriate in a he-

roic poem. Writing in 1675, Hobbes reiterated more than a century of conventional thought when he stated that the virtues of heroic poetry included "Justice and Impartiality. . . . And as far as the truth of Fact can defame a man, so far they be allowed to blemish the reputation of Persons. But to do the same upon Report, or by inference, is below the dignity not only of a Heroe but of a Man."[12] Yet Cowley's political design constantly supersedes aesthetic decorums. He reserves the high style for heroic praise of the nation's imperial past while elsewhere easily adopting features from popular forms of political satire to attack the enemies of England's governing dynasty. Cowley's attempt to fuse these disparate modes, styles, and decorums deserves attention.

In the opening lines, the poem declares its consideration of contemporary events to be an innovation in the neoclassical epic style: "What rage does *England* from it selfe divide / More then Seas doe from all the world beside?" (1.1–2). In defiance of strict poetic theory, the poem will address recent events in the context of the nation's past since this historicization will elevate them to heroic status. The opening is not an entirely conventional epic opening—we might have expected "What rage" to be followed by "Tell Muse" rather than a question mark—for the poem is not an attempt at epic proper. Since *The Civil War* openly recalls formulae used by Daniel to begin his historical epic on English civil war, Cowley evidently knew his poem represented an attempt at generic experimentation. Daniel precedes Cowley in summarizing English history up to the start of the period covered by his poem (1.8–24), but he also opens with the induction "I sing" (1.1) and invocation to the Muse (1.4) proper to epic. Both are missing from Cowley's poem. Although *The Civil War* constantly engages epic conventions, these opening violations direct readers' critical attention to the poem's historical and political concerns.

The familiar Virgilian echo cannot alone establish the poem's political stance. The present tense of the repeated and emphatic verb, *does/doe,* and the interrogative form announce a contemporary problem— nationally divisive rage—which is subsequently elaborated by five short episodes, each contrasting present disunity with former periods of imperial achievement under great monarchs. The present is to be understood as merely an aberration from the past, rather than a set of new and unprecedented political circumstances. The possibility of what we might today call "revolution" is simply not considered. Recent opposition to Stuart policy has no place. Instead of hostility to foreign policy and opposition to Laudian episcopacy, crown monopolies, and Stuart claims to absolutism, Cowley's version of England's imperial past reminds us of battles entirely irrelevant to the politics of Roundway Down or Edge Hill, much less Prince Rupert's cavalry. In the context of a version of national history constructed entirely in the form of a series of past victories obtained under glorious monarchs from Henry II to Queen Elizabeth, current disobedience to the king seems to violate the nation's heroic destiny of successful overseas conquest. As in *On His Majesties Return out of Scotland,* from which *The Civil War* borrows lines and motifs, duty to the blood of English ancestors fuels an emotional and irrational appeal to a past system of patriarchal values which displaces the current political crisis. In one of the most startling images of the poem, Cowley turns life against death and past against present in a paradox characteristic of Stuart absolutist discourse: "Thus our *forefathers* fought, thus bravely bled, / Thus still they live, whilst we alive are dead" (1.65–66).

These opening episodes analyze the current wars by contrasting past and present rhetorically, structurally, and imagistically. Each episode opens with an emphatic denial that displaces the present in favor of the past—"It was not so"—and introduces the historical and negative terms which legitimate the break with epic decorum: the important words are the "was ... not" that necessitate the absent "but ... is." Such negative contrasts evolve structurally, for though the episodes vary in length, each breaks medially into two sections corresponding with past and present content. In the first episode, the westward movement of the royal sun suggests another westward movement, the armies of Henry II to Ireland.[13] Success in imperial adventures is as natural for an English king as the terms of the comparison:

> It was not so when *Henryes* dreadfull name;
> Not *Sword*, nor *Cause,* whole Nations overcame.
> To farthest *West* did his swift conquests run;
> Nor did his glories set, but with the *Sun.*
>
> (1.13–16)

This contrast between the natural past and the degenerate present controls each of the five episodes. The past is a series of heroic monarchs, each of them linked with some natural force which vindicates their political authority:

Henry II	like the sun
Richard I	conquers the moon
Edward III	conquers the oceans
Henry V	master of rain and sun
Elizabeth	mistress of the ocean

The succession of England's monarchs is made to appear, if not exactly transtemporal, then at least as inevitable as the natural phenomena they resemble.

Thus political considerations clearly govern Cowley's epic, especially his selection, suppression, and narrative organization of historical material. In characterizing the current war as a historical dislocation, Cowley typically distinguishes national from classical, biblical, and legendary history in a partisan fashion. He most often reserves allusions to the nation's past for characterizing the Stuart cause, while associating the opposition with fabulous and diabolical figures from classical and biblical mythology—the apparent historicity of the one undermining the legendary status of the other. The chronological series of five English monarchs which opens book 1 memorializes a heroic past when the nation seemed united by glorious victory over foreign enemies. How things were illustrates how things should be, but aren't.

Cowley begins with the victories of Henry II (1154–89) over the Irish. The next episode concerns Henry's son, Richard I (1189–99). But Cowley links the episodes by theme and image in addition to genealogy in order to naturalize patrilinear succession. While Henry's victories in the west resemble the movement of the sun, Richard's conquests overcome the moon of Islam:

> It was not soe, when in the happy *East*
> *Richard,* our *Mars, Venuses* Isle possest.
> 'Gainst the proud *Moon,* Hee th'*English Crosse* displaid,
> Eclypst one *Horne* and th'other paler made,
> When our deare Lives we ventur'd bravely there,
> And dig'd our owne to gaine *Christs Sepulcher.*
>
> (1.21–26)

Cowley contrasts Richard's crusades with the present wars thematically: both wars illustrate the theme of fighting for religion. In the glorious past English Christians captured the Holy Land from Islam; in the present, they engage in sectarian disputes.

> That sacred *Tombe* which should we now enjoy,
> We should with as much zeale fight to destroy!
> The pretious signes of our dead Lord we scorne,
> And see his *Crosse* worse then his *Body* torne!
> Wee hate it now both for the *Greeke,* and *Jew,*
> To us tis *Foolishnes* and *Scandall* too.
> To what with Worship the fond *Papist* falls,
> That the fond *Zealot* a curst *Idoll* calls.
> So twixt their double madnes heres the odds,
> One makes false *Devills,* t'other makes false *Gods.*
>
> (1.27–36)

The satiric texturing here differs from that of a Dryden or a Butler. The elevated expectation of balance and point set up by caesura and antithesis in the first line of the passage is suitably dashed by the unconstrained flatness of the second, as the sacred nobility of the past decays into the zealous language of the present. Although the opening lines of the poem emphasize those features which mark it as an innovation in the art of poetic history writing, *The Civil War* persistently appropriates poetic conventions from historical poems written in opposition to the Stuart dynasty. In times of civil war, poets turn the enemies' weapons against them; in this case the official version ignores recent complaints against the Stuart court—which might have some direct bearing upon the causes of the current civil war—by appropriating features of the language in which those complaints were voiced. Ad hominem religious satire, that staple of Augustan poetics, was begotten by Cowley out of Saltmarsh, Cragge, and Vicars.

When *The Civil War* turns from blame to praise, its diction becomes more dignified, its rhythms more heroically tight and intense. The victories of English kings during the Hundred Years War provide Cowley with the theme for his fourth episode, which links English kings with natural forces in order to stir heroic and patriotic pride:

> It was not soe when *Agin Court* was wonne,
> Under great *Henry* serv'd the *Raine* and *Sun.*
> A Nobler fight the *Sun* himselfe nere knew,
> Not when he stopt his Course a fight to view.
> Then *Death,* old *Archer,* did more skilfull grow;
> And learned to hit more sure from th'*English Bow.*

> Then *France* was her owne Stories sadly taught,
> And felt how *Caesar,* and how *Edward* fought.
>
> (1.51–58)

Here, at least, accurate historical detail gives nobility and weight to the poetic conceit. Henry V's (1413–22) power over the elements is not entirely hyperbolic exaggeration for, as Pritchard points out, "Henry V's archers were aided in their great victory at Agincourt (1415) by the heavy rains preceding the battle, which caused the French cavalry to bog down in the soft ground, and by the sun, which during the crucial period of combat shone in the faces of the French, dazzling them" (p. 128).

The sounds of victories against France ringing in his readers' ears, Cowley evades the embarrassingly long period of civil war which followed Henry V's death—notice how the fourth episode ends with a retrospective glance at Edward rather than the forward movement typical of the other episodes—by leaping ahead to the reign of Elizabeth (1558–1603) where he lands on safer ground.

> It was not soe when the vast Fleete of *Spaine*
> Lay torne and scatter'd ore the injur'd *Maine*.
> Through the proud world a *Virgin* Terror strooke,
> The *Austrian* Crownes and *Romes* seaven *Hills* she shooke.
> To her great *Neptune* homag'd all his Streames,
> And all the wide stretcht *Ocean* was her *Thames*.
>
> (1.59–64)

Elizabeth, not simply a military conqueror exercising power over natural forces like the kings in the previous analogies, becomes a goddess—very much like Nemesis—to whom even Neptune pays homage. Characteristically, Cowley's political verse treats actual events in an increasingly allegorical manner the closer they approach his own times. His *Ode* on the Restoration stands out among poems by other major poets on the event because of its systematic allegorization of the king's return: perhaps he knew his king's father's injunction that poets should "be war of wryting any thing of materis of commoun weill, or uther sic grave sene subiectis (except Metaphorically . . .)."[14]

Cowley's tendencies to allegorize contemporary events, and to satirize his enemies by association with fabulous rather than historical allusions, continue through the closing section of his fifth and final episode.

He compares present-day Englishmen with the Spartii, those fabulous offspring of the serpent's teeth sown by Cadmus,[15] in a vigorous roar of nationalistic pride and martial fervor that he closes off, at sonnet length, with a fine iconographic portrait of his king's divine (because paradoxical) qualities:

> Thus our *forefathers* fought, thus bravely bled,
> Thus still they live, whilst we alive are dead.
> Such Acts they did as *Rome* and *Caesar* too
> Might envy those whom they did once subdue.
> We'are not their *ofspring* sure, our *Heralds* ly;
> But *borne* we know not how, as now we *dy*.
> Their Pretious Blood we could not venture thus;
> Some *Cadmus* sure sow'd *Serpents* Teeth for us.
> We cold not els by mutuall fury fall,
> Whilst *Rhene* and *Sennen* for our Armies call.
> Choose that, or Peace; yee have a *Prince,* ye know,
> As fitt for both, as both are fitte for you:
> Furious as *Lightning* when Warrs *Tempest* came,
> But Calme in *Peace,* calme as a *Lambent flame*.
>
> (1.65–78)

The closing pair of couplets neatly situates the *"Prince"* as that mysterious but absolute presence who both generates and resolves political freedom of choice. Rhetoric and rhythm enforce the paradoxical status of the dynastic leader who alone provides not only the central, though absent, term of the chiasmic inversion in line 76, but also the limiting presence or absolute center—both "furious" and "calme"—which alone can mediate the historical rhythms of the past, from war to peace. Only kings can make sense of the problems of history; only loyalty to that belief can solve the immediate problem caused by the vicious folly of forgetfulness. Once the English people recall their blood debt to their heroic past, they will stop the present rebellion and worship the mystery of their king.

Cowley will again appeal directly to the glorious heroism of long-dead ancestors later in book 3, dramatically putting the appeal into the mouth of his royal hero Charles, addressing his troops before the battle of Newbury: "Your births command yow to orecome or dy; / They their Forefathers wrong unlesse they fly" (3.297–98). Appeals to the irrational ties of blood were common, perhaps, as Lawrence Stone has suggested, because the appeal to kinship ties had particularly strong claim upon people's emotional lives during the late sixteenth and early seventeenth centuries.[16] Certainly some such emotional appeal underlies Cowley's contrast between past and present in dynastic terms.

In any event, Cowley evokes a heroic past restricted to periods of former military glory when English kings and queens had the power to "force from fate a victory." By representing the past in this way Cowley emphasizes present degeneration. The rhetorical insistence of the repeated opening lines, the syntactical trickery, the allegorizing of his own times, the appeals to kinship, the interwoven patterns of natural imagery, and the duplicated structures are all designed to persuade us to accept a collection of otherwise unconnected incidents from the nation's past as though they were normal, historical conditions from which the present is a diabolic aberration. Instances of how the nation used to be, these episodes together construct a model of how the nation should be by conflating selective past with ideal conditions. England's natural condition is historically determined—imperial monarchy under heroic kings and queens.

But the paradoxes of Stuart ideology are clearly only part of the picture. The selectivity and ingenuity with which Cowley so carefully makes the past fit his present design become clearer once we notice how his version of national history in book 2 differs from that in book 1. Instead of analyzing the immediate circumstances of the current wars and demonstrating how they violate the nation's imperial past, Cowley summarizes previous attempts to overthrow established monarchies. With one notable exception, the episodes in book 2 are, like those in book 1, arranged chronologically according to reign. Again, Cowley selects those incidents from the past which comply with his design. This time, instead of imperially successful reigns, he treats those characterized by rebellions against monarchic authority, normally associating the rebels with fabulous and fantastic predecessors. Together the two histories catalogue most of the English monarchs—with a few gaps—since the reign of Henry II.

The catalogue of English rebels occupies the second half of book 2 in a more general history of hell clearly influenced by the antiprelatical satires of 1641, such as those discussed in Chapter 2. By considering English political history within his satirical and heroic description of hell, Cowley can assign a diabolic cause to the current civil war. The parliamentary leaders appear as the last in a long procession of rebels that, starting with Old Testament examples, includes those barons who drafted Magna Charta and ends with the catholic "Powder traitors" of 1605 (2.497). Cowley's hell—which predates and may have influenced Milton's[17]—is not simply a place where rebels happen to congregate, but the source of all rebellions against divine order, and hence of all human suffering, woe, and misery:

> Here Rebell Minds in envious torments ly;
> Must here forever Live, forever Dy.
> Here Lucifer, the mighty Captive reignes,
> Proud midst his Woes, and Tyrant in his Chaines.
> Once Generall of a guilded Hoast of Sp'rites,
> Like Hesper, leading on the spangled nights.
> But downe like Lightning, which him strooke, hee came,
> And roar'd at his first plunge into the flame.
> Myriads of Spirits fell wounded round him there;
> With dropping Lights thick shone the singed aire.
> Since then the dismall solace of their woe,
> Has only binne weake mankind to undoe.
>
> (2.385–96)

Permitting full liberty to his imaginative preoccupation with the nature and horror of rebellion as both a psychological and a physical condition, Cowley describes the torments of the souls in hell with some precision and a certain sadistic relish. Several familiar figures from Old Testament history appear, characterized by their punishments rather than their crimes:

> Davids proud Sonne hangs up in flames by th'haire;
> A thowsand Feinds stand round and wound him there.
> Still with fresh darts his dropping limmes they tore,
> As Joab, and the young men did before.
> . . .
> There Baâshas head weares still a burning Crowne,
> And Zimri, whose wild Spirit came smoaking downe.
> In such feirce flames the Traytour now is fried,
> That hee thinkes those scarce warme, in which hee died.
>
> (2.433–36, 449–52)

The brief intrusion into Zimri's mind here is hardly convincing as psychological realism, but its suggestion—that those who murder kings and usurp their power are ever conscious of their torment—might have offered some rather dubious pleasure to an indignant royalist with sadistic inclinations.

Cowley moves directly from the tortures undergone by Old Testament rebels to those suffered by a long line of English rebels, all of whom were punished for trying to overthrow the established government of their times. There is surely a grim irony in his proud assertion that "of all Lands, (though all sende millions in) / More bountiful then Albion none hath bin" in supplying hell with rebellious souls, and that "this yeres Harvest" was a "richer Crop" than ever before (2.455–56, 502). Why Albion should bring forth rebels as part of her fecundity remains unexplained since explanation might necessarily suggest how the conditions of oppression which generated the current rebellion have also been a traditional element of the nation's constitution. But in Cowley's poem rebellion against the English throne, however powerful, always has been and still is doomed to fail.

Even attempts to resist royal power fill Cowley's text with horror. Turning to Magna Charta, Cowley stresses the treachery of the barons involved by accusing them of conspiring to sell their king and country to France:

> There thowsand stubborne Barons fetterd ly,
> And curse their old vaine noyse of Liberty.
> They who their angry Soveraigne to oppose,
> The hatefull yoake of France and Lewis chose.
> A vaine pretence from Johns bad acts they bring;
> John was a fond wild man, but yet their King.
>
> (2.457–62)

Pritchard points out that Cowley's intent here—and in subsequent lines—is to refute "Parliamentary writers such as Prynne, who made heroes of these men and appealed to their example as precedent for their own rebellion in the name of liberty," and he stresses the importance of Magna Charta in the constitutional disputes of the time (p. 29). Cowley wishes also to stress their eventual failure, in the next world if not in this; and to insist that kings must be obeyed no matter what their actions or personal moral qualities.

The other noble English rebels whom Cowley assigns to hell continue the chronological series. Queen Isabella and her lover, Roger Mortimer, who overthrew Edward II (1307–27), were familiar figures from Marlowe's play who appear in suitably grotesque terms:

> Their scorching lusts, and all their hot desires,
> Are now extinguisht quite by greater fires.
>
> (2.473–74)

Richard II's death in 1400, while he was being held prisoner, was thought by many to have been murder.[18] Since Parliament had ordered Richard's imprisonment, Cowley, more severe than Shakespeare in his judgment, consigns the members of both Houses to hell (2.483–86). He also condemns Richard Neville, the earl of Warwick, who, having aided Edward IV to the throne, later deposed him in favor of Henry VI (2.487–88), as well as Richard III who became king in 1483 after having supposedly killed both Henry VI and Edward V (2.489–92).

Cowley breaks this chronological series once, and then only to maintain class decorum. After so many noble, even regal, rebels, he lumps together the leaders of populist uprisings in a reverse chronological order that makes the most of the cacophonous sounds of their names:

> There too an endlesse multitude is spread,
> By Kets, and Cades, and Tylers thether lead.
> Long darknesse now their Ign'orance does repay;
> Blind, stubborne men, that hether groap'd their way!
>
> (2.493–96)

This history of rebellion in England ends with a reference to the Gunpowder Plot of 1605 (2.497–500) that brings Cowley up to his own times and the Stuart dynasty.[19] As recorded by this poet, all previous attempts to subvert the authority of the English crown led relentlessly to the downfall of those involved. In similar fashion, those currently waging war against Charles doom themselves to follow their predecessors. Again, Cowley represents only those aspects of the past suited to his purpose, interpreting them in conformity with a partisan design. The rest of book 2, following the catalogue of the tormented, describes a council in hell at which the devil urges the infernal powers to stir up rebellion in the souls of seventeenth-century Englishmen.[20] Cowley thus discloses the traces of a historical genealogy within the current war in order to expose its diabolic causes.

COWLEY'S VERSION OF THE PRESENT

While these two serial accounts of England's past illustrate how Cowley comments on current events while referring to the past, other sections of *The Civil War* report contemporary incidents directly as historical facts. The second part of book 1 and the first part of book 2 survey the military campaigns of the months between autumn 1642 and autumn 1643, while the second part of book 3 accounts for the battle of Newbury. In addition to employing various kinds of historical allusion to evaluate recent happenings, Cowley often reminds us of some event that previously occurred at the present sites of civil strife. Generally, he treats recent events no less partially than more distant ones, often requiring that readers already share his view if they are to find the text persuasive.

Cowley often demands that we share, or at least be able to recognize, his values and beliefs before we can understand his treatment of them. When referring to the trial of Strafford, for example, he provides only an indirect evaluation of the event in highly tendentious terms that require our prior acquiescence in his judgment. By recognizing the referent behind the polemical tone, we become tacitly implicated in the poet's point of view. Like other poets of the time, Cowley is openly hostile to the mob. He reviles them in allusions that were, no doubt, assumed to be beyond their understanding but common knowledge to a more informed audience.

> in unjustest wise
> The many-mouthed *Rout* for *Justice* cries.
> They call for *blood* which now I feare do's call,
> For *bloud* againe much louder then them all.
> In sencelesse Clamours and confused Noyse,
> We lost that rare and yet unconquered *voice*.
> So when the sacred *Thracian Lyre* was drown'd
> In the *Bistonian Woemens* mixed Sound,
> The wondering *stones,* that came before to heare,
> Forgot themselves and turn'd his *Murderers* there.
>
> (1.139–48)

As Pritchard points out, the crowds who gathered at Westminster Hall to call for Strafford's execution shouted "Justice" (p. 131), and Cowley expects us to know this in order to understand the lines. Familiarity with the incidental fact is the only way we can positively recognize the reference to Strafford. Knowledge gathered from other poems on Strafford—whether sympathetic or not—would be of little help since they normally depict him as a Marlovian overreacher, a tragic hero who rises to such heights above mere mortals that he is bound to fall.[21] Cowley presents Strafford as does no other poet of the time. Instead of a Phaeton who assumed too great a power for his ability, Cowley's Strafford appears in the more sympathetic role of Orpheus; the classical allusion is apt, for, like the Thracian bard, the English courtier was noted for his oratorical powers.[22] But Cowley's oblique allusion demands that we already recognize the encomiastic reference to Strafford. Cowley continues with a reference to Archbishop Laud that is almost as veiled and full of assumptions:

> The same lowd storme blew the grave *Miter* downe,
> It blew downe that, and with it shooke the *Crowne.*
> Then first a *State* without a *Church* begun;
> Comfort thy Selfe, deare *Church,* for *then* twas donne.
>
> (1.149–52)

Again, readers are implicated simply by recognizing the referent.

And so Cowley's account of the present participates in the events it describes by directing us to read and accept it in ways that will temper our understanding of those events. His representation of the battles of 1642–43 obliges us to accept his belief in an inevitable victory for England's monarch. Once he has, in the opening lines of book 1, characterized the current war by contrast with England's imperial past he reports significant events from campaigns of the previous year. He thus divides recent history into units, many of which have their own histories, and which are arranged into a serial narrative sequence according to chronological and geographical principles like those used by William Camden in his *Britannia* (1586) and adapted to poetry in Drayton's *Polyolbion.*[23] Cowley breaks up the campaigns of the previous year into discrete incidents according to location before arranging them into separate sequences, one each for books 1 and 2. The order of events within each sequence follows chronological and geographical principles to construct a rhetorically persuasive pattern. When Cowley breaks chronology, he maintains coherence by grouping episodes together within larger areas of the nation. Working on a larger scale than Denham in *Cooper's Hill,*

Cowley directs the perspective of Chronology around the entire country to see recent events which he then tabulates topographically.

But frequently Cowley's account of a battle, siege, or other military engagement follows topographical conventions by including specific references to some previous incident which occurred in the same place. By involving local history in this way, Cowley prejudices his treatment of the recent event by past association. He introduces the campaigns in the West Country, for example, with familiar political associations from Arthurian legend:

> The *Saxon* fury to that farre-stretcht place,
> Drove the torne reliques of great *Brutus* race.
> Here they of old did in long safety ly,
> Compast with *Seas,* and a worse *Enemy.*
> Nere till this time, nere did they meet with foes,
> More cruell and more Barbarous, then those.
> Yee noble *Brittaines* who so oft with blood
> Of *Pagan Hosts* have dyed old *Tamars Flood.*
> If any drop of mighty *Uther* still,
> And *Uthers* mightier *Sonne,* your veines does fill,
> Show now that Spirit, till all men thinke by you,
> The doubtfull tales of your great *Arthur* true.
>
> (1.395–406)

Cowley's use of ancient British material depicts current events by means of political links between royalist and Briton, Parliamentarian and Saxon. He uses such linkages again when representing the siege of Exeter by stressing connections between Trojan and British history. Without developing the legendary Trojan history of Exeter—that it was founded by Brute himself[24]—he focuses on the battles and sieges that have taken place there. After the Saxons had usurped power from the old Trojans, came the Danes. Cowley continues the historical series to a victorious English monarch in a passage that illustrates how the history of a place can serve to convince us of his version of history.

> Hether the *Danes* victorious *Poleaxe* came;
> It felt great *Suenoes* rage in blood and flame.
> Yet they the swelling *Norman* durst oppose,
> Till *Heaven* it selfe, declar'ed which side t'had chose.
> Downe at his feet, downe fell th'unbatterd Wall;

> The *Cities Stones* did *Homage* first of all.
> Strange was the sight; yet not soe strange a show
> That they fell then, as that they fell not now.
> Thrice since that time did they a Seidge sustaine;
> First *Courtneys* wrath here tyr'ed it selfe in vaine.
> In vaine did *Warbecks tragick Pageant* here,
> With *Armes* as weake, as his false *clayme,* appeare.
> The *Painted Rose* was here discern'ed too well,
> All his false *Leaves* soone lost their hue and fell.
> Much of white fame did this good action get;
> And *Henries Sword* beares witnesse still of it.
> Alas, thow wisest *King,* what has thow donne?
> They'le use it 'gainst thy best and greatest Sonne.
> Againe they prove their faith, and nobly fight
> 'Gainst *Sword,* and *Famine,* and the *Cornish might.*
> The *Cornish* then *rebell,* the *Cornish fall;*
> Their strength (wee see) and boldnes is not all.
> The *Causes* change now changes both their doomes;
> *Isca* rebells, and *Cornwall* overcomes.
>
> (2.283–306)

While this portrait of the West Country adopts political associations from legal and constitutional disputes of the time by alluding to British legend, it also relies upon and invokes the recent growth of and taste for local history writing. John Stow's *Survey of London* (1598) and Richard Carew's *Survey of Cornwall* (1602) are prominent examples of this important trend in historical research that began toward the end of Elizabeth's reign.[25]

Cowley's treatment of Exeter here links directly with this kind of history, for one of the more systematic examples of the genre is a history of that very city. John Hooker, "alias Vowel," served as chamberlain of Exeter from 1555 until his death in 1601. Afflicted with what was becoming a mania for antiquarian research, Hooker spent much of his working life collecting and cataloguing city records.[26] He is better known, perhaps, for editing and revising Holinshed's *Chronicle* (1577). Hooker's revised edition, for which he hired the services of other antiquarians, appeared in three volumes between 1586 and 1587. Unhappily for Hooker and his fellow workers, some of their additions to the original "relating to contemporary politics raised the wrath of the queen, and caused the edition to undergo serious castration."[27] Among the sections not affected by the censorial paranoia of Elizabeth and her Privy Council was the fruit of Hooker's own research into the local history of Exeter. In volume 3 of the revised Holinshed, untouched by the censor, appears "the description of the citie of Excester, and of the sundrie assaults given to the same: collected and gathered by John Vowell (alias Hooker), gentleman and chamberlaine of the same."[28] The description interrupts Holinshed's account of Devon and Cornwall, just when it is describing the rebellion which took place in the West Country in 1552, during the reign of Edward VI. Hooker's history of his home city was separately published twice, in London (1575) and Exeter (1583). There are, in addition, several manuscript copies in Oxford where Cowley composed his epic.[29]

Whether or not Cowley knew Hooker's work, Exeter's history was clearly celebrated for its rebelliousness. Cowley gives his most extensive description of a city which had not only a rich and varied past, but a detailed written history arranged around the same theme of rebellion. Poet and local historian agree that Exeter was, and always had been, a city famed for rebellion and siege. In Cowley as in Denham, topographical history becomes a strategy of political rhetoric. Like Denham's Windsor, Cowley's Exeter is a "mighty Embleme" that displays those moral qualities with which his account opens. The city itself is "stubborne," "ancient, strong and factious"; all qualities exemplified in the brief history of the city which follows. When the account arrives at contemporary disputes, Cowley conflates the city with its defense of the parliamentary forces in one of his limpest lines: "The *Causes* change now changes both their doomes; / *Isca* rebells, and *Cornwall* overcomes" (2.305–6). More frequently, Cowley represents battles by recounting the history of what else happened there, though sometimes his political attitude is less directly expressed than here. Sometimes he pretends to be on neither side, declaring for peace rather than a bloody victory for either of the embattled parties. Here he uses the same general strategy of finding historical precedents, but this time subordinates it to a literary device much used in the *Polyolbion,* personification of place:

> *Worc'ester* first saw't, and trembled at the View,
> Too well the ills of *civill warr* she knew.
> Twise did the flames of old her towers invade,
> Twise cal'd she in vaine for her owne *Severnes* Ayd.

>   (1.181–84)

Although damaged by war several times, Worcester had indeed been set on fire only twice before—during the reigns of William II in 1088 and Stephen in 1150.[30] Cowley recalls these precedents as items in the memory of a personified city, a memory that reminds the seemingly impartial city to fear the impending battle. Later, when Cowley first introduces Birmingham disparagingly by associating the city with an ancient Midlands tribe, his tone carries contempt: "Ye bold *Cornavian* race, from hence begin / Your *Lesson,* from hence dread th'Effects of *Sinne*" (2.69–70). Royalists did, in general, sneer at Birmingham, but there seems little reason for Cowley to have linked the Cornavii with that contempt. This suggests, presumably, that the city's political support for Parliamentary forces follows a tribal characteristic, in a further instance of some ancient pride, a sin that Prince Rupert will now punish. In fact, Rupert's atrocities against the inhabitants of Birmingham—which Cowley mystifies in suitably indignant terms (1.85–94)—might more justly be called sinful.[31] Lichfield, on the other hand, has historical associations that make it a stronghold of traditional religious authority. The Parliamentary troops who commit blasphemy by violating that past only strengthen their foes:

> Not here, oh, doe not here proud Ensignes spread,
> To'affright the *Ghost* of *Canonized Ced.*
> The soules of thowsand *Bishops* midst yee stand,
> And with heard prayers adde strength to *Ruperts* hand.
>
> (2.101–4)

The souls of dead bishops support, after all, the side of the king and his forces.

Once he has thus broken down the general course of the war into local and regional episodes, Cowley represents the place in historical terms or in more generally allegorical terms that rely on literary and legendary associations for their political import. He transforms Kineton, for instance, where the first major battle of the war took place and where, after a year, Charles and Henrietta Maria were reunited after a long separation, from a place of martial tension (1.207–30) into a locus of peace and harmony (1.491–508). Both of Cowley's descriptions resemble scenes from a court masque which opens in balanced opposition and ends in marital concord and harmony.[32]

The first scene of Cowley's Kineton masque opens just before the battle of October 1642, when the contending armies meet. The passage is worth giving in full for the baroque allegorical detail, the symbolic use of space, the attention to dramatic particulars of costume and scene, and the subordination of artistic concerns to partisan polemic:

> On two faire *Hills* both Armies next are seene,
> Th'affrighted *Valley* sighes and sweats betweene.
> Here *Angells* did with faire expectance stay
> And wisht good thinges to a *King* as mild as *they*.
> There *Fiends* with hungry waiting did abide;
> And curst both but spur'd on the guilty side.
> Here stood *Religion,* her lookes gently sage;
> *Aged,* but more comely for her *age*.
> There *Schisme,* old *Hag,* but seeming young appeares,
> As *snakes* by casting skin renew their yeares.
> Undecent rags of severall dies she wore
> And in her hands torne *Liturgies* she bore.
> Here *Loyalty* an humble *Crosse* displaid,
> And still as *Charles* past by she bowd and prayd.
> *Sedition* there her crimson *Banner* spreads,
> Shakes all her Hands, and roares with all her Heads.
> Her knotty haires were with dire *Serpents* twist,
> And all her *Serpents* at each other hist.
> Here stood white *Truth* and her owne *Host* do's blesse,
> Clad with those *Armes* of *Proofe,* her *Nakednesse*.
> There *Perjuries* like *Canon* roar'd alowd,
> And *Lies* flew thicke like *Cannons* smoaky *Clowd*.
> Here *Learning* and th'Arts met; as much they fear'd,
> As when the *Huns* of old and Goths appear'd.
> What should they doe? unapt themselves to fight,
> They promised noble pens the Acts to write.
> There *Ignorance* advanc'd, and Joyd to spy,
> Soe many that durst fight they knew not why.
> From those who most the slow-sould *Monkes* disdaine,
> From those she hopes for th'old *Monks* Age againe.
> Here *Mercy* waits with sad but gentle looke
> (Never, alas, had she her *Charles* forsooke).
> For *Mercy* on her *friends* to heaven she cries
> Whilst *Justice* pluckes down *Justice* from the Skies.
> *Oppression* there, *Rapine* and *Murther* stood,
> Ready as was the Field to drinke their blood.
> A thousand wronged Spirits amongst them moand,

> And thrice the *Ghost* of mighty *Strafford* groand.
> Now flew their *Canon* thicke through wounded Aire,
> Sent to defend and kill their *Sovereigne* there.
> More than *Hee* them, the *Bullets* fear'd his head,
> And at his feete lay innocently dead.
> They knew not what those men that shot them ment,
> And acted their *pretence,* not their *intent.*
>
> (1.207–50)

On February 3, 1633, ten years before Cowley wrote these lines, Justice had indeed descended in just this fashion at the Banqueting Hall in Whitehall in James Shirley's masque *The Triumph of Peace.* Two years later, Rubens' famous apotheosis of James Stuart, supported by figures of Justice and Religion, and surrounded by Victory, Wisdom, and an angelic host—an emblematic tableau not unlike Cowley's—would decorate the ceiling of that same center of Stuart culture. Cowley's figure of Sedition here reminds us of Inigo Jones's Furies for Davenant's *Salmacida Spolia* of 1640.[33] Shirley's and Davenant's masques typically address precise and immediate political concerns by employing members of their courtly "audience" to perform allegorical speeches in emblematic costumes. In Cowley's text, the allegorical personifications have become conventional-ized echoes of a cultural moment that has passed away. We can, however, note that as David Trotter observes,[34] Cowley balances sets of couplets against each other, thereby setting the opposing forces in contrast: here angels, there fiends, here religion, there schism. At the same time, he uses the prepositions to place himself and his reader directly on the king's side.

A year later, the scene at Kineton changes to the "Place that Fortune did approve, / To bee the noblest *Scene* of *war* and *Love.*" The reunion of the king and queen becomes a historical enactment of the reconcilia-tion of Mars and Venus in Cowley's account, an event complete with royalist cupids who playfully rout the ghosts of Parliamentary troops.[35] Politicization of the landscape by personification, as suggested here by the courtliness of Edgehill the "happy *Mount,*" is common throughout Cowley's poems and the political verse of the time generally. The sites of battles that Cowley claims for royalist victories—such as Powick Bridge and Kineton—appear to be uncommitted, fearful if anything, and gen-erally wish that there were no war (1.181–82, 1.208). Yet towns that support the Parliamentary army—such as Bristol, Exeter, and Birmingham—are invariably portrayed as intending evil (2.216–17, 2.277–78, 2.85–94).

COWLEY AND THE STUART CAUSE

In transforming recent events into poetry almost as they occurred, Cowley uses many different kinds of rhetorical and historical strategies in order to convey, as convincingly as possibly, his own and his party's views. He aims, not simply to glorify the crown, but to legitimate the war itself by showing how it promises victory for the king's side. We need to read *The Civil War* within the general context of a nation taking sides, of men trying to avoid fighting or paying for a war that many of them did not want, and of others whose careers and beliefs depended upon persuading others to fight or pay. For Cowley desires less to relay information than to win and maintain support for the king's army, showing it to be the natural, true, godly side destined to win. In addition to the carefully controlled presentation of selected events, *The Civil War* contains other persuasive techniques, matters of feeling rather than of thinking, aimed at molding our attitude toward the version of events presented.

Pritchard usefully reminds us of "a common epic pattern," found in Tasso and Milton. "In this pattern," he suggests, "the forces of good secure an initial success; there is then an upsurge of the forces of evil, but in the conclusion good achieves an overwhelming triumph" (p. 37). Pritchard makes this suggestion to clarify Cowley's epic pretensions rather than to help analyze the poem's affective design. The pattern he describes owes much to the generic links between epic and tragedy as they were conceived of in mid-seventeenth-century critical theory, especially their common affective purpose.[36] Further, *The Civil War* organizes past and recent history in accordance with an affective design that generates sympathy for the king's cause, arouses indignation at the enemy and their successes, and seeks to convince us of relentless historical movement toward a divinely ordained royalist victory.

From the opening lines of the poem, Cowley's rhetoric has urged us to agree that the times have degenerated by provoking our indignation at present civil discords which deviate from the nation's natural and historical conditions of imperial power. The series of recent military engagements in book 1 channels that indignation into martial euphoria by focusing almost exclusively on the excitement of inevitable royalist victory. But the account of recent fighting that opens book 2 recounts the martyrdom of royalist officers, turning patriotic excitement into desire for revenge. The much lamented death of Sir Bevil Grenvill may have aroused proper heroic fury in book 1:[37]

> Hee sold like *Decius* his devoted breath,
> And left the *Commonwealth* Heyre to his *Death*.
> Haile, mighty *Ghost,* looke from on high and see,
> How much our Hands and Swords remembred thee.
> On *Roundway Downe,* our rage for thy great fall,
> Whet all our Spirits, and made us *Greenvills* all.
>
> (1.467–72)

But his death is immediately transformed into an incentive that promises future victory. In book 2, Cowley retunes his elegiac lyre to a pastoral mode, sounding a more plangent note of regret conventionally evoked by the passing of some rare and precious beauty of nature. He sings the passing of Charles Cavendish:

> At last old *Gainesbrow* his sad fall beheld;
> And all along *Trents* mournfull waters swelld.
> Too few the teares of his owne *Spring* hee thought,
> Too few the waves that thirty *Rivers* brought.
> The sullen Streame crept silent by his shore,
> Mute as the *Fish* his populous current bore.
> Whilst Hee, with thowsand foes strow'ed lifelesse by,
> In all the *triumphs* of brave *Death* did ly.
> Like some fair *Flower,* which *Morne* saw freshly gay,
> In the feilds generall ruine mowne away.
> The *Hyancinth,* or purple *Violet,*
> Just languishing, his coloured *Light* just set.
> Ill mixt it lies amidst th'ignobler *Grasse;*
> The country *daughters* sigh as by'it they passe.
>
> (2.143–56)

This elegiac shift from heroic fury to pastoral consolation has a specific epic precedent in the *Aeneid*.[38] Having engaged sympathy for the royalist dead, Cowley can close his account of military events in book 2 by reminding us that setbacks to a cause often promise future victory. He warns the recalcitrant city of Plymouth to "Beware"

> for if future thinges,
> Nere faile my prophesing *Muse,* in what shee sings,
> Thy conquest soone fame from my pen shall git.

(2.353–35)

With this assurance, Cowley turns from recent history to the council in hell which closes book 2; another topic of epic precedent that invites us to share this poet's scorn for the rebels condemned there. The devil urges infernal spirits to infect the souls of Englishmen with the plague of rebellion. He directs them to London:

> Goe then, hast all to Luds seditious Towne;
> Yee know, and love't, scarce Hell is more your owne.
> There's nothing now your great designe to stay,
> God, and his troubl'esome Spir'its are gonne away.

(2.538–41)

As if without a break, book 3 opens with the arrival and dispersal of these carriers of discord in the city which barred its king:

> Hee spoke, and what hee spoke was soone obeyd;
> Hast to their London prey the Furies made.
> The gapeing ground with naturall joy made roome,
> For this old monstrous burden of her wombe.
> . . .
> The rebell Passions they below unchaine,
> And licence that wild Multitude to raigne.
> Theyr business done, home fled the night and they;
> But scarce could Natures selfe drive on the day.

(3.1–4, 17–20)

Conventional expressions of contempt for London permeated royalist poetry and feeling at the time. As poet of the king's cause, Cowley could hardly avoid arousing savage fury at what many thought to be the center of rebellion. When Cowley was writing, London had already completed what David Underdown calls "its first, and moderate revolution."[39] Royalist contempt for the city that had early and eagerly taken up arms against the king was fierce.[40] To Sir Edward Walker, royalist secretary-at-war and, even in the eyes of other royalists, a great snob,[41] London was "the head and fountain of this detested rebellion."[42] To Clarendon,

London was less a fountain than a "sink of the ill humours of the kingdom." (3.57).

Cowley registers this contempt for London by directing infernal spirits there. He describes their night's work in a mock heroic catalogue that decides various political and religious sectarian movements of the time. Although ordering the sects according to related religious beliefs, he characterizes them all as threats to the established political order rather than to religious orthodoxy. Parliamentary "Traytors," puritan ministers, the ever-hated mob are all satanically infected with fantasies of rebellion:

> Up rose the mighty Traytours, in whose brests,
> The guilt of all our ills soe tamely rests,
> By sleepeing now they'advanc'ed our ruine more,
> Then by long watchings they'had donne oft before.
> Strait, like thick fumes, into their braines arise,
> Thowsand rich slander, thowsand usefull Lies.
> A thowsand arts and thowsand slights they frame
> T'avert the dangers of sweet Peaces name.
> To Westminster they hast, and fondly there,
> Talk, plot, conspire, vote, cov'enant, and declare.
> New feares, new hopes, pretences new they show,
> Whilst ore the wondring Towne their nets they throw.[43]
> Up rose their Preists (the viperous brood that dare
> With their owne mouths their beawteous Mother tare).
> Their walking noysy diligence nere will cease;
> They roare, and sigh, and pray, and eate'gainst peace.
> Up rose the base Mechanicks, and the Rout,
> And cry'd, Noe peace, th'astonisht streets throughout.
> Here, injur'd Church, thy strong avendgment see;
> The same noyse plucks downe Peace, that pluckt down thee.
>
> (3.25–44)

In part, the satire here depends upon erasing those differences in belief, ideology, and political significance that distinguished the various oppositional groups; instead, they are all treated as irrational and diabolic. The lists of verbs (lines 34, 40) characterize both Parliamentarian and minister by suggesting their common tendency to be overactive and erratic: many things at once, as it were, but nothing long. Cowley marches out the combined forces of the satanic army in their various colors and ranks:

> Three thowsand hot-brained Calvinists there came;
> Wild men, that blot their great Reformers Name.
>   . . .
> The Independents their two thowsand sent;
> Who into Raggs the seamelesse Vesture rent.
>   . . .
> The dismall Haer'esy of wild Muncers crew,
> Heither twelve hundred stout Mechanicks drew.
>   (3.59–60, 83–84, 87–88)

And so on, through Brownists (3.111–12), followers of Novatus (3.123–28), Adamites (3.129–36), Pelagians (3.137–42), Arians (3.143–56), and other sects (3.157–86).[44] Cowley insists that this army is held together only by a common bond of rebellion and is contemptible in its lack of any other principle of organization: "Such quarreling Sects, Spirits of soe different kind, / Nothing but loved Rebellion could have joynd" (3.191–92).

The final section of the third book describes the royalist defeat at Newbury, laments royalist losses, and culminates in an elegy for Lord Falkland. It displaces satiric contempt and derision for the enemy in favor of martial fury and rage once again: "Wretches, your losse will now triumphant bee, / You'le Falkland name when wee name Victorie" (3.623–24). But the text ends with a penitential prayer:

> Yet rather, gracious God, stop here thine hand,
> And let this losse excuse our perishing Land,
>   . . .
> Thinke on our sufferings, and sheath then againe;
> Our Sinnes are great, but Falkland too is slaine.
>   (3.639–40, 647–48)

COWLEY'S "TROWBLED MUSE" AND AUGUSTAN POETICS

The view that Cowley abandoned his epic at this point while in the midst of composition may accurately describe events, but may equally prove misleading in assessing and understanding not only what Cowley did achieve, but also the circumstances and constraints conditioning that achievement. Cowley's own account of why he stopped work on the poem, which appears in the preface to his *Poems* of 1656, suggests the causes were primarily political, but also literary. "I have," he writes:

> cast away all such pieces as I wrote during the time of the late troubles, with any relation to the differences that caused them; as among others, *three Books of the Civil War it self,* reaching as far as the first *Battel* of *Newbury,* where the succeeding *misfortunes* of the *party* stopt the *work;* for it is so uncustomary, as to become almost *ridiculous,* to make Lawrels for the *Conquered.*[45]

Taking him at his word, Pritchard observes that the poem "was overtaken by history before it was completed," adding that Cowley "may have been dissatisfied ... with the literary qualities of the work" (pp. 4, 5). Certainly, Cowley did stop writing *The Civil War,* but only after having finished book 3, in length and scope comparable to the other two. Dissatisfied with Pritchard's suggestion, David Trotter has argued that "the poem had begun to fail, had moved into conflict with itself, *before* history started to provide the wrong plot" (p. 18). Trotter aims throughout his discussion of *The Civil War* to advance the cause of organic formalism by "demonstrat[ing] the validity ... of [a] relative disregard of political and social context" (p. 6), a position that enables him to treat the poem as a failure since, apparently, it displays "an irresolvable antagonism between modes" (p. 18).

Clearly *The Civil War* brings together an astonishing variety of generic, modal, and stylistic strategies, shifting from arcadian nostalgia to heroic fury, from pastoral to elegaic, from satire to panegyric. But as Barbara Lewalski has shown in her study of the genres of *Paradise Lost,* an encyclopedic approach to generic inclusiveness was—in keeping with Tasso's *Discourses*—very much the hallmark of Renaissance epic generally.[46] Arguing that *The Civil War* fails because it mixes generic features reveals a misunderstanding of contemporary heroic poetry, both its theory and its practice. Leaving aside the pseudoquestion of whether Cowley's poem "failed" simply because it was unfinished, I would suggest that Renaissance epic theory partly provides the terms in which Cowley's enterprise encountered insuperable problems, and, with Howard Erskine-Hill and Margaret Doody, I would argue that the conditions of English Augustanism are to be found in the literary-political relations of the mid-seventeenth century.

While writing that "the argument of the best epic should be based on history," Tasso warns of the danger of writing on contemporary matters.[47] Significantly, he employs a simile based upon the visual arts:

> Between modern and ancient times, let [the epic poet] choose those of a convenient remoteness from memory, as a painter sets his picture not too

close to our eyes, nor yet so far away that it cannot be recognized, but in the proper lighting at the proper height. (Pp. 52–53)

Since "the action that is to come under the epic poet's art must be noble, illustrious, and great" (p. 42), the poet who attempts an epic on contemporary events will inevitably find himself positioned too close to his subject to be able to see it in its entirety. This, surely, describes Cowley's predicament. And since that subject must be noble, illustrious, and great, a further problem arises that Davenant points out in the "Preface" to his *Gondibert* (1650), a text that owes a good deal to Tasso's *Discourses*. "Men," he writes:

> even of the best education, discover their eyes to be weak when they look upon the glory of Vertue, which is great actions, and rather endure it at a distance than neer, being more apt to believe and love the renown of Predecessors then of Contemporaries, whose deeds, excelling theirs in their own sight, seem to upbraid them, and are not reverenc'd as examples of Vertue, but envy'd as the favours of Fortune.[48]

As Davenant here suggests, a contemporary subject invariably arouses sentiments inappropriate for the dignity of a heroic poem. Rather than epic wonder and admiration at the exceptional virtues of past heroes, the poet who treats recent events in a heroic manner may well arouse envy and resentment. Such a poet necessarily takes sides, though impartiality was, to Hobbes at least, one of the chief virtues of the heroic poem.[49] Within the terms provided by Renaissance epic theory, the problem facing Cowley in *The Civil Wars* was not that of an irreconcilable conflict of modes caused by generic variety, but the need to reconcile partisan interests with the formal requirements of an epic design—how to inscribe royalist victory across the face of the continuing present as though it were the already completed past.

Once victory for Cowley's party became more distant, the scale of contemporary events, his subject, became broader than he might at first have expected. The complete and entire action suited to treatment by heroic poetry expanded beyond the poet's range of vision. With the death of Falkland, Cowley first openly acknowledges his own presence in the poem as more than an apparently impartial observer. He self-consciously draws attention to his own participatory role within the course of continuing events when he reports that

> A Muse stood by me, and just then I writ
> My Kings great acts in Verses not unfit.
> The trowbled Muse fell shapelesse into aire,
> Instead of Inck dropt from my Pen a Teare.

(3. 545–58)

There is nothing else quite like this in the entire text, so personal despite the conventionality of the elegiac topos. Cowley's immediate topic—the death of the royalist general Falkland—does not account for his use of inexpressibility to emphasize the poem's heroic style and subject. With the dissolution of his muse into formlessness the poet enters his own poem in order to admit that his art can no longer record events with which he himself is involved. Cowley's stance has changed from that of poet historian with a pretense of detachment to that of an active agent who admits himself into the events being described. When the unimaginable happens, after the defeat at Newbury where the royalist party lost control of historical forces, the crown's poet appears in his poem, self-consciously confessing that he himself is as much part of the continuing process of history as the events he describes. Within that admission, Cowley further acknowledges the difficulty of an art designed to celebrate the "Kings great acts in Verses not unfit" when the "trowbled Muse fell shapelesse."

As much as Cowley's use of the "heroic" couplet, the unfinished or unfinishable status of his epic fragment deserve serious consideration as an emergent characteristic of English historical poetry once poets seek to treat contemporary events in the high style of the heroic and discover the inadequacy of tropes based on analogy. The epic fragment, the brief epic, the mock epic, the incomplete or unfinished epic, *Annus Mirabilis,* Pope's *Brutus* fragment and his "Opus Magnum," even Cowley's *Davideis;* the piece of an unwritable epic is surely a *typical* form of English historical poetry for two generations of major poets. The English Augustan enterprise centers on just this endeavor to achieve a national epic. Cowley could not finish the epic of England's delivery from forces of Parliamentary darkness by the swords of a Stuart army, but in closing the third book in a revelation of his direct personal involvement with the political events of his poem, he does achieve the only possible form of closure available.[50] And if that very fact casts serious doubt upon his artistry in its reliance on traditional forms, its use of the spatial mode of historical representation, and its expression of overt partisan allegiances to the

Stuart cause, then the key importance of this text in the transitional history of English Augustanism is clear. Cowley sets out to treat contemporary events as a closed narrative. The sequence of events opens with the specific disruption of a prior order and aims for a resolution coinciding with the end of that sequence and the reimposition of order. Hence the ambiguous status of the troubled Muse falling shapeless, for *The Civil War* remains an open text despite its evident attempt to reach a (politically acceptable) closure. Yet its fragmentary or uncompleted character is only partially attributable to its "failure" to provide the ever-deferred but always-expected ending, to the poet's inability to bring a final and complete closed order to bear upon contemporary events, since this "failure" to provide the pleasure of the expected is also an attitudinal problem: how could a humanist like Cowley continue legitimating the slaughter of his countrymen without a more sophisticated argumentative design that would enable him to treat such events in a royalist epic? If we would admire the poetry for fusing so many styles and modes within an overall epic design that signals the crises out of which Augustan heroic, panegyric, and satiric textualities emerge, we might also admires its refusal to allow the poet to continue. How could a native English muse, even of so bloodthirsty a genre as epic, permit Cowley to continue legitimating civil slaughter?

But if we insist that the poem fails nevertheless, then the problem surely lies in the way it views contemporary events with its back to the future even as it anticipates much of what is best in later political poetry. Cowley, we have seen, adopts the conventional position of measuring the present by analogy with the past. When he treats the present directly, he does so by allegorizing or displacing it in the Elizabethan and Jacobean fashion which emphasizes the pageantry of royal life transforming itself perpetually into a symbolic realm of universal signification. This, of course, is Denham's compromise too in the "allegorical" ending of *Cooper's Hill*. If we would speak of Cowley's poem as in any respect a failure, we surely must speak of the tensions between the poet's political partiality and his commitments to a humanist historiography that valorizes a past which is constituted by the will to power of heroic leaders.

Heroes die. In the closing prayer, Cowley gestures toward the future in what is surely an expression of horror at the unknowable, a horror that causes him to recoil and retreat, once again, to a summary of the recent past:

> If this red warre last still, it will not leave,
> Enough behind great Falklands death to greive;
> Wee have offended much, but there has binne
> Whole Hecatombs oft slaughtered for our Sinne.
> Thinke on our sufferings, and sheath then againe;
> Our Sinnes are great, but Falkland too is slaine.
>
> (3.643–48)

In modern German one can distinguish between two senses of *history* available in English as variant meanings of the same word. *Historie* suggest a completed narrative action, associated exclusively with the past, while *Geschichte* "can refer to a process including past, present, and future."[51] This latter sense becomes available with developments in historical theory usually associated with Vico and the eighteenth century. Cowley, by writing on contemporary matters as they happen, finds himself forced to attempt the latter kind of history, but without a model of history as process to guide him. Whether Cowley had continued his poem or not, the difficulty facing his enterprise was the eventual inadequacy of his model of historical representation, one based on the spatialization of historical process in the name of heroic individualism. What Cowley represents as contemporary history—the course of the war from its origins to a future royalist victory—is a foreclosed set of incidents predetermined by his artistic and political design and his consequent commitment to making present events accountable to the past. Cowley's interpretation leads him to portray his own times as one of those periodic alterations from historically normal conditions of monarchic power that have never, previously, succeeded in subverting royal authority.

In the case of poets writing on contemporary events we may modify Carr's formula. The poet's commitment to the analogy with the past determines the point in the historical procession in which the poet finds himself: usually during the early modern period, with his back to the future. The way poets represent current events is finally determined not only by their deliberate partisan purposes, but also by the very manner in which they understand and represent historical process, spatializing temporality through chronology's perspective glass and history's ledger, assuming a sovereignty of vision and historical knowledge that makes radical social transformation unthinkable.

5
The Unprecedented Future

The Historian by running back to Ages past, and then forward to present Affairs, comparing one with the other, can give a verdict of the State, well near Prophetick.

—EDWARD CHAMBERLAIN (1647)[1]

WHEN BRECHT chose to set two of his most important exercises in anti-Aristotelian "epic" theater in the seventeenth century, the choice was by no means arbitrary. If the modern age begins with Galileo looking through his telescope, it does so not only because he revolutionized the possibilities of space, that "last frontier," but because he also posed the potentially more revolutionary question of the as-yet-unimagined future in terms of a scientific problematic. In *Mother Courage* the necessity of war for the advancement of the capitalist mode of production provides the foreground of Brecht's dramatic design—to analyze the Thirty Years War as the crucial episode in the transition from feudalism to capitalism, a class war that signals the victory of those in control of technology and the circuits of "free" trade rather than the generals or armies on either side. His eponymous hero lives off the war by entering the circuits of investment and profit made necessary and possible by the war economy, though in entirely different circumstances from those of the successful professional soldiers or the industrialists and businessmen who manufactured and traded the weapons. If the war ends, Courage will be unemployed. By the time the war ended, many men "not of princely birth" had risen to fame and wealth by becoming generals.[2] When the war was over, most real wealth in Europe had changed hands. In Bohemia alone, the Confiscation Committee "took possession of some 500 estates ... worth an estimated 43 million florins ... no less than two-thirds of all the land in the kingdom."[3] When the war was over, the weapons and allied industries had achieved unprecedented importance and new fortunes had been made; even the great protestant hero Gustavus Adolphus helped finance his entry into the war with profits made from exporting

Swedish copper throughout Europe during the early years of the war.[4] The economics of war demand that the development of productive forces necessarily take the form of the development of destructive forces. Estimates of the percentage of the population killed in European wars indicate a slow rise from 2.5 percent in the twelfth century to 5.9 percent during the sixteenth. With the technological advances in munitions of the seventeenth century, the figure jumps to 15.6 percent, a rise comparable only to that between the nineteenth and the first half of the twentieth century when, once again, technological advances enable the death count to leap from 16.3 percent to 38.9 percent.[5] During the seventeenth century, the real conditions of war dislocated it from its conventional heroic values, or, as Brecht shows, courage became a virtue that civil society could no longer afford.

We have already seen that, in Butterfield's term, "historical mindedness" constantly shifts with alterations in political power and institutions. But belief in heroes seems to have stayed alive in the poetic struggle for control over the national memory. When, during the military and political crises of the 1640s, poets began speculating about what the future might hold, they kept one eye on the past while trying to anticipate an ever imminent, but never quite realized, new age unlike any that had ever been. Nostalgia continues, as in every new age, but hope for the nation's future dominates the poetry of the Commonwealth. This change in historical perspective, from the past to the future, offers to free the poet who, writing on contemporary events as Cowley does in *The Civil War*, finds his muse must desert him when he tries to write about the war. And it provided this freedom without entirely compromising the supposed detachment of the artist from historical conditions.

To imagine the future, poets must not only be well versed in history and politics, they must also be able to invent. In 1656 John Collop writes that the poet

> must have ravell'd times, and Kingdoms through,
> And when the world oreview'd, can make a new.
> A *Plato's* Commonwealth, who can outdo?
> A *Mores* Utopia, and *Atlantis* too.[6]

Writing at the highest moment of the Commonwealth, Collop historicizes the ideal world of the poet's imagination by comparing it with ideal political states, not with cities of God or arcadian fairylands in which

Nature pours forth her bounty to a fortunate people. The fictitious world of the poet's imagination still constitutes an ideal, but it has become a political ideal achieved through human contrivance rather than divine intervention; and it exists in the future, not the irrevocable past.

The appeal to the future dominates the hagiographic and elegiac poetry written on Charles I's execution, often giving rise to outrageous fantasies that placed this unprecedented historical event outside the realm of human possibility. Poets supporting the various interregnum governments and Cromwell's Protectorate exploited the Stuart fashion for neoclassical precedents from imperial Rome as part of a systematic attempt to link Roman republicanism and imperial power with a new age of global civilization and commercial dominion under the new, kingless English republic. This Augustan compromise, the marriage of arms and arts which once seemed impossible to Daniel, becomes central to the heroic poetry of the later seventeenth century. The preconditions of Augustan heroic poetry develop from the political turmoil of the first part of the seventeenth century to become dominant between the execution of Charles Stuart in 1649—an event which temporarily devalued the appeal to the past and the divinity of monarchic dynasties—and the death of Cromwell, the "best of ordinary men," in 1658. While politicians struggled to gain control of what they perceived to be historical forces— the institutions of domestic government, world trade, and pubic opinion—poets set to work speculating about the future.

EXECUTION POEMS, 1649

Among the most often reprinted of the many elegies written about Charles's execution on January 30, 1649, James Graham's epitaph, "Upon the death of King *Charles* the first," written—the legend goes—"with the point of his Sword"—uses direct formal variations that illustrate the intimate link between poetic form and ideological design to express the frustrated rage of the group which has just lost control of the forces of history.[7] To create the feeling appropriate for the public execution of a king, poets must change their art and thereby regain control over the changing times:

> GReat! Good! & Just! could I but rate
> My griefs, and thy too rigid fate,
> I'de weep the world to such a strain
> As it should deluge once again.

> But since thy loud tongu'd blood demands supply
> More from *Briareus* hands than *Argus* eye,
> I'de sing thy obsequies with Trumpets sounds,
> And write thy Epitaph with blood and wounds.

Rejecting the conventional consolation of inexpressible but lachrymose grief, Graham instead transforms the elegiac form itself into a heroic call for military action. Until the "but" of the fifth line, the conditional mood of the octosyllabic lines registers the refusal to become reconciled to another's death common to heroic elegy. The mourner's tears *would,* like a second flood, purge the land of those sinners involved in the king's death, were he to shed them. With the "but," however, mood and verse alter to offer a more adequate response to the king's execution: an unprecedented event requiring artistic innovation. Commitment replaces consolation; redemptive purgation is rejected in favor of revenge; Old Testament history is replaced by Greek legend. In full heroic pentameters, the poet turns to announce that he will emulate the hundred-armed Briareus instead of the hundred-eyed Argus: instead of participating by watching and weeping merely, he will call for action. The poet himself demands an active participation in history, preferring the role of avenging agent rather than that of grief-stricken maker of memorials.

This sense that Charles's execution demanded a new response, one that, in turn, required artistic change and a new sense of the poet's intervention in history, constantly appears in elegiac poems published during the spring of 1649.[8] Reprinted several times, *Chronostichon* expresses a typical view that the execution was without precedent in the whole of Christian history. The poet varies a common pastoral topos:

> Such a Fall
> Great *Christendom* ne're Pattern'd; and 'twas strange
> Earth's Center reel'd not at this dismal *Change*.[9]

"Fall" here works either way, recalling at once the sin against divine law that began human history as well as the dismembered head dropping. Charles's execution overturned the very order of history, tearing apart the symbolic fabric essential to royal hegemony just as Adam broke the original covenant and consigned humanity to history. Other poets represented this shift in the historical paradigm in more secular terms. One thought the execution terrifying because, while it was without precedent,

the political implications could be imagined only too easily—leveling of
the hierarchy leading to anarchy:

> few have levell'd at a Princess fall,
> But such whose claim did for succession call:
> Whose bordering title tyr'd to be kept down,
> Cast trains lesse for his ruine, then his Crown.
> But here the desperate Rebell strikes at sway,
> Not for who shall succeed, but that none may.[10]

Elegists made a great deal of how this king's death was without
historical precedent. To Bishop Henry King, the act was simply "Treason
sublim'd, / That cannot by a parallell be rim'd."[11] He later placed the
king's death in a larger historical context as an event of singular
importance:

> CALL for amazed thoughts, a wounded sense
> And bleeding hearts at our intelligence.
> Call for that Trump of Death, the Mandrake's groan
> Which kills the hearers: this benefits alone
> Our story which through times vast Calendar,
> Must stand without example or repair.[12]

Because this "story" was without past "example or repair," poets
often turned to the future for a perspective that might enable them to
represent Charles's death as a distant past event, seen as if it had taken
place long ago. In characteristically partisan fashion, the poet of *Chronostichon* conflates royalist loss of power with the impending eclipse of the
entire nation. The poet poses as one about to leave a country which, since
its history has been canceled, no longer offers any future for him:

> Farewel sad *Isle!* Farewel! Thy fatal *Glorie*
> Is Summ'd, Cast up, and Cancell'd in this *Storie.*

Yet in several poems, the execution of the king marks the arrival of a
new age. Thomas Pierce compares Charles with Christ since both introduce new eras in human history:

> Posterity will say, he should have dy'd
> No other *Death,* then by being *Crucifi'd.*

> And their renownedst *Epocha* will be
> *Great Charles his Death,* next *Christ's Nativity.*[13]

Another elegist tropes on the king as a singular text that will defy future interpretation:

> Unvalued CHARLS: Thou art so hard a Text,
> Writ in one Age, not understood i'th'next.[14]

Fear that this might happen urged one poet to instruct future historians what they were to say of the dead king:

> But Thou blest CHARLS, whom Historie shall stile
> The *Princelie Proto-Martyr* of this *Isle.*[15]

But against concern for the future or the past, the urgencies of the moment press hard in verses that insist upon the claims of the present:

> NO more of *Annals;* let great Rome grow mute
> In quoting *Catiline,* or recording *Brute:*
> *Britain* now wear's the Sock. . . . [16]

History must be rewritten. As so often with the announcement of new ages even in our times, this one requires not just the reinterpretation but also the rewriting of the past. Pierce agrees and envisages future opinion of those responsible for the king's death. Old Testament allusions used earlier in the decade to represent the corruption of the Stuart regime are turned against those who first uttered them:

> When *future times* shall look what *Plagues* befell
> *Aegypt* and *us,* by way of *Parallel,*
> They'l find at once presented to their *view*
> The *Frogs* and *Lice,* and *Independents* too.
> Onely this *signal difference* will be known
> 'Twixt those *Aegyptian* judgements and our *own,*
> Those were *Gods Armies;* but th'*effect* doth tell
> That these *our Vermin* are the *Host of Hell.*

The desire to rewrite history remained a persistent one, even if it meant pretending that the king had never been executed. While some elegists vicariously consoled themselves by imagining the judgment bound to fall upon those who had taken the king's life, Thomas Fairfax wanted to banish the event from history entirely:

> Oh lett that Day from time be blotted quitt
> And lett beleefe of't in next Age be waved
> In deepest silence th'Act Concealed might
> So that the Kingdoms Credit might be saved.[17]

It is a strange kind of elegy that suggests we pretend the death never took place, but such is the logic of necessity when it comes to "saving" the nation's future "credit."

More piously perhaps, Bishop Henry King wanted to keep the king's death very much part of the historical register. He was among those who were anxious that posterity would judge and condemn those who had seized power.

> England must write such annals of your reign
> Which all records of elder mischiefs stain.[18]

This poet also imagines a new royal age, one that will be governed by the second Charles who must now take over from his dead father:

> And now see! see! another *Phenix* rise!
> From the blest ashes of this Sacrifice!
> A Second CHARLS! who shall in fame asspire,
> And grow more Mightie then his *Princelie Sire.*[19]

Another elegist looks to the future, offering a precedent for the new king's arrival, a Roman one that becomes ubiquitous throughout the political poetry of the second half-century:

> May our young King as wisely build upon
> This bloody ground-work and Foundation,
> As young *Augustus* did on *Casars* blood.
> May glorious triumphs prove his title good.[20]

Whatever their differences in gesture and concern, these elegies consistently look to the future for a perspective suitable for viewing their unprecedented topic. By overtly drawing attention to the regicide as a momentous historical event, they stress its importance as the culmination of a past series of events. Two important consequences of this perspective also characterize the poetry written during the fifties on behalf of the victorious—or guilty—party, which sought to endorse the new regime inaugurated by the king's death. First, the past tends to recede in importance at a time when—as we saw with Cowley's *The Civil War*—it begins to prove inadequate for an understanding of the present. For several hundred years England had been ruled by monarchs; never before had the nation been constituted a republican commonwealth. Barons had rebelled against royal authority. But never before 1649 had the law itself been turned against the life of a king. References to the nation's past, which had been a staple of political poetry during the reigns of the early Stuarts, did not entirely disappear, but were displaced to a large extent by speculation about the nation's future under the new form of government. Second, when poets do refer to the past, they tend now to look back to Rome rather than to England and see, in the institutions and imperial success of the Roman republic, models for what they hope will be England's destiny now that, like Tarquin the Proud, Charles Stuart has been executed. Taken together, these two tendencies remind us how dependent poets still were upon the analogy with the past. The new emphasis on the future becomes a convenient artistic strategy that magnifies the present as being greater than anything that has gone before. Poets may have declared that the king's death marked a radical break with the past, but as they did so they continued ransacking Roman and biblical history for a source of past analogues. However unprecedented the events culminating in Charles's execution might have seemed, they had been brought about by men who "intended to defend what already existed, or was believed to exist," and not as part of a systematically deliberate revolutionary program for the future.[21]

COUNCIL OF STATE POEMS, 1649–1653

When Charles was executed on January 30, political power had already been assumed by the purged Rump Parliament which had voted on January 4

> That the people are, under God, the original of all just power ... that the commons of England, in parliament assembled, being chosen by, and representing the people, have the supreme power in this nation ... that whatsoever is enacted, hath the force of law; and all the people of this nation

are concluded thereby, although the consent and concurrence of king, or house of peers, be not had thereunto.[22]

Advanced in 1642 by extremists like Henry Parker, the theory of popular sovereignty had never before been put into practice by an English government. It is a radical theory, contemptuous of custom and tradition, a theory that enabled the Rump propagandists to ignore the nation's past whenever convenient by ascribing "the original of all just power" to the people, and then arguing from the necessity of present circumstances to justify alterations in governmental and legal institutions: *salus populi, suprema lex.*[23]

But the ideal of popular power created institutional and ideological difficulties too. Political thinkers supporting the new government set out to reform institutions in order to exercise and maintain sufficiently widespread support to secure the new regime. "Nothing," observes Blair Worden in his study of the Rump, "better illustrates the limits of seventeenth-century English radicalism than the faith displayed by reformers of almost every variety in the institutions of parliament."[24] For their part, poets were unaccustomed to praising any but the noblest heroes, let alone assemblies. At various times both poet and statesman would urge the crown on Cromwell, so great was the need for a traditionally heroic head of state whose power could be identified, isolated, and limited by custom, tradition, and law. By the time of Cromwell's death in 1658, divisions among those most concerned with government—Army leaders and Parliamentarians of various interests—proved greater than the newly constituted government could bear. But none of this was clear in 1649.

During the early days of February, directly after the king's death, the Rump set about consolidating their power by constitutional reforms.[25] On the fifth they abolished the House of Lords; on the seventh they declared that "the Office of a King in this nation and Ireland . . . is unnecessary, burthensom, and dangerous to the liberty, safety and publique interest of the people."[26] These revolutionary proceedings were passed as acts of Parliament on March 19 and 17, respectively. The king and Lords safely out of the way, the Commons proceeded to delegate supreme executive and legislative powers to an appointed Council of State by an act of February 13. Besides suppressing attempts to "maintain the pretended Tytle of Charles Stuart, eldest sonne of the late King," this council held power over the army, navy, national trade, internal revenues, foreign policy, and domestic administration for a term of one year.[27]

Monarchy had become oligarchy, the kingdom a commonwealth, the realm a republic.

If royalist poets generally viewed the execution as a turning point in world history, one that caused them anxiety for the future, at least one did not dispute that the transfer of power into the hands of the Council of State had really taken place. After listing the members, and slandering each of them, the author of *Tyrants Triumphant* acknowledges in dismay and horror:

> Yet these be they who must have all the sway,
> These are the Kings the *English* must obey,
> Here are the Pillars of the Common-weale,
> The Power Supream, from whence is no appeale.[28]

A key word here is "Kings," for it indicates one of the major ideological difficulties confronting those apologists of the new regime who faced the task of constructing a new political history adequate to the new form of government. Unlike previous English poets, these had to write in support of a republican oligarchy which had pretty much appointed itself to power rather than a single, dynastic hero who came to power with traditional authority and limitations. Across the face of a national culture traditionally constructed within the heroic tropes of patriarchal monarchy, their task was nothing less than to inscribe the new text of state.[29]

This problem was further complicated by literary practice which had long habituated poets to think of groups of people as fit objects for satire—as in *Tyrants Triumphant* and the third book of Cowley's *Civil War*. Panegyric usually praises only heroic individuals. Although royalist satirists had already singled out Cromwell for satiric attack by the early summer of 1649,[30] he was by no means the exclusive focus of poems written to legitimate the interregnum governments of 1649–54. Before "history and world order had to be re-interpreted to include Cromwell,"[31] they had first to accommodate the annually appointed Council of State that held supreme power until Cromwell's Protectorate began in 1654.

Poets seem, however, to have been both slow and reluctant to respond to the challenge of the new form of government. Most of the political poems published between January 1649 and Cromwell's dissolution of the Rump in April 1654 are royalist satires. Among the few poems celebrating the Commonwealth, three poems by "R. F." published in 1651 stand out as the earliest systematic attempts in verse to legitimate the power of the Council of State, and they do so by reinterpreting history if not world order.[32]

The first, dated February 3 by Thomason, *Mercurius Heliconicus. Or, The Result of a safe Conscience whether It be necessary to submit to the Government now in being,* advances most of this writer's doctrine.[33] Like many partisan poets before and since, "R. F." poses as a reasonable spokesman contemplating the common good and deciding in favor of the de facto regime. He traces all political institutions to their original in Adam at the dawn of human history and proceeds to level traditional hierarchies:

> See Man in *Adam,* and you'le finde that we
> Are but a lineall fraternity,
> Equally free by nature, Kings, and Slaves
> Have the same womb, and exit, birth, and graves.
> Our dust makes no distinction. . . .
>
>   (P. 3)

From this materialist premise of a common human history and final equality, "R. F." advances the Hobbesian doctrine that opens the poem:

> CRownes were but gallant robberies at first.
> And Conquerors heroick theeves that durst
> Attempt the worlds inslaving, why should we
> Repine then to behold a Monarchy
> Rak'd up in dust?
>
>   (P. 3)

Yet if all monarchs are robbers—however heroic—the authority for their political power remains that providence which permits them to assume power in the first place. Only from "The Will of a Creator and the mind / Of Providence . . . / The Sanctions of heaven" and "the hand of fate" are

> All power's thence deriv'd, and that divine
> Decree which first erected, may define,
> And terminate its own Act, and that will
> Prescribe another rule be't good or ill

> To flesh and bloods conception. Present things
> And formes of State must be our Laws & Kings.
>
> (P. 4)

The argument, pointedly, legitimates the de facto rise to power of the Council of State by a Hobbesian providentialism that collapses the present into an originary moment.

Of course, even conservative thinkers of the time tended to acknowledge the authority of de facto power.[34] David Underdown has shown how similar arguments favoring present forms of state were a staple of official policy during 1649, when "much of the Commonwealth's own propaganda was indeed directed to securing the support of the conformists."[35] Though a commonplace by 1651, the argument in "R. F."'s poem reminds us that even radical thought at the time remained predominantly conservative in its historical vision. Tracing political institutions to their origins in Adam might be a historical argument rather than an argument from history; but like many new regimes, the one supported by "R. F." also needed to revise the past in order to vindicate its rise to power. Since the Commonwealth was a republic of sorts, and an institutional innovation in English government, its theorists felt impelled to account for all those centuries when monarchs ruled England.

Henry Parker, another "theoretical predecessor of Hobbes,"[36] provided just such a reinterpretation in the years before "R. F."'s poem. The full title of his work declares the range and purpose of his argument which he closely documents with references to such authorities as Daniel, Speed, Matthew of Paris, Prynne, and Bacon: *The True Portraiture of the Kings of England; Drawn from their Titles, Successions, Raigns and Ends. Or, A Short and Exact Historical description of every King, with the Right they have had to the Crown, and the manner of their wearing of it; especially from WILLIAM the Conqueror. Wherein is Demonstrated, that there hath been no direct succession in the line to create an hereditary right, for six or seven hundred yeers: faithfully collected out of our best Histories, and humbly presented to the Parliament of England.* Parker's argument, based upon an appeal to a former age of liberty, was hardly new. Christopher Hill has examined it in some detail as the notion of the "Norman Yoke."[37] "Is not," Parker asks,

> five or six hundred year enough for *England* to be under the succession of a *Norman* Bastard ... and to be sold with all its liberties, from usurpation

to usurpation, as well as from generation to generation? I need not be very zealous in application, the history is enough to make all wise men consider, by whom we have all this while been governed, and upon what terms; How tyranny and usurpation comes to be adored, if it have but a royall name added to it. (P. 15)

In verse, "R. F." employs a similar argument as the first of two premises supporting the regime which took power at the regicide:

> If then the *Norman* Conquest be decreed
> To cease, and be defunct in such a seed,
> Tis sinne to descant on the Edict [that] brings
> A close to our dispute and bickerings;
> ... If that your Princes fall disgust your hearts
> Conceive it was your sin, not his deserts
> Wip'd him away. And be reform'd in this
> To yeeld obedience to that State that is.
>
> (Pp. 5–6)

This defense of the de facto government rests also on a broad argument from historical determinism that deftly avoids the difficulty of praising an oligarchy by subsuming that praise into a more general defense of things-as-they-are:

> Destiny runs without a supposition,
> Its rule is positive, far from condition.
>
> (P. 7)

There is no denying the force and facts of history, though in practice we can dispense with as much of the past as we need to when defending the current order of things.

When poets of the Commonwealth do look to the past for analogues, they tend to prefer republican Rome to monarchist England. Only the Roman republic could provide images of what England's future might be like—powerful, civilized, imperial, and oligarchic. The most famous of the poems written between 1649 and 1654 on the government, Marvell's *Horatian Ode on Cromwell's Return from Ireland* (1650),[38] em-

ploys a striking parallel between the foundation of Rome's republic and
that of England's commonwealth. The moment of Charles's execution

> was that memorable Hour
> Which first assur'd the forced Pow'r.
>   So when they did design
>   The *Capitols* first Line,
> A bleeding Head where they begun,
> Did fright the Architects to run;
>   And yet in that the *State*
>   Foresaw it's happy Fate.
>
> (1.93)

Commentators agree that these lines refer to a human head found in the
reign of Tarquin, the last Roman king, during excavation for a temple.
"The Temple," observes John Wallace, "was not dedicated until the first
year of the Republic, and, as a prognostication, the head was taken to
mark the end of Rome's infancy, the beginning of the Republic and of
Roman liberty, and, universally, as a sign that Rome would be the head
of a new world empire."[39] Wallace also suggests that constant allusions
to Thomas May's translation of Lucan's *Pharsalia* in the opening lines of
Marvell's *Ode* invite learned readers to draw further comparison between
the English and Roman states.

   Marvell evokes a Roman past to speculate upon England's future
under Cromwell's military leadership. He emphasizes the comparison in
order to forecast the nation's "happy Fate" as imperial leader of the
world:

> What may not then our *Isle* presume
> While Victory his Crest does plume!
>   What may not others fear
>   If thus he crown each Year!
> A *Caesar* he ere long to *Gaul*,
> To *Italy* an *Hannibal*,
>   And to all States not Free
> Shall *Clymacterick* be.
>
> (1.94)

Marvell asks us to judge the present by what, since it resembles the past,
it will bring in the immediate future. Earlier praise of Stuart England

as an arcadian haven cut off from the rest of the world has been replaced with a vision of future global imperium modeled after Rome's past.

An important but relatively neglected poem published shortly after the third Council of State assumed office in December 1651 operates a similar parallel between England and imperial Rome under Julius Caesar. Thomas Manley's *Veni; Vidi; Vici. The Triumphs of the Most Excellent and Illustrious OLIVER CROMWELL* alludes constantly to Greek and Roman history—to the total exclusion of English history—in order to show how recent events in England somehow promise a glorious new age of peace at home and imperial dominion abroad under the military leadership of Cromwell and the political leadership of the new Council of State. The "Gratulatory Song of Peace" which occupies most of *Veni; Vidi; Vici* interprets the New Model Army's recent victories against Charles Stuart's Scottish forces at Dunbar (September 3, 1650) and Worcester (September 3, 1651) as assurances of England's continuous peace and right to world dominion. But to view this poem as being exclusively concerned with Cromwell and his personal claim to power would be to miss the full range of its design, which is, representative of the period and illustrates the more general connections between new forms of government and the new forms of poetry required to legitimate them.

First, *Veni; Vidi; Vici* is not a single poem but a collection of different pieces, largely translated from Payne Fisher's Latin panegyric on Cromwell of the same name (not all of which is in verse). Several pages of prefatory material are followed by a 1,647-line poem variously called the "Song" and "Ode" of peace which recounts the Army's recent victories. Then follow a prose "animadversion," panegyrics to Cromwell and Edward Ludlow, finally an elegy on Henry Ireton. A document of its times, a mixture of various forms, the collection combines historical reportage, personal encomia, and speculation on the future in order to praise the power of the new Council of State and England's military leaders.

Veni; Vidi; Vici appeared at a moment of acute constitutional crisis between Army leaders, particularly involving Cromwell who wanted to dissolve the Rump of the Long Parliament, and the Rump Parliamentarians who opposed further governmental reforms which would threaten their own positions. A partisan work that tries to forge a compromise of sorts, *Veni; Vidi; Vici* clearly prefers the Army version of what should be done. The work probably appeared in late January 1652,[40] shortly after

Cromwell and the Independents compromised their attempts to dissolve Parliament by permitting, instead, the formation of the new Council of State. The work's partisan bias appears most evidently in its glorification of military leaders in the "Song," in the panegyrics, and in the treatment of one of the more radical army Independents, Major General Thomas Harrison, the man who would later lead troops into the House of Commons at Cromwell's command. One of the regicides, Harrison had served on the Council of State during 1651 but was excluded from the nominations for the next year because of his extreme views.[41] Nevertheless, Manley singles him out for praise in the "Song" for his part in the battle of Worcester. The initial *occupatio* characterizes Manley's rhetorical prolixity:

> Nor can I speak enough of what was done
> By thy fam'd vertues gallant *Harrison;*
> That by thy growing merits doest augment,
> Thy *Countreys* honor: neither art thou spent
> With stollen titles studying how to rise,
> But lying vainer honors dost despise,
> Knowing that granted truth, that thou shalt get
> More noble glory, to be *good* then *great.*

> (P. 19)

The conciliatory tone reveals that Manley's sympathy for the Independent cause does not lead him to a polemic against the Parliamentary conservatives. His work, rather, celebrates the authority of the present government. The main poem, in fact, is inscribed "To the All-Worthy . . . JOHN Lord Bradshaw . . . LORD High-President of the Right Hon[able] the Councell of State: as also, To the rest of those ever Renowned Patriots, Sitting Members of the same Right Hon[able] Councell" (sig. Bi[v]). There follows a two-page catalogue of the thirty-two members of the newly vested council other than Cromwell and Bradshaw.[42] *Veni; Vidi; Vici* does not, as Ruth Nevo would have us believe, illustrate the irreconcilable conflict between destiny and Cromwell—portrayed as a conquering hero who "holds the Fates fast bound in iron chains"[43]—for its design vindicates the diverse power of the newly appointed members as the nation's rightful leaders. On this aspect of its purpose, the "Epistle Dedicatory" is emphatic, for, as Manley argues, from such recent victories against the enemies of the "publike liberty . . . it proceedes that war is banisht from our borders." This being the case, asks Manley, "who can but admire so many the elaborate endeavors of the Parliament? Who will gaynsay you the succeeding upholders of our State? Who but will confess the immediate providence and Divine Finger of God to be seen even apparently in the victorious, atcheivements of our Generall; In the acts of our Parliament, the Supreme Authority" (sigs. B3ᵛ-B4).

A second reason why we should hesitate before seeing *Veni; Vidi; Vici* as a panegyric to Cromwell is that the text itself raises the issue of appropriate poetic form several times, thereby reminding us how literary kinds are being mixed. Manley blends praise for the great military hero with glorification of the Council of State by interpreting world events as a foreshadowing of a future age of peace and world imperium for England under the new regime. He denies that he intends to compose a regular panegyric when, toward the end of his "Song," he declares that he has not yet sung Cromwell's praises:

> The time may come, wherein I may declare
> At large the triumphs of your greater war,
> And all your Souldiers famous actions shew,
> Laying them open to the publike view.
>
> (P. 79)

The profession of inside knowledge may, of course, be genuine, but its effect here is to suggest the impartiality and accuracy of the poet's information. Before the poet will disclose the "greater war," however, he must first wait upon the goodwill and benevolence of the Council of State:

> If those most honour'd *Nobles* of the State
> With their great President but animate
> Kindly these first-fruits of my zeale and toyle,
> A new designe may grow from every smile.
>
> (P. 79)

The poet stresses the mixed form of the "Song" by frequently commenting upon his own work, his present "designe," and by his various use of the muses. Such variety in formal features was, of course, considered admirable by aestheticians of the time.[44] In addition to various appeals to all of the muses in general,[45] Manley names Thalia, the muse of pastoral, and Clio, the muse of history. The former is particularly appropriate for a poem variously designated an "ode" and "song" celebrating peace,[46] for, as Manley reminds us, the wars just ended have disturbed England's agricultural economy:

> Til now the earth groan'd through the weight of war,
> Scarce was the care of cattell, use of share;
> The fields were barren and did useless ly,
> Through the neglect of ceasing Husbandry.
>
> (P. 3)

The poet's inspiration by Thalia, however, depends upon the favor of Bradshaw, the man in charge of the nation's economy:

> who of the supream Parliament,
> Art (justice prop) the worthy *President,*
> With the same calmness both of brest and eye
> That you into much greater writings spye,
> Deign but to look at ours, *Thalia* then
> May happen somwhat stop to grace my pen.
>
> (P. 2)

When the poet turns to the Council of State as a whole in the lines immediately following these, however, he admits his difficulty in addressing a group that have altered the political constitution of the nation:

> And you brave *Heroes,* whose grave counsels waite
> Upon the high designments of the State;
>   . . .
> You steere the *English,* you the Pilots are,
> You sit at prow and poope in peace in war
>
>   . . .
> With safe and gentle gales you change the Scene,
> And make a State where Monarchy hath beene;
> Thus free from danger at the last in health
> Arrives ith'port a happy Common-wealth.
> Tell me ye Muses in your milder Vein
> To sing these changes what must be my strain.
> These joy'd retreates no verse can truly sing,
> *Cromwells* return doth nought but raptures bring.
>
> (Pp. 2,3)

The shift of focus here as the poet turns from council to Cromwell enables him to attribute the mixed form of the "Song" to rapture at a conquering hero's victories, which herald a new era in English poetry and politics both. "Pious in Peace and politick in war," Cromwell has

> strongly call'd back Peace from lower shades,
> Whence to the Rulers both and people brought
> Shewes better times to those that better fought.
>
> (P. 4)

In a catalogue of familiar agricultural and rural motifs that describe the return of peace to England's war-torn island (pp. 4, 5), the poet describes how, thanks to Cromwell's victories, poetic and political forms will change together as a sign of the better times ahead. Posing as one fevered by inspiration at Cromwell's deeds, the poet finally regains control of his poem and ends this prolix and digressive encomium to the nation and its hero by chastising Clio for having carried him off into history:

> But stay my Muse, rash *Clio*, whither away?
> Thou know'st not how thy sails plow up the Sea;
> Hold in, and lesser use the winde and Sail,
> At the first setting out Oars best prevail.
>
> (P. 6)

Regardless of the modes the Muses may have carried him into, Manley insists that his poem is the very mixture of kinds inspired by history that celebrates the nation and its governments by recounting their deeds.

Thus Manley celebrates the revival of England's agricultural economy, using pastoral tropes to establish an emotional norm about which many of the "Songs'" shifts of feeling turn. Yet the historical design controls the poem with an interweaving of interpretative and selective reportage and encomia characteristic of historical poetry. The bulk of the "Song" represents the military campaigns of 1650–51 fought between the New Model Army and the Scottish forces supporting Charles Stuart. The poem celebrates Cromwell's victories at Dunbar and Worcester as English conquests against the armies of an aggressive, unjust, and invading foreign nation, Scotland. Unlike the previous wars fought by Cromwell—perhaps those "greater wars" the poet has not yet sung—those of 1650–51 are specifically not civil wars at all, but wars between two distinct foreign nations: he designates Scotland a "nation" and a "country" (pp. 48, 50) distinct from England.

Many Englishmen, it seems, commonly felt his sense of nationalism at the time Manley's poem appeared. It grew during the summer of 1651, before the battle of Worcester, but after Charles had entered England from Scotland at the head of a Scottish army. "It is probable," thought S. R. Gardiner,

> that nearly if not quite a third of the victorious army [at Worcester] consisted of local militia regiments. It was the natural result of the system of war which Charles had elected to conduct. As long as the struggle lay between two English parties, it was left to the regular army on either side to carry on the contest. When it came to an invasion by a Scottish army, masses of Englishmen, who would have held back from exposing their own persons, eagerly threw themselves forward to defend their homes against those who were in that age regarded as foreigners. (1.445–46)

Whether or not anyone eagerly leaped into battle, unprecedented support from local volunteers aided Cromwell's victory. Moreover, Parliamentary propagandists had, while Charles marched with his Scottish troops along the west coast of England, portrayed this as an invasion by a foreign army under the command of a foreign king. In June, shortly after Charles and his army had crossed the border into England, a pamphlet appeared defending the "Rights of the people of England ... against the pretences of the Scottish King."[47] And in the next month a satirical poem—*Old Sayings and Predictions verified and fulfilled touching the Young King of Scotland*—appeared illustrated with a woodcut of "the Scots holding their young Kinges nose to the grindstone."[48] If, early in the century, monarchist panegyrists had celebrated James Stuart's accession to the English throne for uniting nations, Parliamentary writers now turned his grandson's ancestry against him by depicting him as a foreigner with no rights in England.

Manley represents the campaigns of 1650 that ended at Dunbar as part of a foreign war rather than as the continuation of the earlier civil wars fought during the previous decade. In doing so he places these campaigns within a larger design that anticipates a glorious future for England under the new regime, a regime that successfully defends England from foreign enemies. National interest is equated with the interests of the party in power. Manley generously intersperses his account with flattery of Cromwell and the other army leaders, establishing their superiority to most Greek and Roman types (pp. 71–73, 80–85). He directly addresses Cromwell and his imperialistic virtues:

... YOU Great Sir, Greater than *Caesar* are,
The Empire of your Vertues reacheth far,
          • • •
... hating idle sloth, and sinfull peace,
By constant warfare th'*English* [empire] dost encrease.

(P. 72)

The "Song" however also celebrates the Council of State as best able to
govern domestic affairs and turns, in its final pages, to address those
responsible for governing the newly pacified nation. After a prophetic
vision of a future in which lambs lie down with calves and cows feed
with bears (pp. 89–91), the poem ends with an encomium upon Bradshaw, the "parent of our State and President" (p. 91).

Manley's vision of the future unifies peace at home with successful
war abroad. An arcadian haven of peace and prosperity under the new
Council of State, the island nation will conquer and rule the world by
the might of Cromwell's sword. Like most, if not all, new ages, the one
imagined by Manley lies in the imminent future. It exists potentially in
the new political regime which, being most original, is also most just
and hence destined to produce policies conducive to English dominion
over the entire world. Yet Manley's portrait of the future lacks the professed historicity of his earlier reports of recent events which, whatever
their partisan distortions, tell of things that actually occurred. As Manley
looks to the future, he relies increasingly upon fantastic traditions associated with the return of the gold age:

Concord will grow, and all divisions cease,
And all things whisper to the *Brittaines peace*,
Then shall the Woolfe, *that with a fatall eye*
Did meditate before new treachery,
Against the lambe, *his fierceness laid aside*,
Henceforth together safety they reside.

(Pp. 89–90)

After the detailed accounts of Cromwell's military campaigns and amidst
the praise of Bradshaw and the Council of State, the echoes of Virgil's
Fourth Eclogue sound distinctly absurd, hardly masking the poet's inability to imagine the future for himself and for his own times. Indeed,
though variety was considered to be a poetic virtue, we might also consider the self-consciously mixed character of the "Song," and of *Veni;*

Vidi, Vici as a whole, to result from the poet's uncertainty about recent changes in government as much as from current aesthetic theory. Manley's question—"to sing these changes what must be my strain"—may, in fact, be more than a merely rhetorical figure of inexpressibility, for by it this poet hides the uncertainty of his art in an age when whether the future looked hopeful was by no means clear.

Once Cromwell had been appointed head of state in 1654, poets more confidently represented the new age of England's imperium for they could then identify the nation's future with the policies of a single heroic figure who rules wisely and justly. As we saw in Chapter 2, Waller's *Panegyric* of 1655 restores national assurance and pride by heroically celebrating a new age achieved through the power of the new national leader. But without such a central hero to praise, one who personally embodies and controls the national destiny in his own public career, poets like Manley seem to have failed to represent the nation's future in any but the most generalized or fantastic terms. The new age, however unprecedented it might have been, remained inescapably bound to traditional artistic habits of thought and representation, and to a past form of government, one headed by a single, heroic leader.[49]

PROTECTORATE POEMS, 1653–1654

On April 20, 1653, Cromwell ordered troopers into the House of Commons to dissolve the Rump of the Long Parliament which had been in session, in various forms, since 1641.[50] Cromwell's actions ended a period of constitutional dispute that had raged, intermittently, between varying factions within the parliamentary government since Pride's Purge of December 1648 had cleared the House in favor of those responsible for the execution of Charles I some weeks later. When Cromwell dissolved Parliament, hostilities between the army Independents and the greatly reduced House centered on persistent attempts by radicals, such as Thomas Harrison, to break up the Parliament entirely, and those who sought to reform its constitution. Cromwell himself does not seem to have approved of any of the formulas offered, and threatened to resign as Lord General of the Army on April 15. No one else was prepared to accept responsibility, so when he ousted the Rump, he did so as the most powerful political agent in the country, deriving his authority, like Dryden's Almanzor, from his power to do so. The legitimacy of Cromwell's de facto power was immediately accepted by large and influential groups among the nations's political and economic leaders. The Lord Mayor of

London formally recognized Cromwell's authority that very afternoon, and with him went the support of many city merchants and aldermen. Cromwell had complete support from the Army, and though Admiral Blake was initially hostile, Monck and Deane soon swayed the support of naval officers to the cause of the new regime.[51] Even some supporters of Charles Stuart may have seen reason to find hope in Cromwell's actions.[52]

A month later a poem appeared pinned to a wall in the Exchange encouraging Cromwell to accept the crown, an idea that was to persist right up to the time of his death four years later. I give the poem from the transcription which Thomason made that day, May 19:

> Ascend three thrones, great Captaine & Divine
> By the Will of god (O Lion) for th'are thine
> Come priest of god bring oyle, bring robes, & gold
> Bring Crownes & Scepters, itts now high time, unfold
> Your cloister'd baggs, you state cheats, lest the rod
> Of steel & Iron of the King of god
> Chastise you all in's wrath, th[e]n Kneel & pray
> To Oliver the torch of zion Starre of day
> Then shout O Merchants, Citts, & Gentry sing.
> Let all men bare-head cry. God save the King.[53]

For some, the rituals and symbols of episcopacy and monarchy seem never to have died, really. Although Cromwell had no intention of accepting the crown, then or at any time, he did claim that the authority for his power derived directly from the divine will. But he was a practical man ever anxious to delegate power to an executive committee.

After appointing a new Council of State, Cromwell spent the spring and summer of 1653 steering between two wings of army opinion regarding the constitution of the assembly to exercise legislative and executive control. The major proposals both depended upon past models of government. Harrison and his supporters favored a small assembly, appointed by nomination to resemble the Hebrew Sanhedrin. Lambert, together with the more conservative wing, argued in favor of a larger elective body, modeled on the traditional parliamentary system.[54] Hill has argued that Cromwell so far preferred the compromise reached that he viewed the meeting in July of "Barebone's" Parliament "as the highest point of the Revolution." In Hill's term, Cromwell's self-appointed mission was to bring about this very moment. And certainly, in his inaugural speech—to which Hill refers—Cromwell eulogizes the new assembly as "called by God to rule with him and for him," and hints that it begins a new age such as that prophesied by Scripture. "This may," he told them, "be the door to usher-in the Things that God has promised; which have been prophesied; which he has set the hearts of his People to work for. . . . Truly seeing things are thus, that you are at the edge of the Promises and Prophecies."[55]

At the time it may well have seemed that the opening of the new assembly heralded the millenium, for indeed it was an unprecedented Parliament in many respects that might well betoken a revolutionary break with the past. For the first time ever, Parliament sat in the name of the "three Thrones" mentioned by the poem found on 'Change. Although the Instrument of Government later authorized inclusion of thirty Scots and thirty Irish members in Parliament, Gardiner the democrat reminds us that during Barebone's, "neither Scotland, or Ireland, any more than England, had been asked whether they wished to be so represented or not (2:232). Moreover, drawing its authority from God alone, Barebone's rested on no surer political foundation than the power of the Army and of personal loyalty toward the men in command of that power. More like a military despotism than a traditionally elected Parliament, the new government resembled a self-appointed oligarchy, headed by Cromwell. Indeed, as the poet hopes, a willingness to accept Cromwell's personal rule seems to have become increasingly general during the summer and autumn of 1653 as the new government proved inadequate to its tasks.

By December 1, Lambert had offered the crown to Cromwell on the authority of the army. Cromwell refused but, after careful revision, accepted Lambert's proposed constitution—the Instrument of Government—which was then passed by a committee of officers on December 16. However disappointed Cromwell may have been at the failure of Barebone's to bring about the millennium, his acceptance of the Instrument and the title of Protector that went along with it, seemed to many at the time hardly less than a return to monarchy. Gardiner reminds us that Cromwell is the first de facto despot willing to set limits to his own power (2:282). But Hill's is surely a more telling point. The Protectorate ended the possibility of widespread political, social, and religious reform since it constituted a victory of more conservative forces who wished to maintain as much of the past as possible.[56]

The first article of the Instrument gives the Protector more power than had been held by any one man since 1649:

> the supreme legislative authority of the Commonwealth of England, Scotland, and Ireland, and the dominions thereunto belonging, shall be and reside in one person, and the people assembled in Parliament: the style of which person shall be the Lord Protector of the Commonwealth of England, Scotland, and Ireland.[57]

To many at the time, this constitution seemed tantamount to monarchy except for two crucial differences that gained importance after Cromwell's death; the Protector's power lacked the clear restraints which tradition had imposed upon a king; and the succession was not assured by a principle as immediately efficient as the dynastic principle of heredity.[58]

Poets remained surprisingly quiet about Cromwell's appointment: no contemporary poem seems to have been written specifically on this occasion. In June 1654, however, a collection of poems by members of the University of Oxford—*Musarum Oxoniensum Elaiophoria*—appeared on the recent peace treaty signed with the Dutch. None of the English poems in this collection directly treats the political question of Cromwell's Protectorate. As we might expect, most of them celebrate the treaty as the union of two nations, while others praise Cromwell as a heroic general whose victory promises much for the nation's future. They invariably envisage a future of English commercial expansion under a military leader rather than a head of state. Unlike Manley, none of these academic poets wrote in English on the new form of government or on Cromwell's domestic power. They focus instead on a recent military and commercial success and its implications for the national economy. The composite portrait of Cromwell which emerges from the collection reveals a great and glorious military commander securing the nation's commerce, not a supremely powerful head of state.

The English poems in *Musarum Oxoniensum*, including one by John Locke, do little more than rehearse familiar tropes to suit the times, but they thus remind us of poetic commonplaces in royalist poems written during the terminal years of 1649 and 1660. Not only do they adapt figures and ideas from elegies on Charles I, but they also adopt others from panegyric that were used later to celebrate the Restoration of Charles II. But these continuities also represent transformations. Unlike the elegists of 1649, who anxiously created a future perspective from which they could judge the regicide, these Oxford poets forecast a new age of foreign power and untold commercial wealth. To a political prop-agandist writing earlier in 1654, Cromwell's military leadership was proof of the providential sanction for his political power. "Can we imag-ine," asks "E. M." the author of *Protection Perswading Subjection*, "the conquest of three potent Kingdomes [England, Scotland and Ireland] hath been accomplished, and the Conqueror become the Protector thereof, and these great things not done by divine Providence?" (p. 5). And later, "the Lord hath made his Highnesse really and in truth our Protector; how can it be then, but that the name and place of Protector, must most justly belong unto his renowned person?" (p. 20). On the evidence of the English poems in *Musarum Oxoniensum*, however, one would never know that Cromwell was anything more than a victorious general whose victories placed England on the threshold of global com-mercial and imperial dominion.

Cromwell is *"the Worlds great wonder"* (p. 66) that heralds the re-turning golden age (cf. pp. 67, 98). Either like Augustus (p. 59) or beyond parallel (p. 96). he encourages the arts to flourish (p. 61) while uniting in his person the power and skill of both Ulysses and Achilles (p. 67), thereby transforming "Greeke Fables" into "English Historie" (p. 98). One poet defends his foreign policy on religious grounds (p. 66), but for most of the others, simply comparing his deeds with those of classical models as a promise of commercial dominion seemed sufficient legiti-mation (pp. 59, 93, 98). None of these poets—unlike Waller a year later—compares Cromwell to a previous English monarch; though one mentions Agincourt only to dismiss it as a minor victory compared with those of the mighty Protector (p. 66).

Several poets draw attention to the advantages which England now holds with respect to world trade. One points out that *"Merchants* may trade, the *High-shooe* live at ease; / For all men now are bound unto the *Peace"* (p. 89). But this internationalism is not common: other poets are more directly nationalistic in their visions of future world trade. Later to defend the right to property gained by imperial conquest, John Locke argues that under Cromwell's power England has mercantile rights over the entire world. This global power is a creative process. The imperial creator has absolute rights over the new worlds he creates by conquering them:[59]

> Our ships are now most beneficiall growne,
> Since they bring home no spoiles but what's their owne.
> Unto these branchlesse *Pines* our forward spring

Owes better fruit, then Autumn's wont to bring:
Which give not only gemms and Indian ore,
But adde at once whole Nations to our store:
Nay if to make a World's but to compose
The difference of things, and make them close
In mutuall amitie; and cause Peace to creep
Out of the jarring Chaos of the deep:
Our ships doe this, so that whilst others take
Their course about the World, Ours a World Make.

(P. 95)

By 1654 Cromwell had added "not only gemms and Indian ore" but also "whole Nations" to England's "store" by successfully asserting England's authority over Scotland, Ireland, New England, Newfoundland, Virginia, Maryland, the Bermudas, Barbados, and Antigua.

The commercial emphasis in these celebrations of England's rightful dominion over the world confirms Hill's interpretation of the establishment of the Protectorate: when Cromwell accepted the title of Protector some months before the Oxford volume appeared, it signaled a victory for those interested in a stable government that would encourage the expansion of English trade over those who wished to revolutionize England's entire political system.[60]

And indeed, Cromwell's foreign policy has often been cited as one of the greatest achievements of his leadership. Although poets praised the halcyon days of peace under the early Stuarts, the Venetian ambassador wrote in 1640 that England had dwindled from the days of Elizabeth into a "a nation useless to the rest of the world, and consequently of no consideration."[61] Seven years earlier, he had noticed that England "has no minister of her own at any court of Europe." though merchants maintained their own envoy at Constantinople.[62] It was during the fifties that, according to a nineteenth-century historian, "England began to turn definitely from its position as an island chiefly agricultural to a world power chiefly industrial and commercial."[63] And if this sounds Whiggish, Hill has more recently argued that "the governments of the 1650's were the first in English history to have a world strategy."[64] Cromwell's foreign policy was not only conceived on a global scale but also singularly commercial in its interests. It aimed at power over the Dutch for access to India and the Far East, and at power over the Spanish for access to the West Indies and Americas.[65] As early as December 23, less than a week after the Instrument of Government proclaimed Cromwell as Protector, Thurloe writes, "This change (in government) hath a very general acceptance, especially among the lawyers, the ministers and the merchants."[66] During the early years of the Protectorate, England began to take its place as the imperial center of the commercial world. As one Oxford poet wrote:

> Farre now our Shipps their *Canvass Wings* shall stretch,
> And the worlds Wealth to richer *England* fetch.
> Till greater Treasures overspread our Coast
> Then *Tagus*, or *Pactolus* sands do boast.
> With this designe our busy Vessells Range
> About, to make our *Isle* the *Worlds Exchange*.
>
> (P. 98)

This sort of ambition, to turn the British Isles into the commercial center of an imminent global empire will repeatedly appear in poems written to celebrate the return of Charles II in 1660. Hindsight allows us to see how, in their treatment of the past, the poems in *Musarum Oxoniensum* of 1654 look both forward and back, reminding us of royalist poems written on both the regicide and the Restoration. While elegies on Charles I commonly obliterate English history to signify the momentousness of the king's execution, the Oxford poems celebrating Cromwell's military and commercial policy ignore the past, as part of a more general strategy of avoiding questions about domestic government. They broaden instead their historical—and geographical—perspective in order to forecast a future of English world control. And, when these poets do look to the past, they rest their gaze not on national history but on times of Roman—and sometimes Greek—world power and civilization. They take a larger view of history than the Stuart elegists of 1649 by looking further back while also speculating more freely upon the potential of the present.

This more expansive historical perspective, favoring classical models over national ones, characterizes the so-called Augustan or neoclassical aesthetic that modern scholars have variously identified as emerging into dominance through the literature of the Restoration and early eighteenth-century.[67] Some of the reasons for the influence of an aesthetic theory deliberately modeled after imperial, civilized Rome obviously derived from political constraints. While imagining themselves at the start of a new age, these poets never quite imagined a future that wasn't modeled after something familiar from the past. They may have broadened their historical range by looking more to the future, but as their gaze stretched forward in time, it turned back and took its images from the more remote past. The "perspicill" of Chronology, turned in both directions, still saw not the entirety of what was available but what it wanted to see. And what it wanted to see were objects that fit into the ledger book of History, neatly arranged in complete, serial form. Even when looking to the future, those poets were restricted in what they saw by the analogy between past and present—and now future—that provided them with a means of at once understanding and representing history while it also led them to imagine and represent the future as little more than a return to an age of Augustan civilization, culture, and imperium. Such is the power of the daughters of memory. And as Blake knew, it is a political power. Poets often looked to Rome because it provided a republican precedent for Cromwell's England. In so doing they often constructed an idealized vision of Augustan Rome that would assure England's future in the form of a successful state built upon a defeated monarchy that could be hopeful of world dominion.

Developments in aesthetics and poetic practice cannot finally be separated from larger ideological developments that, in turn, are inseparable from developments in political life, thought, and institutions. Nevertheless to interpret Cromwellian poetry by post facto analysis and to judge it, favorably or otherwise, for its anticipation of later, better-known works would surely be inappropriate.[68] Unlike poems praising the early Stuarts, poems in praise of Cromwell typically portray the nation's future rather than its past in order to support "present things and formes of State." Unlike Manley, these poets give specific shape to the future, secure in the leadership of a strong head of state (even if they prefer not to acknowledge that) whose imperial ambitions, divinely supported, will bring about an English Augustan age. They portray a new age inseparably linked with the career of that mortal, conquering hero, who monarchlike, controls the national destiny.

THE MILLENNIAL HERO, 1655–1658

Two poems praising Cromwell, Marvell's *First Anniversary* (1655) and the anonymous *Anglia Rediviva* published in 1658, urge comparison for several reasons. In addition to a common subject, they both display important rhetorical and structural similarities while nevertheless exemplifying differing—if not opposed—political views. Both poets adopt, in some respects, the stance of the deliberative orator who, in Aristotle's

Rhetoric, advances doctrine by showing what it will bring about in the future. In doing so they both adapt structural features of "triumphal form" as Alastair Fowler has described it.[69] In the center of Marvell's poem, commemorating the first year of the Protectorate, the hero ascends in a divine chariot to preside over historical and political forces which he has already subdued to his own control. Marvell defines heroism as control over history, using the triumphal form both to declare the importance of Cromwell's achievements during the first year of his Protectorate and to assure us of their permanence beyond the life of the individual Protector. Three years later, the poet of *Anglia Rediviva* also employs triumphal form, but in strikingly different ways since the design here is to urge Cromwell to accept the crown and thereby restore monarchic government. At the sovereign center of this poem, Cromwell rides out to his coronation and history stops, as it were, while the poet represents, in some detail, two triumphal arches that memorialize his past achievements. Marvell details Cromwell's achievements in order to look beyond them toward the future they assure; the other urges the benefits of a possible next step—Cromwell's coronation—only to leave us there contemplating the past.

Written in December 1654 and published early in 1655, the *Anniversary* demonstrates how Cromwell has brought about the divine will in human history. In both its political and its historical vision, the poem's design is grander than that of any of the other poems written to celebrate an interregnum government or hero. The title as it appears in the 1655 quarto—*The First Anniversary of The Government Under His Highness the Lord Protector*[70]—draws attention to the poem's general purpose more strikingly that does the title found in the folio of 1681, *The First Anniversary of the Government under O. C.*, since the poem legitimates the future promise of the current government more than the personal might and prestige of Cromwell himself, though it does so by praising the Protector's heroic power over the forces of history. In what has already been recognized as, in part, a deliberative poem that offers political counsel, Marvell advises the English Parliament and people that the political reforms already achieved by Cromwell will resolve the political order of the entire world into a single empire ruled by England. The revolution in English political life has global implications. Further, once the harmonious system of government established in England spreads through all nations of the earth, it may put an end to human time and history entirely by inaugurating the millennium.

Christopher Hill has suggested that Cromwell aspired to effect such a revolution on a millennial and, consequently, international scale; though by 1655 such hopes were frustrated by disagreements at home.[71] Like the Oxford poets who celebrated the Dutch treaty of the year before, Marvell dwells on the revolutionary and millennial aspects of the Protectorate while celebrating its commercial achievements. But Marvell does not assure us that the last days are certain to come about. He does not pose exclusively as a prophet but also as a political orator, offering advice by speculating upon what will happen provided that certain policies are adopted. On the one hand Marvell encourages support for the government reformed by Cromwell. On the other he advises Cromwell and members of the government that, to endure beyond Cromwell's leadership and continue the millennial reforms which have begun, they must abolish factionalism in the nation at large and among themselves. If England is to lead a world empire to the last days of human time, then the entire nation and the government in power must follow the poet's advice and move beyond the heroic leadership of an individual. Moreover, the poem both celebrates the glorious future under the government constituted by the Instrument of Government, and argues that only the harmonious form of that government, brought about by Cromwell's power and wisdom, can assure its endurance and latent millennial purpose. Using triumphal form to counterpose and finally transcend current arguments concerning the nature of Cromwell's power, Marvell's poem insists that while Cromwell may be the divine agent who inaugurates an era of English millennial imperium, the future so conceived must not depend upon him alone. That future demands, rather, the continued unity of political interests within the state which he has helped to construct, and the endurance of those harmonious governmental institutions which he has established.

The argumentative design of the *Anniversary* is obviously a complex and sophisticated one that has, accordingly, generated a variety of differing emphases amongst scholarly commentators who have variously privileged certain elements, allusive patterns, and points of engagement with contemporary political disputes, in order to account for the poem as a whole. By focusing attention on Marvell's use of biblical allusions, John Wallace has seen the poem as encouraging Cromwell to restore monarchy by accepting the crown. Joseph Mazzeo and Steven Zwicker have interpreted these allusions differently to argue, respectively, that Marvell wishes us to view Cromwell as a Davidic king and an Old Testament judge. A. J. N. Wilson emphasizes the classical allusions in order to argue that the poem represents Cromwell as a type of Augustus, while Isabel Rivers and Annabel Patterson have variously suggested that Marvell strives to show that Cromwell is all these things and more, a truly unprecedented heroic leader. Warren Chernaik argues that the poem operates on the principle of *concordia discors* in order to celebrate "the liberal principle of division of power."[72] Most recently, Derek Hirst has developed the synthetic emphases and, with Rivers, emphasized the "vividness' of the poem's millenarianism in what is, perhaps, the most thorough treatment of the poem's immediate political contexts to date.[73] Here I would suggest that by looking through and beyond the terms of Marvell's celebration of Cromwell's Protectorate to the overall structure which gives those terms shape and meaning, we can recognize that the design of the *Anniversary* turns attention from Cromwell's undeniable achievements and argues that they must be given enduring constitutional form in a stable government that will survive him. The unprecedented alteration in the historical order which the Protectorate announces is precisely that—a shift away from governmental models requiring heroic leaders who are bound to die. While Cromwell's authority stems from personal qualities, the design of the poem encourages us to see how, by wise constitutional reforms, he has already invested the nation as a whole with those very qualities of active energy.

In the opening of the poem, Marvell attributes to Cromwell an unprecedented control over historical forces because of his personal "Vigour" that is comparable only with the movement of time itself. Unlike all other men and national leaders, Cromwell "alone with greater Vigour runs, / (Sun-like) the Stages of succeeding Suns" (lines 7–8). By the end of the poem Marvell has shown Cromwell to have animated the English nation and its governmental institutions with this same vigorous control over history. Toward the end of the poem a foreign prince laments that "The [English] Nation had been ours, but his one Soul / Moves the great Bulk, and animates the whole" (lines 379–380). Just as Cromwell can outrun other men in the race against time and historical degeneration, so the English nation, reformed by the Protectorate and "animated" with his "one soul," can outrun other nations. The formal movement of the poem transfers energy and historical control from Protector to nation.

In addition to placing and describing Cromwell at the center of an English political state destined to global imperium, the *Anniversary* celebrates the use to which Cromwell had put his mastery over time and history by describing that model of political order which he has estab-

lished in England, one based on cosmic principles of harmony and pro-
portion and aimed at bringing about the millennium. Marvell writes that
Cromwell reconstructs the English state by

> Choosing each Stone, and poysing every weight,
> Trying the Measures of the Bredth and Height;
> Here pulling down, and there erecting New,
> Founding a firm State by Proportions true.
>
> > (Lines 245–48)

"Choosing" and "poysing," Cromwell, like Amphion, unites disparate
political elements into a unified national assembly. the "Proportions true"
of this "firm state" derive from a comprehensive inclusion of many seemingly intractable and mutually opposed forces in a harmonious structure
that resembles, in its architectural dimensions, the Parliamentary assembly seated in the House of Commons:

> The Common-wealth does through their Centers all
> Draw the Circumf'rence of the publique Wall;
> The crossest Spirits here do take their part,
> Fast'ning the Contignation which they thwart;
> And they, whose Nature leads them to divide,
> Uphold, this one, and that the other Side;
> But the most Equal still sustein the Height,
> And they as Pillars keep the Work upright;
> While the resistance of opposed Minds,
> The Fabrick as with Arches stronger binds,
> Which on the Basis of a Senate free,
> Knit by the Roofs Protecting weight agree.
>
> > (Lines 87–98)

Via the pun on "protect," the last couplet here describes the shape of the
entire poem, with Cromwell at the apex of the Parliamentary assembly
that constitutes the state, itself held together by inner supports and tensions and based upon his transference of control over history to the governing body.

Like Noah, Cromwell inherits a world purged of sinners by the
flood of civil war. But Marvell extends the comparison into a contrast:

> Thou, and thine House, like *Noah's* Eight did rest,
> Left by the Wars Flood on the Mountains crest:

> And the large Vale lay subject to thy Will,
> Which thou but as an Husbandman wouldst Till:
> And only didst for others plant the Vine
> Of Liberty, not drunken with its Wine.
>
> (Lines 283–88)

Unlike the license permitted by Noah's drunkenness (lines 291–92), that "sober Liberty" (line 289) which Cromwell's selfless husbandry promotes does not include the divisive kind of democratic liberty demanded by the various sects (lines 289–310). Cromwell, Marvell assures us, expels such "Accursed Locusts" from the state. The poet warns these groups that they must continue to fear the Protector now that the seeming danger from his coaching accident has passed:

> But the great Captain, now the danger's ore,
> Makes you for his sake Tremble one fit more;
> And, to your spight, returning yet alive
> Does with himself all that is good revive.
>
> (Lines 321–34)

But Marvell aims, as Rivers suggests, "to turn millenarianism against the millenarians" (p. 114). As the poem moves toward its triumphal center, it moves from celebrations of Cromwell's just reformations within the nation to legitimations of his personal authority over England and, though this has yet to come about, the entire world. Marvell speculates on the global implications of Cromwell's domestic reforms. With the English state newly reconstituted, Cromwell uses it as an Archimedean *pou stou*, a place to set his foot and turn the world:

> When for his Foot he thus a place had found,
> He hurles e'r since the World about him round;
> And in his sev'ral Aspects, like a Star,
> Here shines in Peace, and thither shoots a War.
>
> (Lines 99–102)

Marvell's argument moves, structurally, inward toward the triumphal center of the poem by duplicating terms, topoi, and metaphors across the poem. Because Cromwell displays the technical skill of a political engineer working on both national and global scales, he alone leads the protestant crusade against Rome, and is the one man capable of leading the

English ship of state during the storms of civil war. His deeds are divinely prompted and may well inaugurate the millennium, a task for which he alone is suited by birth. The Protector's right to world empire is legitimate, Marvell argues, because he has the knowledge, skill, means, and virtue to exercise the necessary power justly. Cromwell's control over the course of human history, and his ability to summon selfless political ingenuity together with native vitality in the divine mission of constructing a timeless world empire that will endure beyond his life, lead directly to his central triumphal ascent out of time.

Marvell maintains emphasis on the future, global implications of Cromwell's present rule by manipulating a topos from pastoral elegy at the linear center of the poem:

> Thou *Cromwell* falling, not a stupid Tree,
> Or Rock so savage, but it mourn'd for thee:
> And all about was heard a Panique groan,
> As if that Natures self were overthrown.
>
> (Lines 201–4)

Marvell elaborates the topos from disturbance in the natural order to disturbance in the universal and cosmic order (lines 205–6), then back to earth where Cromwell's fall creates havoc in the social, religious, and political order of England (lines 207–14). The entire poem turns back at the "But" at the triumphal center of the poem:

> But thee triumphant hence the firy Carr,
> And firy Steeds had born out of the Warr,
> From the low World, and thankless Men above,
> Unto the Kingdom blest of Peace and Love:
> We only mourn'd our selves, in thine Ascent,
> Whom thou hadst left beneath with Mantle rent.
>
> (Lines 214–20)

Cromwell's terrestrial fall was no less than an ascent out of time and human mortality, into eternity. Yet in achieving that ascent, the Protector rends the "Mantle," a trope that has excited much commentary. Margoliouth seems best on its general import—the mantle "does symbolize succession, and the epithet 'rent' no doubt implies retrospective anxiety on Marvell's part ... The prevailing motif is that no one in England can fill Cromwell's place" (1:324–25). But within the larger argument of the poem, no one needs to. Cromwell does not, like others, passively allow the waters of time to close over his head, but embodies the active vigour of Machievellian *virtù*. His fall from the coach was an ascent out of time that rends the entire fabric of England's past. As Hirst has cogently demonstrated, Marvell's millenarianism comes by way of Machiavelli. "The Machiavellian ideal," he writes,

> is also perfectly congruent with the constitutional structure under Cromwell. The protectorate was a commonwealth, that is, a republic, ruled over by a single person whose successors were to have less power than he ... The future of the republic established by Machiavelli's new ruler of the *Discorsi* could only be secure once the people were united in *virtù*. The rent mantle left to the self-regarding nation on Oliver's "ascent" pointed graphically to England's lack of collective *virtù* at this juncture. The passage is an unconcealed warning to Englishment to think on the future, and to mend their ways. (Pp. 37–38)

The mistake over the significance of Cromwell's fall several months before the poem's composition suggests the nation's inability to understand his millennial purpose, power, and destiny.

As the second half of the poem retraces its steps to the poem's final image of Cromwell healing the waters that he yearly troubles, Marvell assures us that the Protector's control over historical forces—manifest in his just political reforms—begins the end of world history. However optimistic this future vision may seem, it is nevertheless only part of the poem's didactic design. Such speculation on the future is appropriate to a deliberative oration—that rhetorical form intended for political persuasion—which advises what to do by describing the future effects of the offered policy. Hence the conditional verbs with which Marvell describes Cromwell's ascent: what *will* happen *if*. The poem's artistic achievement, then, resides in its union of political intention and poetic form: its careful articulation of the structural properties of triumphal form for specific political purposes.

But events gave less cause for optimism than Marvell projected. Old ways of thinking continued to assert themselves. The anonymous author of *Anglia Rediviva*, a poem published three years later, openly urges Cromwell to accept the crown of England and to return the state to a monarchy: the nation's power and glory will be revived—hence the title—

only by such a return. This poet's one concession to recent political events
is that kings are to be appointed by Parliament, not by hereditary succession. Like the *Anniversary*, this poem adapts the structural procedures of
triumphal form but in radically different ways, as we would expect of a
poem advocating so different a political doctrine. Its doctrine, moreover,
impedes its vision of the state, a limitation that appears in its more rig-
idly spatial use of the triumphal pattern.

Like Marvell's poem, *Anglia Rediviva* offers a deliberative account of
current issues by adapting the triumphal form and numerical patterning.
The poem is divided into four cantos of approximately equal length,
each prefaced by a four-line summary, for a total of 888 lines. Canto 1,
including the prefatory summary, is exactly 222 lines long. The linear
center of the poem occurs toward the end of canto 2 and offers a prover-
bial precept which the printer set off from the rest of the text by initial
inverted commas—"Where men do nothing, Titles can't do all." This
central precept comes, appropriately enough, in a brief speech praising
Cromwell for accepting the crown. As this poem is a relatively unfamil-
iar one, it might help to summarize its argument before discussing its
design.

Anglia Rediviva argues that Cromwell should accept the crown because vox populi and vox dei agree that by doing so Cromwell can save
England from unspecified political chaos. But, as the tense of the title
implies, this has already taken place so the poem declares its argument
in a fictitious account of recent events that have, so the story goes, just
occurred. The continuing present is, from the opening, objectified into a
completed past action with a beginning and a final pause as Cromwell,
about to be crowned, considers the two triumphal arches that depict his
achievements.

The first two cantos concern the people's voice and report imaginary
debates in the House of Commons during the course of a day and a half:
yesterday and this morning. Canto 1 reports a debate during which a
figure named Themis—justice—acts as Speaker of the House and advises a return to monarchy as the best principle for national recovery.
Canto 2 describes Cromwell's unanimous appointment the next morning, his modest refusal of the crown, and his final acceptance:

> When seeing all refusall was in vain
> To those, wear full resolved to obtain,
> Forc't, his unwilling shoulders he bowd down,

> To th'Royall Roabs, and head unto the Crown;
> Especially since so great consentment showd
> The voice oth'People was the voice of God:
> From whom then, by their hands deliver'd him,
> He did accept the Royall Diadem.
>
> (P. 19)

This is pure fantasy, but within the temporal logic of the poem, it describes events that took place today, only moments ago.

Cantos 3 and 4 emphasize the authority of vox dei in Cromwell's succession by describing two triumphal arches erected for the coronation, each variously illustrating the providential will working through Cromwell's former deeds. The poem then falls into two sections turning at a triumphal center when Cromwell accepts the crown and sets off on his coronation progress through the streets of London. The central line of the poem occurs in a brief speech praising Cromwell which, we are informed, truly expresses the people's will, for it is delivered by "one more eloquent amongst the rest" who

> In's one voice thus, the voice of all exprest.
> Even such a person, suche a minde as thine
> Brave *Heroe* Empourers had in ancient time;
> When choosing men for Empire onely fit,
> The bravest mind and Person carried it;
> Till by a Tenour worse than *Gavel-kinde*,
> They Empire gave to th'body, not the minde,
> Kings in cold blood, their Active heat quite gone,
> Becoming such chill passive things alone,
> No wonder they and th'Throne together fall
> "Where men do nothing, Titles can't do all.
> But pitty (alas!) rather than envy those,
> For others virtues, not their own are chose;
> Tis Fortune to be Kings as others be,
> Bur onely virtue to be one like thee.
>
> (Pp. 19–20)

As in Marvell's *Anniversary*, the central line of the poem tells us what is not true of Cromwell's sovereignty, "Where men do nothing, Titles can't do all"—while the triumphal center of the poem's larger divisions presents him riding, triumphantly, to his coronation. Here, the printer has even marked the line for us.

The full import of this speech, however, resides in its exposition of the poem's general defense of monarch and the appointment of Cromwell as king. In ancient times, the argument runs, emperors were chosen for superior physical and intellectual powers until, greater emphasis falling on "th' body, not the minde," they became, paradoxically, sterile, "their Active heat quite gone." Such is the kind of lifeless dynastic monarchy that formerly brought about a need for governmental reform in England. But, and this is the core of Themis' polemic in canto 1, "th'abuse away being tan / The lawfull use of Kings should still remain" (p. 6). The political problem that *Anglia Rediviva* constructs in order to offer a solution is that of how to replace ineffective hereditary monarchs with those truly fit to govern. A return to monarchy is appropriate since the nation has become subject to a Parliament "all maim'd and mutilat" (p. 6), one that has already "some disquiet humours in the State / Occasion'd by unskillfulness of some / More skil'd in stirring, than in purging them" (p. 3). The poem's rhetorical stance suggests that all agree on the need to return to monarchy. "Who is't," asks Themis, "that does not see / Our former state of health was Monarchy?" (p. 4). He receives his answer at the end of canto 1 when "unanimously all arose ... / Inclining all with gentle murmuring / to *Themis* vote, for Kingdom. and for King" (p. 11, 12). Canto 1 shows a fictitious Parliament voting for a return to monarchy and presents the reasons why in a deliberative and highly polemical speech: the future requires a return to past forms of government. Canto 2 describes the assembly choosing Cromwell and tells us why they make this selection. The people's will expresses their belief that Cromwell will not be a "King as others be," and the poet then enquires:

> And who now doubts whe're he be king or no
> The people generally have proclaimed so?
> Or who so selly is, to doubt again,
> Where he or no legitimatly raign;
> The Laws confirm, together with th'applause
> Of the whole Kingdome, that confirms those laws.
>
> (P. 20)

The state has become a kingdom again and so ends the second canto. Cromwell's legitimation comes at the triumphal center of the poem.

    The time scheme of the fictious narrative contributes to the poem's triumphal celebration of Cromwell's appointment and deserves comment. A temporal center is every bit as sovereign as a spatial one,[74] and it is at noon today that we find Cromwell issuing forth to his coronation parade at the opening of the third canto. Now, the debate in canto 1 took an entire day before Themis' proposal received unanimous support. "But," as the poet tells us.

> as when this great Fabrique began,
> *God* first did make the world, & then made man:
> So they enough of business did suppose
> For first daies work, the Kingdom to have chose,
> Leaving to'an other day their choyce of King,
> As we t'an other Canto for to sing.
>
> (P. 12)

The poet does not develop the hexaemeric numerology, but the reference indicates the magnitude of the events being described. Canto 2 then opens with the dawn of a new day, but the kingless kingdom has not yet fully recovered from the darkness of previous political confusion:

> NOw morn appear'd, and yet you could not say
> By th'doubtfull light, whether t'were night or day
> As black and white do both in mixture meet,
> And different Sexes i'th' Hermophodite: [sic]
> And now as soon as twi-light they discern'd,
> All hast to th'House, both curious and concern'd.
>
> (P. 9 [17], sig. C)

Light does not properly return to the nation until noon, when the newly appointed king sets out to be crowned at the opening of canto 3:

> ANd now that day more gloriously shone,
> Made gloriouser by's Coronation:
> Even Envie pale companion of night
> And darkness, dazzled with so great a light,
> To caverns subterren Inhabited
> By guilt, and mischief, all astonisht fled,
> Where it absorbing its own venume lay,
> With grief and anguish, quite consum'd away.
> Mean time the coronation pomp set on . . .
>
> (P. 25)

Here, at the triumphal center of the poem and the start of the procession, the fictitious narrative ends, halting the passage of time to describe two monumental arches depicting Cromwell's past achievements. The poet does not take events as far as the coronation itself; that, perhaps, would be too presumptuous, though he does, in the prefatory epistle, inform us:

> If things happen as I have Imagined them, I am both Poet and Prophet too: If not, I am a Poet only, who has more liberty than the Historographer, and his likelihood (most commonly) is more worth than tothers Truth. (Sig. A2)

Instead of an imagined future beyond Cromwell's assumption of royal power, this poet looks back in time to remind us of the great man's past career. The detailed description of the arches represents his achievements to assure us of the future. But this poet imagines the future only by representing the past in the peculiarly static and spatial form of the triumphal arch. Historical process becomes objectified into artistic representation. While the spatially reduplicated structures of Marvell's *Anniversary* formally embody forward movement in time by repetitions of key images, themes, and metaphors, forward movement appears in *Anglia Rediviva* only in the development of the narrative. And that stops at the middle of the second day corresponding to the middle of the poem, halted by the triumphal arches that monumentally and for all time reflect the past as promise for the future.

The "arch of war" in canto 3 is described in considerable visual detail. The quaternary impulse evident in the poem's line numbers and division into four cantos reappears: four pillars sustain the arch. We see it through Cromwell's eyes as he rides to the coronation:

> (High rays'd) the first Triumphant arch of warr
> By fower faire dorick pillars was sustaind,
> As many large compartements contain'd,
> The severall monuments of his victories.
>
> (P. 26)

In a note, the poet informs us that the pillars have triumphal significance and that the other arch, of peace, has four Corinthian pillars (pp. 37–38 n.a.). The masculine Doric pillars, which the ancients thought suited the "Temples of their gods," rise from emblematic bases carved with the "several Towns and Fortresses" Cromwell has conquered (p. 27).

Above the arch, a figure of Victory surmounts a tableau of England:

> each side for greater State,
> Two Sister Kingdoms ranckt beneath her stood;
> She could have us'd like Captives if she wo'd:
> As in a scedule there annex'd was sed,
> *Oliver for England these had conquered.*
>
> (P. 27)

Beneath and above the pillars—presumably arranged as two pairs in a straight line across the front of the arch[75]—the four "large compartments" depict Cromwell's military conquests. Described in chronological series, these scenes are the only instances of historical report in the poem; the rest is entirely fictitious. Cromwell's campaigns in Ireland (pp. 28–29), Scotland (pp. 29–31), and against Charles Stuart at Dunbar and Worcester (pp. 31–21) occupy the first three compartments. The fourth "mongst all the rest of's Triumphs, was / By th'skilfull Artist left . . . vacant." His reason?

> There to insert an other victory,
> Over a far more puissant Enemy;
> Over a far more pertinacious one
> Than all the rest whom he had overcome,
> The Envie of his high Felicity,
> Honours, and Dignities, an Enemy,
> Even *Hercules* after all his Labours past
> Had much ado to overcome at last.
> Such yet's his modesty in bearing u'm.
> That too (no doubt) at last he'ill overcome.
>
> (Pp. 35–36)

Herculean apotheosis may well befit a living hero, but if this poet's only vision of the future under King Oliver I is a victory over envy—who slunk off, it will be recalled, at the start of the coronation procession—alas for England! Having dispensed with dynastic succession, the poet looks to the future and sees only blankness and anxiety similar to that provoked by the uncertain succession at the end of Elizabeth's reign.

The arch of peace in canto 4 does not bode much better for England unless the figures of Peace, Content, Cherfullness, and Plenty—resplendent with her cornucopia—can inspire us with a sufficient sense of bliss to come. The dominant section of this arch depicts an allegorical tableau of the poem's doctrine. Trampling Rumour and Discontent underfoot, Cromwell sits enthroned (pp. 43–44), with figures of Order and Equity on either side (pp. 44–45). Above his head, the divine hand of providence—emerging from a cloud—suspends the crown and announces, *"By me Kings Reign"* (pp. 49–50). As the first half of the poem ended with vox populi, so this ends with vox dei: both in unison proclaim Oliver king of England, and Englishment can put their trust only in the hand of God to provide for their future.

In seventeenth-century Europe generally, heroes were commonly conceived as men whose powerful vision of the future gave them the courage and ability to overcome any and all difficulties that might be encountered in bringing that vision into being. Marvell's portrait of Cromwell in the *Anniversary* shows a man fully in charge of the forces of history, shaping both them and national institutions in order to hasten a clearly defined future of millennial world revolution. In *Anglia Rediviva*, Cromwell appears as an agent of the past, a man suited to command a nation modeled on traditional forms of government, victorious in battle and beneficent at home, but whose future is left blank for it can promise little more than his death and a return to that problem of succession with which the century opened, a problem solvable only by the providential supply of yet another heroic leader. Marvell's achievement is not only in artistic conception and execution, but also in the range and scope of his understanding of England's political and historical situation. Both poets accept the difficult—if not ultimately impossible—challenge of transforming contemporary politics into poetry by attempting to celebrate a historically unprecedented national leader whose personal qualities can hold out little assurance for England's future. And both, appropriately enough, adopt similar procedures of deliberative speculation and triumphal form. Yet it is surely more than merely suggestive that, while Marvell stays close to factual detail, the other poet elaborates fictions, and that Marvell articulates the temporal possibilities of a predominantly spatial pattern of poetic organization in order to imagine a possible future more fully grounded upon a perceptive critique of current events than the other's detailed fabrications permit. Although consistently, yet unobtrusively, advisory, Marvell's poem displays a comprehensive understanding of the intimate links between domestic polity and international affairs, of Cromwell's crucial position as both ruler and reformer of the English state, and of the problem of dynastic succession. Thus he avoids the desperate polemic and eventful failure of vision which the other poet's reactionary monarchism inevitably entails. Marvell's *Anniversary* is itself a triumph, not only of poetic virtuosity, but also of historical imagination: a democratic assembly should stand by itself.

When Cromwell did die, in the same year in which *Anglia Rediviva* appeared, hopes for the new age of an English republican empire, once so confidently expected to follow from the political changes of the Commonwealth, largely faded. Like the scientific revolution of the seventeenth century, as Brecht describes it in his *Life of Galileo*, the political revolution imagined by poets foundered on a commitment to the past which proved integral to their heroic conception of history. Locked into the logic of the past when representing the present and future, political poets could deal only with things that had already taken place, and they needed time-conquering heroes to praise.

When Brecht's Galileo recants his teachings, one of his former disciples cries out, "Unhappy the land that has no heroes!" Galileo corrects him: "No. Unhappy the land that is in need of heroes."[76]

Epilogue

Toward the Restoration . . .

When a royal hero came down the line in May 1660 it didn't prove very difficult to generate a great deal of cultural excitement over the event. By the time of the coronation eleven months later, well over a hundred separately printed poems had appeared celebrating the king's return. The printing presses seem to have taken hardly any time to begin producing the ballads, news sheets, sermons, proclamations, songs, pamphlets, and histories which modern readers have since learned to expect from state occasions involving royalty. Here details of the day-to-day events were variously chronicled and what one recent historian calls the "natural" questions were addressed: what sort of man was Charles? what sort of king would he make? would he be fair? would he temper justice with mercy?[1] In terms of contemporary printed accounts, the Restoration must be the most heavily textualized, the most written-about event of the English revolution. But that in itself is perhaps less surprising than the way readers interested in the events of 1660 should still be so easily taken in by the myths and mystifications generated by that flurry of cultural production. What is there to make us believe that these were the natural questions other than that, simply by addressing them, the official accounts printed at the time invite us to ask them thereby making us, as readers, subject to the very discourse they were so busily naturalizing?[2]

Many of the English poems published at the time agree with other contemporary accounts and offer us the familiar image of rapt and giddy celebrations, of carnivalesque outbursts and highly orchestrated state displays, such as we find recorded by Pepys, Evelyn, and news sheets of the time. For some, the king's return doubtless seemed a glorious Maytime of ribbons and banners in the sunlight, of carousing amidst the bonfires and rumps roasting in the city streets after dark.[3] But not for all. While the king's return provided the chance for just the sort of celebration which made it difficult to be seen disapproving,[4] not everyone can have thought that the return to monarchy in 1660 was necessarily a good thing. In *The World Turned Upside Down,* Christopher Hill urged the cause of women and employees, pointing out that "by 1660 a majority of the men of property had come to see a lot" in the view that "true liberty" was knowing "by a certain law that our wives, our children, our servants, our goods are our own."[5] More recently David Underdown's study of political culture at the Restoration has encouraged us "not [to] exaggerate either the unanimity or the spontaneity of the celebrations. Many a genteel fellow-traveller who had only recently climbed aboard the royalist bandwagon would doubtless have been willing to desert Charles."[6]

Women, and women's rights, had a specially bad time after the Restoration. It was as if the insecurity of the new regime spilled over to feed already existing male anxieties. After the considerable advances women had made during the 1640s and 1650s, Restoration culture proved amazingly hostile to women. "In London, at least," Underdown reminds us, "women had demonstrated and petitioned on political matters, with or without the consent of their husbands." In arguing that "patriarchal order had been further subverted by sects which permitted women to preach, vote as church members, and disobey unconverted husbands," he still does something of a disservice to the memory of those sectarian women, who didn't need the authority of a "sect" to "permit" them to take their lives into their own hands.[7] But with the defeat of revolution, all that began changing. Ecclesiastical courts soon reopened and began enforcing their control over women by regulating family relations and sexual practices. Anne Caseley of Kenton in Devon was ordered to do public penance in her parish church for being an unmarried mother. Gilbert and Elioner [*sic*] Remphrey of Shirwell Clerk in the same county were ordered to confess publicly before "three clerics [to] their sin of fornication with each other before marriage." The accusation of witchcraft reappeared in the church courts as a credible legal category useful for punishing women. In Exeter on July 19, depositions were registered against a widow, Bridget Wotton, charging "that the accused caused the death of several pigs, and sickness in several women, by sorcery, using a toad as a familiar spirit."[8]

Poems celebrating the Restoration were often scurrilous and antiwoman, expressing the same fear of women's power that marks satires attacking sectarian women. It is a misleading commonplace of literary history that every aspiring poet who penned verses on the occasion did

so to celebrate the joyousness of Charles's return, since not all of them
were unreservedly celebratory and many expressed unwholesome desires
and appetites:

> Rejoyce Great Brittain, now, for Kings there's none
> Shall govern thee, but *Charles,* and he alone
> Will Peace and Plenty to this Nation bring,
> Who is the Son of *Charles* thy martyr'd KING.
> The *Rump* of Traytors (that did sore so high
> To spill the blood of sacred Majesty)
> Are now defunct, Poor Whore shee's brought a Bed
> Of a long Tayl, but neither brains nor Head.

In texts like this one, *The Famous Tragedie of the Life and Death of Mris
Rump,* the celebratory poetics of praise soon wear thin, giving way to
bizarre fantasies about the productivity of women's bodies that suggest a
very dark side to the rejoicing. After the Restoration, prurient fascination
with and fear of female sexuality combine with delight in generalized
slander and personal attack to become dominant features of political
poetry, as in the lines above from the epilogue to a text that purports to
have been "presented on a burning Stage at *Westminster* the 29th of *May,*
1660." While it is highly unlikely that *The Famous Tragedie of the Life
and Death of Mris Rump. Shewing How She was brought to Bed of a Monster
With her terrible Pangs, bitter Teeming, hard Labour, and lamentable Travell
from Portsmouth to Westminster, and the great misery she hath endured by her
ugly, deformed, ill-shapen, base-begotten Brat or Imp of Reformation* was
ever performed, much less on the day of Charles's arrival in London, this
publication nicely illustrates how printed verse both supplied and generated the need for new literary forms at the change in government by
displacing the contradictions of Stuart ideology into sensational narratives, such as gynophobic fantasies involving unnatural births.[9] For this
text of a play that no one ever imagined would be performed is every bit
as much a part of the poetic discourse of the Restoration as a formal
panegyric like Dryden's *Astraea Redux.* The *Famous Tragedie* tells us how,
finding herself to be pregnant, Mrs. Rump repents for her past sins before vomiting up the blood she has carried within her for the last eleven
years. With each bout of retching, she confesses to a further crime committed against the divine order of monarchy, as if the king returned

primarily in order to punish those responsible for usurping royal prerogative. Low comic dialogue, violent misogynist satire, parody of a puritan
repentance narrative, the visceral appeal of grotesque and disfiguring
revenge: these are the characteristic features of a text that was as integral
a part of the poetic discourse legitimating the Restoration as the more
decorous neoclassical panegyrics of a Dryden or a Waller.

In 1660 the return of monarchy was as much a cultural crisis of
textual representation as it was a political crisis of social representation.
Full of contradictions and gaps, riddled with tensions, Restoration culture quickly mobilized many different psychic, political, and poetical
registers seeking to reinscribe monarchic ideology in ways that would
make the king's return seem acceptable and unquestionable. David
Lloyd's specially up-dated edition of *Eikon Basilike* triumphantly claims
"Royal History Compleated: 1660" on the commemorative frontispiece.[10]
But in that year monarchy came back as a significantly fractured discursive field, clearly far from complete, and evidently in need of the cultural
legitimacy which the printed word seemed most capable of providing.[11]
Amidst the printed writings of 1660, alongside the rapturous expressions
of joy, the king's return was also being inscribed as an occasion for vent-
ing hostilities and righteous indignation. Readers were encouraged to
imagine the pleasures of some pretty vicious scenes. Pro-Stuart writers
engaged in systematic mystifications of monarchic authority that reveal
just how eager they were to authenticate their own control over the
printed word since it was peculiarly capable of setting conditions to
which royal power would be held accountable. This, at least, is the burden of personal satiric attack in *A Rope for Pol, Or, A Hue and Cry after
Marchemont Nedham. The late Scurrilous News-writer,* one of the more
interesting publications of the summer since, as the title goes on to explain, this is nothing less than "a Collection of [Nedham's] horrid Blas-
phemies and Revilings against the King's Majesty, his Person, his Cause,
and his Friends; published in his weekly *Politicus.*" Reprinting attacks
on a new king might once have seemed like a very strange way to generate hatred of their author. But in 1660 the copy was available, easy to
reissue, and during that summer there could be little doubt that it would
sell. The preface, however, complicates this rationale even as it offers it,
by dwelling not on the legitimacy of monarchy but on the power of print,
and by complaining of the way "unconsidering readers" often mistake
print for the truth.

It has been made a Question long agoe, whether more mischief then ad-
vantage were not occasion'd to the Christian world by the Invention of
Typography. But never was any Question more fully determin'd then this
has been of late years in these Nations. We have seen the Hierarchy of the
Church of *England* traduce'd and profan'd by the Writings of zealous In-
cendiaries. . . . In the State we have seen Sedition and Rebellion defended
and propagated in full Treatises, Murder, Treachery, Rapine, Perjury, Ambition, Tyranny, Oppression, Perfidiousnesse justify'd and applauded. . . .
Writings of this strain, and many others as they have been the issue of
trayterous and pestilent minds, so they have been brought into the world
and propagated by the assistance of the Presse. But what was by others
singly attempted in several waies, has been in all practis'd by the late Writer
of *Politicus, Marchemont Nedham,* whose scurrilous Pamphlets flying every
Week into all parts of the Nation, 'tis incredible what influence they had
upon numbers of unconsidering persons, who have a strange presumption
that all must needs be true that is in Print.

                                                            (Sigs. [a2–a2ᵛ])

Just what were the pleasures to be derived from reading Nedham's attacks on the king, his person, and his cause? What sort of reader had
come into being by 1660 who, wanting to read about the new king,
would want to read this sort of thing? Maybe everything printed isn't
necessarily the truth just because it is printed; how else could Nedham's
attacks on Charles be reprintable? Although *A Rope for Pol* was published as part of the celebrations welcoming Charles, these statements
indicate its more precise location and intervention within a public discourse of printed texts that was not only helping to generate and autho-
rize specific kinds of public interest in the king, but was thereby demonstrating the satirist's claims about how enormously powerful the press
had become in affairs of state, and that such power was independent of
royal authority. A wise reader knew that print did not signify truth,
always: but that very unreliability would seem to be a condition of the
authority which, by 1660, print had already established for itself. Not
always true but nevertheless powerful: such is the logic of representation
underwriting the reinstitutionalization of royal authority.

Amidst the euphoric reestablishment of cultural controls centered
on the mysterious, visceral appeals of royal power, there was little that
opposition poets could do during 1660 but remain silent. Even the view
from Scotland, which offered a pastoral voice of critical opposition, suffered from the intoxication of the times. The full title of *Grampius Con-*

gratulation ([Edinburgh ?], 1660) recalls how a self-consciously plain style gave the pastoral opposition its traditionally radical edge—*In plain Scots Language*—but then alludes to the Stuart conceit of the triple crown/nation—*To His Majesties Thrise Happy Return.* The verses are not in dialect yet offer a deliberately rough style that crashes rhymed couplets about inside what are printed to look like irregular strophes. In case we miss the point, on the second page we are told:

> What if we mirrie made by water,
> Mingled with *Enthean* fire shall clatter?
> No Treason's here: our noise and din
> Shall greater be far than our sin.
>
> (Sig. A2ᵛ)

This sort of crude ethnic satire doesn't exactly invite readers to identify with the persona, but it does suggest how the possibility of oppositional poetry was erased when its own language was being taken over and collapsed into the irrationality and unthinking condition necessary to an acceptance of the Restoration. Milton, who surely understood these matters better than most, knew not even to try opposing the king's return in poetry. During the autumn of 1659, while there was still a chance of "a second English Revolution,"[12] Milton trusted to prose. "Between October 1659 and April 1660," Hill reminds us, "Milton put forward no less than six variants of his plan for averting a restoration of monarchy, and always the idea behind the changes was to make a commonwealth more widely accepted."[13] But those members of Parliament who, in late January, set the Restoration in motion by inviting Monck's army into London seem not to have been reading Milton.[14] Perhaps they were too busy for ideas, already too caught up imagining what it would be like to invite a king back, too fascinated by fantasies of their own power to be persuaded by rational argument.

The cultural euphoria of 1660, the strong and persistent appeal of and to an irrationality that was evidently necessary to mediate the contradictions of Charles's return, depended on more than ethnic humor and sensational sexist fantasies. To legitimate the Restoration, to make sure fellow travelers stayed on that bandwagon, it was evidently necessary to rely upon the logic of undecidability as if the self-deconstruction of historical claims about the king's return were an essential condition of its legitimacy. In 1662, John Gauden, who had been appointed bishop of

Exeter during the autumn of 1660, published *The Strange and Wonderfull Visions and Predictions of William Juniper of Gosfield in Essex, relating to the Troubles of England*. It contains the following report:

> To all these he added, at that time, which was Five or Six years at least before the Kings happy restauration; this last Vision or Dream, which he thus told me: He thought (said he) I was in such a large Field, and looking about me, I saw from the East a very goodly *Lion* coming at a stately pace; on the *West* I saw all sorts of Beasts coming towards him, with all reverent and lowly behaviour, crouching and fawning. The *Lion* advanced till he came into the midst of the Field, and the highest place of it, there he sate down on his hinder part with such *Majesty,* as seemed to keep all the Beasts in aw; they came in very lowly manner toward him, prostrating themselves, and at last they lay on the ground quietly round about him, but at a good distance; The *Lion* using no revenge upon any of them, sate composed in great state and quiet.
>
> I said, *Goodman Juniper,* this seems to import the Kings peaceable and happy return again to his Kingdom, and that we may live to see all people subject to him. *He replyed,* Sir, I no thing doubt of that; God will certainly Restore his Majesty, and subdue his enemies; though I may not live to see it, yet your *Worship* may.
>
> (Pp. 13–14)

Gauden knew about rewriting history. Back in 1655 or 1656, about the time the Commonwealth was becoming Cromwell's Protectorate, an ordinary Englishman was dreaming about his king coming back. As an instance of the continuing need to erase the memory of revolution by historicizing the Restoration, the passage is interesting for a number of reasons; the conventional yet conveniently relevant solar movement of the king who comes from the east and receives tribute from the west, the unquestioning assumption that revenge is somehow part of the story, the way desire for the king's return displaces the revolutionary past. And then there is that stylish clumsiness over the he/I pronouns governing the vision—"he thus told me: He thought (said he) I was"—which returns after the report, strategically transformed into a heavily class-coded disagreement over how to interpret the dream. Gauden, who had probably taken a leading hand in the production of the *Eikon Basilike* back in 1649, was experienced in the ways of producing cultural discourse on behalf of Stuarts named Charles. He clearly understood how to employ printed texts for naturalizing the mysteries of monarchy. Throughout his framing comments in the book, he adopts a generally skeptical view of dreams and prophecies while insisting that Goodman William Juniper had no ulterior motives or designs in his visions.

Now when a bishop who claims that he doesn't believe in prophetic visions nevertheless publishes a report of a workingman's dream as evidence of the legitimacy of monarchy in which he manifestly wants his readers to believe, we should suspect there are some pretty odd things going on besides the erasure of the revolutionary past by the phantasmagoria of strange and wonderful dreams. For one, existing class contradictions are being displaced and contained by the continuing ideological struggle for authority over knowledge production. For another, future class conflict is being rendered unthinkable. So much depends on those beasts from the west. Where the skeptical bishop reads the possibility of them both living "to see all people subject" to the restored monarch, the dreamer, who would have no public voice if it weren't for the prelate's allowing him this access to print, is permitted to contradict himself. While announcing that he "no thing" doubts of what the bishop says, he makes it clear that he expects to die before becoming one of those subjects. Perhaps that's the same thing as the king subduing his enemies; so much depends on what Goodman Juniper could not say. The world, having been turned upside down, is not being put to rights again in any simple way. Whatever the arrival of Charles meant, it was no simple return.

I am suggesting that we still tend to think of the Restoration the way we were told to. In 1660, at least, it was what we would now call a large-scale media event, one that involved the production of a great deal of commemorative publishing.[15] In much the same ways that television and print coverage leading up to the Royal Wedding in 1981 distracted attention from the ways Thatcher's police were, during those sunny June days, manipulating the class riots in Brixton so that anyone not involved would imagine they were racially rather than politically generated, the production of political poetry had become an integral part and necessary form of a public discourse largely managed by commercially minded printers and professional writers, a class that included but was not restricted to bishops and other dependents of the king. Like previous royal entries, Charles's return depended on a great deal of theatricality, and the reopening of the theaters has long been taken as the central cultural event of 1660. But we should not forget that the Restoration was also the first royal occasion that could, and indeed had to, make use of an already established commercial printing industry that employed people who had become fully aware of their political power. Under these conditions, poetry assumed both constitutive and critical functions precisely because in praising returning monarchy poets knew they were establishing structures of ideals and expectations to which the new regime would be held accountable.

In this time of celebration and suspicion, of uncertainty and fear, most of the English poems published between the king's return and his coronation reassure their readers—those secured by the Act of Indemnity, at least—that everything would be well since the king was in control again. So the broader historical significance of the poems written to celebrate the Restoration is their mediation of this double view by publicly providing terms in which Charles's return becomes imaginatively acceptable.[16] Poems celebrating the Restoration display a remarkable insistence on continuity, not only with traditional royalist ideology, but also with changes in attitude accomplished during the revolutionary decades. Even the most pro-Stuart panegyrists put limits to royal power implicitly if not directly. Why should they have ignored the degree to which the political demands of their readers had been shaped by the last twenty years? There would have been little point in ignoring the compelling memory of the last king's spectacular death, or in pretending that people would not remember Worcester. If the execution and interregnum had demonstrated the undeniably secular basis of and consequent limits to royal power, it was always possible to appeal to divine judgment and recuperate royal defeat into even more glorious victory.[17] Alongside celebrations of the benefits of monarchy, the debate over liberty continued.[18] And there were changes in foreign policy. Harrington and Cromwell had so far revised the theory and practice of British foreign policy that the adventure of imperial expansion appears publicly as part of the national destiny and no longer a matter of royal prerogative.[19]

The Restoration put an end to many revolutions, but not those in historical thinking and textual production. Among the most typical gestures of Restoration panegyric is one learned from the oppositional poets of the 1630s and 1640s who, writing against the grain of Stuart absolutism, insisted that the national identity depended upon foreign policy. By associating Charles with the growth of British trade and empire, poets in 1660 continued a line of argument from Cromwellian panegyric which had celebrated mercantile expansion during the 1650s. So much had the image of monarchy changed from the days of James. In arguing that Charles is an unprecedented kind of king, Richard Flecknoe's "Portrait" suggests that it wasn't just the image that had changed. The emphasis falls on how Charles is different because of his education in foreign courts, which is one way of recuperating his exile:

> Nor shall you e'er in any person finde
> A great strength of body and of minde;
> Which with long Travel ha's improved so,
> He knows what e're befits a Prince to know;
> Not learnt from th'dead, but from the world, & men,
> Those living *Authors;* and ha's studied them,
> So as each Nations Wisdom he does know,
> And each one's Language to express it too.
> Whence he compar'd to other Princes, sit
> Dully at home, and nothing know but it,
> Seems just like some huge Gallion does come
> From farthest Indies, richly laden home.[20]

Flecknoe surely knew Marvell's *First Anniversary* and Waller's celebrated *Panegyric on My Lord Protector.* But Dryden also wrote of Charles's "too, too active age," and argued that his exile was really an education in becoming a shrewd world leader. The oppositional poets of the 1630s and 1640s who criticized Stuart pacifism had tended to represent the adventure of overseas expansion as the nostalgic recovery of a glorious chivalric past.[21] Cromwellian panegyrics of the 1650s more explicitly celebrated the virtues of mercantilism and overseas expansion as the conditions of his success. At the Restoration, Dryden was not the only poet to praise Charles by instructing him to adopt policies that would increase British control of world trade, though *Astraea Redux* advocates a singularly bloodthirsty foreign policy involving a speedy trade war against the Dutch. One balladeer of the time agreed that the Restoration will be a good thing if it increases trade, but did not agree about the means:

> Our *Exchange* shall bee filled with Merchants from far
> 'Tis better to deal in good Traffick than war
> With all Neighbour Nations wee'l shake hands in peace
> By that means our treasure and trade will increase
> > With *France* and with *Spain*

> Wee'l make leagues again
> Wee thank them for *succouring* our Soveraign
> *May all the rich pleasures that ever were reckon'd*
> *Attend on the Person of King Charls the second.*[22]

Poets writing to celebrate the king's return agreed about some things and disagreed about others. Auden was surely thinking of large-scale and immediate changes when he observed that poetry makes nothing happen. Certainly no poet could have prevented the Restoration if Milton couldn't; and he tried in prose. But without poetry, the Restoration might not have succeeded. It certainly wouldn't have been the same.

. . . AND BEYOND

We need a new history of the production, reproduction, and reception of "English" poetry in the seventeenth century, one based on an analysis of changes in the relations of cultural production that will avoid the depoliticization of formalistic accounts or the simplifications likely to result from master narratives such as the transition from feudalism to capitalism central to classical Marxist historiography. Rethinking literary history from a relations-of-production model will situate seventeenth-century poetry between the capitalization of land tenure on the one hand, and the political economies of mercantile expansion on the other.[23] Operating a politicized analysis of "genre," "ideology," and "history," rather than formalist categories of author, oeuvre, and the canon, a new history of seventeenth-century English poetry will attend to "protestant" poetics as central to the discursive crisis of masculinity inscribed by Reformation gender ideologies and by the new virility of empire which the Restoration helped enunciate. It will trace the emergence of modern sexual divisions and gender formations within the general interpellation of the imperial reading subject to contributing to our understanding of the gender and class fantasies which print culture made possible in early modern England. It will employ the perspectives of a feminist materialism sufficiently nuanced to account for the historically specific poetic forms that underwrite particular social and political orders by the discontinuous articulation of race, class, and gender hierarchies. It will examine the "making" of gender- and class-specific English-reading publics. It will recuperate the forms of resistance, assimilation, and silencing experienced by pro-woman and women poets. And it will emphasize the instrumentality of printing amidst broader technological developments that were making possible the inauguration and establishment of those sociocultural practices, values, and structures of desire that enabled British imperial hegemony by constructing the normative expectations of "first-world" readers.

Notes

Works Cited

Index

Notes

Preface

1 Billy Bragg, *Between the Wars* (London: Chrysalis, 1984), side B; his version of "The Digger's Song" also appeared on an EP of the same name. See also Red London, *This is England* (London: Razor Records, 1984), side 2, and The Gang of Four, *Solid Gold* (London: Warner Brothers, 1981).

2 Interview, cited Paul Graham, "March of the New Puritans" *Sunday Times Magazine,* March 13, 1988, p. 68.

3 For a critique of recent theories of "the reader" and an introduction to the need for an *intertextual* approach to the problem of how Renaissance texts help form their readers, see Maureen Quilligan's *Milton's Spenser: The Politics of Reading* (Ithaca: Cornell University Press, 1983), chap. 1.

4 See Ullrich Langer, "Gunpowder as Transgressive Invention in Ronsard," in *Literary Theory / Renaissance Texts,* ed. Patricia Parker and David Quint (Baltimore: Johns Hopkins University Press, 1986), pp. 96–114.

5 Walter Benjamin, "The Work of Art in the Age of Mechanical Reproduction," *Illuminations,* trans Harry Zohn, ed. Hannah Arendt (1968; rpt. New York: Schocken, 1969), pp. 218–19.

6 Elizabeth Eisenstein, *The Printing Press as an Agent of Change: Communications and Cultural Transformations in Early-Modern Europe,* 2 vols. (Cambridge: Cambridge University Press, 1979).

7 Richard Helgerson, "Milton Reads the King's Book: Print, Performance, and the Making of a Bourgeois Idol," *Criticism* 29 (1987): 1–26.

8 Simon Barker, "Images of the Sixteenth and Seventeenth Centuries as a History of the Present," in *Literature, Politics and Theory: Papers from the Essex Conference, 1976–84,* ed. Francis Barker, Peter Hulme, Margaret Iverson, and Diana Loxley (London: Methuen, 1986), pp. 173–89. And see Margot Heinemann, "How Brecht Read Shakespeare," in *Political Shakespeare: New Essays in Cultural Materialism,* ed. Jonathan Dollimore and Alan Sinfield (Manchester: Manchester University Press, 1985), pp. 202–30.

9 Cited by Barker, "Images of the Sixteenth and Seventeenth Centuries," p. 185.

10   See Timothy J. Reiss, *The Discourse of Modernism* (Ithaca: Cornell University Press, 1982).

11   Jon Klancher, *The Making of English Reading Audiences, 1790–1832* (Madison: University of Wisconsin Press, 1987), p. 6. Although concerned primarily with the English romantics, Klancher's study offers a useful paradigm for understanding the construction of reading audiences, particularly the sense of possible "mis"-reading, in the seventeenth century. "Interpretation," he writes, "attends *all* uses of a text, it requires a guarantee of institutional authority capable of ruling in, and ruling out, the possible readings made by possible audiences" (p. 6). The mechanisms or apparatuses of this "institutional authority" are precisely what are at issue in the debate over Lucan's *Pharsalia* discussed in Chapter 1, for the binary opposition poetry/history concerns different kinds of textual claims to the truth. The most common institution of control operating in seventeenth-century Britain was clearly the training in the classics that both produced and problematized this sort of grand generic scheme. It was a necessary task of Renaissance humanism thus to co-locate a secular canon of Greek and Roman authors against the canon of sacred scriptures by means of distinguishing their referential status. How could the representation of a world—or an epistemology, as Derrida would have it—in a text by a Homer or a Virgil be mistaken for that of a Moses or a Saint Paul? However central and pervasive the control over intepretation exercised by generic regulation might have been, other social controls besides access to education, such as censorship, access to a press, as well as residual class contempt for publishing one's writings, would further distinguish the seventeenth from later centuries.

12   Catherine Belsey, *John Milton: Language, Gender, Power* (Oxford: Blackwell, 1988), p. 14.

Introduction

1   See the Epigraph, which comes from Christopher Hill, "The Pre-Revolutionary Decades," *The Collected Essays,* Vol. 1: *Writing and Revolution in Seventeenth-Century England* (Amherst: University of Massachusetts Press, 1985), p. 3. A similar argument, again directed at historians rather than literary scholars, is made throughout Lauro Martines' theoretical considerations in *Society and History in English Renaissance Verse* (Oxford: Blackwell, 1985), which seeks to persuade historians that they should and must consider poetry as part of the historical record with which they are concerned. In "Literature and the English Revolution," *The Seventeenth Century* 1 (1986): 15–30, Hill replies that this work is already being done by certain literary historians.

2 For a theoretically sophisticated justification of reading allusions to Virgil in seventeenth-century English poetry politically, see Annabel Patterson, *Pastoral and Ideology: Virgil to Valéry* (Berkeley and Los Angeles: University of California Press, 1987), chap. 3.

3 I owe this observation to Christopher Hill. For discussion of Milton's attempts to prevent the Restoration by strategic last-minute planning, see Hill, *Milton and the English Revolution* (New York: Viking, 1977), p. 199. For a discussion of *Paradise Lost* as a commentary upon Restoration politics, see Mary Ann Radzinowicz, "The Politics of *Paradise Lost*," in *Politics of Discourse: The Literature and History of Seventeenth-Century England,* ed. Kevin Sharpe and Steven Zwicker (Berkeley and Los Angeles: University of California Press, 1987): 204–29.

4 For a summary of the general debate, see T. K. Rabb and Derek Hirst, "Revisionism Revised: Two Perspectives on Early Stuart Parliamentary History," *Past and Present* 92 (1981): 55–78, 79–99.

5 Dominick LaCapra, *Rethinking Intellectual History: Texts, Contexts, Language* (Ithaca: Cornell University Press, 1982), p. 25.

6 Ibid., p. 30.

7 Jonathan Goldberg, *James I and the Politics of Literature* (Baltimore: Johns Hopkins University Press, 1983).

8 Maureen Quilligan, *Milton's Spenser: The Politics of Reading* (Ithaca: Cornell University Press, 1983). See Ann R. Jones's political reading of Nashe's *The Unfortunate Traveller* for the most incisive introduction to a demotic Renaissance text in terms of Bahktinian "heteroglossia" and Kristevan "intertextuality" in "Inside the Outsider: Nashe's *Unfortunate Traveller* and Bakhtin's Polyphonic Novel," *English Literary History* 50 (1983): 61–81. This problem of the literary historian identifying with the view from above most seriously marks Barbara Lewalski's magisterial *Protestant Poetics and the Seventeenth-Century Religious Lyric* (Princeton: Princeton University Press, 1979) which manages to ignore the important protestant lyrics of John Cragge, John Saltmarsh, John Vicars, and George Wither, to name only a few.

9 Cited by Perry Anderson, in *Lineages of the Absolutist State* (1974; rpt. London: Verso, 1980), p. 23.

10 For a defense of this position, and a careful working through of its implications for reading early modern biographical texts, see Judith B. Anderson, *Biographical Truth: The Representation of Historical Persons in Tudor-Stuart Writing* (New Haven: Yale University Press, 1984).

11 See Ruth Nevo, *The Dial of Virtue: A Study of Poems on Affairs of State in the Seventeenth Century* (Princeton: Princeton University Press, 1963); C. V. Wedgewood, *Poetry and Politics under the Stuarts* (Cambridge: Cambridge University Press, 1968); Isabel Rivers, *The Poetry of Conservatism, 1600–*

1745: A Study of Poets and Public Affairs from Jonson to Pope (Cambridge: Rivers Press, 1973); Earl Miner, *The Metaphysical Mode from Donne to Cowley* (Princeton: Princeton University Press, 1969), *The Cavalier Mode from Jonson to Cotton* (Princeton: Princeton University Press, 1971), *The Restoration Mode from Milton to Dryden* (Princeton: Princeton University Press, 1974); Steven Zwicker, *Dryden's Political Poetry* (Providence: Brown University Press, 1972) Michael McKeon, *Politics and Poetry in Restoration England: The Case of Dryden's "Annus Mirabilis"* (Cambridge: Harvard University Press, 1975); Michael Wilding, *Dragon's Teeth: Literature in the English Revolution* (Oxford: Clarendon Press, 1987).

12 John Wallace, *Destiny His Choice: The Loyalism of Andrew Marvell* (Cambridge: Cambridge University Press, 1968); Christopher Hill, *Milton and the English Revolution* (New York: Viking, 1977); George MacFadden, *Dryden the Public Writer, 1660–1685* (Princeton: Princeton University Press, 1977); Annabel Patterson, *Marvell and the Civic Crown* (Princeton: Princeton University Press, 1978); Warren Chernaik, *The Poet's Time: Politics and Religion in the Work of Andrew Marvell* (Cambridge: Cambridge University Press, 1983); Steven Zwicker, *Politics and Language in Dryden's Poetry: The Arts of Disguise* (Princeton: Princeton University Press, 1984).

13 See Quilligan, *Milton's Spenser,* and Arthur Marotti, *John Donne: Coterie Poet* (Madison: University of Wisconsin Press, 1986).

14 See Stephen Orgel, *The Jonsonian Masque* (1965; rpt. New York: Columbia University Press, 1981); Margot Heinemann, *Puritanism and Theatre: Thomas Middleton and Opposition Drama under the Early Stuarts* (Cambridge: Cambridge University Press, 1980); Lisa Jardine, *Still Harping on Daughters: Women in Drama in the Age of Shakespeare* (Brighton: Harvester, 1983); Jonathan Dollimore, *Radical Tragedy: Religion, Ideology and Power in the Drama of Shakespeare and His Contemporaries* (Chicago: University of Chicago Press, 1984); Catherine Belsey, *The Subject of Tragedy: Identity and Difference in Renaissance Drama* (London: Methuen, 1986); Walter Cohen, *Drama of a Nation: Public Theater in Renaissance England and Spain* (Ithaca: Cornell University Press, 1985); Leonard Tennenhouse, *Power on Display: The Politics of Shakespeare's Genres* (London: Methuen, 1987); and Martin Butler, *Theatre and Crisis, 1632–1642* (Cambridge: Cambridge University Press, 1984). See also the collections of essays in *Alternative Shakespeares,* ed. John Drakakis (London: Methuen, 1985), and *Political Shakespeare: New Essays in Cultural Materialism,* ed. Jonathan Dollimore and Alan Sinfield (Manchester: Manchester University Press, 1985).

15 The key work here is Stephen Greenblatt's *Renaissance Self-Fashioning from More to Shakespeare* (Chicago: University of Chicago Press, 1980), but no less important is Richard Helgerson's *Self-Crowned Laureates: Spenser, Jon-*

son, Milton and the Literary System (Berkeley: University of California Press, 1983).

16 See James Turner, *The Politics of Landscape: Rural Scenery and Society in English Poetry, 1630–1660* (Oxford: Blackwell, 1978); David Norbrook, *Poetry and Politics in the English Renaissance* (London: Routledge and Kegan Paul, 1984); Annabel Patterson, *Censorship and Interpretation: The Conditions of Writing and Reading in Early Modern England* (Madison: University of Wisconsin Press, 1984), and *Pastoral and Ideology.*

Chapter 1: Poetry, History, and Seventeenth-Century English Culture

1 See Steven Zwicker's development of the terms of political "disguise" in the poetics of the time in his *Politics and Language in Dryden's Poetry: The Arts of Disguise* (Princeton: Princeton University Press, 1984). The term was first developed in Max Novak, ed., *English Literature in the Age of Disguise* (Los Angeles: William Andrews Clark Memorial Library, University of California Press, 1977). For recent interest in the history/poetry distinction by literary historians of seventeenth-century England, see John Wallace, Introduction to *The Golden and Brazen World: Papers in Literature and History, 1650–1800* (Berkeley and Los Angeles: University of California Press, 1985); Janel Mueller, "The Mastery of Decorum: Politics as Poetry in Milton's Sonnets," *Critical Inquiry* 13 (1987): 475–508; and Kevin Sharpe and Steven Zwicker, Introduction to *Politics of Discourse: the Literature and History of Seventeenth-Century England* (Berkeley and Los Angeles: University of California Press, 1987).

2 Perry Anderson, *Lineages of the Absolutist State* (1974; rpt. London: Verso, 1980), pp. 113–42. See also Nicos Poulantzas, *Political Power and Social Classes,* trans. Timothy O'Hagan et al. (London: Verso, 1982), pp. 157–72, and Brian P. Levack, "Law and Ideology: The Civil Law and Theories of Absolutism in Elizabethan and Jacobean England," in *The Historical Renaissance: New Essays on Tudor and Stuart Literature and Culture* ed. Heather Dubrow and Richard Strier (Chicago: University of Chicago Press, 1988), pp. 220–41.

3 See Ted Benton's introduction to Louis Althusser's concept of "interpellation," which posits the social constitution of "the subject and its subjection" in relation with the "Absolute Subject" of ideology, in *The Rise and Fall of Structural Marxism* (New York: St. Martin's, 1984), esp. pp. 173–99; the phrase is from p. 197. Compare Diane Macdonnell, *Theories of Discourse: An Introduction* (Oxford: Blackwell, 1986), pp. 36–42, and Althusser's own formulation in "Ideology and Ideological State Apparatuses," *Lenin and Phi-*

losophy and Other Essays, trans. Ben Brewster (London: Monthly Review, 1971), pp. 127–86.

4 In *Literacy and the Social Order: Reading and Writing in Tudor and Stuart England* (Cambridge: Cambridge University Press, 1981), pp. 42–61, David Cressy questions the assumption that the great increase in book production during the seventeenth century necessarily implies growth in the reading public.

5 See F. Smith Fussner, *The Historical Revolution: English Historical Writing and Thought, 1580–1640* (London: Routledge and Kegan Paul, 1964). In these comments regarding the development of historiography in seventeenth-century England, I have also relied upon the following: Arthur B. Ferguson, *Clio Unbound: Perception of the Social and Cultural Past in Renaissance England* (Durham: Duke University Press, 1979); Donald Kelley, *Foundations of Modern Historical Scholarship: Language, Law, and History in the French Revolution* (New York: Columbia University Press, 1970); and F. J. Levy, *Tudor Historical Thought* (San Marino, Ca.: Huntington Library, 1967). Joseph Levine's "Ancients, Moderns, and History: The Continuity of English Historical Writing in the Later Seventeenth Century," in *Studies in Change and Revolution: Aspects of English Intellectual History,* ed. Paul Korshin (Menston, Yorks: Scolar Press, 1972), pp. 43–75, offers an opposing account.

6 See *Richard II,* ed. Peter Ure (1956; rpt. London: Methuen, 1966), pp. lvii–lxii.

7 Stephen Greenblatt, "Invisible Bullets: Renaissance Authority and Its Subversions, *Henry IV* and *Henry V,*" in *Political Shakespeare: New Essays in Cultural Materialism,* ed. Jonathan Dollimore and Alan Sinfield (Manchester: Manchester University Press, 1985), p. 45.

8 Franco Moretti, "Tragic Form and the Deconsecration of Sovereignty," in *Signs Taken for Wonders: Essays in the Sociology of Literary Forms* (London: Verso, 1983), pp. 42–82. See also Walter Cohen, *Drama of a Nation: Public Theater in Renaissance England and Spain* (Ithaca: Cornell University Press, 1985).

9 Barry Reay, Introduction to *Popular Culture in Seventeenth-Century England* (New York: St. Martin's, 1985), p. 4.

10 Edmund Bohun translated Degory Wheare's 1623 lectures as *The Method and Order of Reading both Civil and Ecclesiastical Histories* in 1685 (rpt. 1694, 1698). For contemporary discussions of the reading and writing of history and poetry, see also Sir Thomas Elyot, *The Booke of the Governor,* ed. S. E. Lehmberg (1962; rpt. London: Dent, 1966, p. 228; Thomas Lanquet, *An Epitome of Chronicles*) (1549, rpt. 1559), sig. Aiii, and his edition of *Cooper's Chronicle* (1560), sig. A; Roger Ascham, *Ascham's English Works,* ed. W. A. Wright (Cambridge: Cambridge University Press, 1904), p. 213; *The Basili-*

con Doron of King James VI, ed. James Craigie (London: Blackwood, 1944), 1:151–52; James Cleland, *Heropaedia, of the Institution of a Young Nobleman* (1607), p. 83; Henry Peacham, *The Complete Gentleman,* ed. Virgil B. Heltzel (Ithaca: Cornell University Press, 1962), pp. 56–65; Alexander Ramsey, *The Gentleman's Companion; or, a Character of True Nobility and Gentility* (1672), pp. 14–16; Jean Gailhard, *The Complete Gentleman; or, Directions for the Education of Youth* (1678), pp. 43–48; Thomas Hearne, *Ductor Historicus, or, A Short System of Universal History* (1698), sig. A1ᵛ; Robert Norton's translation of Camden's *The History of the Princess Elizabeth* (1630), sig. A; and Richard Braithwait, *A Survey of History* (1638), p. 56. Among modern studies, see Levy, *Tudor Historical Thought,* pp. 167–236, and H. S. Bennett, *English Books and Readers, 1603–1640* (Cambridge: Cambridge University Press, 1970), pp. 179–89. For European backgrounds, see Leonard F. Dean, "Bodin's *Methodus* in England before 1625," *Studies in Philology* 39 (1942): 160–66, and "Sir Francis Bacon's Theory of Civil History Writing," *English Literary History* 8 (1941): 161–83; Julian M. Franklin, *Jean Bodin and the Sixteenth-Century Revolution in the Methodology of Law and History* (New York: Columbia University Press, 1963); George H. Nadel, "History as Psychology in Francis Bacon's Theory of History," *History and Theory* 5 (1966): 275–87; and Richard Schlatter's introduction to his edition of *Hobbes's Thucydides* (New Brunswick, N.J.: Rutgers University Press, 1975).

11 Thomas Bearde, *The Theatre of God's Judgements* (1597), sigs. A4ᵛ–A5. See also Louis B. Wright, *Middle-Class Culture in Elizabethan England* (Chapel Hill: University of North Carolina Press, 1935), pp. 297–338.

12 Pierre Amyot, preface to North's translation of Plutarch's *Lives* (1579), sig. +iii. See Richard S. Ide, "Chapman's *Caesar and Pompey* and the Uses of History," *Modern Philology* 82 (1985): 256.

13 On Ralegh's *History,* see Leonard Tennenhouse, "Sir Walter Ralegh and the Literature of Clientage," in *Patronage in the Renaissance,* in ed. Guy Lytle and Stephen Orgel (Princeton: Princeton University Press, 1981), pp. 249–58. C. A. Patrides' introduction to his edition of *The History of the World* (Philadelphia: Temple University Press, 1971) offers useful background information, but is marked by a rather desperate attempt to force Ralegh's work into strict adherence to a Christian providentialism.

14 John Dryden, "Life of Plutarch," *Of Dramatic Poesy and Other Critical Essays,* ed. George Watson, 2 vols. (London: Dent, 1968), 2:4.

15 John Speed, *History of Great Britain* (1623 ed.), sig. A5.

16 Richard Crashaw, *The Poems English, Latin, and Greek,* ed. L. C. Martin (Oxford: Clarendon Press, 1927), p. 463. Isaacson's title page and these verses are also discussed by Paul K. Alkon, "Johnson and Chronology," in *Greene Centennial Studies,* ed. Paul J. Korshin and Robert R. Allen (Charlottesville: University of Virginia Press, 1984), pp. 144–45.

17 William Davenant, Preface to *Gondibert,* in *Critical Essays of the Seventeenth Century,* ed. Joel Spingarn, 3 vols. (Oxford: Clarendon Press, 1908), 1:11.

18 Braithwait, *A Survey of History,* p. 2.

19 Owen Feltham, *Resolves* (the so-called "eighth" edition of 1661), p. 122.

20 J. P. Sullivan, *Literature and Politics in the Age of Nero* (Ithaca: Cornell University Press, 1985), p. 20.

21 Frederick Ahl, Martha A. Davis, and Arthur Pomeroy, "Silius Italicus," in *Aufstieg und Niedergang der römischen Welt,* Vol. 32.4, ed. Hildegard Temporini and Wolfgang Haase (Berlin: De Gruyter, 1986), pp. 2502–3.

22 On the transmission of Aristotle's *Poetics* in England via the Italian commentators, see Marvin T. Herrick, *The Poetics of Aristotle in England* (New Haven: Yale University Press, 1930).

23 See Frederick Ahl, *Lucan: An Introduction* (Ithaca: Cornell University Press, 1976), pp. 35–47, 333–65, and passim.

24 *Boccaccio on Poetry: Being the Preface and the Fourteenth and Fifteenth Books of Boccaccio's Genealogia Deorum Gentilium in an English Version,* trans. Charles G. Osgood (Princeton: Princeton University Press, 1930), p. 132; see pp. 173–74 for earlier commentators.

25 Scaliger, *The Poetics,* in *Critical Theory since Plato*, ed. Hazard Adams (New York: Harcourt, 1971), p. 141.

26 Castelvetro, *The Poetics* in Adams, *Critical Theory,* p. 145.

27 Pierre de Ronsard, *Les Oeuvres de Pierre de Ronsard: Texte de 1587,* ed. Isidore Silver, 8 vols. (Chicago: University of Chicago Press, 1967), 4:18.

28 Carlo Signio, *De Dialogo* (1562), cited in Bernard Weinberg, *A History of Literary Criticism in the Italian Renaissance,* 2 vols. (Chicago: University of Chicago Press, 1961), 1:483.

29 Camillo Pellegrino, *Replica alla riposta de gli Accademici della Crusca* (1585), cited in Weinberg, *History of Literary Criticism,* 2:1019.

30 Torquato Tasso, *Discourses on the Heroic Poem,* trans. Mariella Cavalchini and Irene Taylor (Oxford: Clarendon Press, 1973), p. 54.

31 John Dryden, "The Author's Apology for Heroic Poetry and Poetic Licence," prefixed to the 1677 edition of *The State of Innocence,* in *Of Dramatic Poesy,* 1:201.

32 Cited in Edward W. Tayler, ed., *Literary Criticism of Seventeenth-Century England* (New York: Knopf, 1967), p. 372. For comparisons between Lucan and Virgil made earlier in the century, see Henry Peacham, "Of Poetry," from *The Compleat Gentleman* (1622) in Springarn, *Critical Essays,* 1:127–28, and William Alexander's defense of Lucan in his *Anacrisis* (1634?), in Spingarn, *Critical Essays,* 1:183.

33 "From the Conversations of Ben Jonson and William Drummond of Hawthornden, 1619," in Spingarn, *Critical Essays,* 1:212.

34 "To my chosen Friend, The learned Translator of Lucan, Thomas May,

Esquire," in *Lucan's Pharsalia: Or The Civill Warres of Rome, betweene Pompey the great, and Julius Caesar,* translated by Thomas May (1627), sig. a7.

35 William Davenant, Preface to *Gondibert,* in Spingarn, *Critical Essays,* 2:3.

36 Thomas Hobbes, *Answer to Davenant,* in Spingarn, *Critical Essays,* 2:56.

37 *The Poems of John Dryden,* ed. James Kinsley, 4 vols. (Oxford: Clarendon Press, 1958), 1:44.

38 John Dryden, "Of Heroic Plays," in *Of Dramatic Poesy,* 1:160.

39 Thomas Rymer, *Preface to Rapin* (1674), in Spingarn, *Critical Essays,* 2:171.

40 Sir William Temple, "Of Poetry," in Spingarn, *Critical Essays,* 3:84.

41 See Christopher Hill, *Intellectual Origins of the English Revolution* (1965; rpt. Oxford: Clarendon Press, 1982), p. 150.

42 "Quintilian comments that Lucan is a better model for orators than for poets: 'magis oratoribus quam poetis imitandis' (*Inst. Or.* 10.1.90)." Ahl, *Lucan,* p. 75.

43 See Ahl, *Lucan,* pp. 58–61, and Robert Tucker, "Lucan and the French Revolution: The *Bellum Civile* as a Political Mirror," *Classical Philology* 66 (1971): 6–16.

44 *Lucan's Pharsalia,* trans. Thomas May (1627), sig. A2^v.

45 On the political context and implications of May's *Continuation,* see the brief but pithy account in Howard Erskine-Hill's *The Augustan Idea in English Literature* (London: Arnold, 1983), pp. 183–98, and R. T. Bruère's discussion of the 1640 Latin version in "The Latin and English Versions of Thomas May's *Supplementum Lucani,*" *Classical Philology* 44 (1949): 145–63, which argues that May altered his English version in keeping with his subsequent change in political affiliation.

46 An earlier version of the line, comparing Virgil with Lucan, appeared in some verses describing the title page of May's 1627 translation: "*Maro . . . /* Thy favour'd *Muse* did finde a different fate: / Thou gott'st *Augustus* love, he *Nero's* hate." *Lucan's Pharsalia,* title page.

47 First published in *The Essayes of a Prentise in the Divine Art of Poesie* (Edinburgh, 1584), and reprinted in *The Poems of James VI. of Scotland,* ed. James Craigie, 2 vols. (Edinburgh: Blackwood, 1955–58), 1:62.

48 Annabel Patterson, *Censorship and Interpretation: The Conditions of Writing and Reading in Early Modern England* (Madison: University of Wisconsin Press, 1984), p. 14.

49 On Ralegh's circle and Gorges' place in it, see Hill, *Intellectual Origins,* pp. 131–224. See also William Hunt, "Spectral Origins of the English Revolution: Legitimation Crisis in Early Stuart England," in *Reviving the English Revolution: Reflections and Elaborations on the Work of Christopher Hill,* ed. Geoff Eley and William Hunt (London: Verso, 1988), pp. 305–32.

50 Roy Strong, *Henry Prince of Wales and England's Lost Renaissance* (London: Thames and Hudson, 1986), p. 41.

51 *The Poems of James VI,* 1:79. The passage is also cited in Patterson, *Censorship and Interpretation,* p. 20, a study to which this section is generally indebted.

52 See Christopher Hill, "Radical Prose in Seventeenth Century England: From Marprelate to the Levellers," *Essays in Criticism* 32 (1982): 95–118.

53 *A Declaration and Resolution of the Lords and Commons assembled in Parliament, in Answer to the Scots Declaration* (1642), p. 1.

54 *A Remonstrance Or The Declaration Of the Lords and Commons, now Assembled in Parliament, 26. of May. 1641* (1642), p. 1.

55 *His Majesties Answer to a Printed Book, Entituled A Remonstrance, or, The Declaration of the Lords and Commons now assembled in Parliament, May 26. 1642* (1642), p. 2.

56 *A Remonstrance of the Lords and Commons Assembled in Parliament, Or, The Reply of both Houses, to a printed Book, under His Majesties name, Called, His Majesties Answer to a Printed Book* (1642), p. 16.

57 See, for instance, *The Protestation and Declaration of Divers Knights, Esquires, Gentlemen, and Free-holders of the Counties of Lincolne and Nottingham: Against the unjust oppressions and inhumane proceedings of William Earle of New-castle and his Cavaleers* ("sent to be printed at *London,*" 1643), p. 6; and William Walwyn, *The Compassionate Samaritan* (1644), p. 35, cited in Hill, *Intellectual Origins,* p. 113. See Kevin Sharpe and Steven Zwicker, Introduction to *Politics of Discourse* (Berkeley and Los Angeles: University of California Press, 1987), who claim that "not until the 1650s do we find the word [i.e., *party*] commonly associated with the taking of sides in a political contest," (p. 7), citing *OED.*

58 Samuel Daniel, *The Civil Wars,* ed. Laurence Michel (New Haven: Yale University Press, 1958), book 1, stanza 6.

59 For an illuminating discussion of Milton's disatisfaction with the spatial view of history as the basis for epic poetry, see Gordon Teskey's "Milton's Choice of Subject in the Context of Renaissance Critical Theory," *English Literary History* 53 (1986): 53–72, esp. 57–58.

60 Fulke Greville was writing *Mustapha* on the same theme, though subsequent events prompted him to revise parts of it as his *A Treatise of Monarchy,* an examination of the origins and nature of kingship. See R. A. Rebholz, *The Life of Fulke Greville, First Lord Brooke* (Oxford: Clarendon Press, 1971), pp. 147–54, 200–201.

61 On opposition to Stuart neoclassicism, see Malcolm Smuts, "The Political Failure of Stuart Cultural Patronage," in *Patronage in the Renaissance,* ed. Guy F. Lytle and Stephen Orgel (Princeton: Princeton University Press, 1981), pp. 165–87.

62 Throughout *Pastoral and Ideology* (Berkeley and Los Angeles: University of California Press, 1987), Annabel Patterson argues that the structural choice

which Virgilian pastoral offers between exile and complicity might/should be read as an allegory for the constitution of a tradition of intellectual life in the West that has, in recent decades, been taken up by academic literati.

63 C. H. Firth, "The Ballad History of the Reign of James I," *Transactions of the Royal Historical Society,* 3d ser. 5 (1911): 29.

64 In 1612 the future archbishop contributed two poems to *Iusta Oxoniensum,* a collection of verses on the death of Prince Henry by members of the University of Oxford. For discussion of Locke's contribution to the 1654 Oxford collection—*Musarum Oxoniensum Elaiophoria*—see Chapter 5.

65 John W. Draper observes that propagandistic elegies on behalf of the "puritans" did not begin until the death of the earl of Essex in 1646; see *A Century of Broadside Elegies* (London: Ingpen and Grant, 1928), pp. xv–xviii.

66 Cited by Michel, ed., *The Civil Wars,* p. 6. See also p. 341 for other contemporary comparisons between Daniel and Lucan.

67 "The Epistle Dedicatorie" of 1609, *The Civil Wars,* p. 69.

68 Ann Baynes Coiro, *Robert Herrick's "Hesperides" and the Epigram Book Tradition* (Baltimore: Johns Hopkins University Press, 1988), p. 42. See pp. 30–42 for Coiro's reading of "The Argument of his Book" which outlines her larger argument by drawing attention to the nexus of generic innovation and complex political commentary in this initial poem. For a contextualized reading of the politics of Herrick's lines and parts of *The Hesperides,* see Leah S. Marcus, "Herrick's *Hesperides* and the 'Proclamations made for May,'" *Studies in Philology* 76 (1979): 49–74, and, for a comprehensive historicist account of the politics of Herrick's poetry, her *The Politics of Mirth: Jonson, Herrick, Milton, Marvell and the Defense of Old Holiday Pastimes* (Chicago: University of Chicago Press, 1986).

69 Robert Herrick, *Poetical Works,* ed. L. C. Martin (Oxford: Clarendon Press, 1956), p. 5.

70 Douglas Bush, *English Literature in the Earlier Seventeenth Century,* 2d ed. (Oxford: Clarendon Press, 1962), p. 117.

71 On "The Hock Cart," see James Turner, *The Politics of Landscape* (Oxford: Blackwell, 1979), pp. 150–51, and Coiro, *Herrick's "Hesperides,"* pp. 156–58.

72 Coiro, *Herrick's "Hesperides,"* p. 4.

73 On the didactic nature of all poetic genres at this time, see Michael McKeon, *Poetry and Politics in Restoration England* (Cambridge: Harvard University Press, 1975), pp. 6–8.

74 Richard Corbett, *The Poems of Richard Corbett,* ed. J. A. W. Bennett and H. R. Trevor-Roper (Oxford: Clarendon Press, 1955), p. 85.

75 George Puttenham, *The Arte of English Poesie,* ed. G. D. Willcock and Alice Walker (1936; rpt. Cambridge: Cambridge University Press, 1970), pp. 45, 46.

76 See Samuel R. Gardiner, *History of England from the Accession of James I. to*

the Outbreak of the Civil War, 1603–1642, 10 vols. (London: Longmans, Green, 1883–84), 7:160–67; and Alan G. R. Smith *The Emergence of a Nation State: The Commonwealth of England, 1529–1660* (London: Longmans, 1984), pp. 277–84.

77 Among the many works of social and economic history that have helped to shapes these comments, see Robert Ashton, *The City and the Court, 1603–1643* (Cambridge: Cambridge University Press, 1979), *The Crown and the Money Market, 1603–1640* (Oxford: Clarendon Press, 1960); and Derek Hirst, *The Representatives of the People?* (Cambridge: Cambridge University Press, 1978). For a different position, see Kevin Sharpe's account in his "The Personal Rule of Charles I," in *Before the Civil War: Essays in Early Stuart Politics and Government,* ed. Howard Tomlinson (New York: St. Martin's, 1984), pp. 53–78.

78 The development of political opposition and of "parties" in early modern England has been the topic of much heated debate recently: for a general survey of the controversy, see Simon Adams, "Faction, Clientage and Party Politics, 1550–1603," *History Today* 32 (1982): 33–39. My use of the term "partisan" to describe poems that advocate the interests of one social group within the nation might offend some, but it nevertheless seems a clear and precise enough term for the formations I am here describing. For possible objections, see Mark Kishlansky, *The Rise of the New Model Army* (Cambridge: Cambridge University Press, 1979), pp. 15–20, and the same author's "The Emergence of Adversary Politics in the Long Parliament," *Journal of Modern History* 49 (1977): 617–40. See Sharpe and Zwicker, Introduction to *Politics of Discourse,* who comment on the "partisan" as a weapon (p. 7).

79 Gerrard Winstanley, *The Law of Freedom and Other Writings,* ed. Christopher Hill (Harmondsworth: Penguin, 1973), p. 393.

80 *I Thank You Twice* (1647), rpt. in W. W. Wilkins, ed., *Political Ballads of the Seventeenth and Eighteenth Centuries,* 2 vols. (London: Longmans, 1860), 1:54.

81 Thomas Carew, *Poems,* ed. Rhodes Dunlap (Oxford: Clarendon, 1949), p. 77. For the important political implications of the Virgilian discourse, see Patterson, *Pastoral and Ideology,* pp. 147–56, and Michael Parker, "Carew's Political Pastoral: Virgilian Pretexts in the 'Answer to Aurelian Townsend,'" *John Donne Journal* 1 (1982): 101–16.

82 David Norbrook, *Poetry and Politics in the English Renaissance* (London: Routledge and Kegan Paul, 1984), p. 222.

83 Derek Hirst, *Authority and Conflict: England, 1603–1658* (London: Arnold, 1986), p. 176. The best accounts of the Thirty Years War in English remain Michael Roberts, *Gustavus Adolphus: A History of Sweden, 1611–1632,* 2 vols. (London: Longmans, Green, 1953, 1958), and Herbert Langer, *The Thirty Years War,* trans. C. S. V. Salt (Poole, Dorset: Blandford, 1980).

84 *Barrington Family Letters,* ed. Arthur Searle, Camden Fourth Series, Vol. 28 (London: Royal Historical Society, 1983), p. 236.

85 Folke Dahl, "Amsterdam—Cradle of English Newspapers," *The Library,* 5th ser. 4 (1949): 174. See also Gardiner, *History of England,* 7:206.

86 For evidence of the Spanish influence in the banning of the newsbooks, see Dahl, "Amsterdam—Cradle of English Newspapers," pp. 174–76. Dahl reprints the Star Chamber decree, p. 173. On Charles's foreign policy at this time, see Gardiner, *History of England,* 7:173–208, though Roberts in *Gustavus Adolphus* claims that "Charles himself could scarcely be said to have a foreign policy at all" (2:430). On the larger question of the political consequences of Charles's "personal rule" as an incentive to the outbreak of war, see Smith, *Emergence of a Nation State,* pp. 277–99.

87 The date of *An Elegie upon the death of Gustavus Adolphus, King of Swethland* by "J. R." (presumably John Russell) among the Thomason Tracts in the British Library has caused confusion, but is probably also 1633 and not 1640 as suggested in the *Catalogue of the Pamphlets . . . Collected by George Thomason, 1640–1661,* ed. George Fortescue, 2 vols. (London: British Museum, 1908), 1:5. *The Great and Famous Battel of Lutzen, Fought betweene the renowned King of Sweden, and Walstein* "faithfully translated out of the French Coppie," a prose tract in the Huntington Library, also appeared in 1633, though the colophon does not indicate place of publication or date of printing.

88 Despite the title page—which claims "London, printed by *I. L.* for *Nath. Butter* and *Nicholas Bourne*"—a colophon on p. 164 of the third part of *The Swedish Intelligencer* reads "Printed with all necessary priviledge. In *Lisbon.* By *Antonio Alvarez.* 1633. Febr. 16" (sig. X^v). The exact provenance of these works is otherwise obscure, but Dahl reports that the "first and second parts were issued before Oct., 1632" (i.e., before the Star Chamber decree banning foreign news) in his *Bibliography of English Corantos and Periodical Newspapers, 1620–1642* (London: Bibliographical Society, 1952), p. 221.

89 I have come upon only one instance of this edition with the additional title page as quoted here; it is in the British Library at shelfmark 1478.bbb.6.

90 See appropriate entries in John Venn and J. A. Venn, *Alumni Cantabrigienses. Part One: From the Earliest Times to 1751* (Cambridge: Cambridge University Press, 1924), Vol. 3, and C. M. Neale, *The Early Honours Lists (1498–9 to 1746–7) of the University of Cambridge* (Bury St. Edmunds: Groom, 1909).

91 Gardiner, *History of England,* 6:102–3, 7:172.

92 Ibid., 5:297–300.

93 Ibid., 7:176–77.

94 Ibid., 7:183–91.

95 Ibid., 7:196–97.

96 Arthur Searle, Introduction to *Barrington Family Letters,* p. 2.

97   Cited in Gardiner, *History of England,* 7:207.

98   See R. C. Munsden, "James I and 'the growth of mutual distrust': King, Commons, and Reform, 1603–1604," in *Faction and Parliament,* ed. Kevin Sharpe (Oxford: Clarendon Press, 1978), pp. 43–72, esp. pp. 62–65.

99   On poetic and literary responses to the union, see Patterson, *Censorship and Interpretation,* pp. 65–66.

100 John Clapham, *Elizabeth of England,* ed. E. P. Reed and C. Reed (Philadelphia: University of Pennsylvania Press, 1951), pp. 118, 119.

101 Joshuah Sylvester, "Corona Dedicatoria: Clio," in his *Divine Weeks* (1605 ed., sig. A4), rpt. in *The Divine Weeks and Works of Guillaume de Saluste, Sieur du Bartas,* ed. Susan Snyder, 2 vols. (Oxford: Clarendon Press, 1979), 2:888.

102 Morgan Coleman, [*The genealogies of King James I.*] (1608), line 38. For other poems on this issue, see F. J. C. Hearnenshaw, *English History in Contemporary Poetry* (1913; rpt. London: Historical Association, 1969), pp. 9–11, and see Norbrook's important chapter "The Spensarians and King James, 1603–16," in *Poetry and Politics,* pp. 195–214.

103 Richard Rowlands [Verstegan], "Verses of the Authors concerning this his worke," in *A Restitution of Decayed Intelligence* (1628), sig. ***3ᵛ.

104 Patterson, *Pastoral and Ideology,* p. 151.

Chapter 2: English Poetry and the Struggle for a National History

1   Jonathan Goldberg, *James I and the Politics of Literature* (Baltimore: Johns Hopkins University Press, 1983), p. 117.

2   See George deForest Lord, *Classical Presences in Seventeenth-Century English Poetry* (New Haven: Yale University Press, 1987). The reference to Jameson in this context is borrowed from Annabel Patterson, without whose *Pastoral and Ideology: Virgil to Valéry* (Berkeley and Los Angeles: University of California Press, 1987) I wrote this chapter the way I did (see p. 76). Had Patterson's study been available I would doubtless have designed my project differently. The chapter on pastoral in seventeenth-century England, provocatively entitled "Going Public," is specially useful and interesting on the class politics of intellectual life and production.

3   On Bacon's importance for the English revolution, see Christopher Hill, *Intellectual Origins of the English Revolution* (1965; rpt. Oxford: Clarendon Press, 1982), chap. 3: "Francis Bacon and the English Parliamentarians," pp. 85–130. See also Anthony Grafton and Lisa Jardine, *From Humanism to the Humanities* (Cambridge: Harvard University Press, 1986).

4   See Mark Gould's revisionist account of *Revolution in the Development of Capitalism: The Coming of the English Revolution* (Berkeley and Los Ange-

les: University of California Press, 1987) for a brilliant sociological recuperation of economic determination in the final instance. Gould's thesis, that seventeenth-century England experienced several revolutions not in the transition from feudalism to capitalism but as the result of ruptures internal to the development of an already-nascent capitalist mode of production, unfortunately ignores questions of the sexual division(s) of labor. This seems damaging since a key move in his argument (as I understand it) depends upon what Gould calls the "natural development from a capitalism dominated by the extraction of absolute surplus value—manufacturing rooted in simple cooperation—to capitalism dominated by the extraction of relative surplus value—manufacturing dominated by complex cooperation and finally machine capitalism" (pp. 114–15). Were Gould to consider the history of women's work at the time, I suspect, he would have to revise not only that "natural development" but also the "simple cooperation." But if he does not seem to have read Alice Clark's *Working Life of Women in the Seventeenth Century* (1919; rpt. London: Cass, 1968), much less has he considered important recent studies that demonstrate the importance of women and their (unpaid) work to any history of labor (e.g., Mary Prior, "Women and the Urban Economy: Oxford, 1500–1800," in *Women in English Society, 1500–1800,* ed. Mary Prior [London: Methuen, 1985], pp. 93–117). For some provocative comments on how georgic "naturalizes" both "poetic creation" and "the process of an empire's creation," see Jane Tylus, "Spenser, Virgil, and the Politics of Poetic Labor," *English Literary History* 55 (1988): 55 and passim.

5 J. G. A. Pocock, "Languages and Their Implications: The Transformations of the Study of Political Thought," *Politics, Language and Time* (New York: Atheneum, 1973), p. 15, cited in Goldberg, *James 1,* p. 115.

6 John Dryden, *Poems,* ed. James Kinsley, 4 vols. (Oxford: Clarendon Press, 1958), 2:869. Laud's description of the syllabus at Westminster during the early part of the century gives us some indication of how Virgil was taught and read: "Betwixt one to 3, that lesson which, out of some author appointed for that day, had been by the M^r expounded unto them (out of Cicero, Virgil, Hom^r Eurip; Isoc; Livie, Sallust, &c.) was to be exactlie gone through by construing and other grammatical waies, examining all the rhetoricall figures and translating it out of verse into prose, or out of prose into verse; out of g^r into lat: or out of lat. into G^r. Then they were enjoyned to commit that to memorie against ye next morning." The passage here is quoted from the transcription in John Sergeaunt, *Annals of Westminster School* (London: Methuen, 1898), p. 280.

7 Gayatri Chakravorty Spivak, "Explanation and Culture: Marginalia," *Humanities in Society* 2 (1979): 214; reprinted in *In Other Worlds: Essays in Cultural Politics* (London: Methuen, 1987), p. 114.

8 Josephine Waters Bennett, "Britain among the Fortunate Isles," *Studies in Philology* 53 (1956); 114. And see Ann Baynes Coiro, *Robert Herrick's "Hesperides" and the Epigram Book Tradition* (Baltimore: Johns Hopkins University Press, 1988), pp. 6–8.

9 Arthur Golding's translation cited by Bennett, "Britain among the Fortunate Isles," p. 117.

10 Quoted by Bennett, "Britain among the Fortunate Isles," p. 117.

11 William Shakespeare, *Cymbeline,* ed. J. M. Nosworthy (1955; rpt. London: Methuen, 1969), 3.4.139–42.

12 See Nosworthy, ed. *Cymbeline,* p. 117.

13 Samuel Daniel, *The Civil Wars,* ed. Laurence Michel (New Haven: Yale University Press, 1958), 1.67–68; references from this edition are to book and stanza.

14 Morgan Coleman, [The genealogies of King James I. and Queen Anne, his wife, from the Conquest] (1608).

15 Ben Jonson, *Love Freed From Ignorance and Folly,* in *A Book of Masques,* ed. Norman Sanders (Cambridge: Cambridge University press, 1967), p. 140. Sanders discusses the varying dates of composition and performance, pp. 73–74.

16 George Chapman, *The Masque of the Inner Temple,* in *The Plays of George Chapman: The Comedies,* ed. T. M. Parrott, 2 vols. (1910–14; rpt. New York: Russell and Russell, 1961), 2:447.

17 David Norbrook, *Poetry and Politics in the English Renaissance* (London: Routledge and Kegan Paul, 1984), pp. 204–5.

18 Samuel Daniel, *Complete Works in Verse and Prose,* ed. Alexander B. Grossart, 5 vols. (1885; rpt. New York: Russell and Russell, 1963), 1:72.

19 See Arthur Marotti, "'Love is Not Love': Elizabethan Sonnet Sequences and the Social Order," *English Literary History* 49 (1982): 399.

20 Richard Crashaw, *The Poems English, Latin, and Greek,* ed. L. C. Martin (Oxford: Clarendon, 1927), p. 180.

21 [Edmund Bolton], *London, King Charles His Augusta* (1648), pp. 8, 9 [page 8 is mispaginated 6]. Although published in 1648—Thomason dated his copy March 7—this work is almost certainly a translation of a Latin poem written between 1631 and 1632; see Thomas Blackburn, "Edmund Bolton's *London, King Charles His Augusta, or City Royal,*" *Huntington Library Quarterly* 25 (1978): 315–23. For a fuller discussion of this poem, see the next chapter.

22 Peter Stallybrass, "Patriarchal Territories: The Body Enclosed, in *Rewriting the Renaissance,* ed. Margaret Ferguson, Maureen Quilligan, and Nancy Vickers (Chicago: University of Chicago Press, 1986), p. 129.

23 It is tempting to follow the *DNB* entry for Hopkins which indicates that he had Jacobite learnings. However, Alice E. Jones thinks not; see her "Note on Hopkins," *Modern Language Notes* 5 (1940): 191–94.

24 See Christopher Hill, *Antichrist in Seventeenth-Century England* (Oxford: Clarendon, 1971); Bernard S. Capp, *The Fifth Monarchy Men: A Study in Seventeenth-Century Millenarianism* (London: Faber, 1972); and Katharine R. Firth, *The Apocalyptic Tradition in Reformation Britain, 1530–1645* (Oxford: Clarendon, 1979).

25 Joshuah Sylvester, trans., *The Divine Weeks and Works of Guillaume de Saluste, Sieur du Bartas,* ed. Susan Snyder, 2 vols. (Oxford: Clarendon, 1979), 1:463.

26 For an excellent summary of the history of this metaphor, see Peter Ure's introduction to his "Arden" edition of *Richard II* (1956; rpt. London: Methuen, 1966), pp. li–lvii.

27 George Puttenham, *The Arte of English Poesie,* ed. G. D. Willcock and Alice Walker (1936; Cambridge: Cambridge University Press, 1970), p. 38. On the use of low style and "rude speeches" as a disguise for commenting on contemporary political matters, see Norbrook's discussion of pseudo-Chaucerian texts in *Poetry and Politics,* pp. 42–43 and passim.

28 A similar portrait of Albion as "Great Britain" with sceptre and cornucopia appears on the title page to Drayton's *Polyolbion* of 1612. This is reproduced in *The Comely Frontispiece: The Emblematic Title-page in England, 1550–1660* (London: Routledge and Kegan Paul, 1979), where Margery Corbett and Ronald Lightbown incorrectly observe that "for the only time in her career" Albion appears "notably young and beautiful" (p. 156).

29 See Richard Helgerson, "Milton Reads the King's Book: Print, Performance, and the Making of a Bourgeois Idol," *Criticism* 29 (1987): 1–25, which discusses James's antitheatrical bias as an integral element of his claims to absolutism. "Though James does often use the familiar image, already a favorite of Elizabeth's, of the ruler as "set high on a stage," it is always with an uncomfortable sense, quite unlike Elizabeth's, of being rudely peered at and usually with an accompanying denial of the very nature of theatrical representation. He plays no part. Instead he is always and absolutely himself" (p. 5).

30 For the controversy over James, see Wallace Notestein's defense of the traditional view that he was "a foolish man" in *The House of Commons, 1604–1610* (New Haven: Yale University Press, 1971), p. 504, and the revisionist position in Robert Zaller, *The Parliament of 1621* (Berkeley and Los Angeles: University of California Press, 1971), and Robert E. Ruigh, *The Parliament of 1624* (Cambridge: Harvard University Press, 1971). See also William Hunt, "Spectral Origins of the English Revolution: Legitimation Crisis in Early Stuart England," in *Reviving the English Revolution,* ed. Geoff Eley and William Hunt (London: Verso, 1988), pp. 305–32; Derek Hirst, "Unanimity in the Commons," *Journal of Modern History* 50 (1978): 51–71; Alan Smith, "Constitutional Ideas and Parliamentary Developments," in *The Reign of James VI and I,* ed. Alan Smith (London: Macmillan, 1973), pp.

160–76; Robert Zaller, "The Concept of Opposition in Early Stuart England," *Albion* 12 (1980): 211–34; Kevin Sharpe's Introduction to *Faction and Parliament* (Oxford: Clarendon Press, 1978); Conrad Russell, *Parliaments and English Politics, 1621–1629* (1979; rev. ed. Oxford: Clarendon Press, 1982); and Norbrook, *Poetry and Politics,* p. 198.

31 At James's death in 1625 there were 128 members of the House of Lords; there were only 81 when he acceded in 1603. "As the number of spiritual Lords remained constant at twenty-six," observes Alan Smith, "the increase was due to James's lavish creations of new hereditary peerages, a policy which had almost doubled the number of secular Lords by the time of his death." "Constitutional Ideas," p. 170.

32 On the legal disputes between the royal prerogative and the court's various privileges, see J. R. Tanner, *English Constitutional Conflicts* (1928; rpt. Cambridge: Cambridge University Press, 1962), pp. 18–25; J. G. A. Pocock, *The Ancient Constitution and the Feudal Law* (Cambridge: Cambridge University Press, 1957), passim; and J. R. Jones, "The Crown and Courts in England," in *The Reign of James VI and I,* pp. 177–94.

33 Although royal patents granting monopolies to court favorites were a constant source of discontent during James's reign—except among those who received them, we may presume—they were of special interest and importance at the time when Slatyer's work appeared. "They have become so ordinary," wrote John Chamberlain in July 1620, "that there is no end, every day bringing forth some new project or other.... In truth the world doth even groan under the burden of these perpetual patents, which are become so frequent that whereas at the king's coming in, there were complaints of eight or nine monopolies then in being, they are now said to be multiplied to so many scores." Cited in Thomas Birch, ed., *The Court and Times of James I,* 18 vols. (London: Colburn, 1849), 2:205. One balladeer of about this time attacked "the briske Sickafanticall Courtier, / That by begging Monoplies rise." *The French Shipper,* in *The Pepys Ballads,* ed. Hyder Rollins, 8 vols. (Cambridge: Harvard University Press, 1929), 1:143. One of the first actions of the 1621 Parliament was to try to expel two of its own members—Robert Flood and Giles Mompesson—for holding what many considered to be illegal (i.e., crown patented) monopolies. Their celebrated trials were part of a series of attacks, led by the aged Coke, against abuses of the royal prerogative. See Samuel R. Gardiner, *History of England from the Accession of James I. to the Outbreak of the Civil War, 1603–1642,* 10 vols. (London: Longmans, Green, 1883–84) 4:39–45. Alan Smith comments that "the upshot of the debates was the Act of Monopolies of 1624, the first statutory limitation of the royal prerogative and as such a landmark in constitutional history." "Constitutional Ideas," p. 175.

34 On this aspect of James's character and career there has been little disagree-

ment. "James's sincere, idealistic love of peace," writes Alan Smith, "is not in doubt and his aims in foreign policy, after he had concluded what is generally held to be a sensible and honourable settlement with Spain in 1604 [see next note], were to remain on terms of friendship with all foreign powers and to make England (and himself) the peacemaker and arbiter of Europe." Introduction to *The Reign of James VI and I,* p. 15. Gerald Howat observes in *Stuart and Cromwellian Foreign Policy* (London: Black, 1974), p. 15, that the king himself had a hand in writing a tract entitled *The Peace-Maker, or Great Britainnes Blessing* which had appeared in 1619, two years before Slatyer's *History.*

35 Even the Treaty of London of August 1604, by which James ended the long Spanish war that he had inherited with the crown, was not well received at the time. "The proclamation of peace," writes Gardiner, "in the City, was for the most part received in sullen silence, only broken here and there by exclamations of 'God preserve our neighbours in Holland and Zealand!'" *History of England,* 1:214; and see Smith, "Constitutional Ideas," p. 165, and S. L. Adams, "Foreign Policy and the Parliaments of 1621 and 1624," in *Faction and Parliament,* pp. 139–71.

36 War had broken out in 1618 when the Austrian emperor invaded Bohemia enabling Catholic Spain to seize the Protestant Palatinate while Frederick—James's son-in-law—was occupied in Bohemia. "Popular opinion in England," writes Godfrey Davies in *The Early Stuarts* (1937; rev. ed. Oxford: Clarendon Press, 1959), "whole-heartedly adopted Frederick's side, but the king stood aloof from this enthusiasm" (pp. 56–57). See *The King and Queen of Bohemia* (1622–23?) rpt. in *Pepys's Ballads,* 1:2–4.

37 Howat, *Stuart and Cromwellian Foreign Policy,* p. 28. See Tanner, *English Constitutional Conflicts,* pp. 48–49, and Alan Smith, "Constitutional Ideas," p. 164.

38 Tanner, *English Constitutional Conflicts,* p. 47, and Alan Smith, "Constitutional Ideas," p. 174.

39 Recent historians tend to emphasize the independence of the men vying for political influence in the nation and thus to see them less as members of easily identifiable groups than as men with divisible allegiances. In *London on the Outbreak of the Puritan Revolution* (Oxford: Clarendon Press, 1971), pp. 2–3, Valerie Pearl demonstrates that even so seemingly coherent a group as the aldermen of London—whose influence over national policy and the economy was considerable—was made up of men who did not simply oppose or support the king, but who varied among themselves over any given issue. But poets at the time did not have, or probably desire, the resources or the hindsight of modern historians. And however clear it might be that they lacked the ability to perceive the fine lines dividing groups and individuals, they most commonly wrote of the men involved as antagonistic

either toward royal policy or toward those in opposition. Even poems praising individual men tend to treat them as members of group interests as in
Jonson's "To Jephson," in *Poems,* ed. Ian Donaldson (London: Oxford University Press, 1975), p. 68, and Dryden's "To My Honor'd Kinsman, John
Driden," in *Poems,* 4:1529–35.

40 For a recent assessment that refers to the major works, see Derek Hirst,
    "Court, Country, and Politics before 1629," in *Faction and Parliament,* pp.
    105–37.

41 See Nicholas Breton's *The Court and the Country* (1618), a dialogue which
    rehearses most of the commonplaces.

42 Frank Kermode, *English Pastoral Poetry* (1952; rpt. New York: Norton,
    1972), p. 17.

43 John Barrell and John Bull, eds., *A Book of English Pastoral Verse* (New York:
    Oxford University Press, 1975), p. 142.

44 Sir Richard Fanshawe, *Shorter Poems and Translations,* ed. N. W. Bawcutt
    (Liverpool: Liverpool University Press, 1964), pp. 5–9. See Patterson, *Pas-
    toral and Ideology,* pp. 148–50, for discussion of Fanshawe's debts to Meli-
    boeus in this poem.

45 Giles Fletcher, *Works,* ed. F. S. Boas, 3 vols. (Cambridge: Cambridge Uni-
    versity Press, 1908–9), 1:226. The lines are from Fletcher's poem which
    appeared in *Epicidium Cantabrigiense* of 1612. In 1648, Mildmay Fane wrote
    of the nation as a garden in military terms that indicate a typical commit-
    ment to monarchic forms of government: England is "The Garden of the
    world, wherin the Rose, / In chiefe Commanded." "Anglia Hortus," in *Otia
    Sacra* (1648), p. 133.

46 But see Lawrence Stone and Jeanne C. Fawtier-Stone, *An Open Elite: En-
    gland, 1540–1880* (Oxford: Clarendon Press, 1984), and, for examples of the
    new feminist history of the period, see Roberta Hamilton, *The Liberation of
    Women: A Study of Patriarchy and Capitalism* (1978; rpt. London: Allen and
    Unwin, 1982), and the essays in *Women in English Society, 1500–1800,* espe-
    cially Mary Prior's "Women and the Urban Economy: Oxford, 1500–1800"
    (pp. 93–117), which includes a study of William Davenant's family, and
    Marie B. Rowlands, "Recusant Women: 1560–1640" (pp. 149–80). Elaine
    Hobby's recent *Virtue of Necessity: English Women's Writing, 1649–1688* (Lon-
    don: Virago, 1988) dispels any residual belief that Stuart women were really
    "chaste, silent and obedient."

47 *The Poems of James VI. of Scotland,* ed. James Craigie, 2 vols. (Edinburgh:
    Blackwood, 1955–58), 2:178.

48 See Derek Hirst, *Authority and Conflict: England, 1603–1658* (London: Ar-
    nold, 1986), p. 7.

49 Alan G. R. Smith, *The Emergence of a Nation State,* p. 279.

50 Gardiner, *History of England,* 8:67; see also H. F. Kearney, *The Eleven Years'*

Tyranny of Charles I (London: Historical Association, 1962), and Alan Smith, *Emergence of a Nation State,* pp. 277–84.

51 G. R. Hibbard, "The Country House Poem," *Journal of the Warburg and Courtauld Institutes* 19 (1956): 159–73.

52 Raymond Williams, *The Country and the City* (1973; rpt. New York: Oxford University Press, 1975), p. 27. And see William Cain, "The Place of the Poet in Jonson's 'To Penshurst' and 'To My Muse,' " *Criticism* 21 (1979): 34–38.

53 For the best analysis of "Penshurst" as a social text, see Don E. Wayne's *Penshurst: The Semiotics of Place and the Poetics of History* (Madison: University of Wisconsin Press, 1984), esp. 23–44, and passim.

54 *The Poetical and Dramatic Works of Thomas Randolph,* ed. W. Carew Hazlitt (London: Reeves and Turner, 1875), pp. 578–79. The *Ode* was first publishd in 1638.

55 See Alan Smith, *Emergence of a Nation State,* pp. 277–99, and Anthony Fletcher, *The Outbreak of the English Civil War* (London: Arnold, 1981).

56 See Earl Miner, *The Cavalier Mode from Jonson to Cotton* (Princeton: Princeton University Press, 1971), pp. 164–204.

57 Thomas Carew, *Poems,* ed. Rhodes Dunlap (1949; rpt. Oxford: Clarendon Press, 1970), p. 77.

58 John Russell, *The Two Famous Pitcht Battels of Lypsich and Lutzen* (Cambridge, 1634), p. 31.

59 The phrase is from Jonson's "An Epistle to a Friend, to Persuade Him to the Wars," *Poems,* p. 155.

60 William Lithgow, *Scotlands Welcome To Her Native Sonne, and Soveraigne Lord, King Charles* (Edinburgh, 1633), sig. B2.

61 See Lithgow's *A Most Delectable, and True, Discourse of a Peregrination in Europe, Asia, etc.* (1614) which was reprinted four times before 1640.

62 Crashaw, *Poems,* p. 178.

63 Carew, *Poems,* pp. xli–xlii

64 Edmund Waller, *Poems,* ed. George Thorn-Drury, 2 vols. (London: Bullen, 1901), 1:82.

65 See Christopher Hill, "Censorship and English Literature," *The Collected Essays,* Vol. 1: *Writing and Revolution in Seventeenth-Century England* (Amherst: University of Massachusetts Press, 1985), pp. 40–50.

66 As Hill comments, "Milton's friend the bookseller George Thomason tried to buy a copy of every book and pamphlet published during these exciting times. In 1640 he purchased twenty-two items; in 1642, 1966," *Collected Essays,* p. 40. These figures, presumably, rely on the analysis offered by George Fortescue in the Preface to the *Catalogue of the Pamphlets. . . . Collected by George Thomason* (2 vols. [London: British Museum, 1908]), which indicates that the figure for 1641 was 717 (p. xxi). These numbers exclude manuscripts and newspapers; including the latter, the total figures for

printed items are slightly higher—22 for 1640, 721 for 1641, and 2,133 for 1642.

67 George Barlow, verses in the Oxford University collection, *Eucharistica Oxoniensia: In Exoptatissimum & Auspicatissimim Caroli* (Oxford, 1641), sig. A3.

68 See *Eucharistica Oxoniensia*, sigs. A1, A2, a2, a3, a3ᵛ, a4ᵛ, b3, b3ᵛ, b4, b4ᵛ, c, c3, à2.

69 Alan Smith, *Emergence of a Nation State*, pp. 231, 399–400; Gardiner, *History of England*, 9:6; and Elizabeth R. Foster, "The Procedure of the House of Commons against Patentees and Monopolies, 1621–1624," in *Conflict in Stuart England: Essays in Honour of Wallace Notestein*, ed. W. A. Aiken and B. D. Henning (New York: New York University Press, 1960), pp. 57–85.

70 *The Foure Ages of England: Or, The Iron Age* (1648), p. 19. This work was attributed to Cowley.

71 *The Frogges of Egypt, Or The Caterpillers of the Common-Wealth truely Dissected and laid open* (1641), sig. A2.

72 The device of the card game doubtless owes something to the memory of a celebrated court case involving a monopoly on playing cards back in 1603; see Hirst, *Authority and Conflict*, p. 120.

73 Margaret Doody, *The Daring Muse: Augustan Poetry Reconsidered* (Cambridge: Cambridge University Press, 1985), pp. 45–46.

74 On the use of language and imagery of the carnivalesque to invert and subvert political relations, see David Underdown, *Revel, Riot, and Rebellion: Popular Politics and Culture in England, 1603–1660* (Oxford: Clarendon Press, 1985), and Peter Stallybrass, "'We feaste in our Defense': Patrician Carnival in Early Modern England and Robert Herrick's 'Hesperides,'" *English Literary Renaissance* 16 (1986): 234–52.

75 See also A. B. [Alexander Brome?], *A Canterbury Tale. Translated out of Chaucer's old English Into our Now Usual Language,* and Henry Walker's *The Friers Lamenting, For his not Repenting,* both published in September 1641; John Cragge's *A Prophecy Concerning the Earle of Essex* of December 1641; *A Discovery of the Jesuites Trumpery* and Thomas Stirry's emblematic *A Rot Amongst the Bishops, or, A Terrible Tempest in the Sea of Canterbury,* both of which appeared during 1641. Anti-catholic poems that appeared in 1642 include Richard Overton's *New Lambeth Fayre Newly Consecrated and Presented by The Pope Himselfe* of March; John Taylor's *The Apprentices Advice to the XII. Bishops lately accused of High Treason, by the Honourable Assemblies of both Houses,* "printed," according to the title page, "in the new yeare of the Bishops feare" (January 1642); and Taylor's *A Delicate, Dainty, Damnable Dialogue, Between the Devill and a Jesuite* of April.

76 See Fletcher, *Outbreak of the English Civil War,* pp. 91–110.

77 Cited in the *DNB* entry for Vicars.

78 Bernard Capp, "The Fifth Monarchists and Popular Millenarianism," in

Radical Religion in the English Revolution, ed. J. F. McGregor and Barry Reay (1984; rpt. Oxford: Oxford University Press, 1986), pp. 166–67.

79 But see John Taylor's *England's Comfort, and Londons Joy: Expressed in the Royall, Triumphant, and Magnificent Entertainment of our Dread Soveraigne Lord, King Charles, at his blessed and Safe returne from Scotland on Thursday the 25. of Novemb. 1641* (p. 7), which—following the story from 2 Samuel 19. 41-42—offers the parallel between Scotland / England and Judah / Israel in their competitive love for King David / Charles.

80 Anthony à Woods, *Athenae Oxoniensis* (1692 ed.), 2:86.

81 Michel Foucault, "Film and Popular Memory: An Interview with Michel Foucault," trans. Martin Jordin, quoted by Keith Baker, "Memory and Practice: Politics and the Representation of the Past in Eighteenth-Century France," *Representations* 11 (1985): 134.

82 Samuel Butler, *Hudibras, In Three Parts,* ed. Zachary Grey, 2 vols. (London, 1806), 1:123 (book 1, canto 1, line 646).

83 Abraham Cowley, *The Civil War* (1642–43), ed. Alan Pritchard (Toronto: University of Toronto Press, 1973), 1.1–2. Subsequent references are to book and line.

84 *The Foure Ages of England* (1648), p. 27.

85 Douglas Bush calls this work "a small landmark in the development of Augustan neoclassicism." *English Literature in the Earlier Seventeenth Century,* 2d ed. (Oxford: Clarendon Press, 1962), p. 106.

86 See my "Poetry as History: The Argumentative Design of Dryden's *Astraea Redux,*" *Restoration* 4 (1980): 54–64.

87 Stephen Jones, "To his friend the Author," prefixed to Russell's *The Two Famous Pitcht Battels* (1634), sig. ¶¶4. See also *The Great and Famous Battel of Lutzen, fought betweene the renowned King of Sweden, and Walstein* [1633], p. 39, where the anagram is also spelled out.

88 Howard Erskine-Hill, "Augustans on Augustanism: England, 1659–1759," in *Of Private Vices and Public Benefits,* ed. Johan N. Schmidt (Frankfurt: Lang, 1979), pp. 7–34.

89 James Turner discusses this in Denham's *Cooper's Hill;* see *The Politics of Landscape* (Oxford: Blackwell, 1979), pp. 49–61.

90 Richard Corbett, *The Poems of Richard Corbett,* ed. J. A. W. Bennett and H. R. Trevor-Roper (Oxford: Clarendon Press, 1955), pp. 34, 35.

Chapter 3: Representing the Past

1 This is not to suggest that we should abandon genre as an analytical concept but rather, following Jauss, that we should attend to its historical variability as a shifting horizon of expectations rather than as a system of classification; see Hans Robert Jauss, "Literary History as a Challenge to Literary Theory,"

New Literary History 2 (1970): 7–37, and for recent essays proving that genre studies are alive and well, see Barbara Lewalski, ed., *Renaissance Genres: Essays on Theory, History, and Interpretation* (Cambridge: Harvard University Press, 1986).

2 Raymond Williams, *Marxism and Literature* (Oxford: Oxford University Press, 1975), p. 183; see also pp. 149 and 176.

3 On the religious legitimation of the personal or inner voice at the time, see Nigel Smith, *Perfection Proclaimed: Language and Literature in English Radical Religion, 1640–1660* (Oxford: Clarendon, 1988). As Smith points out, the matter is of considerable importance for understanding the history of women's writing and social presence at the time. For a discussion of how the social achievements made by sectarian women during the civil wars were reversed at the Restoration, see the introduction to my edition of Poullain de la Barre's *The Woman As Good as the Man: Or, the Equality of Both Sexes* (Detroit: Wayne State University Press, 1988), pp. 24–45.

4 George Puttenham, *The Arte of English Poesie*, ed. G. D. Willcock and Alice Walker (1936; rpt. Cambridge: Cambridge University Press, 1970), p. 39.

5 Jan van Dorsten, "Literary Patronage in Elizabethan England: The Early Phase," in ed. Guy Lytle and Stephen Orgel (Princeton: Princeton University Press, 1981), p. 194.

6 John Hall, dedication to Charles Alleyn's *The Battailes of Crescey and Poictiers* (1631), sig. A2ᵛ.

7 John Dryden, *Poems,* ed. James Kinsley, 4 vols. (Oxford: Clarendon Press, 1958), 1:44.

8 On the incorporation of the Great Fire into *Annus Mirabilis,* see the California edition of Dryden's *Works,* ed. H. R. Swedenberg et al., 20 vols. (Berkeley and Los Angeles: University of California Press, 1956–), 1:257–58.

9 Thomas Blackburn, "Edmund Bolton's *London, King Charles His Augusta, or City Royal,*" *Huntington Library Quarterly* 25 (1978): 315–23.

10 Holograph copy of a letter by Bolton to the mayor and aldermen of London, dated September 1, 1632, cited by Blackburn, "Edmund Bolton's *London,*" p. 317.

11 Bolton's proposal is discussed by F. Smith Fussner, *The Historical Revolution* (London: Routledge and Kegan Paul, 1964), p. 106. See also Ethel M. Portal, *Bolton and the Academe Roial* (London: British Academy, 1915); Philip Sykes, "Politics and Historical Research in the Early Seventeenth Century," in *English Historical Scholarship in the Sixteenth and Seventeenth Centuries,* ed. Levi Fox (London: Oxford University Press, 1956), pp. 49–72; and J. Hunter, "An Account of the Scheme for Erecting a Royal Academy in England," *Archaeologia* 32 (1847): 132–49.

12 The use of arguments from etymology in solving historical questions was

widespread at the time; a great deal of widely circulating books like Camden's *Britannia* (1586) and John Speed's *Historie of Great Britain* (1611) is given over to learned discussion of place names. The practice was so common that Bolton himself inveighs against it in his *Hypercritica* (c. 1618).

13 George Fortescue, ed., *Catalogue of the Pamphlets ... Collected by George Thomason, 1640–1661*, 2 vols. (London: British Museum, 1908), 1:588–89.

14 On the "importance of an exact chronology in determining what any given text was likely to mean to its audience at the time of its appearance," see Annabel Patterson, *Censorship and Interpretation* (Madison: University of Wisconsin Press, 1984), p. 47.

15 On the tangled political disputes involving the citizens of London and Parliament at this time, see Robert Ashton, *The English Civil War: Conservatism and Revolution* (New York: Norton, 1981), pp. 312–52; Alan G. R. Smith, *The Emergence of a Nation State* (London and New York: Longman, 1984), pp. 314–19; A. S. P. Woodhouse, Introduction to *Puritanism and Liberty* (1938; rpt. London: Dent, 1986), pp. 14–35; H. N. Brailsford, *The Levellers and the English Revolution,* ed. Christopher Hill (1961; rpt. London: Spokesman, 1983), pp. 247–53, 317–30. For the numerous ballads published between January and May treating the relations between Charles and the city of London, see Joseph Frank, *Hobbled Pegasus: A Descriptive Bibliography of Minor English Poetry, 1641–1660* (Albuquerque: University of New Mexico Press, 1968), pp. 194–205.

16 The full dedication reads: "To the sacred Majestie of Charles, By the Grace of God, King of Great Britainne, France, And Ireland. Defender of the Faith, &c. This Historicall Poem, Borne by His Command, and not to live but by his gratious acception, is humbly dedicated by the author." Thomas May, *The Reigne of King Henrie the Second* (1633), title page.

17 For a brief discussion of poems written on the Restoration that took an unfavorable view of the event, see my "An Edition of Poems on the Restoration," *Restoration* 11 (1987): 117–21.

18 *The Poems and Letters of Andrew Marvell,* 3d ed. rev. Pierre Legouis, 2 vols. (1972; rpt. Oxford: Clarendon Press, 1976), 1:218. The king's need to borrow money is recorded by Pepys in his entry for May 16, 1660, *The Diary of Samuel Pepys,* ed. Robert Latham and William Matthews, 11 vols. (Berkeley and Los Angeles: University of California Press, 1980–83), 1:143.

19 Robert Weimann, "*Fabula* and *Historia:* The Crisis of the 'Universall Consideration' in *The Unfortunate Traveller,*" *Representations* 8 (1984), p. 18.

20 See Joseph Frank's important study *The Beginnings of the English Newspaper* (Cambridge: Harvard University Press, 1961), the same author's *Cromwell's Press Agent: A Critical Biography of Marchamont Nedham* (Lanham, Md.: University Press of America, 1980), and James R. Sutherland's *The Restoration Newspaper and Its Development* (Cambridge: Cambridge University

Press, 1986). R. S. Crane and F. B. Kaye's *A Census of British Newspapers and Periodicals, 1620–1800* (1927; rpt. London: Holland House, 1979) still provides an invaluable quantitative guide to the growth of serial publications.

21 See David Douglas, *English Scholars, 1660–1730* (1939; rev. London: Eyre and Spottiswoode, 1951), and Royce Macgillivray, *Restoration Historians and the English Civil War* (The Hague: Martinus Nijhoff, 1974).

22 In *British Autobiography in the Seventeenth Century* (New York: Columbia University Press, 1969), Paul Delaney traces the development of both secular and religious autobiography in the century.

23 I find the phrase "historical consciousness" in a posthumous essay by Herbert Butterfield, "The Establishment of a Christian Historiography," where it is associated with a general secularization of historical thought during the Christian era that culminates in the seventeenth century when "science" was finally able to "free men from the necessity of regarding spirits as the source of some of the motions . . . of the physical universe." *The Origins of History,* ed. Adam Watson (New York: Basic Books, 1981), pp. 176–77. This sounds rather "Whiggish" coming as it does from the man who gave us the term and the critique.

24 See Achsah Guibbory, *The Map of Time: Seventeenth-Century English Literature and Ideas of Pattern in History* (Urbana: University of Illinois Press, 1986), which argues that the major canonical poets of the century—Jonson, Donne, Milton, and Dryden—deployed strategic mixtures of three dominant historical schemes: progress, decay, and recurrence.

25 On analogy as a key to the grid of Renaissance epistemology, see Michel Foucault, *The Order of Things: An Archaeology of the Human Sciences* (1966; rpt. New York: Random House, 1973), pp. 21–23.

26 Ben Jonson, "To Sir Robert Wroth," *Poems,* ed. Ian Donaldson (London: Oxford University Press, 1975), p. 63.

27 *The Poetical Works of Robert Herrick,* ed. L. C. Martin (Oxford: Clarendon Press, 1956), p. 211.

28 Cited by John Barrell and John Bull, eds., in *A Book of English Pastoral Verse* (New York: Oxford University Press, 1975), p. 141.

29 See also John Wallace's important essay "'Examples Are Best Precepts': Readers and Meaning in Seventeenth-Century Poetry," *Critical Inquiry* 1 (1974): 273–90.

30 For a detailed account of the incident and its importance, see S. L. Goldberg, "Sir John Hayward, 'Politic' Historian," *Review of English Studies,* n.s. 6 (1955): 233–44.

31 See May McKisack, *Medieval History in the Tudor Age* (Oxford: Clarendon Press, 1971), and J. R. Hale, *The Evolution of British Historiography* (New York: Meridian, 1964).

32 Sir Thomas Blundeville, *The true order and Methode of wryting and reading*

Hystories (1574), sig. A4ᵛ. Citations are to this edition. H. G. Dick reprinted this important work in "Heywood's True Method," *Huntington Library Quarterly* 3 (1940): 149–69.

33 These figures are all listed as representing these qualities in Joshua Poole's *English Parnassus* (1657), pp. 534, 234, 230, 229, 283, 235, 277, 279, 243.

34 See Roberta Brinkley, *Arthurian Legend in the Seventeenth Century* (Baltimore: Johns Hopkins University Press, 1932), pp. 55–59, 102–3. For a more detailed discussion, see J. G. A. Pocock, *The Ancient Constitution and the Federal Law* (Cambridge: Cambridge University Press, 1957).

35 Morgan Coleman, [*The genealogies of King James I.*] (1608). Brinkley discusses Tudor claims via British ancestry, *Arthurian Legend,* p. 2.

36 Milton writes, "who *Arthur* was, and whether ever any such reign'd in *Britain,* hath bin doubted heeretofore, and may again with good reason." *Works,* ed. Frank A. Patterson et al., 20 vols. (New York: Columbia University Press, 1931–40), 10:127–28. See also P. F. Jones, "Milton and the Epic Subject from British History," *Publications of the Modern Language Association* 42 (1927): 901–9.

37 Richard Rowlands, *A Restitution of Decayed Intelligence* (1628), sig. xxx3ᵛ.

38 See Zera S. Fink, *The Classical Republicans: An Essay in the Recovery of a Pattern of Thought in Seventeenth-Century England* (Evanston: Northwestern University Press, 1945), p. 69.

39 There seems to be no reason to infer, as Brinkley does in *Arthurian Legend,* p. 74, that it was reissued for that purpose. It was published in Cambridge, later a Parliamentary stronghold, but neither of the two men responsible for the reissue supported the Parliamentary cause. Abraham Wheelock, Reader in Anglo-Saxon and librarian of the University Library, did keep his fellowship until his death in 1653, so he was not among those staunch royalists who lost their places under the interregnum governments. Yet in 1641, only three years before *Archaionomia* came out, he had been among the contributors to *Irenodia Cantabrigiensis,* a collection of academic verses celebrating the peace which Charles had made with Scotland (sigs. A3ᵛ–A4). Sir Roger Twysden, by contrast, did much of his work preparing additional materials for the new issue of Lambarde while in prison for his royalist sympathies. A first cousin of Sir Henry Vane, Twysden had represented Kent in the Short Parliament at which time he had supported opposition to Stuart absolutism. "As with a number of the more enlightened country gentlemen of his time, the law of the constitution was a favorite study, and it was the conclusion he drew from it that inspired him to resist any infringement of ancient right from whatever quarter it might come" (*DNB*); see also Frank W. Jessup, *Sir Roger Twysden, 1597–1672* (London: Cresset, 1965).

40 According to Fussner, Bolton's work as an antiquarian "was tied to the

rights of monarchy" (*Historical Revolution*, p. 106). Even his theoretical treatise *Hypercritica* betrays "an excessive diffidence toward monarchical authority" (p. 168).

41 Richard I, one of the great national heroes even today, was popular with
    balladeers during the seventeenth century; see *St. George's Commendation*
    (1612) in Hyder E. Rollins, ed., *The Pepys Ballads*, 8 vols. (Cambridge: Har-
    vard University Press, 1929), 1:45; *A Princely Song of King Richard*, in Rich-
    ard Johnson's *The Golden Garland* (1620), sigs. A8–B3. See also Michael
    Drayton, *Polyolbion*, book 9, in *Works*, ed. William Hebel et al., 5 vols.
    (Oxford: Shakespeare Head, 1961), and Abraham Cowley, *The Civil War*,
    ed. Alan Pritchard (Toronto: University of Toronto Press, 1973), 1.21–26.
    Victor of the battle of Agincourt, Henry V is still regarded as one of the
    great English conquerors. In addition to the accounts given of him in
    Shakespeare, *The Cronycle* (1590?) calls him "wyse and ryght manly, in
    peace and warre." See also Thomas Heywood, *Troia Britannica* (1690), sig.
    G3ᵛ; Drayton, *The Battle of Agincourt* (1627), *Works*, 3:9–72; Cowley, *The
    Civil War*, 1.51–58; and *Anglia Rediviva* (1658), pp. 7, 15. The ballads written
    on Agincourt are worthy of independent study; see Rollins, *Pepys Ballads*,
    1:45 and 2:51.

42 On Edward II, in addition to Marlowe's play, see Cowley, *The Civil War*,
    2.226, 2.469, and *Anglia Rediviva* (1658), p. 13. On Richard, see Cowley, *The
    Civil War*, 2.489, and *A Discourse By Way of Vision* in *English Writings*, ed.
    A. R. Ward, 2 vols. (Cambridge: Cambridge University Press, 1905–6),
    2:346.

43 On Roger Mortimer, see Drayton, *Mortimeriados* (1596), in *Works*, 1:368–69
    and passim, and notes to *The Barons Wars* in *Works*, 5:63–69.

44 On Simon de Montfort, see Cowley, *The Civil War*, 2.463–468, and Drayton,
    Polyolbion, in *Works*, 4:430–31.

45 There is an early account of Tyler's insurrection in John Berner's translation
    of Froissart's *Chronicle* which appeared in 1524–25, cited by A. M. Kinghorn
    in *The Chorus of History* (London: Blandford, 1971), pp. 32–34. Subsequent
    prose accounts appeared in 1642 and 1658 as royalist admonitions against
    popular rebellion. See *The Just Reward of Rebels* (1642) and Cleveland's *The
    Rustick Rampant* (1658). One of the earliest seventeenth-century poets to
    treat Tyler is Thomas Deloney. The tenth canto of his *Strange Histories* of
    1602 consists of a ballad, "The Rebellion of Wat Tyler and Jack Straw." Tyler
    also appears in a 1626 ballad entitled *A Brave Warlike Song*, reprinted in
    Rollins, *Pepys Ballads*, 2:54–62. Finally, we might notice that Charles himself
    warned the commons that if their Nineteen Propositions of June 1642 were
    instituted, and "all power ... vested in the House of Commons ... this
    splendid and excellently distinguished form of government [would] end in
    a dark, equal chaos of confusion, and the long line of our many noble

ancestors in a Jack Cade or a Wat Tyler." Cited by J. P. Kenyon, *The Stuart Constitution, 1603–1688* (Cambridge: Cambridge University Press, 1966), p. 22. For an excellent general study, see Charles Paulson, *The English Rebels* (London: Journeymen, 1984).

46 In "The Ballad History of the Reign of James I," (*Transactions of the Royal Historical Society*, 3d ser. 5 [1911]:21–61), C. H. Firth notes that of nine ballads on the Gunpowder Plot listed soon after the event, only one survives. The Gunpowder Plot was, however, the subject of a manuscript poem by Cleveland written in the early 1640s; see *The Poems of John Cleveland*, ed. Brian Morris and Eleanor Withrington (Oxford: Clarendon Press, 1967), pp. 72–73. See also Midmay Fane's "Ad Angliam in quinti Novembris," in *Otia Sacra* (1648), pp. 62–63. The plot was also the subject of numerous references in poems of the middle decades. In addition to John Vicars' poem discussed in Chapter 2, see the following: Cowley, *The Civil War*, 2.497; Richard Corbett, "Iter Boreale" (1648), *Poems*, ed. J. A. W. Bennett and H. R. Trevor-Roper (Oxford: Clarendon, 1967), p. 36; Alexander Ross, *England's Threnodie* (1648), p. 2. And see also the following prose accounts: *A Modell of the Fireworks* (1647); John Turner, *A Commemoration* (1654); and Thomas Spenser, *England's Warning Peece* (1658).

47 See Cowley, *The Civil War*, 1.37–50, and Edmund Waller's *Panegyric to My Lord Protector*, in *Poems*, ed. George Thorn-Drury, 2 vols. (London: Bullen, 1901), 2:10–17.

48 Richard Niccols, eds., *The Mirour for Magistrates* (1610), sigs. Yy5–Zz5; William Warner, *Albions England* (1602), p. 24; and Drayton, *Polyolbion*, in *Works*, 5:333.

49 Samuel Daniel, *The Civil Wars*, ed. Laurence Michel (New Haven: Yale University Press, 1958), 1.15.

50 Sir John Denham, *The Poetical Works*, ed. T. H. Banks, 2d ed. (Hamden, Conn.: Archon, 1969), p. 85.

51 This procedure clearly anticipates a structural feature of "progress" poems, a genre that was emerging at the time which typically traces the historical evolution of some abstract quality rather than dynastic succession. See R. H. Griffith, "The Progress Pieces of the Eighteenth Century," *Texas Review* (now *Studies in English Literature*) 5 (1920): 218–23; Mattie Swayne, "The Progress Piece in the Seventeenth Century," *Studies in English Literature* 16 (1936): 84–92; and my "So What *does* Thomas Gray's *Progress of Poesy* have to do with Progress?" *Postscript: Publication of the Philological Association of the Carolinas* 2 (1985): 67–74.

52 On the Baconian challenge to humanist epistemology, see Timothy J. Reiss, *The Discourse of Modernism* (Ithaca: Cornell University Press, 1982), pp. 198–225 and passim, and Lisa Jardine, *Francis Bacon and the Art of Discourse* (Cambridge: Cambridge University Press, 1974).

53 See my "Poetry as History: The Argumentative Design of Dryden's *Astraea Redux*," 54–55 and passim.

54 Fussner, *Historical Revolution*, p. 178.

55 Daniel was anxious that his work should not be thought to carry unwarranted topical associations. He carefully excised several references to the earl of Essex after that lord fell from favor at court; see Joan Rees, *Samuel Daniel* (Liverpool: Liverpool University Press, 1964), pp. 132–35.

56 Dedication to Mary, countess of Pembroke, in Daniel *The Civil Wars*, p. 67.

57 James Shirley, *The Dramatic Works and Poems*, ed. William Gifford and Alexander Dyce, 6 vols. (London: Murray, 1833), 6:279.

58 John Saltmarsh, "To his Ingenious *Friend* Master *Russel*, upon his Heroick *Poem*," prefixed to John Russell's *The Two Famous Pitcht Battels of Lypsich and Lutzen* (Cambridge, 1634), sig. 3ᵛ. In his fine study of Saltmarsh in *The World of the Ranters: Religious Radicalism in the English Revolution* (London: Lawrence and Wisehart, 1970), pp. 45–69, A. L. Morton misses this dedicatory poem which predates Saltmarsh's *Poemata Sacra* of 1636. The omission is of some interest since the poem suggests a militant edge to Saltmarsh's sensibility before 1641—when Morton suggests he became radicalized (p. 41)—and helps to explain Saltmarsh's autobiographical comment about "the bondage of a troubled conscience at times, for the space of about twelve years" in his *Free Grace* of 1645 (cited Morton, p. 50).

59 Jonathan Swift, *The Prose Writings*, ed. Herbert Davis, 15 vols. (Oxford: Blackwell, 1939–68), 12:264.

60 C. V. Wedgewood, *Poetry and Politics under the Stuarts* (Cambridge: Cambridge University Press, 1968), p. 34.

61 David Norbrook, *Poetry and Politics in the English Renaissance* (London: Routledge and Kegan Paul, 1984), p. 207.

62 See Lauro Martines' discussion of the important lexical studies of pronoun use in English Renaissance poetry undertaken by Giorgio Melchiori, *Society and History in English Renaissance Verse* (Oxford: Blackwell, 1985), pp. 109–12.

63 See, also, Cowley's "The Muse," *The Works of Mr Abraham Cowley* (1681), p. 24.

64 *Thanks to the Parliament*, in *Cavalier and Puritan*, ed. Hyder E. Rollins (New York: New York University Press, 1923), p. 140. The examples of grievances listed in the stanza suggest the ballad belongs to the months just before the outbreak of war. Between Strafford's imprisonment in November 1640 and the raising of the king's standard at Nottingham in August 1642, Parliamentary leaders kept the Commons busy with complaints directed against Charles's economic policies, including all of those measures mentioned in the ballad. See S. R. Gardiner, *History of England, 1603–1642*, 10 vols. (London: Longmans, 1883–84), 7:71–74, 9:140, 238, and F. C. Montague, *The History of England* (London: Longmans, 1907), p. 119.

65 Annabel Patterson, *Pastoral and Ideology* (Berkeley and Los Angeles: University of California Press, 1987), p. 151.

66 "I think," said Sir Edward Coke in 1628, "the Duke of Buckingham is the cause of all our miseries," cited by Gardiner, *History of England,* 6:305, a charge that had been voiced in the House of Commons two years earlier. See also Godfrey Davies, *The Early Stuarts* (1937; 2d ed. Oxford: Clarendon Press, 1959), pp. 63–67. On Buckingham's wars, see J. P. Kenyon's chapter "Buckingham and War" in *Stuart England* (Harmondsworth: Penguin, 1978), pp. 75–106. On the costs of the wars, see Gardiner, *History of England,* 6:219, and Robert E. Ruigh, *The Parliament of 1624* (Cambridge: Harvard University Press, 1971), pp. 257–302.

67 See Davies, *Early Stuarts,* p. 63, and *Calendar of State Papers [CSP], Venetian, 1625–1626,* p. 495, *CSP, Venetian, 1628–1629,* p. 128.

68 For the peace negotiations, see Martin J. Havran, *Caroline Courtier: The Life of Lord Cottington* (Columbia: University of South Carolina Press, 1973), pp. 92–102.

69 Edward Hyde, Earl of Clarendon, *The History of the Rebellion,* ed. W. Dunn Macray, 6 vols. (Oxford: Clarendon Press, 1888), 1:93.

70 *Irenodia Cantabrigiensis,* sigs. K–K^v. Notable among other English poems in this collection is Cleveland's "Upon the Kings Return from Scotland," sigs. L^v–L2.

71 See John H. Timmis, *Thine is the Glory* (University: University of Alabama Press, 1974), for a cryptoroyalist account of Strafford's "tragedy" that usefully provides transcriptions of most of the important documents.

72 "Charles insisted on visiting the northern kingdom," writes Davies, "because he had made up his mind to try to win over the Scottish leaders by personal persuasion." *Early Stuarts,* p. 106.

73 Abraham Cowley, *English Writings,* ed. A. R. Ward, 2 vols. (Cambridge: Cambridge University Press, 1905–6), 1:23.

74 Ibid., 1:22.

75 For anti-Scottish feeling, see, for example, the following ballads by Martin Parker: *A True Subjects Wish* (1640), *Britain's Honour* (1640), *News From Newcastle* (1640), *Good News from the North* (1640), all in Rollins, *Cavalier and Puritan,* pp. 84–106.

76 The formula of peace at home through war abroad was a commonplace one that still seems effective. For major exemplary statements of the principle, see Henry IV's advice to Hal in *Henry IV, Part Two,* 4.4.203–15, and Denham's *Cooper's Hill,* in *Poetical Works,* p. 74. See also G. R. Waggoner, "An Elizabethan Attitude toward Peace and War," *Philological Quarterly* 33 (1954): 20–33.

77 E. H. Carr, *What Is History?* (1961; Harmondsworth: Penguin, 1977), pp. 35–36. The proposition follows in general ways Benedetto Croce's familiar paradox that all history is contemporary history. This was first formulated

in his *Theory and History of Historiography,* trans. Douglas Ainslie (London: Harrap, 1921), pp. 11–12, and developed in *History as the Story of Liberation,* trans. Sylvia Spragge (New York: Norton, 1941), p. 19 and passim.

Chapter 4: Contemporary History and Epic Form

1 Dominick LaCapra, *Rethinking Intellectual History: Texts, Contexts, Language* (Ithaca: Cornell University Press, 1982), p. 57.

2 John N. King, *English Reformation Literature: The Tudor Origins of the Protestant Tradition* (Princeton: Princeton University Press, 1982), p. 6.

3 Martin Parker, *An Exact Description Of the manner how his Majestie and his Nobles went to the Parliament, on Munday, the thirteenth of Aprill, 1640,* in *Cavalier and Puritan,* ed. Hyder E. Rollins (New York: New York University Press, 1923), p. 78.

4 Abraham Cowley, *The Civil War,* ed. Alan Pritchard (Toronto: University of Toronto Press, 1973), 1.1–2.

5 See Pritchard's introduction for a full history of the text.

6 *The Foure Ages of England* (1648), p. 37.

7 This passage from *The Military Memoir of Colonel John Birch* is cited by Paul Hardacre, *The Royalists during the Puritan Revolution* (The Hague: Martinus Nijhoff, 1956), p. 1. The propaganda war to attract the impartial and undecided was especially fierce at the time of Cowley's poem. See Hardacre, *Royalists,* pp. 2–6, and *The Resolution of the Women of London* (1642).

8 Although returned MP for the 1656 Parliament, Birch was secluded until after Cromwell's death when he joined the Council of State that planned the Restoration. In 1660 he was one of six commisioners appointed to disband the army. See John Booker, ed., *A History of the Ancient Chapel of Birch, in Manchester Parish,* Chetham Society Publications, Vol. 47 (Manchester, 1859), pp. 109–10, 113.

9 The poem's immediate political importance is hard to evaluate. Cowley evidently considered the work sufficiently well known to be worth retracting ten years after he had, supposedly, abandoned work on it. His own role in the political events of the time is obscure. David Underdown, in *Royalist Conspiracy in England, 1649–1660* (1960; rpt. Hamden, Conn.: Archon, 1971), p. 207 n. 10, has dismissed Cowley from any complicity in engineering the Restoration. The coded letters which Cowley was once thought to have written, and which are now among the Clarendon State Papers in the Bodleian, were, according to Underdown, written by Sir John Cooper; for transcripts of the letters, see Arthur Nethercott, *Abraham Cowley: The Muse's Hannibal* (1931; rpt. New York: Russell and Russell, 1967), pp. 312–13.

10 Herbert Butterfield, *Man on his Past* (1955; rpt. Boston: Beacon, 1960), p. 17.

11 Among the many examples of the diabolic instigation of rebellion against monarchy in *Rump: Or, An Exact Collection of the Choycest Poems and Songs,* 2 vols. (1662), see especially "The Parliaments Pedigree" (1:24); "A Monster to be seen at Westminster" (1:85); "The Publique Faith" (1:124–26); "In imitation of *Come my Daphne,* a Dialogue between *Pluto* and *Oliver*" (1:339–40); "The Bloody Bed-roll, or Treason displayed in its Colours" (1:343–50); "The Devills Arse a Peake: or, Satans beastly part" (2:96–99); "A New Kickshaw for the queasie Stomack of Sathan and all that fight under his Banner" (2:162–65); and see also *The Devils Cabinet-Councell discovered: or, The Mistery and Iniquity of the Good Old Cause* (1660).

12 Thomas Hobbes, "The Vertues of an Heroique Poem," preface to *Homers Odyssees* in *Critical Essays of the Seventeenth Century,* ed. Joel Spingarn, 3 vols. (Oxford: Clarendon Press, 1908), 2:70.

13 At the time Cowley was writing there had been constant trouble in Ireland since the outbreak of rebellion there in October 1641. See Edward Hyde, Earl of Clarendon, *The History of the Rebellion,* ed. W. Dunn Macray, 6 vols. (Oxford: Clarendon Press, 1888), 4:23–30. In *The Puritan and the Papist,* Cowley himself attacks the Parliamentary leaders for their Irish policy in more specific terms, accusing them of exploiting the Irish for personal gains: "Your *Covetousnesse* let gasping Ireland tell, / Where first the *Irish Lands,* and next ye *sell* / The *English Bloud;* and raise *Rebellion* here, / With that which should supress, and quench it there." *English Writings,* ed. A. R. Ward, 2 vols. (Cambridge: Cambridge University Press, 1905–6), 2:155.

14 *The Poems of James VI of Scotland,* ed. James Craigie, 2 vols (Edinburgh: Blackwood, 1955–58), 1:79.

15 See the opening to book 3 of Ovid's *Metamorphoses.* According to other accounts, the warriors fight only after Cadmus throws a stone among them. In a more general context than Cowley's, the fable appears in *The Foure Ages of England* (1648) (p. 27), to suggest a parallel between the civil war and the beginning of the iron age.

16 Lawrence Stone, *The Family, Sex and Marriage in England, 1500–1800* (New York: Harper, 1977), pp. 29–30, 89–90.

17 *The Civil War,* p. 53, n. 5.

18 Ibid., p. 159.

19 The Gunpowder Plot was the subject of many ballads written in 1605–6; see previous chapter n. 46. Encouraging fear of catholic plots was a major device of radical polemics during the 1640s; see Brian Manning, *The English People and the English Revolution* (London: Heinemann, 1976), pp. 21–45. In the first edition of his *Epistolae Ho-Elianae* of 1645, James Howell reminded readers of the plot (sig. A3ᵛ). But in 1654, John Turner published his *A Commemoration, or A Calling to Minde of the great and Eminent Deliverance From the Powder-Plot* because, apparently: "*England* alas almost hath

quite forgot / The great deliverance from the Powder-plot; / Great mercies are, when they're past and gon, / Laid aside, and buried in oblivion" (p. 1).

20 An anonymous broadside, probably issued in Oxford, called *Pyms' Juncto,* purports to describe the inner workings of Parliament at this time. Thomason dated his copy May 8. See Falconer Madan, *Oxford Books,* 3 vols. (Oxford: Clarendon Press, 1895–1931), #1340. Toward the end of the satire, Pym calls upon infernal forces to help his party: "Rise *Synna, Sylla, Marius, Gracchus* Ghost, / With the rest of the whole Mechanick Host, / *Romes* greatest Earth-quakes, and this little trunck / Make with your desperate Spirits deeply drunk, / Up from your drousie urnes, the Ghost of those / My Ancestors that *Richard* did depose, / Drop fresh into my breast, my soul inspire, / And strongly actuate me with your fire, / That theirs thus mixt with my Malitious Gall, / Mine may with theirs fully possesse you all." The poem was reprinted in *Rump* (1662), from which I have quoted, 1:6. Cowley, who was in Oxford at the time, may well have known the poem, though the topos was well-worn by the 1640s. In *A Satyre Against the Cavaliers* (1642), the satirist instructs the cavaliers: "Call up those busie ghosts that once did thrive / In mischiefe like your selves, but not out-live / Their work, gallant *Cethegus,* and the rest, / Whose glorious hopes plum'd with *Romes* wealth, and drest, / Soar'd high, and ventured themselves, and all, / To give themselves, or *Rome* a funerall." Evidently, like so many of these devices, this one could work equally well for any party.

21 The poet of the anonymous *Verses: Lately written by Thomas Earl of Strafford* (1641) treats him as a Phaeton "Who with ambitious wings did fly / In *Charles* his Waine too loftily," rpt. in *A Century of Broadside Elegies,* ed. John W. Draper (London: Ingpen and Grant, 1928), #7. Other contemporary poems on Strafford that represent his rise and fall as a tragic movement include: Sir Richard Fanshawe, "On the Earle of Strafford's Tryall," *Shorter Poems and Translations,* ed. N. W. Bawcutt (Liverpool: Liverpool University Press, 1964), pp. 67–68; Sir John Denham, "On the Earl of Straffords Tryal and Death," *Poetical Works,* ed. T. H. Banks, 2d ed. (Hamden, Conn. Archon, 1969), pp. 153–54; John Cleveland, "Epitaph on the Earl of Strafford," *Poems,* ed. Brian Morris and Eleanor Withrington (Oxford: Clarendon Press, 1967), p. 66; Laurence Price, "The True Manner of the Life and Death of Sir Thomas Wentworth," rpt. in *Cavalier and Puritan,* pp. 119–24; John Lookes, *Keep Thy Head on Thy Shoulders, and I will keep Mine,* rpt. in *Cavalier and Puritan,* pp. 125–31; and Thomas Herbert, *An Elegie upon the Death of Thomas Earle of Strafford* (1641). Fanshawe, it is worth nothing, served under Strafford in Ireland.

22 So Denham: "Such was his force of Eloquence, to make / The Hearers mor concern'd than he that spake." *Poetical Works,* p. 154.

23 Camden's importance in the development of English historiographical

method can hardly be overestimated. The *Britannia* alone, first published in Latin, was reprinted in 1586, 1590, 1594, 1600, and 1607. Philemon Holland's English translation, which made the work more generally available and suggests something of the popular demand for English history, appeared in 1610 with reissues in 1637 and 1695. See Stuart Piggott, *William Camden and the "Britannia"* (London: British Academy, 1953), and Hugh Trevor-Roper, *Queen Elizabeth's First Historian: William Camden* (London: Cape, 1971). Camden's emphasis on places as both topographical and historical sites had already entered English poetry; see J. A. W. Bennett and H. R. Trevor-Roper, eds., *The Poems of Richard Corbett* (Oxford: Clarendon Press, 1955), pp. 118–19, for a list of poems in the subgenre describing a scholar's journey through the country, and James Turner's catalogue of "iter" poems in "The Matter of Britain," *Notes & Queries*, n.s. 25 (1978): 514–24.

24 *The Civil War*, p. 155.

25 On the rise of local history, see Fussner, *Historical Revolution*, pp. 211–229.

26 See the *DNB* entry, and F. Smith Fussner, *The Historical Revolution* (London: Routledge and Kegan Paul, 1964), p. 34, and Wallace T. MacCaffey, *Exeter, 1540–1640* (Cambridge: Harvard University Press, 1958), pp. 272–73.

27 See *DNB* entry for Hooker.

28 Camden, *Britannia* (1586), p. 107.

29 The *DNB* lists three manuscript copies, Ashmole MS. 762 and Cotton Titus F. vi. 88 in Oxford at the Bodleian, and M. D. N. #41 in the Library of the College of Arms.

30 *The Civil War*, p. 133.

31 The city of Birmingham had opposed the king even before he raised his banner at Nottingham in 1642. Charles was thwarted in attempts to gain possession of Coventry because three hundred men from Birmingham had gone there "to defend it against the king's forces." It was reported at the time that these men "first stirred up those of Coventry to resist the king." *A Letter written from Walshall* (1643), dated April 3 by Thomason. Birmingham was also hated by royalists for supplying the Parliamentary army of the earl of Essex with 15,000 swords manufactured there, while refusing to sell any to the king's agents (Clarendon, *Rebellion*, 6:83, 7:31). Cowley refers to this incident at 2.71–74. When royalist troopers entered the town, they destroyed the blademill where the disputed arms had been manufactured and set fire to much of the town, destroying enough houses and buildings to leave hundreds homeless. Prince Rupert's atrocious treatment of the city sparked off a pamphlet war that could not have gone unnoticed by Cowley, though he presents the barbarity as just retribution. See Manning, *English People*, pp. 200–206.

32 C. V. Wedgewood comments on the masque-like qualities of this passage.

Poetry and Politics under the Stuarts (Cambridge: Cambridge University Press, 1968), p. 76.

33 See James Shirley, *The Triumph of Peace* (1633) in *A Book of Masques,* ed. Norman Sanders (Cambridge: Cambridge University Press, 1964), p. 297: "a third Cloud, of various colour from the other two, begins to descend toward the middle of the Scene with somewhat a more swifter motion, and in it sat a person representing Dice, or Justice, in the midst, in a white robe and a mantle of satin, a fair long hair curled with a coronet of silver pikes, white wings and buskins, a crown imperial in her hand." The best study of Jacobean Whitehall is D. J. Gordon, "Rubens and the Whitehall Ceiling," *The Renaissance Imagination,* ed. Stephen Orgel (Berkeley and Los Angeles: University of California Press, 1975), pp. 25–50. Inigo Jones's drawings are reproduced in *A Book of Masques,* figure 30. Illustrations of Rubens' ceiling are often reproduced as, for example, in Antonia Fraser, *King James* (New York: Knopf, 1976), p. 176.

34 David Trotter, *The Poetry of Abraham Cowley* (London: Macmillan, 1979), pp. 10–11.

35 The theme of Cupid as a harbinger of death has been explored by Erwin Panofsky in *Studies in Iconology* (1939; rpt. New York: Harper and Row, 1972), pp. 124–25. It provided the theme for Shirley's masque *Cupid and Death* of 1635; see Harris' introduction in *A Book of Masques,* pp. 373–79.

36 See Richard H. Perkinson, "The Epic in Five Acts," *Studies in Philology* 43 (1946): 465–81.

37 In addition to an Oxford collection, *Verses on the Death of the Right Valiant Sr Bevill Grenvill* (Oxford, 1643), see the elegy by Martin Lluellyn in his collection *Men Miracles* (Oxford, 1646), p. 116.

38 Pritchard notices that the flower metaphor at lines 140–44 follows the description of Pallas' funeral in book 11 of the *Aeneid* (*The Civil War,* pp. 152–53).

39 David Underdown, *Pride's Purge: Politics in the Puritan Revolution* (Oxford: Clarendon Press, 1971), p. 42. See also Valerie Pearl, *London on the Outbreak of the Puritan Revolution* (Oxford: Clarendon Press, 1971), pp. 107–59.

40 The trained bands of London had gathered to display their strength in May 1642; Clarendon, *Rebellion,* 5:139. There had been considerable antagonism toward the royalist cause in London before this, however. See Manning, *English People,* pp. 1–98.

41 Sir Edward Walker served under Charles I as secretary of war and later as Garter Knight of Arms. He remained staunchly faithful to the Stuarts throughout the interregnum and directed the coronation ceremony for Charles II. His vanity and pride caused him to be disliked by many, including Clarendon: *DNB.*

42 Manning, *English People,* p. 196; see also pp. 196–98 for an account of the charges that royalist thinkers made against the city.

43 See Sandra Billington, "An Horatian Ode—Charles I and the Army as Actors," *Notes & Queries,* n.s. 25 (1978): 513, on the use of nets by morality play devils and Marvell's *Horation Ode.*

44 See *The Civil War,* pp. 164–69 for notes on the sects.

45 Cowley, *English Writings,* 1:9.

46 Barbara K. Lewalski, *"Paradise Lost" and the Rhetoric of Literary Forms* (Princeton: Princeton University Press, 1985), pp. 3–6.

47 Tasso, *Discourses on the Heroic Poem,* trans. Mariella Cavalchini and Irene Taylor (Oxford: Clarendon Press, 1973), p. 34.

48 William Davenant, Preface to *Gondibert,* in Spingarn, *Critical Essays,* 2:11.

49 See "The Vertues of an Heroique Poem," his preface to *Homer's Odyssees* (1675), in Spingarn, *Critical Essays,* 2:71–72, 73.

50 Without, that is, Lucan's sense of how to turn your enemies' victory against itself by emphasizing the sacrifices which that "victory" entails. See Frederick Ahl, *Lucan: An Introduction* (Ithaca: Cornell University Press, 1976), p. 67 and passim. A detailed study of Lucan's *Pharsalia,* translations into English by Sir Arthur Gorges, Thomas May, and Nicholas Rowe, Daniel's *The Civil Wars,* and Cowley's *The Civil War* would make a valuable contribution to our understanding of poetry and politics in revolutionary England. Allan Pritchard offers some useful observations about literary parallels between *Pharsalia* and Cowley's epic (pp. 40–42), but they depend on a reading of Lucan's text that Ahl's *Lucan* and J. P. Sullivan's *Literature and Politics in the Age of Nero* (Ithaca: Cornell University Press, 1985) render politically uninformed.

51 Raymond Williams, *Keywords* (New York: Oxford University Press, 1976), p. 119.

Chapter 5: The Unprecedented Future

1 The epigraph comes from the title page to the 1660 reprint of Edward Chamberlain's *The Late Warre Parallel'd. Or, A Brief Relation of the five years Civil Warres of Henry the Third, King of England, with the event and issue of that unnatural Warre, and by what course the Kingdom was then styled again* (first published in 1647) as a translated version of a Latin tag which preserves the visual metaphor for describing the historian's activities: "Qui respicit quae fuerunt, & inspicit quae sunt, prospicit etiam quae futura sunt."

2 Tilly, Wallenstein, and Montecuccoli in the Empire, Turenne and Condé in France, Spinola in Italy, and the great Swedish commanders Wrangel, Horn, Banér, and Tortensson are among those who rose to positions of considerable power from low beginnings; see Herbert Langer, *The Thirty Years War,* trans. C. S. V. Salt (Poole, Dorset: Blandford, 1980), p. 158.

3 By the end of the war, 680 disenfranchised noble families had joined townsmen and "tens of thousands of parish priests, teachers, peasants, merchants

and artists" in seeking asylum as political refugees; "20,000 houses were abandoned in Lower Austria alone." Langer, *Thirty Years War,* p. 133. The great engraver Wenceslaus Hollar was among the first wave of refugees, leaving Prague in 1627.

4 Ore mining and smelting centers in the Harz mountains, Upper Palatinate, and elsewhere flourished; increasingly large profits were possible from trading in copper, iron, lead, sulphur, and saltpeter; manufacturing and trading families living in the great cities of Danzig, Nuremberg, Hamburg, Bremen, Amsterdam, and Frankfort became rich and sometimes titled; families of arms dealers, like the Kletts of Zurich, merely became richer. See Langer, *Thirty Years War,* pp. 161–64, 167–68.

5 Langer, *Thirty Years War,* p. 8.

6 John Collop, "The Poet," in *Poems,* ed. Conrad Hiberry (Madison: University of Wisconsin Press, 1962), p. 38.

7 James Graham, "Upon the death of King *Charles* the first," in *Arcana Imperii: Or, The Casquet-Royall* (1660), p. 422; the legend appears at the bottom of the page in this version, which is quoted here. The legend also appears with the version given in *Reliquae Sacrae Carolinae* (The Hague, 1651), pp. 316–17. A variant text is given in Helen Gardiner, ed., *The New Oxford Book of English Verse* (New York: Oxford University Press, 1972), p. 309. For further discussion of the importance of the poems written on Charles's execution, especially their discursive links with poems written celebrating the Restoration, see my "The King on Trial: Judicial Poetics and the Restoration Settlement," *Michigan Academician* 17 (1985): 375–88.

8 I have passed by works, such as *Stipendariae Lachrymae* (The Hague, 1654) and Katherine Philips' "Upon the Double Murder of King Charles I, in answer to a libellous Copy of Rymes by Vavasour Powell," *Poems* (1664), which are retrospective.

9 *Chronostichon,* rpt. in *Vaticinium Votivum* (1649), p. 49. Harold Brooks in "Rump Songs," *Proceedings of the Oxford Bibliographical Society* 5 (1940): 296, lists single issues of this poem and suggests that it might be by Payne Fisher.

10 "An Elegie on the Meekest of Men," in *Momentum Regale* (1649), p. 5.

11 Henry King, "A Deep Groan Fetched at the Funerall of Charles the First," in *Monumentum Regale* (1649), p. 33.

12 Henry King, *An Elegy upon the most Incomparable King Charles the First,* rpt. in *Minor Poets of the Caroline Period,* ed. George Saintsbury, 3 vols. (1905; rpt. Oxford: Clarendon Press, 1968), 3:255.

13 [Thomas Pierce], *Caroli,* rpt. in *Monumentum Regale,* p. 26.

14 Unsigned and untitled elegy among "Severall Verses made by Divers Persons upon His Majesties Death," in *Reliquae Sacrae Carolinae,* p. 315.

15 "To the Sacred Memory," in *Vaticinium Votivum,* p. 37.

16 "To the Sacred Majesty of that Late High and Mightie Monarch, Charles the First," in *Vaticinium Votivum,* p. 36.

17 Thomas Fairfax, "On the Fatal day Jan: 30 1648," in "The Poems of Thomas Third Lord Fairfax," ed. Edward B. Reed, *Transactions of the Connecticut Academy* 14 (1909): 281.

18 Henry King, *An Elegy upon . . . Charles the First,* in Saintsbury, *Minor Poets,* 3:260.

19 "To the Sacred Memory," in *Vaticinium Votivum,* p. 38.

20 *Two Elegies,* cited in Joseph Frank, *Hobbled Pegasus* (Albuquerque: Universitiy of New Mexico Press, 1968), p. 225.

21 Christopher Hill, *God's Englishman: Oliver Cromwell and the English Revolution* (1970; rpt. New York: Harper, 1972), p. 211.

22 *Commons Journal,* cited Godfrey Davies, *The Early Stuarts, 1603–1660* (1937; 2d ed. Oxford: Clarendon Press, 1959), p. 160. See the discussion by Perez Zagorin, *A History of Political Thought in the English Revolution* (London: Routledge and Kegan Paul, 1954), pp. 79–83.

23 See Zagorin, *History of Political Thought,* p. 5.

24 Blair Worden, *The Rump Parliament, 1648–1653* (1974; rpt. Cambridge: Cambridge University Press, 1978), p. 139.

25 See Worden, *Rump Parliament,* pp. 163–210.

26 *Acts and Ordinances of the Interregnum, 1642–1660,* ed. C. H. Firth and R. S. Rait, 3 vols. (London: H.M.S.O., 1911), 2:19. See also S. R. Gardiner, *History of the Commonwealth and Protectorate, 1649–1660,* 6 vols. (London: Longmans, Green, 1894), 1:4; and S. R. Gardiner, ed., *Constitutional Documents of the Puritan Revolution, 1625–1660,* (1906; 3d ed. Oxford: Clarendon Press, 1968), pp. 384–88.

27 *Acts and Ordinances,* 2:3. The act appointing a Council of State is reproduced in Gardiner, *Constitutional Documents,* pp. 381–83.

28 Cited by Frank, *Hobbled Pegasus,* p. 243.

29 Zera S. Fink, *The Classical Republicans: An Essay in the Recovery of a Pattern of Thought in Seventeenth-Century England* (Evanston: Northwestern University Press, 1945), remains the best introduction to the limits of "republican" thought at the time.

30 Attacks on Cromwell were common throughout the period. The following were all published during the spring and early summer of 1649: *A Coffin for King Charles: A Crowne for Cromwell: A Pit for the The People,* and *The State's New Coin,* both in *Political Ballads of the Seventeenth and Eighteenth Centuries,* ed. W. W. Wilkins, 2 vols. (London: Longmans, 1860), 1:79–85, 1:94–95, and see also *Balaam's Asse, or The City-Feast for Cursing the King: And Blessing Oliver; A Sad Sigh, With Some Heart-Cracking Groanes;* and *The Loyall Subjects Jubilee, or Cromwell's Farewell to England.*

31 Ruth Nevo, *The Dial of Virtue* (Princeton: Princeton University Press, 1963), p. 75.

32 The author of these poems is not the Robert Fletcher who wrote the volume of verse *Ex Otio Negotium* (1656) as Frank suggests in *Hobbled Pegasus,* p.

273. See D. H. Woodward, ed., *The Poems and Translations of Robert Fletcher* (Gainesville, Fla.: University of Florida Press, 1970), p. 9.

33 See also *Mercurius Heliconicus #2* (February 12, 1651) and *Radius Heliconicus* published the same month. Two other poems that shed light on this period are *Somnium Cantabrigiense* (1650), and *A Word of Counsel to the Disaffected* (1651).

34 See Zagorin, *History of Political Thought,* pp. 66–71, 91–94, 123–29.

35 David Underdown, *Pride's Purge* (Oxford: Clarendon Press, 1971), p. 262.

36 Christopher Hill, *The World Turned Upside Down* (New York: Viking, 1972), p. 125. On Parker's political thought and career, see J. W. Allen, *English Political Thought, 1603–1644* (London: Methuen, 1944), pp. 426–35; W. K. Jordan, *Men of Substance* (1942; rpt. New York: Octagon, 1967), pp. 140–47; and Zagorin, *History of Political Thought*, p. 5.

37 Christopher Hill, "The Norman Yoke," in *Puritanism and Revolution* (1958; rpt. London: Panther, 1969), pp. 58–125.

38 I follow the dating given by Margoliouth in *The Poems and Letters of Andrew Marvell,* 2 vols. (1972; rpt. Oxford: Clarendon Press, 1976), 1:295.

39 John Wallace, *Destiny His Choice* (Cambridge: Cambridge University Press, 1968), p. 84. See the note in *Poems and Letters of Andrew Marvell*, 1:300.

40 The work obviously postdated Ireton's death, which occurred on November 7, and the assumption of office by the new Council of State on December 1. Thomason dated his copy February 8 (i.e., 18), 1652.

41 Harrison was friendly with the Leveller John Lilburne in 1648, espoused Fifth Monarchist principles, and came to oppose Cromwell during the Protectorate. See Gardiner, *Commonwealth and Protectorate,* 1:471–77; Christopher Hill, *The Experience of Defeat* (New York: Viking, 1984), pp. 69–77, 303–7; and my "The King on Trial," pp. 377–79.

42 The names listed—sigs. B2–B2^v—correspond, with only two exceptions, to those members of the council appointed to serve on committees on December 2. The names of Isaac Pennington, an alderman of London who had been a member of the council of 1649, and Sir Peter Wentworth, do not appear as subcommittee members: *Calendar of State Papers [CSP], Domestic, 1649–1650,* p. 6, *CSP, Domestic, 1651–1652,* p. 43. However, the two previous councils both had several members not appointed for 1652, none of whom appear in the lists given in Manley's poem.

43 Nevo, *Dial of Virtue,* p. 82.

44 See H. V. S. Ogden, "Variety and Contrast in Seventeenth-Century Aesthetics and Milton's Poetry," *Journal of the History of Ideas* 10 (1949): 159–82.

45 Manley clearly has the muses as a group in mind; one of the errata listed for page 39 corrects "Muse" to "Muses" (*Veni; Vidi; Vici,* sig. A4^v).

46 The title page calls the poem a "song," but the running heads and the epigraph refer to it as an "ode."

47 *Anglia Liberata* (1651), title page.

48 The engraving is reproduced in Maurice Ashley, *Oliver Cromwell and His World* (New York: Putnam, 1972), p. 75.

49 Many perceived Cromwell's appointment as little more than a return to monarchy. Published shortly after Cromwell was formally invested, *Britannia Triumphalis* (1654) describes the period from Charles's execution to Cromwell's personal rule as a movement "from the end of one Monarchy to the beginning of another" (p. 207). This writer's view that monarchy is "the darling of the multitude" (p. 5) may or may not express general feeling at the time, but does express a sense common to many poems written in support of the Protectorate.

50 See Underdown, *Pride's Purge;* Worden, *Rump Parliament;* and Austin Woolrych, *Commonwealth to Protectorate* (Oxford: Clarendon, 1982).

51 Gardiner, *Commonwealth and Protectorate,* 2:217–18.

52 See *The House Out of Doors* (1653), rpt. in Wilkins, *Political Ballads,* 1:100–104.

53 Thomason, E. 697. (17). Gardiner also transcribes the poem in *Commonwealth and Protectorate,* 2:228, with several variants, and mentions two other copies of the poem. The verses clearly became a popular and rather formulaic expression of support for the idea of monarchy. A four-line manuscript in the Bodleian turns the opening and closing lines to a call for the Restoration: "Rise up brave Worthy for thou art divine / Receive Three Kingdomes which are justly Thyne: / And you brave Merchants with the Gentry sing / Viv' le Roy Long live the King" (MS Ashmole 36,37 f.165). The idea of King Oliver was by no means novel. *The Cities Welcome* of 1647—two years before Charles was executed—ironically declares: "There's no such thing as Charles our King, / We here renounce him ever; / We'll have no king but thee, sweet Noll, / Or Tom Fairfax, that glorious feather," rpt. in Wilkins, *Political Ballads,* 1:67.

54 Gardiner, *Commonwealth and Protectorate,* 2:221–22, and Woolrych, *Commonwealth to Protectorate,* pp. 352–78.

55 Hill, *God's Englishman,* p. 139. I have quoted Cromwell's speech from Thomas Carlyle's edition *Cromwell's Letters and Speeches,* 5 vols. (London: Chapman and Hall, 1873), 3:225, 226.

56 Hill, *God's Englishman,* p. 149.

57 Gardiner, *Constitutional Documents,* p. 405.

58 As Clarendon was later to observe of Cromwell's appointment: "And in this manner, and with so little pains, this extraordinary man, without any other reason than because he had a mind to it, and without the assistance, and against the desire of all noble persons or men of quality, or of three men who in the beginning of the troubles, were possessed of three hundred pounds land by the year, mounted himself into the throne of three king-

doms, without the name of a king, but with a greater power and authority than had been ever exercised or claimed by any king; and received greater evidence and manifestation of respect and esteem from all the kings and princes in Christendom. . . ." *Rebellion,* 14:26.

59 See John Locke, *Two Treatises of Civil Govrnment,* ed. W. S. Carpenter (1924; rpt. London: Dent, 1967), pp. 130–35.

60 Not all modern historians have been so sanguine about Cromwell's success. For an excellent introductory summary of the controversy over Cromwell's foreign policy during the 1650s, see Alan G. R. Smith, *The Emergence of a Nation State* (London and New York: Longman, 1984), pp. 333–38, which cites the major critics of Hill's view which, nevertheless, best seems to fit the poetic evidence.

61 *CSP, Venetian, 1640–1642,* p. 78.

62 *CSP, Venetian, 1632–1636,* p. 110.

63 Abbot, cited by Hill, *God's Englishman,* p. 167.

64 Hill, *God's Englishman,* p. 166.

65 Ibid., pp. 156, 165–66.

66 Quoted by Hill, *God's Englishman,* p. 149.

67 See Howard D. Weinbrot, *Augustus Caesar in "Augustan" England* (Princeton: Princeton University Press, 1978), pp. 3–8, for a summary of discussions of English "Augustanism," and Howard Erskine-Hill, *The Augustan Idea in English Literature* (London: Arnold, 1983), for a comprehensive survey of how the tradition was transmitted.

68 Such seems to be the appraisal of Ruth Nevo who, in *Dial of Virtue,* discovers in the "content and approach" of Cromwellian elegies, "every indication of the subsiding of conflict, the lessening of acute ideological tension. There is evident in them an abstraction of the idea of heroic virtue from the mesh and tug of revolutionary events, revolutionary decisions. In this abstraction is to be found the germ of the heroic, which, divorced from specific historical or political contexts, can henceforth be applied to fictitious characters in imaginary situations, as in the heroic drama." Pp. 136–37.

69 Alastair Fowler, *Triumphal Forms: Structural Patterns in Elizabethan Poetry* (Cambridge: Cambridge University Press, 1970), pp. 80–84.

70 This section of Bodleian MS. Eng. poet. d.49 is reprinted thus in *Andrew Marvell: Miscellaneous Poems 1681* (1969; rpt. Menston: Scolar Press, 1973), Appendix.

71 Hill, *God's Englishman,* pp. 139–66. See also Underdown, *Pride's Purge,* p. 259.

72 Wallace, *Destiny His Choice,* pp. 69–105; Joseph A. Mazzeo, "Cromwell as Davidic King," *Renaissance and Seventeeneth-Century Studies* (New York: Columbia University Press, 1964), pp. 183–208; Steven Zwicker, "Models of Governance in Marvell's 'The First Anniversary,'" *Criticism* 16 (1974): 1–12;

A. J. N. Wilson, "Andrew Marvell's 'The First Anniversary,'" *Modern Languages Review* 69 (1974): 254–73; Isabel Rivers, *The Poetry of Conservatism, 1600–1745* (Cambridge: Rivers Press, 1973), pp. 109–915; Annabel Patterson, *Marvell and the Civic Crown* (Princeton: Princeton University Press, 1978), pp. 68–90; and Warren L. Chernaik, *The Poet's Time: Politics and Religion in the Work of Andrew Marvell* (Cambridge: Cambridge University Press, 1983), pp. 42–55—the phrase is cited from p. 55. See also John Dixon Hunt, *Andrew Marvell: His Life and Writings* (London: Elek, 1978), pp. 126–32.

73 Derek Hirst, "'That Sober Liberty': Marvell's Cromwell in 1654," in *The Golden and Brazen World: Papers in Literature and History, 1650–1800*, ed. John M. Wallace (Berkeley and Los Angeles: University of California Press, 1985), pp. 17–53—the phrase cited appears on p. 35. See also Rivers, *Poetry of Conservatism*, p. 114.

74 Fowler, *Triumphal Forms*, p. 91.

75 As in the Italian arch erected for the coronation of James, an engraved illustration of which appears in Stephen Harrison's *The Archs of Triumph* (1603), sig. D2, reproduced in Graham Parry, *The Golden Age Restor'd: The Culture of the Stuart Court, 1603–1642* (Manchester: Manchester University Press, 1981), p. 14. This shows large compartments behind two sets of pillars. For a seventeenth-century illustration of pictorial bases, see the title-page engraving to Edmund Bolton, *Nero Caesar* (1627).

76 Bertolt Brecht, *The Life of Galileo*, trans. Desmond Vesey (1960; London: Methuen, 1971), pp. 107, 108.

Epilogue

1 See Carolyn Edie, "News from Abroad: Advice to the People of England on the Eve of the Stuart Restoration," *Bulletin of the John Rylands Library* 76 (1984): 383.

2 See, for example, Harold Weber's recent claim that "we find it difficult to grasp not only the immense significance of Charles' Restoration, but the sheer wonder of it, its inexplicable mystery to those who lived through it." "Representations of the King: Charles II and His Escape from Worcester," *Studies in Philology* 85 (1988): 489.

3 In addition to familiar accounts by Pepys and Evelyn, see *The Public Intelligencer* 7 (May 8, 1660), p. 106; *The Parliamentary Intelligencer* 23 May 28–June 4, 1660), pp. 358–60; and Anthony Sadler, *The Subject's Joy for the Kings Restoration* (1660). Bonfires figure prominently in several Restoration poems including the following: *Anglia Rediviva: A Poem on His Majesties most joyfull Reception into England* (1660), p. 2; Abiel Borfet, *Postliminia Caroli II. The Palingenesy* (1660), p. 8; Thomas Forde, "Upon his Sacred

Majesties most happy Return," in *Virtus Rediviva. A Panegyrick on King Charles I., with severall other peeces from the same pen* (1660; rpt. 1661), p. 22; *The Glory of These Nations, being a brief Relation of King Charles's Royal Progresse from Dover to London* [1660], rpt. in *Political Ballads Published In England during the Commonwealth,* ed. Thomas Wright (London: Percy Society, 1841), pp. 223–28; and Samuel Willes, *To the King's Most Sacred Majesty upon his happy and glorious return* (1660), p. 2.

4 In *Mercurius Aulicus* for the last week of May, we read of how one Mr. Dashwood was "sundenly [*sic*] surprised by death ... and that it was suggested he had spoke reproachful words against the King." We are assured that "his whole Family holds a perfect abhorency and detestation of disloyalty." *Mercurius Aulicus* 7 (May 21–28, 1660), p. 56. And we need only think of Edmund Ludlow's stirring memoirs of danger, uncertainty, and flight, or of the extensive publication of confessional and trial material throughout 1660, to recognize the discursive signs of a modern form of social control. See *The Memoirs of Edmund Ludlow* (London, 1751), pp. 341–64, and Edmund Ludlow, *The Voyce From the Watch Tower. Part Five: 1660–1662,* ed. A. B. Worden, Camden Series Vol. 21 (London: Royal Historical Society, 1978); Christopher Hill, *The Experience of Defeat* (New York: Viking, 1984), pp. 69–83; and my "The King on Trial: Judicial Poetics and the Restoration Settlement," *Michigan Academician* 17 (1985): 375–88.

5 See Christopher Hill, *The World Turned Upside Down* (New York: Viking, 1972), pp. 347–48, quoting Sir Thomas Aston on "true liberty" from *A Remonstrance against Presbytery* (1641), sig. M4^v.

6 David Underdown, *Revel, Riot, and Rebellion: Popular Politics and Culture in England, 1603–1660* (Oxford: Clarendon Press, 1985), p. 272.

7 Underdown, *Revel, Riot, and Rebellion,* p. 286. Elaine Hobby pointed this tendency out to me as a habit inherited from Keith Thomas' important essay "Women and the Civil War Sects," *Past and Present* 13 (1958): 42–62. On women as the organizers of their own congregations, see Claire Cross, " 'He-Goats before the Flocks': A Note on the Part Played by Women in the Founding of Some Civil War Churches," in *Popular Belief and Practice,* ed. G. J. Cumming and Derek Baker, Studies in Church History, Vol. 8 (Cambridge: Cambridge University Press, 1972), pp. 192–202.

8 Minute Book of the Exeter General Quarter Sessions, 1660–1672, ff.1,2. I wish to thank P. W. Thomas, assistant librarian at the Exeter Cathedral Library, who in 1984 made me a gift of his library's spare copy of a mimeographed descriptive catalogue, "Charles II and the Restoration: An Exhibition to Commemorate the Tercentenary of the Restoration of the Monarchy held in The Chapter House, Exeter held 18–28 May, 1960," from which I quote, p. 49. The cases involving bastardy and cohabitation are cited from p. 37.

9 See also, for instance, Ralph Astell—uncle of the celebrated protofeminist

Mary Astell—whose *Vota, Non Bella. New-Castel's Heartie Gratulation To Her Sacred Soveraign King Charles the Second; On His Now Glorious Restauration To His Birth-right Power* (Newcastle, 1660) is one of the more fascinating poems of the year. It plays with epithalamic tropes by personifying Newcastle as a "black Northern Lass" (p. 4) who feels herself compelled, despite her sense of unworthiness in contrast with the southern ladies, to write about the king's return. The central metaphor of the text, however, represents Charles's return as a rebirth following the twelve years' labors of Britain "To be Deliver'd of a *Soveraign*" (p. 11). The conceit allows Astell to figure George Monck as "that Noble Instrument" which Heaven sent "from the North . . . / T'obstetricate" (p. 12). For another poet's use of the epithalamic metaphor to advise Britain to prepare herself as a bride in anticipation of receiving the king her bridegroom, see "Upon His Majesties most happy restauration to his Royall Throne in Brittaine," manuscript verses in the Bodleian (Firth b.20, fol. 140) incorrectly ascribed to Katherine Philips, which are transcribed and discussed in my "What Is a Restoration Poem?" in *TEXT 3*, ed. David Greetham and W. Speed Hill (New York: AMS, 1987), pp. 331–40.

10 I quote from a variant leaf added to the copy in the University Library, Cambridge (shelfmark Syn. 7.66.103).

11 See Laura Brown, "The Ideology of Restoration Poetic Form: John Dryden," *Publications of the Modern Language Association* 97 (1982): 395–407, and Nicholas Jose, *Ideas of the Restoration in English Literature, 1660–1671* (Cambridge: Harvard University Press, 1984).

12 Ronald Hutton, *The Restoration: A Political and Religious History of England and Wales, 1658–1667* (Oxford: Clarendon, 1985), p. 121.

13 Christopher Hill, *Milton and the English Revolution* (New York: Viking, 1977), p. 199.

14 Following Hutton, "If there was a moment at which the republic became doomed, it was when the purged Parliament invited Monck's army to London." *Restoration*, p. 120.

15 Deserving of special attention in this respect are the large folio volumes produced in English, Dutch, and French versions by Adrian Vlack at the Hague. The English version, translated by Sir William Lower, is entitled *A Relation in Form of [sic] Journal, of the Voiage and Residence which the most Excellent and most Mighty Prince Charls the II King of Great Britain, &c, hath made in Holland, from the 25 of May to the 2 of June, 1660* and contains several engraved illustrations of Charles being entertained by Dutch and other European leaders. Lower appended some poems explaining each of the illustrations. The illustrations are absent from the one Dutch copy I have examined (British Library, shelfmark 1564.69[2]), but it ends with a poem in Dutch to Charles by Jan Westerboen.

16 See Barry Reay's useful application of Antonio Gramsci's notion of "hege-

mony"—the means by which dominant class ideologies grasp and control public consent—to the culture of early modern England in his Introduction to *Popular Culture in Seventeenth-Century England* (New York: St. Martin's, 1985), pp. 17–21.

17 See, among others, Henry Bold, *St. George's Day Sacred to the Coronation of His Most Excellent Majesty and ever Glorious Prince, Charles the II* (1660), p. 5; Abraham Cowley, *Ode Upon the Blessed Restoration* (1660), stanza 14; John Crouch, *To His Sacred Majesty: Loyall Reflections* (1661), sig. A4ᵛ; Thomas Higgons, *A Panegyrick to the King* (1660), p. 8; and Willes, *To the King's Most Sacred Majesty,* p. 7.

18 See especially the poem by Edward Littleton beginning "Free-men we cannot; Slaves we will not be: / Subjects we are. That's all the liberty / That we desire, or can contain." *Britannia Rediviva* (Oxford, 1660), sigs. A4ᵛ–Bb. See also Giles Duncombe's "Repentance for the Murther of Charles the Martyr. And The Restauration of *Charles,* the II is the only Balm to cure *Englands* Distractions," *Scutum Regale: The Royal Buckler* (1660), sig. Dd 5ᵛ.

19 See Christopher Hill, "Some Conclusions," *The Collected Essays,* Vol. 1: *Writing and Revolution in Seventeenth-Century England* (Amherst: University of Massachusetts Press, 1985), pp. 317–34.

20 Richard Flecknoe, "The Pourtrait of His Majesty, Made a Little before His Happy Restauration," which first appeared in *Heroick Portraits* (1660), sig. B2.

21 See Roy Strong, *Henry Prince of Wales and England's Lost Renaissance* (London: Thames and Hudson, 1986).

22 *Englands Joy in a Lawful Triumph* (1660).

23 See T. H. Aston and C. H. E. Philpin, eds., *The Brenner Debate: Agrarian Development in a Pre-Industrial Europe* (Cambridge: Cambridge University Press, 1985).

Works Cited

Primary Sources

Place of publication for early printed books is London unless otherwise stated.

Adams, Hazard, ed. *Critical Theory since Plato.* New York: Harcourt, 1971.

Aleyn, Charles. *The Battailes of Crescey, and Poictiers under the leading of King Edward the Third of that Name.* 1631. Reprint 1633.

Aleyn, Charles. *The Historie of that Wise and Fortunate Prince, Henrie, of that name the Seventh, King of England.* 1638.

Amyot, Pierre. Preface to North's translation of Plutarch's *Lives.* 1579.

Anglia Liberata, or, the Rights of the people of England maintained against the pretences of the Scotish King. 1651.

Anglia Rediviva: Or, England Revived. An Heroick Poem. 1658.

Anglia Rediviva: A Poem on His Majesties most joyfull Reception into England. 1660.

Arcana Imperii: Or, The Casquet-Royall. 1660.

Ascham, Roger. *Ascham's English Works.* Ed. W. A. Wright. Cambridge: Cambridge University Press, 1904.

Astell, Ralph. *Vota, Non Bella. New-Castel's Heartie Gratulation To Her Sacred Soveraign King Charles the Second: On His Now Glorious Restauration To His Birth-right Power.* Newcastle, 1660.

B., A. [Alexander Brome?]. *A Canturbury Tale. Translated out of Chaucer's old English Into our Now Usual Language.* 1641.

B., T. *Newes from Rome. Or a Relation of the Pope and his Patentees Pilgrimage into Hell, with their entertainment, and the Popes returne backe againe to Rome.* 1641.

Balaam's Asse, Or, The City-Fast For Cursing the King and Blessing Oliver. 1649.

Barre, Poullain de la. *The Woman As Good as the Man: Or, the Equality of Both Sexes.* Ed. G. M. MacLean. Detroit: Wayne State University Press, 1988.

Barrell, John, and John Bull, eds. *A Book of English Pastoral Verse.* New York: Oxford University Press, 1975.

The Barrington Family Letters. Ed. Arthur Searle. Camden Fourth Series, Vol. 28. London: Royal Historical Society, 1983.

Beard, Thomas. *The Theatre of God's Judgements.* 1597.

Blundeville, Sir Thomas. *The true order and Methode of wryting and reading Hystories.* 1574.

Boccaccio, Giovanni. *Boccaccio On Poetry: Being the Preface and the Fourteenth and Fifteenth Books of Boccaccio's Genealogia Deorum Gentilium in an English Version.* Trans. Charles G. Osgood. Princeton: Princeton University Press, 1930.

Bold, Henry. *St. George's Day Sacred to the Coronation of His Most Excellent Majesty and ever Glorious Prince, Charles the II.* 1660.

[Bolton, Edmund]. *London, King Charles His Augusta, or, City Royal.* 1648.

Bolton, Edmund. *Nero Caesar, or Monarchie Depraved.* 1627.

Borfet Abiel. *Postliminia Caroli II. The Palingenesy.* 1660.

Bragg, Billy. *Between the Wars.* London: Chrysalis Records, 1984.

Braithwait, Richard. *The Scholler's Medley, or, an Intermixt Discourse upon Historical and Poetical Relations.* 1614. Reprinted as *A Survey of History: or, A Nursery for Gentry,* 1638.

Brecht, Bertolt. *The Life of Galileo.* Trans. Desmond Vesey. 1960. Reprint London: Methuen, 1971.

Breton, Nicholas. *The Court and the Country.* 1618.

Britannia Triumphalis; A Brief History of the Warres and other State Affairs of Great Britain. 1654.

Butler, Samuel. *Hudibras, In Three Parts.* Ed. Zachary Grey. 2 vols. London, 1806.

Cambridge, University of. *Epicidium Cantabrigiense.* Cambridge, 1612.

Cambridge, University of. *Irenodia Cantabrigiensis.* Cambridge, 1641.

Cambridge, University of. *Voces Votivae Ab Academicis Cantabrigiensibus.* Cambridge, 1635.

Camden, William. *Britannia.* 1586.

Camden, William. *The Historie of the most renowned and victorious princesse Elizabeth late Queene of England.* Trans. R[obert] N[orton]. 1630.

Carew, Richard. *The Survey of Cornwall.* 1602.

Carew, Thomas. *The Poems of Thomas Carew.* Ed. Rhodes Dunlap. 1949. Reprint Oxford: Clarendon Press, 1970.

Chamberlain, Edward. *The Late Warre Parallel'd. Or, A Brief Relation of the five years Civil Warrs of Henry the Third, King of England, with the event and issue of that unnatural Warre, and by what course the Kingdom was then styled again.* 1647. Reprint 1660.

Chapman, George. *The Plays of George Chapman: The Comedies.* Ed. T. M. Parrott. 1910–14. 2 vols. Reprint New York: Russell and Russell, 1961.

Clapham, John. *Elizabeth of England*. Ed. E. P. Reed, and C. Reed. Philadelphia: University of Pennsylvania Press, 1951.

Clarendon, Edward Hyde, Earl of. *The History of the Rebellion and Civil Wars in England*. Ed. W. Dunn Macray. 6 vols. Oxford: Clarendon Press, 1888.

Cleland, James. *Heropaedia, of the Institution of a Young Nobleman*. Oxford, 1607.

Cleveland, John. *The Poems of John Cleveland*. Ed. Brian Morris and Eleanor Withrington. Oxford: Clarendon Press, 1967.

Coleman, Morgan. [*The genealogies of King James I. and Queen Anne, his wife, from the Conquest*]. 1608.

Collop, John. *The Poems of John Collop*. Ed. Conrad Hiberry. Madison: University of Wisconsin Press, 1962.

Corbett, Richard. *The Poems of Richard Corbett*. Ed. J. A. W. Bennett and H. R. Trevor-Roper. Oxford: Clarendon Press, 1955.

Cowley, Abraham. *The Civil War*. Ed. Allan Pritchard. Toronto: University of Toronto Press, 1973.

Cowley, Abraham. *The English Writings of Abraham Cowley*. Ed. A. R. Ward. 2 vols. Cambridge: Cambridge University Press, 1905–6.

Cowley, Abraham. *The Works of Mr. Abraham Cowley*. 1681.

Cragge, John. *Great Britains Prayers in This Dangerous Time of Contagion*. 1641.

Cragge, John. *A Prophecy Concerning the Earle of Essex That Now Is*. 1641.

Crashaw, Richard. *The Poems English, Latin, and Greek of Richard Crashaw*. Ed. L. C. Martin. Oxford: Clarendon Press, 1927.

Cromwell, Oliver. *Oliver Cromwell's Letters and Speeches*. Ed. Thomas Carlyle. 5 vols. London: Chapman and Hall, 1873.

The Cronycle of all the Kynges: that have Reygned in Englande: Sythe the Conquest of Wyllyam Conqueroure. [1590?].

C[rouch], J[ohn]. *A Mixt Poem, Partly Historicall, Partly Panegyricall, Upon the Happy Return of His Sacred Majesty Charls the Second*. 2 variant printings, 1660.

Crouch, John. *To His Sacred Majesty: Loyall Reflections*. 1661.

Daniel, Samuel. *The Civil Wars*. Ed. Laurence Michel. New Haven: Yale University Press, 1958.

Daniel, Samuel. *The Complete Works in Verse and Prose of Samuel Daniel*. Ed. Alexander B. Grossart. 1885. 5 vols. Reprint New York: Russell and Russell, 1963.

A Declaration and Resolution of the Lords and Commons assembled in Parliament, in Answer to the Scots Declaration. 1642.

Deloney, Thomas. *Strange Histories; consisting of ballads and other poems principally by Thomas Deloney*. 1602. Reprint 1607.

Denham, Sir John. *The Poetical Works of Sir John Denham*. Ed. T. H. Banks. 2d ed. Hamden, Conn.: Archon, 1969.

The Devils Cabinet-Councell discoverd; or, The Mistery and Iniquity of the Good Old Cause. 1660.

A Discovery of the Jesuites Trumpery, newly packed out of England. 1641.

Draper, John W., ed. *A Century of Broadside Elegies.* London: Ingpen and Grant, 1928.

Drayton, Michael. *The Works of Michael Drayton.* Ed. William Hebel et al. 5 vols. Oxford: Shakespeare Head, 1961.

Dryden, John. *Of Dramatic Poesy and Other Critical Essays.* Ed. George Watson. Reprint 2 vols. 1962. London: Dent, 1968.

Dryden, John. *The Poems of John Dryden.* Ed. James Kinsley. 4 vols. Oxford: Clarendon Press, 1958.

Dryden, John. *The Works of John Dryden.* Ed. H. R. Swedenberg et al. 20 vols. Berkeley and Los Angeles: University of California Press, 1956–.

Duncombe, Giles. *Scutum Regale, the Royal Buckler.* 1660.

Elyot, Sir Thomas. *The Booke of the Governor.* Ed. S. E. Lehmberg. 1962. Reprint London: Dent, 1966.

Englands Joy in a Lawful Triumph. 1660.

F., R. *Mercurius Heliconicus. Or, The Result of a safe Conscience whether It be necessary to submit to the Government now in being.* 1651.

F., R. *Mercurius Heliconicus. Or, A Short Reflection of Moderne Policy.* 1651.

F., R. *Radius Heliconicus: Or, the Resolution of a Free State.* 1651.

Fairfax, Thomas. "The Poems of Thomas Third Lord Fairfax." Ed. Edward B. Reed. *Transactions of the Connecicut Academy* 14 (1909): 237–90.

The Famous Tragedie of the Life and Death of Mris Rump. Shewing How She was brought to Bed of a Monster With her terrible Pangs, bitter Teeming, hard Labour, and lamentable Travell from Portsmouth to Westminster, and the great misery she hath endured by her ugly, deformed, ill-shapen, base-begotten Brat or Imp of Reformation. 1660.

Fane, Mildmay. *Otia Sacra: Optima Fides.* 1648.

Fanshawe, Sir Richard. *Shorter Poems and Translations.* Ed. N. W. Bawcutt. Liverpool: Liverpool University Press, 1964.

Feltham, Owen. *Resolves, Divine, Morall, Politicall.* The "eighth" edition of 1661.

Firth, C. H., and R. S. Rait, eds. *Acts and Ordinances of the Interregnum, 1642–1660.* 3 vols. London: H.M.S.O., 1911.

Flecknoe, Richard. *Heroick Portraits.* 1660.

Fletcher, Giles. *The Works of Giles Fletcher.* Ed. F. S. Boas. 3 vols. Cambridge: Cambridge University Press, 1908–9.

Fletcher, Robert. *Ex Otio Negotium.* 1656.

Fletcher, Robert. *The Poems and Translations of Robert Fletcher.* Ed. D. H. Woodward. Gainesville, Fla.: University of Florida Press, 1970.

Forde, Thomas. "Upon his Sacred Majesties most happy Return." In *Virtus Re-*

diviva. A Panegyrick on King Charles I., with severall other peeces from the same pen. 1660. Reprint 1661.

The Foure Ages of England, Or, The Iron Age. 1648.

The Frogges of Egypt: Or The Caterpillers of the Common-Wealth truely Dissected and laid open. 1641.

Gailhard, Jean. *The Complete Gentleman; or, Directions for the Education of Youth.* 1678.

The Gang of Four. *Solid Gold.* London: Warner Brothers, 1981.

Gardiner, Helen, ed. *The New Oxford Book of English Verse.* New York: Oxford University Press, 1972.

Gardiner, S. R., ed. *Constitutional Documents of the Puritan Revolution, 1625–1660.* 1906. 3d ed. Oxford: Clarendon Press, 1968.

Gauden, John. *The Strange and Wonderfull Visions and Predictions of William Juniper of Gosfield in Essex, Relating to the Troubles of England.* 1662.

The Glory of These Nations, being a brief Relation of King Charles's Royal Progresse from Dover to London. [1660]. Reprinted in Wright, *Political Ballads*, pp. 223–28.

Gorges, Sir Arthur, trans. *Lucan's Pharsalia: Containing The Civill Warres between Caesar and Pompey.* 1614.

Grampius Congratulation In plain Scots Language To His Majesties Thrise Happy Return. [Edinburgh?], 1660.

The Great and Famous Battel of Lutzen, Fought betweene the renowned King of Sweden, and Walstein. [1633].

Harrison, Stephen. *The Archs of Triumph Erected in honor of the High and mighty prince James. the first of that name king of England and the sixt of Scotland. at his Majesties Entrance and passage through his Honorable Citty & Chamber of London. upon the 15th day of march 1603.* 1603.

Hearne, Thomas. *Ductor Historicus: or, A Short System of Universal History.* 1698.

Hearneshaw, F. J. C. *English History in Contemporary Poetry: Court and Parliament, 1558 to 1668.* 1913. Reprint London: Historical Association, 1969.

Herbert, Edward, Baron of Cherbury. *The Life and Reigne of King Henrie the Eighth.* 1649.

Herbert, Thomas. *An Elegie upon the Death of Thomas Earle of Strafford.* 1641.

Herrick, Robert. *The Poetical Works of Robert Herrick.* Ed. L. C. Martin. Oxford: Clarendon Press, 1956.

Heywood, Thomas. *Troia Britanica: Or, Great Britaines Troy.* 1690.

Higgons, Thomas. *A Panegyrick to the King.* 1660.

His Majesties Answer to a Printed Book, Entituled A Remonstrance, or, The Declaration of the Lords and Commons now assembled in Parliament, May 26. 1642. 1642.

Hobbes, Thomas. *Hobbes's Thucydides.* Ed. Richard Schlatter. New Brunswick, N.J.: Rutgers University Press, 1975.

Hopkins, Charles. *Boadicea, Queen of Britain.* 1697.

Howell, James. *Epistolae Ho-Elianae.* 1645.

I Thank You Twice. 1647. Reprinted in Wilkins, *Political Ballads,* 1:54.

Isaacson, Henry. *Saturni Ephemerides: sive Tabula Historico-Chronologica.* 1633.

James VI and I. *The Basilicon Doron of King James VI.* Ed. James Craigie. 2 vols. London: Blackwood, 1944.

James VI and I. *The Essayes of a Prentise in the Divine Art of Poesie.* Edinburgh, 1584.

James VI and I. *The Poems of James VI. of Scotland.* Ed. James Craigie. 2 vols. Edinburgh: Blackwood, 1955–58.

Johnson, Richard, ed. *The Golden Garland.* 1620.

Jonson, Ben. *Poems.* Ed. Ian Donaldson. London: Oxford University Press, 1975.

The Just Reward of Rebels. 1642.

Kermode, Frank, ed. *English Pastoral Poetry: From the Beginnings to Marvell.* 1952. Reprint New York: Norton, 1972.

The King and Queen of Bohemia. [1622–1623?]. Reprinted in Rollins, *Pepys Ballads,* 1:2–4.

Lambarde, William. *Archaionomia.* 1568. Reprint Cambridge, 1644.

Lambeth Faire: Wherein you have all the Bishops Trinkets set to sale. 1641.

Lanquet, Thomas. *Cooper's Chronicle.* 1560.

Lanquet, Thomas. *An Epitome of Chronicles.* 1549. Reprint 1559.

A Letter written from Walshall by a Worthy Gentleman to his Friend in Oxford, concerning Birmingham. 1643.

Lithgow, William. *A Most Detectable, and True, Discourse of a Peregrination in Europe, Asia, etc.* 1614.

Lithgow, William. *Scotlands Welcome To Her Native Sonne, and Soveraigne Lord, King Charles.* Edinburgh, 1633.

[Lloyd, David]. *Eikon Basilike.* 1649. Reprint 1660.

Lluellyn, Martin. *Men Miracles, with Other Poems.* Oxford, 1646.

Locke, John. *Two Treatises of Civil Government.* Ed. W. S. Carpenter. 1924. Reprint London: Dent, 1967.

The Loyall Subjects Jubilee, or Cromwell's Farewell to England. 1649. Ludlow, Edmund. *The Memoirs of Edmund Ludlow.* London, 1751.

Ludlow, Edmund. *The Voyce From the Watch Tower. Part Five: 1660–1662.* Ed. A. B. Worden. Camden Series Vol. 21. London: Royal Historical Society, 1978.

M., E. *Protection Perswading Subjection.* 1654.

Machiavel. As He lately appeared to his deare Sons, the Moderne Projectors. 1641.

Manley, Thomas. *Veni; Vidi; Vici; The Triumphs of the Most Excellent and Illustrious Oliver Cromwell.* 1651.

Marvell, Andrew. *Andrew Marvell: The Complete Poems.* Ed. Elizabeth Donno. 1971. Reprint Harmondsworth: Penguin, 1976.

Marvell, Andrew. *Andrew Marvell: Miscellaneous Poems 1681.* 1969. Reprint Menston: Scolar Press, 1973.

Marvell, Andrew. *The Poems and Letters of Andrew Marvell.* Ed. H. M. Margoliouth. 3d ed. rev. Pierre Legouis and E. E. Duncan-Jones. 1972. 2 vols. Reprint Oxford: Clarendon Press, 1976.

May, Thomas, trans. *Lucan's Pharsalia: Or The Civill Warres of Rome, betweene Pompey the great, and Julius Caesar.* 1627.

May, Thomas. *The Reigne of King Henry the Second.* 1633.

May, Thomas. *The Victorious Reigne of King Edward the Third.* 1635.

Mercurius Aulicus 7. May 21–28, 1660.

Milton, John. *The Poems of John Milton.* Ed. John Carey and Alastair Fowler. London: Longmans, 1968.

Milton, John. *The Works of John Milton.* Ed. Frank A. Patterson et al. 20 vols. New York: Columbia University Press, 1931–40.

A Modell of the Fireworks to be presented in Lincolnes-Inne Fields on 5 Nov. in commemoration of the Gunpowder Treason. 1647.

Monumentum Regale, or A Tombe Erected for that Incomparable and Glorious Monarch, Charles the First, King of Great Britaine, France and Ireland &c. 1649.

The New Model Army. *No Rest for the Wicked.* London: EMI Records, 1985.

Niccols, Richard, ed. *A Mirour for Magistrates.* 1610.

Overton, Richard. *New Lambeth Fayre Newly Consecrated and Presented by The Pope Himselfe.* 1642.

Oxford, University of. *Britannia Rediviva.* Oxford. 1660.

Oxford, University of. *Eucharistica Oxoniensia: In Exoptatissimum & Auspicatissimim Caroli.* Oxford. 1641.

Oxford, University of. *Iusta Oxoniensum.* Oxford, 1612.

Oxford, University of. *Musarum Oxoniensum Elaiophoria.* Oxford, 1654.

Oxford, University of. *Verses on the Death of the Right Valiant Sr Bevill Grenvill.* Oxford, 1643.

A Pack of Patentees. Opened. Shuffled. Cut. Dealt. And Played. 1641.

Parker, Henry. *The True Portraiture of the Kings of England; Drawn from their Titles, Succession, Raigns and Ends.* 1650.

Parker, Martin. *An Exact Description Of the manner how his Majestie and his Nobles went to the Parliament, on Munday, the thirteenth of Aprill, 1640. to the comfortable expectations of all Loyall Subjects.* 1640.

The Parliamentary Intelligencer 23. May 28–June 4, 1660.

The Peace-Maker, or Great Britainnes Blessing. 1619.

Peacham, Henry. *The Complete Gentleman.* Ed. Virgil B. Heltzel. Ithaca: Cornell University Press, 1962.

Pepys, Samuel. *The Diary of Samuel Pepys.* Ed. Robert Latham and William Matthews. 11 vols. Berkeley and Los Angeles: University of California Press, 1970–83.

Philips, Katherine. *Poems.* 1664.

Poole, Joshua. *The English Parnassus.* 1657.

The Protestation and Declaration of Divers Knights, Esquires, Gentlemen, and Free-holders of the Counties of Lincolne and Nottingham: Against the unjust oppressions and inhumane proceedings of William Earle of Newcastle and his Cavaleers. 1643.

The Public Intelligencer 7. May 8, 1660.

Puttenham, George. *The Arte of English Poesie.* Ed. G. D. Willcock and Alice Walker. 1936. Reprint Cambridge: Cambridge University Press, 1970.

Pyms' Juncto. Oxford, 1642.

R., J. [John Russell?]. *An Elegie upon the death of Gustavus Adolphus, King of Swethland.* [1633].

Ralegh, Sir Walter. *The History of the World.* 1614. Ed. C. A. Patrides. Philadelphia: Temple University Press, 1971.

Ramsey, Alexander. *The Gentleman's Companion; or, a Character of True Nobility and Gentility.* 1672.

Randolph, Thomas. *The Poetical and Dramatic Works of Thomas Randolph.* Ed. W. Carew Hazlitt. London: Reeves and Turner, 1875.

Red London. *This Is England.* London: Razor Records, 1984.

Reliquae Sacrae Carolinae: Or, The Works of that Great Monarch And Glorious Martyr King CHARLS the I. The Hague, 1651.

A Remonstrance of the Lords and Commons Assembled in Parliament, Or, The Reply of both Houses, to a printed Book, under His Majesties name, Called, His Majesties Answer to a Printed Book. 1642.

A Remonstrance Or The Declaration Of the Lords and Commons, now Assembled in Parliament, 26. of May. 1641. 1642.

The Resolution of the Women of London wherein they declare their hot zealle in sending their husbands to the Warres. 1642.

Rollins, Hyder E., ed. *Cavalier and Puritan: Ballads and Broadsides Illustrating the Period of the Great Rebellion, 1640–1660.* New York: New York University Press, 1923.

Rollins, Hyder E., ed. *The Pepys Ballads.* 8 vols. Cambridge: Harvard University Press, 1929.

Ronsard, Pierre de. *Les Oeuvres de Pierre de Ronsard: Texte de 1587.* Ed. Isidore Silver. 8 vols. Chicago: University of Chicago Press, 1967.

A Rope for Pol, Or, A Hue and Cry after Marchemont Nedham. The late Scurrilous News-writer. 1660.

Ross, Alexander. *Englands Threnodie. Or A briefe and Homely Discoverie of some jealousies and grievances, under which the Kingdom at present groaneth.* 1648.

Rowlands, Richard [Verstegan]. *A Restitution of Decayed Intelligence: In Antiquities concerning the most notable and Renowned English Nation.* 1605. Reprint 1628.

Rump: Or, An Exact Collection of the Choycest Poems and Songs Relating to the Late Times. 2 vols. 1662.

Russell, John. *The Two Famous Pitcht Battles of Lypsich and Lutzen.* Cambridge, 1634.

A Sad Sigh, With Some Heart-Cracking Groanes. 1649.

Sadler, Anthony. *The Subject's Joy For the Kings Restoration.* 1660.

Saintsbury, George, ed. *Minor Poets of the Caroline Period.* 1905. 3 vols. Reprint Oxford: Clarendon Press, 1968.

Saltmarsh, John. *Poemata Sacra.* 1636.

Sanders, Norman, ed. *A Book of Masques.* Cambridge: Cambridge University Press, 1967.

A Satyre Against the Cavaliers: Penned in Opposition to the Satyre against the Separatists. 1642.

Shakespeare, William. *Cymbeline.* Ed. J. M. Nosworthy. 1955. Reprint London: Methuen, 1969.

Shakespeare, William. *Henry IV, Part Two.* Ed. A. R. Humphreys. 1966. Reprint London: Methuen, 1970.

Shakespeare, William. *Richard II.* Ed. Peter Ure. 1956. Reprint London: Methuen, 1966.

Shirley, James. *The Dramatic Works and Poems of James Shirley.* Ed. William Gifford and Alexander Dyce. 6 vols. London: Murray, 1833.

Slatyer, William. *The History of Great Britanie from the first peopling of this Iland to this present Raigne of our happy and peacefull Monarke K. James.* 1621.

Somnium Cantabrigiense, or A poem upon the death of the late King. Cambridge, 1650.

Speed, John. *Historie of Great Britain.* 1611.

Speed, John. *History of Great Britain.* 1623.

Spenser, Thomas. *England's Warning Peece: or, The History of the Gun-Powder Treason.* 1658.

Spingarn, Joel, ed. *Critical Essays of the Seventeenth Century.* 3 vols. Oxford: Clarendon Press, 1908.

Stipendariae Lachrymae. The Hague. 1654.

Stirry, Thomas. *A Rot Amongst the Bishops, or, A Terrible Tempest in the Sea of Canterbury.* 1641.

Stow, John. *Survey of London.* 1598.

The Swedish Intelligencer. London [and Lisbon?], 1632–33.

Swift, Jonathan. *The Prose Writings of Jonathan Swift.* Ed. Herbert Davis. 15 vols. Oxford: Blackwell, 1939–68.

Sylvester, Joshuah. *The Complete Works.* Ed. Alexander B. Grossart. 2 vols. Reprint New York: AMS Press, 1967.

Sylvester, Joshuah, trans. *The Divine Weeks and Works of Guillaume de Saluste, Sieur du Bartas.* Ed. Susan Snyder. 2 vols. Oxford: Clarendon Press, 1979.

Tasso, Torquato. *Discourses on the Heroic Poem.* Trans. Mariella Cavalchini and Irene Taylor. Oxford: Clarendon Press, 1973.

Tayler, Edward W., ed. *Literary Criticism of Seventeenth-Century England.* New York: Knopf, 1967.

Taylor, John. *The Apprentices Advice to the XII. Bishops lately accused of High Treason, by the Honourable Assemblies of both Houses.* 1642.

Taylor, John. *A Delicate, Dainty, Damnable Dialogue, Between the Devill and a Jesuite.* 1642.

Taylor, John. *Englands Comfort, and Londons Joy: Expressed in the Royall, Triumphant, and Magnificent Entertainment of our Dread Soveraigne Lord, King Charles, at his blessed and Safe returne from Scotland on Thursday the 25. of Novemb. 1641.* 1641.

Thanks to the Parliament. [1641]. In Rollins, *Cavalier and Puritan,* p. 140.

Turner, John. *A Commemoration, or A Calling to Minde of the great and Eminent Deliverance from the Powder-Plot.* 1654.

Two Elegies: The One on His Late Majesty, the Other on Arthur Lord Capel. 1649.

"Upon His Majesties most happy restauration to his Royall Throne in Brittaine." MS verses, Bodleian Firth b.20, fol. 140.

Vaticinium Votivum: Or, Palaemon's Prophetick Prayer. 1649.

Verses on the Death of the Right Valiant Sr Bevill Greenvill. Oxford, 1646.

Verstegan. *See* Rowlands.

Vicars, John. *Englands Remembrancer, or, A thankfull acknowledgement of Parliamentary Mercies to our English-Nation.* 1641.

Vicars, John. *Mischeefes Mysterie: Or, Treason's Master-peece.* 1617.

Vicars, John. *November the 5. 1605. The Quintessence of Cruelty, Or, Master-peice of Treachery, the Popish Pouder-Plot, Invented by Hellish-Malice, Prevented by Heavenly-mercy.* 1641.

Virgil. *The Pastoral Poems.* Ed. and trans. E. V. Rieu. Harmondsworth: Penguin, 1961.

Walker, Henry. *The Friers Lamenting, For his not Repenting.* 1641.

Waller, Edmund. *The Poems of Edmund Waller.* Ed. George Thorn-Drury. 2 vols. London; Bullen, 1901.

Warner, William. *Albions England. A Continued Historye of the same Kingdome from the Originals of the first Inhabitants thereof.* 1586. Reprint 1589, 1592, 1596, 1602.

Wheare, Degory. *The Method and Order of Reading both Civil and Ecclesiastical Histories.* Trans. Edmund Bohun. 1685. Reprint 1694, 1698.

Wilkins, W. W., ed. *Political Ballads of the Seventeenth and Eighteenth Centuries.* 2 vols. London: Longmans, 1860.

Willes, Samuel. *To the King's Most Sacred Majesty upon his happy and glorious return.* 1660.

Winstanley, Gerrard. *The Law of Freedom and other Writings.* Ed. Christopher Hill. Harmondsworth: Penguin, 1973.

Wits Recreations. 1640.

Woods, Anthony à. *Athenae Oxoniensis.* 2 vols. Oxford, 1692.

A Word of Counsel to the Disaffected. 1651.

Wright, Thomas, ed. *Political Ballads Published in England during the Commonwealth.* London: Percy Society, 1841.

Secondary Sources

Adams, Simon. "Faction, Clientage and Party Politics, 1550–1603." *History Today* 32 (1982): 33–39.

Adams, Simon. "Foreign Policy and the Parliaments of 1621 and 1624." In Sharpe, *Faction and Parliament,* pp. 139–71.

Ahl, Frederick. *Lucan: An Introduction.* Ithaca: Cornell University Press, 1976.

Ahl, Frederick; Martha A. Davis; and Arthur Pomeroy. "Silius Italicus." In *Aufstieg und Niedergang der römischen Welt,* ed. Hildegard Temporini and Wolfgang Haase, 32.4: 2492–2561. Berlin: De Gruyter, 1986.

Aiken, W. A., and B. D. Henning, eds. *Conflict in Stuart England: Essays in Honour of Wallace Notestein.* New York: New York University Press, 1960.

Alkon, Paul K. "Johnson and Chronology." In Korshin and Allen, *Greene Centennial Studies*, pp. 142–58.

Allen, J. W. *English Political Thought, 1603–1644.* London: Methuen, 1944.

Althuser, Louis. "Ideology and Ideological State Appartuses." In *Lenin and Philosophy and Other Essays,* trans. Ben Brewster. London: Monthly Review, 1971.

Anderson, Judith B. *Biographical Truth: The Representation of Historical Persons in Tudor-Stuart Writing.* New Haven: Yale University Press, 1984.

Anderson, Perry. *Lineages of the Absolutist State.* 1974. Reprint London: Verso, 1980.

Ashley, Maurice. *Oliver Cromwell and His World.* New York: Putnam, 1972.

Ashton, Robert. *The City and the Court, 1603–1643.* Cambridge: Cambridge University Press, 1979.

Ashton, Robert. *The Crown and the Money Market, 1603–1640.* Oxford: Clarendon Press, 1960.

Aston, T. H., and C. H. E. Philpin, eds. *The Brenner Debate: Agrarian Development in Pre-Industrial Europe.* Cambridge: Cambridge University Press, 1985.

Baker, Keith. "Memory and Practice: Politics and the Representation of the Past in Eighteenth-Century France." *Representations* 11 (1985): 134–64.

Barker, Francis; Peter Hulme; Margaret Iverson; and Diana Loxley, eds. *Literature, Politics and Theory: Papers from the Essex Conference, 1976–1984.* London: Methuen, 1986.

Barker, Simon. "Images of the Sixteenth and Seventeenth Centuries as a History of the Present." In Barker, Hulme, Iverson, and Loxley, *Literature, Politics and Theory,* pp. 173–89.

Belsey, Catherine. *John Milton: Language, Gender, Power.* Oxford: Basil Blackwell, 1988.

Belsey, Catherine. *The Subject of Tragedy: Identity and Difference in Renaissance Drama.* London: Methuen, 1986.

Benjamin, Walter. *Illuminations.* Trans Harry Zohn. Ed. Hannah Arendt. 1968. Reprint New York: Schocken, 1969.

Bennett, H. S. *English Books and Readers, 1603–1640.* Cambridge: Cambridge University Press, 1970.

Bennett, Josephine Waters. "Britain among the Fortunate Isles." *Studies in Philology* 53 (1956): 114–49.

Benton, Ted. *The Rise and Fall of Structural Marxism.* New York: St. Martin's, 1984.

Billington, Sandra. "An Horatian Ode—Charles I and the Army as Actors." *Notes & Queries,* n.s. 25 (1978): 513.

Birch, Thomas, ed. *The Court and Times of James I.* 18 vols. London: Colburn, 1849.

Blackburn, Thomas. "Edmund Bolton's *London, King Charles His Augusta, or City Royal.*" *Huntington Library Quarterly* 25 (1978): 315–23.

Booker, John, ed. *A History of the Ancient Chapel of Birch, in Manchester Parish.* Chetham Society Publications, Vol. 47. Manchester, 1859.

Brailsford, H. N. *The Levellers and the English Revolution.* Ed. Christopher Hill. 1961. Reprint London: Spokesman, 1983.

Brinkley, Roberta. *Arthurian Legend in the Seventeenth Century.* Baltimore: Johns Hopkins University Press, 1932.

Brooks, Harold. "Rump Songs." *Proceedings of the Oxford Bibliographical Society* 5 (1940): 283–304.

Brown, Laura. "The Ideology of Restoration Poetic Form: John Dryden." *Publications of the Modern Language Association* 97 (1982): 395–407.

Bruère, R. T. "The Latin and English Versions of Thomas May's *Supplementum Lucani.*" *Classical Philology* 44 (1949): 145–63.

Bush, Douglas. *English Literature in the Earlier Seventeenth Century.* 2d ed. Oxford: Clarendon Press, 1962.

Butler, Martin. *Theatre and Crisis, 1632–1642.* Cambridge: Cambridge University Press, 1984.

Butterfield, Herbert. *Man on His Past.* 1955. Reprint Boston: Beacon, 1960.

Butterfield, Herbert. *The Origins of History.* Ed. Adam Watson. New York: Basic Books, 1981.

Cain, William. "The Place of the Poet in Jonson's 'To Penshurst' and 'To My Muse.'" *Criticism* 21 (1979): 34–38.

Capp, Bernard S. "The Fifth Monarchists and Popular Millenarianism." In McGregor and Reay, *Radical Religion,* pp. 165–89.

Capp, Bernard S. *The Fifth Monarchy Men: A Study in Seventeenth-Century Millenarianism.* London: Faber, 1972.

Carr, E. H. *What Is History?* 1961. Reprint Harmondsworth: Penguin, 1977.

"Charles II and the Restoration: An Exhibition to Commemorate the Tercentenary of the Restoration of the Monarchy held in The Chapter House, Exeter held 18–28 May, 1960." [Exeter, 1960].

Chernaik, Warren. *The Poet's Time: Politics and Religion in the Work of Andrew Marvell.* Cambridge: Cambridge University Press, 1983.

Clark, Alice. *Working Life of Women in the Seventeenth Century.* 1919. Reprint London: Cass, 1968.

Cohen, Walter. *Drama of a Nation: Public Theater in Renaissance England and Spain.* Ithaca: Cornell University Press, 1985.

Coiro, Ann Baynes. *Robert Herrick's "Hesperides" and the Epigram Book Tradition.* Baltimore: Johns Hopkins University Press, 1988.

Corbett, Margery, and R. W. Lightbown. *The Comely Frontispiece: The Emblematic Title-page in England, 1550–1660.* London: Routledge and Kegan Paul, 1979.

Crane, R. S., and F. B. Kaye. *A Census of British Newspapers and Periodicals, 1620–1800.* 1927. Reprint London: Holland House, 1979.

Cressy, David. *Literacy and the Social Order: Reading and Writing in Tudor and Stuart England.* Cambridge: Cambridge University Press, 1981.

Croce, Benedetto. *History as the Story of Liberation.* Trans. Sylvia Spragge. New York: Norton, 1941.

Croce, Benedetto. *Theory and History of Historiography.* Trans. Douglas Ainslie. London: Harrap, 1921.

Cross, Claire. " 'He-Goats Before the Flocks': A Note on the Part Played by Women in the Founding of Some Civil War Churches." In *Popular Belief and Practice,* ed. G. J. Cumming and Derek Baker, pp. 192–202. Studies in Church History, Vol. 8. Cambridge: Cambridge University Press, 1972.

Dahl, Folke. "Amsterdam—Cradle of English Newspapers." *The Library,* 5th ser. 4 (1949): 166–78.

Dahl, Folke. *Bibliography of English Corantos and Periodical Newspapers, 1620–1642.* London: Bibliographical Society, 1952.

Davies, Godfrey. *The Early Stuarts, 1603–1660.* 1937. 2d ed. Oxford: Clarendon Press, 1959.

Davis, Martha A. *See* Ahl.

Dean, Leonard F. "Bodin's *Methodus* in England before 1625." *Studies in Philology* 39 (1942): 160–66.

Dean, Leonard F. "Sir Francis Bacon's Theory of Civil History Writing." *English Literary History* 8 (1941): 161–83.

Delaney, Paul. *British Autobiography in the Seventeenth Century.* New York: Columbia University Press, 1969.

Dick, H. G. "Heywood's True Method." *Huntington Library Quarterly* 3 (1940): 149–69.

Dollimore, Jonathan. *Radical Tragedy: Religion, Ideology and Power in the Drama* of Shakespeare and His Contemporaries. Chicago: University of Chicago Press, 1984.

Dollimore, Jonathan, and Alan Sinfield, eds. Political Shakespeare: New Essays in Cultural Materialism. Manchester: Manchester University Press, 1985.

Doody, Margaret. The Daring Muse: Augustan Poetry Reconsidered. Cambridge: Cambridge University Press, 1985.

Dorsten, Jan van. "Literary Patronage in Elizabethan England: The Early Phase." In Lytle and Orgel, Patronage in the Renaissance, pp. 191–206.

Douglas, David. English Scholars, 1660–1730. 1939. 2d ed. London: Eyre and Spottiswoode, 1951.

Drakakis, John, ed. Alternative Shakespeare. London: Methuen, 1985.

Dubrow, Heather, and Richard Strier, eds. The Historical Renaissance: New Essays on Tudor and Stuart Literature and Culture. Chicago: University of Chicago Press, 1988.

Edie, Carolyn. "News from Abroad: Advice to the People of England on the Eve of the Stuart Restoration." Bulletin of the John Rylands Library 76 (1984): 382–407.

Eisenstein, Elizabeth. The Printing Press as an Agent of Change: Communications and Cultural Transformations in Early-Modern Europe. 2 vols. Cambridge: Cambridge University Press, 1979.

Eley, Geoff, and William Hunt, eds. Reviving the English Revolution: Reflections and Elaborations on the Work of Christopher Hill. London: Verso, 1988.

Erskine-Hill, Howard. The Augustan Idea in English Literature. London: Arnold, 1983.

Erskine-Hill, Howard. "Augustans on Augustanism: England, 1659–1759." In Schmidt, Of Private Vices, pp. 7–34.

Ferguson, Arthur B. Clio Unbound: Perception of the Social and Cultural Past in Renaissance England. Durham, N.C.: Duke University Press, 1979.

Ferguson, Margaret W.; Maureen Quilligan; and Nancy J. Vickers, eds. Rewriting the Renaissance: The Discourses of Sexual Difference in Early Modern Europe. Chicago: University of Chicago Press, 1986.

Fink, Zera S. The Classical Republicans: An Essay in the Recovery of a Pattern of Thought in Seventeenth-Century England. Evanston: Northwestern University Press, 1945.

Firth, C. H. "The Ballad History of the Reign of James I." Transactions of the Royal Historical Society, 3d ser. 5 (1911): 21–61.

Firth, Katharine R. The Apocalyptic Tradition in Reformation Britain, 1530–1645. Oxford: Clarendon, 1979.

Fletcher, Anthony. The Outbreak of the English Civil War. London: Arnold, 1981.

Fortescue, George, ed. Catalogue of the Pamphlets, Books, Newspapers, and Manuscripts Relating to the Civil War, the Commonwealth, and Restoration, Collected by George Thomason, 1640–1661. 2 vols. London: British Museum, 1908.

Foster, Elizabeth R. "The Procedure of the House of Commons against Patentees and Monopolies, 1621–1624." In Aiken and Henning, *Conflict in Stuart England,* pp. 57–85.

Foucault, Michel. *The Order of Things: An Archaeology of the Human Sciences.* 1966. Reprint New York: Random House, 1973.

Fowler, Alastair. *Triumphal Forms: Structural Patterns in Elizabethan Poetry.* Cambridge: Cambridge University Press, 1970.

Fox, Levi, ed. *English Historical Scholarship in the Sixteenth and Seventeenth Centuries.* London: Oxford University Press, 1956.

Frank, Joseph. *The Beginnings of the English Newspaper.* Cambridge: Harvard University Press, 1961.

Frank, Joseph. *Cromwell's Press Agent: A Critical Biography of Marchamont Nedham.* Lanham, Md.: University Press of America, 1980.

Frank, Joseph. *Hobbled Pegasus: A Descriptive Bibliography of Minor English Poetry, 1641–1660.* Albuquerque: University of New Mexico Press, 1968.

Franklin, Julian M. *Jean Bodin and the Sixteenth-Century Revolution in the Methodology of Law and History.* New York: Columbia University Press, 1963.

Fraser, Antonia. *King James.* New York: Knopf, 1976.

Fussner, F. Smith. *The Historical Revolution: English Historical Writing and Thought, 1580–1640.* London: Routledge and Kegan Paul, 1964.

Gardiner, Samuel R. *History of England from the Accession of James I. to the Outbreak of the Civil War, 1603–1642.* 10 vols. London: Longmans, 1883–84.

Gardiner, Samuel R. *History of the Commonwealth and Protectorate, 1649–1660.* 6 vols. London: Longmans, Green, 1894.

Goldberg, Jonathan. *James I and the Politics of Literature.* Baltimore: Johns Hopkins University Press, 1983.

Goldberg, S. L. "Sir John Hayward, 'Politic' Historian." *Review of English Studies,* n.s. 6 (1955): 233–44.

Gordon, D. J. *The Renaissance Imagination.* Ed. Stephen Orgel. Berkeley and Los Angeles: University of California Press, 1975.

Gould, Mark. *Revolution in the Development of Capitalism: The Coming of the English Revolution.* Berkeley and Los Angeles: University of California Press, 1987.

Grafton, Anthony, and Lisa Jardine. *From Humanism to the Humanities: Education and the Liberal Arts in Fifteenth- and Sixteenth-Century Europe.* Cambridge: Harvard University Press, 1986.

Graham, Paul. "March of the New Puritans." *Sunday Times Magazine,* March 13, 1988, p. 68.

Greenblatt, Stephen. "Invisible Bullets: Renaissance Authority and Its Subversions, *Henry IV* and *Henry V.*" In Dollimore and Sinfield, *Political Shakespeare,* pp. 18–47.

Greenblatt, Stephen. *Renaissance Self-Fashioning from More to Shakespeare.* Chicago: University of Chicago Press, 1980.

Greetham, David, and W. Speed Hill, eds. *TEXT 3*. New York: AMS, 1987.

Griffith, R. H. "The Progress Pieces of the Eighteenth Century." *Texas Review* (now *Studies in English Literature*) 5 (1920): 218–23.

Guibbory, Achsah. *The Map of Time: Seventeenth-Century English Literature and Ideas of Pattern in History*. Urbana: University of Illinois Press, 1986.

Hale, J. R. *The Evolution of British Historiography*. New York: Meridian, 1964.

Hamilton, Roberta. *The Liberation of Women: A Study of Patriarchy and Capitalism*. 1978. Reprint London: Allen and Unwin, 1982.

Hardacre, Paul. *The Royalists during the Puritan Revolution*. The Hague: Martinus Nijhoff, 1956.

Havran, Martin J. *Caroline Courtier: The Life of Lord Cottington*. Columbia: University of South Carolina Press, 1973.

Hearneshaw, F. J. C. *English History in Contemporary Poetry*. 1913. Reprint London: Historical Association, 1969.

Heinemann, Margot. "How Brecht Read Shakespeare." In Dollimore and Sinfield, *Political Shakespeare,* pp. 202–30.

Heinemann, Margot. *Puritanism and Theatre: Thomas Middleton and Opposition Drama under the Early Stuarts*. Cambridge: Cambridge University Press, 1980.

Helgerson, Richard. "Milton Reads the King's Book: Print, Performance, and the Making of a Bourgeois Idol." *Criticism* 29 (1987): 1–26.

Helgerson, Richard. *Self-Crowned Laureates: Spenser, Jonson, Milton and the Literary System*. Berkeley: University of California Press, 1983.

Herrick, Marvin T. *The Poetics of Aristotle in England*. New Haven: Yale University Press, 1930.

Hibbard, G. R. "The Country House Poem of the Seventeenth Century." *Journal of the Warburg and Courtauld Institutes* 19 (1956): 159–73.

Hill, Christopher. *Antichrist in Seventeenth-Century England*. Oxford: Clarendon, 1971.

Hill, Christopher. *The Collected Essays,* Vol. 1: *Writing and Revolution in Seventeenth-Century England*. Amherst: University of Massachusetts Press, 1985.

Hill, Christopher. *The Experience of Defeat: Milton and Some Contemporaries*. New York: Viking, 1984.

Hill, Christopher. *God's Englishman: Oliver Cromwell and the English Revolution*. London: Weidenfeld and Nicolson, 1970.

Hill, Christopher. *Intellectual Origins of the English Revolution*. 1965. Reprint Oxford: Clarendon Press, 1982.

Hill, Christopher. "Literature and the English Revolution." *Seventeenth Century* 1 (1986): 15–30.

Hill, Christopher. *Milton and the English Revolution*. New York: Viking, 1977.

Hill, Christopher. *Puritanism and Revolution*. 1958. Reprint London: Panther, 1969.

Hill, Christopher. "Radical Prose in Seventeenth-Century England: From Marprelate to the Levellers." *Essays in Criticism* 32 (1982): 95–118.

Hill, Christopher. *The World Turned Upside Down: Radical Ideas during the English Revolution*. New York: Viking, 1972.

Hirst, Derek. *Authority and Conflict: England, 1603–1658.* London: Arnold, 1986.

Hirst, Derek. "Court, Country, and Politics before 1629." In Sharpe, *Faction and Parliament,* pp. 105–37.

Hirst, Derek. *The Representatives of the People? Voters and Voting under the Early Stuarts*. Cambridge: Cambridge University Press, 1978.

Hirst, Derek. " 'That Sober Liberty': Marvell's Cromwell in 1654." In Wallace, *The Golden and Brazen World,* pp. 17–53.

Hirst, Derek. "Unanimity in the Commons." *Journal of Modern History* 50 (1978): 51–71.

Hobby, Elaine. *Virtue of Necessity: English Women's Writing, 1649–1688.* London: Virago, 1988.

Howat, Gerald. *Stuart and Cromwellian Foreign Policy.* London: Black, 1974.

Hunt, John Dixon. *Andrew Marvell: His Life and Writings.* London: Elek, 1978.

Hunt, William. "Spectral Origins of the English Revolution: Legitimation Crisis in Early Stuart England." In Eley and Hunt, *Reviving the English Revolution,* pp. 305–32.

Hunter, J. "An Account of the Scheme for Erecting a Royal Academy in England." *Archaeologia* 32 (1847): 132–49.

Hutton, Ronald. *The Restoration: A Political and Religious History of England and Wales, 1658–1667.* Oxford: Clarendon Press, 1985.

Ide, Richard S. "Chapman's *Caesar and Pompey* and the Uses of History." *Modern Philology* 82 (1985): 255–68.

Jameson, Fredric. *The Political Unconscious: Narrative as a Socially Symbolic Act.* Ithaca: Cornell University Press, 1981.

Jardine, Lisa. *Francis Bacon and the Art of Discourse.* Cambridge: Cambridge University Press, 1974.

Jardine, Lisa. *Still Harping on Daughters: Women in Drama in the Age of Shakespeare.* Brighton, U. K.: Harvester, 1983.

Jardine, Lisa. *See* Grafton.

Jauss, Hans Robert. "Literary History as a Challenge to Literary Theory." *New Literary History* 2 (1970): 7–37.

Jessup, Frank W. *Sir Roger Twysden, 1597–1672.* London: Cresset, 1965.

Jones, Alice E. "A Note on Hopkins." *Modern Language Notes* 5 (1940): 191–94.

Jones, Ann R. "Inside the Outsider: Nashe's *Unfortunate Traveller* and Bakhtin's Polyphonic Novel." *English Literary History* 50 (1983): 61–81.

Jones, J. R. "The Crown and Courts in England." In Smith, *The Reign of James VI and I,* pp. 177–94.

Jones, P. F. "Milton and the Epic Subject from British History." *Publications of the Modern Language Association* 42 (1927): 901–9.

Jordan, W. K. *Men of Substance: A Study of the Thought of Two English Revolutionaries.* 1942. Reprint New York: Octagon, 1967.

Jose, Nicholas. *Ideas of the Restoration in English Literature, 1660–1671.* Cambridge: Harvard University Press, 1984.

Kearney, H. F. *The Eleven Years' Tyranny of Charles I.* London: Historical Association, 1962.

Kelley, Donald. *Foundations of Modern Historical Scholarship: Language, Law, and History in the French Revolution.* New York: Columbia University Press, 1970.

Kenyon, J. P. *The Stuart Constitution, 1603–1688: Documents and Commentary.* Cambridge: Cambridge University Press, 1966.

Kenyon, J. P. *Stuart England.* Harmondsworth: Penguin, 1978.

Kermode, Frank. *English Pastoral Poetry.* 1952. Reprint New York: Norton, 1972.

King, John N. *English Reformation Literature: The Tudor Origins of the Protestant Tradition.* Princeton: Princeton University Press, 1982.

Kinghorn, A. M. *The Chorus of History: Literary-Historical Relations in Renaissance Britain.* London: Blandford, 1971.

Kishlansky, Mark. "The Emergence of Adversary Politics in the Long Parliament." *Journal of Modern History* 49 (1977): 617–40.

Kishlansky, Mark. *The Rise of the New Model Army.* Cambridge: Cambridge University Press, 1979.

Klancher, Jon. *The Making of English Reading Audiences, 1790–1832.* Madison: University of Wisconsin Press, 1987.

Korshin, Paul J., ed. *Studies in Change and Revolution: Aspects of English Intellectual History.* Menston, Yorks.: Scolar Press, 1972.

Korshin, Paul J., and Robert R. Allen, eds. *Greene Centennial Studies.* Charlottesville: University of Virginia Press, 1984.

LaCapra, Dominick. *Rethinking Intellectual History: Texts, Contexts, Language.* Ithaca: Cornell University Press, 1982.

Langer, Herbert. *The Thirty Years War.* Trans. C. S. V. Salt. Poole, Dorset: Blandford, 1980.

Langer, Ullrich. "Gunpowder as Transgressive Invention in Ronsard." In Parker and Quint, *Literary Theory / Renaissance Texts,* pp. 96–114.

Levack, Brian P. "Law and Ideology: The Civil Law and Theories of Absolutism in Elizabethan and Jacobean England." In Dubrow and Strier, *The Historical Renaissance,* pp. 220–41.

Levine, Joseph. "Ancients, Moderns, and History: The Continuity of English Historical Writing in the Later Seventeenth Century." In Korshin, *Studies in Change,* pp. 43–75.

Lewalski, Barbara K. *"Paradise Lost" and the Rhetoric of Literary Forms.* Princeton: Princeton University Press, 1985.

Lewalski, Barbara K. *Protestant Poetics and the Seventeenth-Century Religious Lyric*. Princeton: Princeton University Press, 1979.

Lewalski, Barbara K., ed. *Renaissance Genres: Essays on Theory, History, and Interpretation*. Cambridge: Harvard University Press, 1986.

Lord, George deForest. *Classical Presences in Seventeenth-Century English Poetry*. New Haven: Yale University Press, 1987.

Lytle, Guy, and Stephen Orgel, eds. *Patronage in the Renaissance*. Princeton: Princeton University Press, 1981.

MacCaffrey, Wallace T. *Exeter, 1540–1640: The Growth of an English Country Town*. Cambridge: Harvard University Press, 1958.

Macdonell, Diane. *Theories of Discourse: An Introduction*. Oxford: Blackwell, 1986.

MacFadden, George. *Dryden the Public Writer, 1660–1685*. Princeton: Princeton University Press, 1977.

Macgillivray, Royce. *Restoration Historians and the English Civil War*. The Hague: Martinus Nijhoff, 1974.

McGregor, J. F., and Barry Reay, eds. *Radical Religion in the English Revolution*. 1984. Reprint Oxford: Oxford University Press, 1986.

McKeon, Michael. *Politics and Poetry in Restoration England: The Case of Dryden's "Annus Mirabilis."* Cambridge: Harvard University Press, 1975.

McKisack, May. *Medieval History in the Tudor Age*. Oxford: Clarendon Press, 1971.

Machiavel. As He lately appeared to his deare Sons, the Moderne Projectors. 1641.

MacLean, Gerald M. "An Edition of Poems on the Restoration." *Restoration* 11 (1987): 117–21.

MacLean, Gerald M. "The King on Trial: Judicial Poetics and the Restoration Settlement." *Michigan Academician* 17 (1985): 375–88.

MacLean, Gerald M. "Poetry as History: The Argumentative Design of Dryden's *Astraea Redux*." *Restoration* 4 (1980): 54–64.

MacLean, Gerald M. "So What *does* Thomas Gray's *Progress of Poesy* Have to Do with Progress?" *Postscript: Publication of the Philological Association of the Carolinas* 2 (1985): 67–74.

MacLean, Gerald M. "What Is a Restoration Poem? Editing a Discourse, Not an Author." In Greetham and Hill, *TEXT 3*, pp. 319–46.

Madan, Falconer. *Oxford Books: A Bibliography of Printed Works Relating to the University and City of Oxford*. 3 vols. Oxford: Clarendon Press, 1895–1931.

Manning, Brian. *The English People and the English Revolution*. London: Heinemann, 1976.

Marcus, Leah S. "Herrick's *Hesperides* and the 'Proclamations made for May.'" *Studies in Philology* 76 (1979): 49–74.

Marcus, Leah S. *The Politics of Mirth: Jonson, Herrick, Milton, Marvell and the Defense of Old Holiday Pastimes*. Chicago: University of Chicago Press, 1986.

Marotti, Arthur. *John Donne: Coterie Poet.* Madison: University of Wisconsin Press, 1986.

Marotti, Arthur. "'Love is Not Love': Elizabethan Sonnet Sequences and the Social Order." *English Literary History* 49 (1982): 396–428.

Martines, Lauro. *Society and History in English Renaissance Verse.* Oxford: Blackwell, 1985.

Mazzeo, Joseph A. *Renaissance and Seventeenth-Century Studies.* New York: Columbia University Press, 1964.

Miner, Earl. *The Cavalier Mode from Jonson to Cotton.* Princeton: Princeton University Press, 1971.

Miner, Earl. *The Metaphysical Mode from Donne to Cowley.* Princeton: Princeton University Press, 1969.

Miner, Earl. *The Restoration Mode from Milton to Dryden.* Princeton: Princeton University Press, 1974.

Montague, F. C. *The History of England: From the Accession of James I, to the Restoration.* London: Longmans, 1907.

Moore-Smith, G. C. "Aurelian Townsend." *Modern Language Notes* 12 (1917):422–23.

Moretti, Franco. *Signs Taken for Wonders: Essays in the Sociology of Literary Forms.* London: Verso, 1983.

Morton, A. L. *The World of the Ranters: Religious Radicalism in the English Revolution.* London: Lawrence and Wisehart, 1970.

Mueller, Janel. "The Mastery of Decorum: Politics as Poetry in Milton's Sonnets." *Critical Inquiry* 13 (1987): 475–508.

Munsden, R. C. "James I and 'the growth of mutual distrust': King, Commons, and Reform, 1603–1604." In Sharpe, *Faction and Parliament,* pp. 43–72.

Nadel, George H. "History as Psychology in Francis Bacon's Theory of History." *History and Theory* 5 (1966): 275–87.

Neale, C. M. *The Early Honours Lists (1498–9 to 1746–7) of the University of Cambridge.* Bury St. Edmunds: Groom, 1909.

Nethercott, Arthur. *Abraham Cowley: The Muse's Hannibal.* 1931. Reprint New York: Russell and Russell, 1967.

Nevo, Ruth. *The Dial of Virtue: A Study of Poems on Affairs of State in the Seventeenth Century.* Princeton: Princeton Universitiy Press, 1963.

Norbrook, David. *Poetry and Politics in the English Renaissance.* London: Routledge and Kegan Paul, 1984.

Notestein, Wallace. *The House of Commons, 1604–1610.* New Haven: Yale University Press, 1971.

Novak, Max, ed. *English Literature in the Age of Disguise.* Los Angeles: William Andrews Clark Memorial Library, University of California Press, 1977.

Ogden, H. V. S. "Variety and Contrast in Seventeenth-Century Aesthetics and Milton's Poetry." *Journal of the History of Ideas* 10 (1949): 159–82.

Orgel, Stephen. *The Jonsonian Masque.* 1965. Reprint New York: Columbia University Press, 1981.

Panofsky, Erwin. *Studies in Iconology.* 1939. Reprint New York: Harper and Row, 1972.

Parker, Michael. "Carew's Politic Pastoral: Virgilian Pretexts in the 'Answer to Aurelian Townsend.'" *John Donne Journal* 1 (1982): 101–16.

Parker, Patricia, and David Quint, eds. *Literary Theory / Renaissance Texts.* Baltimore: Johns Hopkins University Press, 1986.

Parry, Graham. *The Golden Age Restor'd: The Culture of the Stuart Court, 1603–1642.* Manchester: Manchester University Press, 1981.

Patterson, Annabel. *Censorship and Interpretation: The Conditions of Writing and Reading in Early Modern England.* Madison: University of Wisconsin Press, 1984.

Patterson, Annabel. *Marvell and the Civic Crown.* Princeton: Princeton University Press, 1978.

Patterson, Annabel. *Pastoral and Ideology: Virgil to Valéry.* Berkeley and Los Angeles: University of California Press, 1987.

Paulson, Charles. *The English Rebels.* London: Journeyman Press, 1984.

Pearl, Valerie. *London on the Outbreak of the Puritan Revolution.* Oxford: Clarendon Press, 1971.

Perkinson, Richard H. "The Epic in Five Acts." *Studies in Philology* 43 (1946): 465–81.

Piggott, Stuart. *William Camden and the "Britannia."* London: British Academy, 1953.

Pocock, J. G. A. *The Ancient Constitution and the Feudal Law.* Cambridge: Cambridge University Press, 1957.

Pocock, J. G. A. *Politics, Language and Time.* New York: Atheneum, 1973.

Pomeroy, Arthur. *See* Ahl.

Portal, Ethel M. *Bolton and the Academe Roial.* London: British Academy, 1915.

Poulantzas, Nicos. *Political Power and Social Classes.* Trans. Timothy O'Hagan et al. London: Verso, 1982.

Prior, Mary. "Women and the Urban Economy: Oxford, 1500–1800." In Prior, *Women in English Society,* pp. 93–117.

Prior, Mary, ed. *Women in English Society, 1500–1800.* London: Methuen, 1985.

Quilligan, Maureen. *Milton's Spenser: The Politics of Reading.* Ithaca: Cornell University Press, 1983.

Quilligan, Maureen. *See* Ferguson.

Rabb, T. K., and Derek Hirst. "Revisionism Revised: Two Perspectives on Early Stuart Parliamentary History." *Past and Present* 92 (1981): 55–78, 79–99.

Radzinowicz, Mary Ann. "The Politics of *Paradise Lost.*" In Sharpe and Zwicker, *Politics of Discourse,* pp. 204–29.

Reay, Barry, ed. *Popular Culture in Seventeenth-Century England.* New York: St. Martin's, 1985.

Reay, Barry. *See* McGregor.

Rebholz, R. A. *The Life of Fulke Greville, First Lord Brooke.* Oxford: Clarendon Press, 1971.

Rees, Joan. *Samuel Daniel.* Liverpool: Liverpool University Press, 1964.

Reiss, Timothy J. *The Discourse of Modernism.* Ithaca: Cornell University Press, 1982.

Rivers, Isabel. *The Poetry of Conservatism, 1600–1745: A Study of Poets and Public Affairs from Jonson to Pope.* Cambridge: Rivers Press, 1973.

Roberts, Michael. *Gustavus Adolphus: A History of Sweden, 1611–1632.* 2 vols. London: Longmans Green, 1953, 1958.

Rowlands, Marie B. "Recusant Women: 1560–1640." In Prior, *Women in English Society,* pp. 149–80.

Ruigh, Robert E. *The Parliament of 1624.* Cambridge: Harvard University Press, 1971.

Russell, Conrad, ed. *The Origins of the English Civil War.* London: Macmillan, 1973.

Schmidt, Johan N., ed. *Of Private Vices and Publick Benefits.* Frankfurt: Lang, 1979.

Sergeaunt, John. *Annals of Westminster School.* London: Methuen, 1898.

Sharpe, Kevin. "The Personal Rule of Charles I." In Tomlinson, *Before the Civil War,* pp. 53–78.

Sharpe, Kevin, ed. *Faction and Parliament: Essays on Early Stuart History.* Oxford: Clarendon Press, 1978.

Sharpe, Kevin, and Steven Zwicker, eds. *Politics of Discourse: The Literature and History of Seventeenth-Century England.* Berkeley and Los Angeles: University of California Press, 1987.

Sinfield, Alan. *See* Dollimore.

Smith, Alan G. R. "Constitutional Ideas and Parliamentary Developments." In Smith, *The Reign of James VI and I,* pp. 160–76.

Smith, Alan G. R. *The Emergence of a Nation State: The Commonwealth of England, 1529–1660.* London and New York: Longman, 1984.

Smith, Alan G. R., ed. *The Reign of James VI and I.* London: Macmillan, 1973.

Smith, Nigel. *Perfection Proclaimed: Language and Literature in English Radical Religion, 1640–1660.* Oxford: Clarendon, 1988.

Smuts, Malcolm. "The Political Failure of Stuart Cultural Patronage." In Lytle and Orgel, *Patronage in the Renaissance,* pp. 165–87.

Spivak, Gayatri Chakravorty. "Explanation and Culture: Marginalia." *Humanities in Society* 2 (1979): 201–21. Reprinted in *In Other Worlds: Essays in Cultural Politics,* pp. 103–17. London: Methuen, 1987.

Stallybrass, Peter. "Patriarchal Territories: The Body Enclosed." In Ferguson, Quilligan, and Vickers, *Rewriting the Renaissance,* pp. 123–42.

Stallybrass, Peter. "'We feaste in our Defense': Patrician Carnival in Early Modern England and Robert Herrick's 'Hesperides.'" *English Literary Renaissance* 16 (1986): 234–52.

Stone, Lawrence. *The Family, Sex, and Marriage in England, 1500–1800.* New York: Harper, 1977.

Stone, Lawrence, and Jeanne C. Fawtier-Stone. *An Open Elite: England, 1540–1880.* Oxford: Clarendon Press, 1984.

Strong, Roy. *Henry Prince of Wales and England's Lost Renaissance.* London: Thames and Hudson, 1986.

Sullivan, J. P. *Literature and Politics in the Age of Nero.* Ithaca: Cornell University Press, 1985.

Sutherland, James R. *The Restoration Newspaper and Its Development.* Cambridge: Cambridge University Press, 1986.

Swayne, Mattie. "The Progress Piece in the Seventeenth Century." *Studies in English Literature* 16 (1936): 84–92.

Sykes, Philip. "Politics and Historical Research in the Early Seventeenth Century." In Fox, *English Historical Scholarship,* pp. 49–72.

Tanner, J. R. *English Constitutional Conflicts.* 1928. Reprint Cambridge: Cambridge University Press, 1962.

Tennenhouse, Leonard. *Power on Display: The Politics of Shakespeare's Genres.* London: Methuen, 1987.

Tennenhouse, Leonard. "Sir Walter Ralegh and the Literature of Clientage." In Lytle and Orgel, *Patronage in the Renaissance,* pp. 249–58.

Teskey, Gordon. "Milton's Choice of Subject in the Context of Renaissance Critical Theory." *English Literary History* 53 (1986): 53–72.

Thomas, Keith. "Women and the Civil War Sects." *Past and Present* 13 (1958): 42–62.

Timmis, John H. *Thine Is the Glory: The Trial for Treason of Thomas Wentworth, Earl of Strafford, First Minister to King Charles I, and Last Hope of the English Crown.* University: University of Alabama Press, 1974.

Tomlinson, Howard, ed. *Before the Civil War: Essays in Early Stuart Politics and Government.* New York: St. Martin's, 1984.

Trevor-Roper, Hugh. *Queen Elizabeth's First Historian: William Camden.* London: Cape, 1971.

Trotter, David. *The Poetry of Abraham Cowley.* London: Macmillan, 1979.

Tucker, Robert. "Lucan and the French Revolution: The *Bellum Civile* as a Political Mirror." *Classical Philology* 66 (1971): 6–16.

Turner, James. "The Matter of Britain." *Notes & Queries,* n.s. 25 (1978): 514–24.

Turner, James. *The Politics of Landscape: Rural Scenery and Society in English Poetry, 1630–1660.* Oxford: Blackwell, 1979.

Tylus, Jane. "Spenser, Virgil, and the Politics of Poetic Labor." *English Literary History* 55 (1988): 53–78.

Underdown, David. *Pride's Purge: Politics in the Puritan Revolution.* Oxford: Clarendon Press, 1971.

Underdown, David. *Revel, Riot, and Rebellion: Popular Politics and Culture in England, 1603–1660.* Oxford: Clarendon Press, 1985.

Underdown, David. *Royalist Conspiracy in England, 1649–1660.* 1960. Reprint Hamden, Conn.: Archon, 1971.

Venn, John, and J. A. Venn. *Alumni Cantabrigienses. Part One: From the Earliest Times to 1751.* 4 vols. Cambridge: Cambridge University Press, 1922–24.

Vickers, Nancy J. *See* Ferguson.

Waggoner, G. R. "An Elizabethan Attitude toward Peace and War." *Philological Quarterly* 33 (1954): 20–33.

Wallace, John. *Destiny His Choice: The Loyalism of Andrew Marvell.* Cambridge: Cambridge University Press, 1968.

Wallace, John. "'Examples Are Best Precepts': Readers and Meaning in Seventeenth-Century Poetry." *Critical Inquiry* 1 (1974): 273–90.

Wallace, John, ed. *The Golden and Brazen World: Papers in Literature and History, 1650–1800.* Berkeley and Los Angeles: University of California Press, 1985.

Wayne, Don E. *Penshurst: The Semiotics of Place and the Poetics of History.* Madison: University of Wisconsin Press, 1984.

Weber, Harold. "Representations of the King: Charles II and His Escape from Worcester." *Studies in Philology* 85 (1988): 489–509.

Wedgewood, C. V. *Poetry and Politics under the Stuarts.* Cambridge: Cambridge University Press, 1968.

Weimann, Robert. "*Fabula* and *Historia:* The Crisis of the 'Universall Consideration' in *The Unfortunate Traveller.*" *Representations* 8 (1984): 14–29.

Weinberg, Bernard. *A History of Literary Criticism in the Italian Renaissance.* 2 vols. Chicago: University of Chicago Press, 1961.

Weinbrot, Howard D. *Augustus Caesar in "Augustan" England: The Decline of a Classical Norm.* Princeton: Princeton University Press, 1978.

Wilding, Michael. *Dragon's Teeth: Literature in the English Revolution.* Oxford: Clarendon Press, 1987.

Williams, Raymond. *The Country and the City.* 1973. Reprint New York: Oxford University Press, 1975.

Williams, Raymond. *Keywords: A Vocabulary of Culture and Society.* New York: Oxford University Press, 1976.

Williams, Raymond. *Marxism and Literature.* Oxford: Oxford University Press, 1975.

Wilson, A. J. N. "Andrew Marvell's 'The First Anniversary.'" *Modern Languages Review* 69 (1974): 254–73.

Wing, Donald, et al., eds. *Short-Title Catalogue of Books Printed in England, Scotland, Ireland, Wales, and British America and of English Books Printed in Other Countries, 1641–1700.* 2d ed. 3 vols. New York: MLA, 1972–88.

Woodhouse, A. S. P. *Puritanism and Liberty.* 1938. Reprint London: Dent, 1986.

Woolrych, Austin. *Commonwealth to Protectorate.* Oxford: Clarendon, 1982.

Worden, Blair. *The Rump Parliament, 1648–1653.* 1974. Reprint Cambridge: Cambridge University Press, 1978.

Wright, Louis B. *Middle-Class Culture in Elizabethan England.* Chapel Hill: University of North Carolina Press, 1935.

Zagorin, Perez. *A History of Political Thought in the English Revolution.* London: Routledge and Kegan Paul, 1954.

Zaller, Robert. "The Concept of Opposition in Early Stuart England." *Albion* 12 (1980): 211–34.

Zaller, Robert. *The Parliament of 1621.* Berkeley and Los Angeles: University of California Press, 1971.

Zwicker, Steven. *Dryden's Political Poetry.* Providence: Brown University Press, 1972.

Zwicker, Steven. "Models of Governance in Marvell's 'The First Anniversary.'" *Criticism* 16 (1974): 1–12.

Zwicker, Steven. *Politics and Language in Dryden's Poetry: The Arts of Disguise.* Princeton: Princeton University Press, 1984.

Index